THE DEADLIEST INDIAN WAR IN THE WEST

THE SNAKE CONFLICT, 1864-1868

THE DEADLIEST INDIAN WAR IN THE WEST
THE SNAKE CONFLICT, 1864-1868

GREGORY MICHNO

CAXTON PRESS
Caldwell, Idaho
2007

Library of Congress Cataloging-in-Publication Data

Michno, Gregory, 1948-
  The Deadliest Indian War in the West : the Snake Conflict, 1864-1868 / Gregory Michno.
     p. cm.
  Includes bibliographical references and index.
  ISBN 978-0-87004-460-1 (pbk.)
  1. Snake War, 1864-1868. 2. Paiute Indians--Wars. 3. Shoshoni Indians--Wars. I. Title.

  E83.864.M53 2007
  978'.02--dc22

                              2007023865

COVER

"Three Forks," by Jim D. Nelson.
www.jdnelsonportraits.com

Lithographed and bound in the United States of America by
CAXTON PRESS
Caldwell, Idaho
174322

TABLE OF CONTENTS

ILLUSTRATIONS

PREFACE

The Snake War is one of the least known of the many white vs. Indian conflicts that occurred in the American West during the nineteenth century. For a century and more, Americans have relished tales of the underdog and celebrated lost causes. We appreciate and praise those who have fought the good fight. The classic imagery of the Indian wars focuses on the war-bonneted horsemen of the Great Plains, sweeping down on a gallant band of soldiers making a last stand. The picture was presented thousands of times in drawings, paintings, histories, novels, and movies. Most Americans are very familiar with some of the soldiers of yesteryear, such as Sheridan, Mackenzie, Crook, Miles, and Custer, and the famous chiefs, like Sitting Bull, Red Cloud, Geronimo, Cochise, and Crazy Horse. Few have heard of Paulina, Weahwewa, Howluck, or Ocheho, and to most people, Winnemucca is simply the name of a lonely stop on the Nevada Interstate.

These men were "Snakes," and the 1864-1868 war with them and their people was the deadliest Western Indian war in American history in terms of loss of human lives. The word "Snake" was a collective one given to several bands of Bannocks, Shoshonis, and Paiutes, some that had once lived along the Snake River, had not signed treaties with the white men, and resisted incursions into their homelands longer than other tribes in the region. The tribal and band lines were fluid, with people intermarrying, moving, and living freely in a vast region of the Great Basin and Columbia Plateau in the Northwest. Most of the great Western overland routes bypassed their central homelands; the Oregon Trail skirted it to the north and the California Trail to the south. Were it not for the vagaries of river courses and mountain chains, a final showdown with the Snakes would probably have occurred years earlier. As it was, these Indians, considered more "primitive" and less of an obstacle by some, put up one of the best fights of any of the Western tribes. As underdogs fighting with forlorn hope, they lost almost every battle, yet persevered with remarkable tenacity and endurance. The end was probably inevitable, but the struggle should not be relegated to history's dustbin.

Perhaps the most famous of the military's Snake War players was Lt. Colonel George Crook. Upon hearing of his death, General William T. Sherman pronounced that Crook "was the greatest Indian-fighter and manager the army of the United States ever had." Crook learned his trade and rose to prominence during the Snake War. Although this book takes exception to all of the praise heaped upon Crook for his Snake War accomplishments, it does concur with a contemporary assessment of the war itself. One of

Crook's aides, Lieutenant John G. Bourke, served with him from 1871 to 1883. Bourke attended the Military Academy during the Snake War and missed the fighting, but he was well aware of its significance. It was where his idol, Crook, got his experience fighting the "Pi-Utes and Snakes" in "a campaign of which little has been written, but which deserves a glorious page in American history as resulting in the complete subjugation of a fierce and crafty tribe. . . ."[1] Since Bourke wrote those words more than a century ago, the Snake War has rarely gotten its page in history.

There were a number of people who helped in preparing the manuscript. Thanks to my wife, Susan, who spent many hours researching and proof reading. Thanks to Kelley Broome and Jeff Broome, who found many pages of documents from RG 393 and the Indian Depredation Claims in the National Archives. I appreciate the help of the folks at the Idaho, Oregon, and Nevada Historical Societies who located documents and photos. Thanks to Jerry Greene in Arvada, Colorado, for use of several items in his research collection, and to Layton Hooper of Fort Collins, Colorado, for reading the manuscript. I am grateful to the folks at the Longmont, Colorado, Public Library, for their help in ordering newspaper materials and for the hours of allowing me to monopolize their microfilm readers. Thanks to Steve Lent at the Bowman Museum, Crook County, Oregon Historical Society, for photos and documents. Thanks also to those at the Huntington Library, San Marino, California, for help in locating historical documents. Special thanks goes to Wayne Cornell, editor at Caxton Press, for his cordiality, promptness, and enthusiasm for my writing projects.

Note

1 Bourke, *On the Border With Crook*, vi, 253.

INTRODUCTION

Seldom can a man predict the future. It must have been a serendipitous combination of personal experience, observation, study, insight, and luck, by which Colonel George Wright made his prescient report to General Winfield Scott on October 10, 1860. Wright, who had succeeded General William S. Harney as commander of the Department of Oregon just three months earlier, foretold with uncanny accuracy, the coming conflict with the "Snake" tribes.

> *The Snakes (including the Root Diggers, Mountain Snakes, Bannocks, &c.) though composed of many bands who wander over the wide extent of country...are not formidable in proportion to their numbers. They have ever been a source of annoyance from their thieving propensities and their habits of lurking around immigration parties...to steal animals, cutting off small parties or individuals.... They have rarely attacked troops... although acts of plunder and hostility had been committed by them during nearly the whole period.... Frequent military expeditions must be expected among these Indians, and these involve long and painful marches through a nearly desert country...expensive and harassing to the troops. Long scouts are made without ever seeing at one time more than a single Indian family. The difficulty we have in advancing is that we have no fixed objective point. We pursue an invisible foe without a home or anything tangible to strike at. The hardships these Indians undergo in war differ little from their privations in peace.... They unite and disperse without inconvenience. Victories can easily be gained over such an enemy, but they will rarely prove decisive. . . . Hence, their final conquest must be a work of time and patience.*[1]

Without realizing it, Wright had nearly summed up the day-to-day experience of the coming Snake War of 1864 to 1868. He did not know he would be describing the deadliest Indian war in the American West.

Note

1 Sen. Exec. Doc. No. 1, "Affairs in the Department of Oregon," (Serial 1079, Washington, D.C., 1861), II: 141-42. Cited in Knuth, "Cavalry in the Indian Country," 117-18.

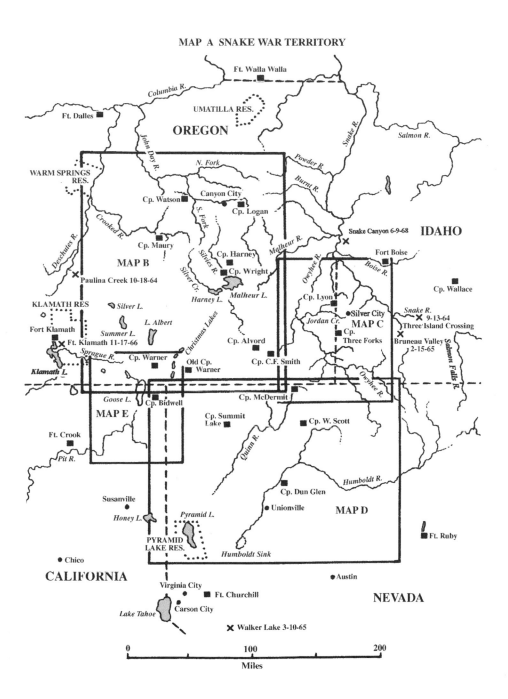

MAP A SNAKE WAR TERRITORY

MAP B

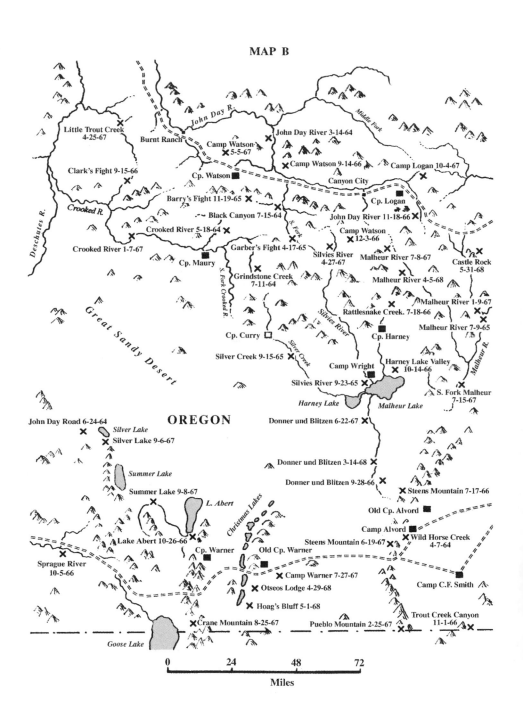

Little Trout Creek 4-25-67

Burnt Ranch

John Day R.

Middle Fork

John Day River 3-14-64

Camp Watson 5-5-67

Camp Watson 9-14-66

Camp Logan 10-4-67

Clark's Fight 9-15-66

Cp. Watson

Canyon City

Crooked R.

Barry's Fight 11-19-65

Cp. Logan

Deschutes R.

Black Canyon 7-15-64

S. Fork

John Day River 11-18-66

Crooked River 5-18-64

Camp Watson 12-3-66

Crooked River 1-7-67

Garber's Fight 4-17-65

Silvies River 4-27-67

Malheur River 7-8-67

Castle Rock 5-31-68

Cp. Maury

S. Fork Crooked R.

Grindstone Creek 7-11-64

Malheur River 4-5-68

Great Sandy Desert

Rattlesnake Creek. 7-18-66

Malheur River 1-9-67

Malheur River 7-9-65

Cp. Curry

Silver Creek 9-15-65

Silvies River

Silver Creek

Cp. Harney

Malheur R.

Camp Wright

Harney Lake Valley 10-14-66

Silvies River 9-23-65

S. Fork Malheur 7-15-67

Harney Lake

Malheur Lake

John Day Road 6-24-64

Silver Lake

OREGON

Donner und Blitzen 6-22-67

Silver Lake 9-6-67

Summer Lake

Donner und Blitzen 3-14-68

Summer Lake 9-8-67

Donner und Blitzen 9-28-66

Steens Mountain 7-17-66

L. Abert

Old Cp. Alvord

Camp Alvord

Christmas Lakes

Lake Abert 10-26-66

Cp. Warner

Old Cp. Warner

Steens Mountain 6-19-67

Wild Horse Creek 4-7-64

Sprague River 10-5-66

Camp Warner 7-27-67

Camp C.F. Smith

Otseos Lodge 4-29-68

Hoag's Bluff 5-1-68

Crane Mountain 8-25-67

Pueblo Mountain 2-25-67

Trout Creek Canyon 11-1-66

Goose Lake

| 0 | 24 | 48 | 72 |

Miles

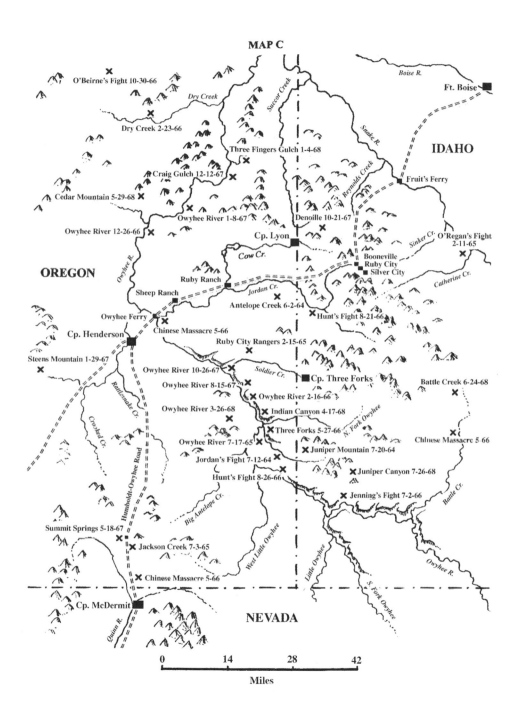

MAP C

O'Beirne's Fight 10-30-66

Dry Creek

Boise R.

Ft. Boise

Dry Creek 2-23-66

Three Fingers Gulch 1-4-68

IDAHO

Succor Creek

Snake R.

Reynolds Creek

Craig Gulch 12-12-67

Cedar Mountain 5-29-68

Fruit's Ferry

Owyhee River 1-8-67

Denoille 10-21-67

Owyhee R.

Owyhee River 12-26-66

Cp. Lyon

Sinker Cr.

O'Regan's Fight 2-11-65

OREGON

Cow Cr.

Booneville
Ruby City
Silver City

Ruby Ranch

Catherine Cr.

Sheep Ranch

Jordan Cr.

Owyhee Ferry

Antelope Creek 6-2-64

Hunt's Fight 8-21-66

Cp. Henderson

Chinese Massacre 5-66

Steens Mountain 1-29-67

Ruby City Rangers 2-15-65

Rattlesnake Cr.

Owyhee River 10-26-67

Soldier Cr.

Cp. Three Forks

Battle Creek 6-24-68

Crooked Cr.

Owyhee River 8-15-67

Owyhee River 2-16-66

Owyhee River 3-26-68

Indian Canyon 4-17-68

N. Fork Owyhee

Three Forks 5-27-66

Chinese Massacre 5-66

Humboldt-Owyhee Road

Owyhee River 7-17-65

Juniper Mountain 7-20-64

Jordan's Fight 7-12-64

Juniper Canyon 7-26-68

Hunt's Fight 8-26-66

Big Antelope Cr.

Jenning's Fight 7-2-66

Battle Cr.

Summit Springs 5-18-67

West Little Owyhee

Little Owyhee

Owyhee R.

Jackson Creek 7-3-65

Chinese Massacre 5-66

S. Fork Owyhee

Cp. McDermit

NEVADA

Quinn R.

| 0 | 14 | 28 | 42 |

Miles

XV

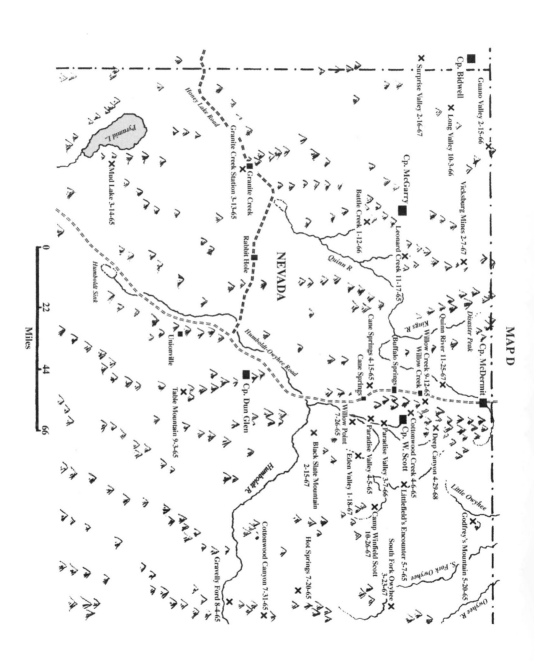

MAP D

Guano Valley 2-15-66
Cp. Bidwell
Long Valley 10-3-66
Surprise Valley 2-16-67

Cp. McDermit

Vicksburg Mines 2-7-67

Pyramid L.

Honey Lake Road

Granite Creek Road

Granite Creek Station 3-13-65

Mud Lake 3-14-65

Granite Creek

Cp. McGarry

Leonard Creek 11-17-65

Battle Creek 1-12-66

Quinn R.

NEVADA

Rabbit Hole

Humboldt Sink

Kings R.

Quinn River 11-25-67

Disaster Peak

Willow Creek 9-12-65
Willow Creek

Deep Canyon 4-29-68

Cottonwood Creek 4-6-65

Buffalo Springs

Cane Springs 4-15-65
Cane Springs

Willow Point 7-26-65

Paradise Valley 3-7-66

Paradise Valley
Eden Valley 1-18-67

Cp. W. Scott

Littlefield's Encounter 5-7-65

Camp Winfield Scott 10-26-67

South Fork Owyhee 3-23-67

Little Owyhee

Godfrey's Mountain 5-20-65

Owyhee R.

S. Fork Owyhee

Humboldt-Owyhee Road

Unionville

Table Mountain 9-3-65

Cp. Dun Glen

Black Slate Mountain 2-15-67

Hot Springs 7-20-65

Humboldt R.

Cottonwood Canyon 7-31-65

Gravelly Ford 8-4-65

0   22   44   66

Miles

MAP E

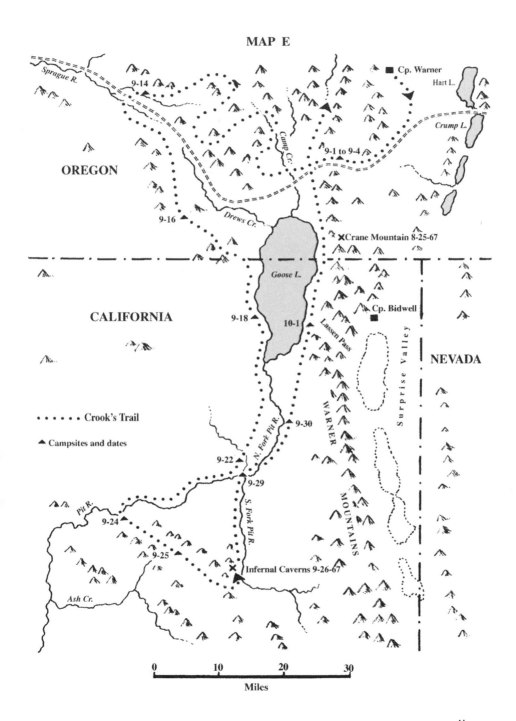

Sprague R.

9-14

OREGON

Camp Cr.

■ Cp. Warner

Hart L.

Crump L.

9-1 to 9-4

9-16

Drews Cr.

✗Crane Mountain 8-25-67

Goose L.

CALIFORNIA

9-18   10-1

Cp. Bidwell

Lassen Pass

NEVADA

• • • • • Crook's Trail

▲ Campsites and dates

WARNER

Surprise Valley

9-30

N. Fork Pit R.

9-22

9-29

S. Fork Pit R.

Pit R.

9-24

MOUNTAINS

9-25

✗Infernal Caverns 9-26-67

Ash Cr.

0   10   20   30

Miles

From Nevada's Black Rock Desert, *Caxton Press, 1978*
Winter March in the Guano Valley.

Chapter 1

ORGANIZING FOR WAR

T he soldiers who would be involved in much of the early fighting in the Snake War were reluctant combatants for the most part. In Oregon, which became a state in 1859, many took their cue from Governor John Whiteaker, a pro-slavery Democrat, who opposed suppression of the Rebellion by force. When the opening guns of the Civil War were fired at Fort Sumter on April 12, 1861, most of the federal troops in the area were sent east. By late spring there were fewer than 700 regulars in the entire northwest.

On May 11, President Abraham Lincoln called for 75,000 volunteers, but Governor Whiteaker did not respond. Instead, later that same month he argued that the South could never be conquered, and since Oregonians came from every state in the Union, she should not send her men to fight. He favored a military policy of defense, of protecting the state's borders, and providing safety for emigrants and travelers. "Beware of making a war for the ultimate or immediate extinction of slavery," he told the people. Illuminating the racial attitude that he shared with many people of the time, he added, "Have a care that in freeing the Negro you do not enslave the white man."[1]

Colonel George W. Wright, 9th Infantry, in charge of the District of Oregon, waited in vain until September for the state to take action, and then requisitioned the governor for one company of volunteer cavalry. Whiteaker called for eighty-eight men, charged the federal government $1,985 for expenses, but only enrolled twelve men. Wright tired of the game, and on the authority of the War Department, took the initiative to recruit the 1st Oregon Cavalry. He appointed Thomas R. Cornelius, colonel; Reuben F. Maury, lieutenant colonel; and Charles S. Drew and J. S. Rinearson as majors, and told them to form a regiment of cavalry. Even so, few men could see the sense in joining up for $31 per month for each man, using his own horse, to patrol the frontier, when wages elsewhere were good and there were new mining strikes being made in Oregon, Nevada, and Idaho. The military spirit of the state seemed to have gone with the regulars, and as late as the spring of 1862, there were only six companies ready for duty. Most of them came from the more populated "Webfoot" country west of the Cascades. Captain George B. Currey recruited half of Company E east of the Cascades. Maury

1

raised Companies A and D, and Cornelius raised B and E. Three other fractional companies were started, and then consolidated into C and F. Colonel Wright accepted the "regiment" with only six full companies. It took another year before one more unit, Company G, was recruited, and even that came as a result of combining two partial units raised by Lieutenants John F. Noble and Henry C. Small. In May 1862, Companies A through F were ordered to their new headquarters at Fort Walla Walla in Washington Territory, and to the Nez Perce and Salmon River mining districts to protect emigrants and miners. Company F spent its term of service at Fort Lapwai, and Company C stayed at Fort Klamath. Of the men who did enlist, almost all of them hoped that one day they would be sent to fight in the great battles in the East. That they were not, said Lieutenant James A. Waymire, "is the misfortune and not the fault of the Oregon volunteers."[2]

Washington Territory, which did not become a state until 1889, with a lower population than Oregon, provided more soldiers, although not without help. Colonel Justus Steinberger filled out his First Washington Territory Infantry by going to California and recruiting eight companies. Impatient over the lack of response to his recruiting efforts, Cornelius resigned as colonel of the Oregon Cavalry in July 1862. Steinberger, also commander of the District of Oregon until replaced by Brigadier General Benjamin Alvord, was senior to Lieutenant Colonel Maury. As a result, for most of its term the Oregon Cavalry was under command of an infantry officer from another territory, which did not help recruiting in Oregon. Maury was not commissioned colonel until April 1865.

Nevada, which became a state in 1864, furnished two units. In April 1863, General Wright, now commanding the Department of the Pacific, requested Nevada to furnish two regiments each of cavalry and infantry, but there were not enough men in Nevada interested in fighting when there was plenty of money to be made in the mines, plus, horses cost twice what they did in California, and were very scarce. Captain E. B. Zabriskie formed Company A, 1st Nevada Cavalry, in Silver City. Captains Noyes Baldwin, H. Dalton, and Milo George recruited Companies B, C, and D, in Virginia City and Gold Hill. Capt. Robert Lyon enlisted Company E in Genoa, Carson City, and Silver City, while Captain J. W. Calder formed Company F in Aurora. The last company was not formed until April 1864. There never were enough troops for a regiment. Companies A, B, and C of the 1st Battalion of Cavalry were organized at Fort Churchill in June 1863, and all were mustered out in July 1866. The 1st Battalion of Nevada Infantry was organized at Churchill in December 1863, and mustered out in December 1865. As late as spring of 1864, the infantry only had parts of six companies, totaling less than 200 men. Both units, even though undermanned and stretched thin, took a large part in patrolling the overland trails and fighting Indians.

Author's photo

Ruins of Fort Churchill Nevada.

Idaho Territory, which became a state in 1890, had no officially organized units. On numerous occasions, however civilians created *ad hoc* companies for protection and to fight Indians.

In comparison, California, a state in 1850, supplied nearly 17,000 men to the war effort. Besides the eight companies for Washington Territory, it sent 500 men as part of the quota for Massachusetts. Formed during the war years were the 1st and 2nd California Cavalry, the 1st through 8th California Infantry, the 1st Battalion of Native California Cavalry, and the 1st Battalion of California Mountaineers. They served across the length and breadth of the West, and several of the units were involved in the Snake War.[3]

Californians did plenty of fighting. The majority of whites who joined the military from the western states and territories were not natives, but were immigrants from Missouri or east of the Mississippi River. There was probably nothing intrinsically unique about Californians to make them so comparatively pugnacious, but there was probably something unique to the character of men who left the East to face the dangers and uncertainties of crossing a wilderness to start a new life in a far-off land. Likely, these were men of daring, generally idealistic and patriotic, and not afraid to stand up for a cause and willing to fight for what they thought was right.

Most Californians, like some of the Oregon volunteers, wanted to go east to fight. Men of the 3rd California Infantry, selected to occupy Utah Territory, were not happy with the assignment. They wanted to leave the West "for the purpose of tramping upon the sacred soil of Virginia," said Chaplain John A. Anderson. Seven hundred men, then in Nevada's Ruby Valley in September 1862, had hearts pulsing "vigorously with the patriotic desire to serve their country in shooting traitors instead of eating rations and

3

freezing to death around sage brush fires." They were so serious, Colonel Patrick E. Connor reported, that the regiment authorized the paymaster to withhold $30,000 of its pay, if the government would only send them east. They would even pay their own passage from California to Panama, if the withheld pay was insufficient. It was quite an affirmation of martial ardor, in paying for the "privilege of going to the Potomac and getting shot." Nevada Governor James W. Nye and Oregon Governor Addison C. Gibbs both offered to pay all expenses to send a couple of companies east to fight. It was not to be. The response from the War Department was emphatic: "We do not want to bring troops from the Pacific coast." Westerners would spend their time fighting in the west.[4]

Chapter 1 notes

1 Carey, *History of Oregon*, 626-27.

2 Carey, *History of Oregon*, 628-29, 634-35; Bensell, *Quiet on the Yamhill*, x; Dyer's Compendium, pt.3, 1556; John M. Drake Papers, Oregon Historical Society, MSS 80.

3 Carey, *History of Oregon*, 630; Angel, *History of Nevada*, 267-68; Orton, *Records of California Men*, 5, 7-12; Dyer's Compendium. Pt. 3, 1345. See Appendix C for further information concerning California's soldiers.

4 Rogers, *Soldiers of the Overland*, 25-27; Hunt, *Army of the Pacific*, 354.

Chapter 2

THE GREAT BASIN AND ITS INDIAN TRIBES

During the year of 1863, Indian Superintendent James D. Doty was busy making treaties with several tribes. In June, the Nez Perce signed a treaty at Fort Lapwai, Idaho Territory. In July, the Eastern Shoshoni signed an agreement at Fort Bridger, and the Northwestern Shoshoni signed at Box Elder, all in Utah Territory. In October, Western Shoshoni signed a treaty at Ruby Valley, Nevada Territory, Gosiutes signed in Tooele Valley in Utah Territory, and the Bannocks and Fort Hall Shoshonis signed at Soda Springs, Idaho Territory.[1]

With the apparently successful treaties concluded in 1863, peace prospects may have looked hopeful for the upcoming year, but peace was not to be attained. There were a number of reasons, among them being the geographical nature of the country and the structure of the Indian tribes. The Snake War took place almost entirely in the northern Great Basin and along the southern edge of the Columbia Plateau, encompassing southwestern Idaho, central and southeastern Oregon, northwestern Nevada, and northeastern California. The Great Basin is nearly surrounded by uplands. On the east are the Wasatch Mountains; on the west, the Sierra Nevada; on the north, the Columbia Plateau; and on the south, the Colorado Plateau. The rivers flow from the cup-like rim toward the center, sinking into depressions called "sinks." For decades, explorers were confused by the Basin's topography, and maps were drawn showing a great river that somehow had to lead across the wasteland and to the Pacific Ocean. It did not exist. It took John C. Fremont, on his second expedition of 1843-44, in which he roughly circumnavigated the Basin's boundary, to finally verbalize and solve the mystery. The vast interior of the West was a land of interior drainage, truly a "great basin," and he first named it so.[2]

The Basin once contained great Ice-Age lakes, now almost all dried and gone, with the Great Salt Lake being the largest remnant. Situated in the rain shadow of the Sierra Nevada and Cascades, the Great Basin is a desert, with an average rainfall of less than ten inches per year. The little rain that falls leads to the creation of temporary lakes, called playas, which dry up in the summer and leave hard, smooth, alkaline valley floors. The Basin is called a "cold desert," mainly because of primarily winter precipitation, snow, and freezing temperatures. Although temperatures may fall below zero in the winter, they can reach 100 degrees in the summer, and in the southern Basin, in the Mojave Desert, temperatures can reach 120 degrees. The Great Basin has the fewest plant and animal species of all the desert regions in the country, with the ubiquitous sagebrush on better-drained uplands and shadscale at lower, poorly drained saline sites. Some pinyon and juniper grow at higher elevations. Sagebrush and shadscale are home to chipmunks, mice, jackrabbits, kangaroo rats, packrats, gophers, badgers, coyotes, and antelope. The Basin is crossed by dozens of north-south trending mountain ranges, making east-west travel difficult. The high mountains range from 7,000 to 10,000 feet in elevation, divided by low dry valleys, which give the area another name: the Basin and Range Province.[3]

The Great Basin culture area was home to several tribes of the Uto-Aztecan language family, including the Shoshoni, Ute, Paiute, Gosiute, and Bannock. With few large mammals present, they were primarily small-game hunters and gatherers of seeds, nuts, roots, berries, and insects. Because they rooted around in the ground for food, some of the bands came to be called "Diggers," by whites who considered themselves culturally superior. Because of poor food and water supplies, the people usually traveled in small bands, or family groups, large enough for protection, but not too large to quickly use up the limited resources of a particular area. They generally lived in small, cone-shaped structures called wickiups, made of wooden frames with brush or reed coverings. Occasionally, bands would congregate for communal rabbit, antelope, or grasshopper drives, but for the most part they traveled in isolated groups with little community rites or tribal identity.[4]

With rough topography, harsh temperatures, scarce water, poor vegetation, alkaline soils, and limited wildlife for game or domestication, the Basin was a tough place in which to live. In Oregon, the portion of the state west of the Cascades, and east in the Basin, were two distinct entities. White Oregonians west of the mountains were called Webfoots, for having to live almost constantly immersed in rain and water, while in the east, heat, cold, and drought were the problems. The native populations eked out a very tentative existence, walking a fine line between survival and disaster. When whites began trekking across the land, sometimes wastefully using the scarce resources available, the tribes were forced to resist or die.

The fragmented structure of the tribes meant that there was no single leader to negotiate for them. The U.S. government might make treaties with several bands, and congratulate itself for a good job, but the treaties did not include all the bands. Even if the omitted bands had knowledge of a treaty, they would not have considered it binding on them. Each band would have to be either negotiated with or defeated separately before a permanent peace was realized. Whites, who believed they had made peace, were often rudely awakened by an attack by Indians still at war, and they thought that the

6

Indians were dishonest and treacherous as a result. Retaliation would lead to another attack; the cycle appeared endless.

The great difficulty in negotiating with all the bands is illustrated by their sheer numbers and geographical dispersion. In the east, from South Pass to Bear Lake, the Eastern Shoshoni numbered about 2,000 people in the 1840s when the first large white emigrations began passing through the territory. The Eastern Shoshoni, however, were a horse people from the Plains culture, lived for the most part outside the Great Basin, and did not figure much in the Snake War. West of them, centered at Fort Hall in eastern Idaho, about 1,000 Fort Hall Shoshonis lived, with about 800 Bannocks. The Bannocks were Northern Paiutes who had intermarried with the Shoshoni and allied with them during times of war. They also were a horse culture, but caught fish lower down the Snake River at Shoshone Falls and dug roots in Idaho's Camas Prairie. Located at several Oregon-California Trail crossroads, the Fort Hall Shoshoni and Bannock were actively involved in many of the emigrant attacks in the 1850s and 1860s.[5]

North of Fort Hall in the Salmon River Mountains lived about 1,800 Lemhi Shoshoni. They were off the beaten path and played little part in the Snake War. The Northwestern Shoshoni lived in today's northern Utah and southeast Idaho, and numbered about 1,500 people at the time of the 1863 treaties. They consisted of ten bands, under Chiefs Pocatello, Sanpitch, Sagwitch, Tosowitz, Toomantso, Tasowitz, Takuetoonah, Yahnoway, Pahragoosahd, Omrshee, and Weerahsoop. This group combined traits of the Plains and Great Basin cultures. Located on major trails, and within the lands that the Mormons selected as their new Zion, the Northwestern Shoshonis were alternately friends and enemies of emigrants and Mormons.

In south-central and southwest Idaho lived the Boise and Bruneau Shoshoni. These bands of about 300 people each, were more sedentary, catching salmon in the Snake River, and digging roots on the Camas Prairie. They participated in many emigrant attacks and were involved in the Snake War. Their attack on the Utter-Van Ornum party in 1860, pressured the Office of Indian Affairs and the U.S. military to do something about the warring Indians in the Snake River country. North of these bands, the Weiser Shoshoni, under Chief Eagle Eye (Igrai), lived along the headwaters of the Payette and Weiser Rivers. They tried to remain peaceful and stay out of the white man's way.[6]

The Gosiutes lived southwest of the Great Salt Lake, from Tooele Valley to the Deep Creek Mountains in present-day eastern Nevada. These 900 people lived in one of the most desolate regions of the West and were the epitome of the "Diggers" that the whites so despised. Mormons took over some of their lands in the east, and the Pony Express and Overland Mails built stage stations through their territory, causing them great hardship. They had fought back in the Paiute War of 1860, and in several isolated skirmishes since then. Some of the bandleaders were Tabby, Adaseim, Tintsa-pa-gin, and Harray-nup.

West of the Gosiutes, about 8,000 Western Shoshonis lived from the Ruby Mountains and along the Humboldt River to the north bend in the vicinity of present-day Winnemucca, Nevada. Many Western Shoshonis were unlucky enough to live on the Humboldt River, which became the main thoroughfare for the California emigrants. The little grass that was to be had was quickly eaten or trampled by thousands of head of livestock. Leaders included Temoke, Mo-hoa, To-nag, Sower-egah, Pon-gemah, Toso-wean-tsogo, and Buck. Twelve chiefs signed the Ruby Valley Treaty in 1863, but they were mostly from bands that resided in Ruby Valley and near the Humboldt, and only represented a portion of the Western Shoshoni. All of the Shoshoni bands numbered about 17,000 people.[7]

Beyond the Western Shoshoni to the Sierra Nevada Mountains were the Northern Paiutes (Paviotso), a loose confederation of about 8,000 people, falling into a dozen groupings, including the Hunipui (Bear Killers), Walpapi (Mountain People), Wahtatkin (Pony Stealers), Kidutokado (Bird People), Pohoi (Wild Sage People), Tukaricka (Sheep Killers), Togwingani (Antelope Hunters), and Lohim (Juniper People). Some of the major Indian leaders and bands in the Snake War included the following:

Bad Face (Winnemucca, Wobitsawahkah)
Big Man/Bigfoot (Howluck, Howlark, Oulux, Oualuck, Nampa)
Cougar Tail (Tahretoonah)
Fish Man (Numaga)
Fox (Wahi)
Gray Head (Tosarke)
Has No Horse (Ocheho, Ochoco, Otsehoe, Chochoco, Cheeoh)
Horse Stopper/Horse Trap (Hadaspoke)
Left Hand (Oytes, Otis, Owits)
Little Rattlesnake (Sieta, Chihiki)
No Ribs (Kewatsana, Kepoweetka)
Pony Blanket (Egan, Ehe-gant)
Sweet Root (Pasego, Pasigo, Potsego, Pashego)
War Spirit (Paulina, Paulini, Paunina, Polini)
Wolf Dog (Weahwewa, Wewawewa, Weahweah, Wewa)

It has been said that the Eastern Shoshonis once had closer ties with the Western Shoshonis and Paiutes, but a power struggle after the cholera death of Red Wolf in 1852, caused a split in the alliance. Gourd Rattler (Washakie) rode off to the Wyoming country, while Weahwewa, a Hunipui, seized the leadership in the Great Basin. By the time of the white man's Civil War, Weahwewa and Ocheho were the main leaders of the Paviotso Confederacy, and Paulina and Winnemucca were two of the leading war chiefs. With the end of the Paiute War of 1860, many of the defeated Indians who once made Pyramid Lake, and the Carson and Truckee Rivers their homes, fled north, away from the Humboldt River roads, to Nevada's barren Black Rock Desert and Smoke Creek Desert, and to Oregon and Idaho. Increasing pressures from the Paiutes moving north, led to more fighting with other Oregon tribes.[8]

The northern Great Basin and Snake River Indians were generally lumped together by the whites in one category as "Snakes." In the southern Basin, they were the "Diggers." Introduction of the horse in the Basin made the bands more mobile and increased their ability to raid, fight, and relocate. The availability of grass in the northern Basin provided forage for the horses, while its scarcity in the south, meant that the bands there could never become a horse culture. Thus, the "Snakes" generally put up a more successful resistance than the "Diggers," but no matter where they went and whatever label was placed on them, the Indians were in a continuous fight for survival.

Chapter 2 notes

1 Kappler, *Treaties*, 843-53, 859-60.
2 Cline, *Exploring the Great Basin*, 214-15.
3 Mares, *Deserts*, 252-53.
4 Waldman, *North American Indian*, 38-39.
5 Madsen, *Shoshoni Frontier*, 4-6.
6 Madsen, *Shoshoni Frontier*, 7-9; Corless, *Weiser Indians*, 12, 40.
7 Madsen, *Shoshoni Frontier*, 10-11; Kappler, *Treaties*, 853, 860; Crum, *Road on Which We Came*, 25-26.
8 Corless, *Weiser Indians*, 41-42; Madsen, *Shoshoni Frontier*, 11; Egan, *Sand in a Whirlwind*, xvi, xx; Ruby and Brown, *Pacific Northwest*, 201; Trenholm, *Shoshonis*, 3-6; Ontko, *Thunder Over the Ochoco III*, 7-8, 453-6. Ontko's study, relying much on oral tradition, can be illuminating from the Indian point of view, but its many inaccuracies with military names, dates, and places means it must be used with caution. Ontko claims Has No Horse (Ocheho) was the main leader; Kee, *Ocheho and Ochoco*, 38-40, claims Ocheho was a secondary leader, who acknowledged both Paulina and Weahwewa as principal chiefs above him.

Chapter 3
ANTECEDENTS TO THE 1864 WAR

In addition to the harsh physical geography of the land and the fragmented tribal structure, a major contributing cause of the war was the increasing influx of whites to the territory. There was no specific incident that touched off the conflict—no Minutemen firing at Concord Bridge or bombardment at Fort Sumter—yet the fighting did not spring up in a vacuum; it was part of a continuing conflict that ebbed and flowed over the years.

Explorers, trappers, and traders had penetrated the area for five decades, but they seldom stayed and only had a minor impact on the land. The tens of thousands of emigrants and gold-seekers who coursed through in the 1840s and 1850s were a more serious threat. Generally, they were only passing through on their way to the coast, but they used up precious water, flora, and fauna, and killed Indians who may have been raiding, or may just have been curious to see these strange white people walking across their lands. The mere exercise of passing through the territory led to scores of emigrant attacks and wars, as mentioned above. The early population growth and fighting along the Pacific coast showed that the frontier line did not advance smoothly in an east-west progression. Americans "jumped" from the Midwest to the forested Pacific slope, leaving about 1,500 miles of mountain and desert to be filled in by later settlement. The gap, crossed by several tenuous trails, was long and dangerous. Forts needed to be built to protect the travelers, the mail, and the communication routes.

Emigrants and travelers were always at risk while traveling to Oregon and California. Some of the most dangerous parts of the Overland Trail were in Idaho. In October 1851, Shoshonis killed eight men in a pack train near Fort Hall. In August 1854, Shoshonis and Bannocks hit several emigrant trains, including the Lake, Perry, and Ward parties along the Snake River, killing about twenty-one people. In July 1859, Indians killed five emigrants from the Shepherd train on the Hudspeth Cutoff, and the next month near American Falls of the Snake, Shoshonis attacked the Miltimore Train, killing and mutilating eight travelers. In September 1860, the Utter-Van Ornum Wagon Train met a horrible fate on the Snake River; when the Indians were finished with them, twenty-nine of the party were dead from bullets or starvation, or in captivity. At Massacre Rocks along the Snake River in August 1862, Shoshonis and Bannocks fell on several wagon trains, killing ten travelers. The next month at City of Rocks, Indians jumped the McBride-Andrews Train, killing six.

In present-day Washington in 1847, Cayuse massacred eleven civilians at the Whitman Mission. In Nevada, near Humboldt Wells in August 1857, Paiutes attacked the Holloway Train, killing six. In September 1862, Paiutes attacked and killed about twenty-three people from four emigrant families near Gravelly Ford. In September 1852, on the Applegate Cutoff on the California-Oregon border near Tule Lake, Modocs attacked an emigrant train, killing an estimated sixty-two people. In revenge, the following month Ben Wright recruited a company of miners and attacked the Modoc village near Black Bluff, just inside Oregon, killing about forty-one Indians.

Small bands of travelers were not the only ones in danger. The northern Great Basin and Pacific Northwest was home to several "wars." In Washington, there was the Cayuse War of 1848, and the Yakima War from 1855 to 1858. In southwest Oregon, the Rogue River War raged on and off from 1851 to 1856. In Utah in the 1850s occurred the Walker War and the Tintic War. In Nevada in 1860, the short, but violent, Paiute War flared up. There were fights at Williams Station and the Truckee River, and in May, about 76 white volunteers lost their lives at the Pyramid Lake Battle. The war flashed up and down the Pony Express route, with fights at Dry Creek Station, Willow Creek Station, and Egan Canyon Station. Several Express riders were killed on the lonely, empty stretches across the Great Basin. There were also dozens of other fights in the area, not specifically related to a particular war.[1]

The Paiutes of central and southeast Oregon had been comparatively isolated from the whites. The initial Oregon Trail bypassed their lands to the north and the California Trail was far to the south. In 1845, about 200 families were persuaded at Fort Hall, to try a new cutoff to Oregon, to bypass the hard haul over the Blue Mountains and reach the Willamette Valley by way of the Malheur River. Stephen H. Meek was enlisted as the guide, but he lost the way, led them into the Harney Basin and across lands so desolate that most of the Indians avoided them. People and livestock died from drinking alkaline water, and an epidemic fever killed others. About twenty died. Bitterness against Meek grew so intense that the guide fled, and the emigrants made their way to the John Day and Deschutes Rivers on their own, finally reaching The Dalles in October.

The episode may have been forgotten as just another unfortunate overland incident, except that on August 25, possibly on one of the tributaries of the John Day, three young men in search of their stock, knelt down to quench their thirst in a small stream. They picked up 15-20 pebbles in the creek that displayed an unusual color. When they showed the stones to other members of the train, they pronounced them to be "copper." When someone asked,

Wayne Cornell photo

Site of the attack on the Utter-Van Ornum wagon train in 1860. Twenty-nine men, women and children were either killed by Indians or died of starvation. The north face of the Owyhee Mountain range can be seen in the distance.

"Was there much of it?" One of the boys replied, "We could have filled one of these blue buckets."

One of the train's members, Mrs. Fisher, kept a single nugget and the train continued its journey. All was forgotten until three years later when gold was discovered in California, and Mrs. Fisher had the nugget assayed and discovered that it was actually gold. When the initial gold bonanzas of California began to play out, interest in the lost "Blue Bucket" mine increased. In 1861, Californians David Littlefield, Henry Griffin, William Stafford, and G. W. Scriver, with about 60 men, left the Willamette Valley and headed east, trying to follow Meek's old trail in reverse and locate the gold. After months of bad luck and arguments, the band disintegrated, with almost all of them returning to the Willamette. The four Californians and a few others hung on until October, when Griffin sunk a hole three feet deep and struck gold. The place was called Griffin Gulch and was located several miles southwest of present-day Baker, Oregon. The rush to the Blue Mountains was on, and by 1862, miners were swarming along the Burnt, Powder, and John Day Rivers.[2]

Even before the miners established themselves in the region, in September 1861, Daniel Chaplin, Green Arnold, and Charles Fox arrived in the Grande Ronde Valley, intending to set up a trade house to sell supplies to the emigrants. The Leasey and Brown Families arrived about the same time. The encampment of those who intended to remain for the winter numbered about 20 people, and Benjamin Brown's cabin was said to be the first one erected

13

in the region. It was built along the Oregon Trail and was the beginning of LaGrande. The influx of settlers and miners to eastern Oregon began a new round of confrontations with the native tribes. No longer were whites just passing through—they were staying.[3]

Additional discoveries of gold in the Fort Lapwai region in 1860, brought miners to what would become Idaho's Orofino District. The Nez Perce, perhaps realizing the futility of trying to keep the miners out, agreed to let them prospect north of the Clearwater. Even so, miners spread south and discovered gold in the Salmon River Country, establishing the towns of Elk City and Florence in 1861. In 1862, a party of men from the north Idaho diggings, under Tom Turner and Moses Splawn, headed south to look for new wealth. They had no luck at first, and the party split up, while another group under George Grimes joined in. Some continued southeast into the Boise Basin, eventually striking color in August 1862, and leading to the establishment of the Idaho City mines. The news flashed and thousands of miners poured into the region.

As the Boise Basin began to fill up, other prospectors explored the area and mines were developed on the Middle Fork of the Boise River in 1863. The same year, men moved into the Owyhee Mountains south of the Snake River. In May, Michael Jordan and twenty-nine men in search of the "Blue Bucket" mine found color in the mountains and along the creek that would later bear Jordan's name. Within two days of the news of the discovery, about 2,000 men left Boise Basin to throng to the new Owyhee District, with the development of the mining towns of Ruby City and Silver City.[4]

More roads crossed the area. In order to avoid the steep trail over the Blue Mountains, in 1859 an attempt was made to construct a new wagon road from The Dalles to the Snake River. Captain Henry D. Wallen, 4th Infantry, with three companies of dragoons and infantry, numbering about 190 men, plus horses, mules, oxen, and wagons, set out on his assignment. He was ordered to ascend the John Day River to its headwaters in the Blue Mountains, cross the divide and descend the Malheur River to its junction with the Snake. It was rough going to the upper John Day, but nearly impossible to find a smooth wagon route down the canyons of the upper Malheur. Wallen completed the trip, but realized his route could not be practicably used by wagons.[5]

Even so, the Northern Paiute's country was again pierced, and they were ready to retaliate. The next year, Major Enoch Steen, 1st Dragoons, led an expedition to continue Wallen's explorations and find a better route. He detached Captain Andrew J. Smith, with Company C, to construct a road from Harney Lake southeast to Raft River. On June 29, 1860, Paiutes attacked Smith 20 miles from the Owyhee River. Smith reported killing one Indian and wounding several, with no loss of his own. Nevertheless, he decided it was too dangerous to continue, pulled back to Harney Lake, and sent for

A. R. Bowman Museum, Crook County Historical Society, Prineville, Oregon
The Dalles, Oregon, on the Columbia River, 1860.

Steen. Steen's 100 dragoons, with sixty-five artillerymen as reinforcements, moved southeast of Harney Lake to a long range of snowy mountains. Steen traveled south along the escarpment that now bears his name, and on August 8 surprised a small band of Indians. The soldiers chased the Indians down narrow, dangerous canyons for about 6,000 feet to the desert valley below, with nothing to show but the loss of a mule. Colonel George W. Wright, in charge of the Department of Oregon, declared in September that the "routes of immigration were rendered perfectly safe," and called off operations for the season. Later that same month occurred the above-mentioned Utter-Van Ornum disaster.[6]

Concerned because his sanguine assessment had been proven wrong, Wright, on October 10, 1860, penned the omniscient missive to General Winfield Scott, detailed above, warning of a long, hard, war of attrition to come. Unknowingly, Wright had just summarized the upcoming Snake conflict.

Although little used by emigrants, there was traffic over the Wallen-Steen roads when gold was discovered along the Burnt and Powder Rivers, and even more so when precious metals were found in the Canyon City area of the upper John Day in 1862. Freighters, wagons, packmules, and miners rolled in. In the early 1860s, Canyon City's population grew to about 5,000, making it the largest city in Oregon, until surpassed by Portland in 1865. In 1862, Paiutes killed several miners on a tributary of the South Fork John Day, since called Murderers Creek. In 1863, they attacked a pack train 15 miles outside of Canyon City. Whites in the area petitioned Oregon Governor Addison C. Gibbs for protection, and he sent Company B, 1st Oregon Cavalry, to Canyon City in July 1863.[7]

15

To the south, along the Humboldt River, the Gravelly Ford emigrant massacre in September 1862, prompted a retaliatory expedition. Major Edward McGarry with Company H, 2nd California Cavalry, left newly constructed Fort Ruby on September 29, to look for hostile Indians. The next day, Captain Samuel P. Smith and Company K joined him and they searched along the Humboldt. On October 5, they arrived at Gravelly Ford, near the present-day town of Beowawe, Nevada. Colonel Patrick E. Connor had ordered McGarry to "destroy every male Indian whom you may encounter."

McGarry sent patrols up and downriver, while the main command moved upstream. On October 9, the soldiers brought in three Indians and McGarry took their weapons. Somehow they broke free and all three were shot and wounded. Fearing they would escape again, McGarry said, "I ordered the guard to fire and they were killed on the spot."

On October 11, about ten miles in advance of McGarry, Captain Smith caught fourteen Indians. After disarming them, they broke free and jumped into the Humboldt River, whereupon Smith fired, killed nine of them, and brought two women back to camp. On the same day, Lieutenant George D. Conrad brought in three Indians and a child. The next day, Captain Daniel McLean brought in a male and female captive, and Lieutenant C. D. Clark returned with one, while yet another was captured that evening.

McGarry told them, through the interpreter, that he would let two of them go to bring in all the Indians who had been guilty of murdering emigrants, but if they did not return that night he would kill all the prisoners. The Indians, perhaps wisely, did not return, and true to his word, McGarry shot four of the remaining males. He released the women and child to spread the word that if they did not desist from killing emigrants he would return next summer and destroy them all.

On October 15, as McGarry moved up the Humboldt, Lieutenant Conrad and Lieutenant Darwin Chase captured eight more Indians. After being disarmed, the Indians attempted to escape and all eight were shot and killed. McGarry continued to City of Rocks and traveled north of the Salt Lake, where he arrived at Camp Douglas on October 28. He had ruthlessly killed twenty-four Indians on his hunting expedition.[8]

In November 1862, Major McGarry took a detachment of 2nd California Cavalry out of Camp Douglas to the settlements of Cache Valley, along Bear River. There he met Mr. Zacheus Van Ornum, the uncle of a boy captured in the attack on the Van Ornum Wagon Train in 1860, who had information about the Indians who had his nephew. McGarry was told that Chief Bear Hunter and his band of Shoshonis had the boy, and the major rode through the night to surround the camp.

Notwithstanding McGarry's precautions, he found the camp deserted, but later in the morning, more than 30 warriors approached, making defiant gestures. McGarry divided his command in three squads and pursued them

A. R. Bowman Museum, Crook County Historical Society, Prineville, Oregon
Freight wagon on The Dalles to Canyon City Road, 1883.

up a canyon. The Indians opened fire on Lieutenant Conrad's party, and McGarry halted his advance, firing from long range. He killed three Indians in the two-hour fight. When Bear Hunter signaled with a white flag of truce, McGarry allowed him to come in to talk.

Had Bear Hunter known of McGarry's previous record with hostages, he probably would not have trusted him. The chief and four others were collared, while the others were ordered to return with the captive boy. Surprisingly, they did return with the child the next day, and McGarry released his prisoners. The rescued child was Reuben Van Ornum.

The following month, after Shoshonis were accused of stealing emigrant cattle near the Bear River Ferry west of Brigham City, Colonel Connor again sent Major McGarry and 100 2nd California Cavalrymen to investigate. He arrived at Empey's Ferry at dawn on December 6, ready "to give them a little taste of the fighting qualities of the Volunteers."

The Indians had cut the ferry rope, but McGarry left his horses behind and crossed the troops on a scow. He caught only four Shoshonis, but sent word to the rest, that if they did not deliver up the stolen stock by noon the next day, the prisoners would be shot. The Shoshonis packed up and headed out, and McGarry, as he had done on his Humboldt Expedition, promptly shot the hostages. It took fifty-one shots to kill four bound men, and the bodies "tumbled into the river."[9]

A climax to the fighting along the overland trails in Utah, Idaho, and Nevada was provided by the California volunteers who had enlisted during the Civil War to fight Rebels, but ended up guarding the long, exposed roads that tenuously connected the Pacific coast states to the East. On January 29, 1863, Colonel Patrick E. Connor led his troops from Camp Douglas, Utah

17

Territory, against the Shoshoni village of Bear Hunter and Sagwitch, who were camped in a bend of Bear River near present Preston, Idaho. The village held about 450 Indians, with about 200 warriors. Conner, with Company K, 3rd California Infantry, Companies A, H, K, and M, 2nd California Cavalry, two howitzers, and a train of fifteen wagons, had about 260 men.

When Connor splashed across the icy Bear River, the Shoshonis, in prepared defensive positions along the banks of Beaver (Battle) Creek, were ready for him. In a half-hour frontal attack, Connor's soaked and freezing men lost ten killed and twenty wounded. He then sent out flanking companies to threaten the Indians' rear and seal off any retreat avenues. Up to this point, the Shoshonis had the best of the fight, but the flank attacks caused many to try to flee. The soldiers picked off those escaping, shooting many as they tried to swim the frigid river, while the handful of staunch defenders decided to sell their lives as dearly as possible in the willows along the creek that ran through the village.

It was a hard-fought battle that lasted four hours. The troops counted 224 Indian bodies on the field, including that of Bear Hunter. About 160 women and children and 175 horses were captured and the village was destroyed. Connor was hurt too: twenty-one killed or mortally wounded and forty-six wounded, and seventy-five men with frostbitten limbs. The battle broke the power of the Shoshonis in the Cache Valley and Bear River area, and one by one bands began to come in to surrender.[10]

Before treaties could be drawn up, the Gosiutes to the west were involved in a short war. On March 22, 1863, they attacked Eight Mile Station in eastern Nevada, killed the employees and ran off the stock. The eastbound stage was next. Gosiute bullets and arrows killed the driver, "Happy Harry" Harper, and one of the passengers drove the wildly running team nine miles to Deep Creek Station. Captain Samuel P. Smith and his California Cavalry unsuccessfully searched for the raiding Indians.[11]

In May 1863, Captain Smith was operating out of Fort Ruby with most of Company K, 2nd California Cavalry. Using Shoshoni scouts, Smith searched the Schell Creek Mountains, went down Steptoe Valley, and discovered the Indians camped near Duck Creek. Smith attacked at dawn on May 4, achieving complete surprise. Only two Indians escaped, while twenty-four were left dead on the battlefield.

Smith waited at the site, anticipating that other Gosiutes would arrive. That afternoon, five more rode in unaware that the soldiers were waiting for them. Smith ordered a charge, and all five Gosiutes were killed. He then marched east over the Schell Creek Range and into Spring Valley. Moving at night, Smith came to a boggy area called Cedar Swamp, about 50 miles south of Spring Creek Station. At daybreak on May 6, he attacked. Marshy ground hindered the charge, enabling many Indians to get away. Even so, the hard-fighting troopers of Company K killed twenty-three Gosiutes with only one of their own men wounded. Smith then circled north, scouting for Indians all the way, and returned to Fort Ruby on May 10.[12]

Captain Smith was back in the saddle the next month, and with a detachment of 2nd California Cavalry, jumped a small party of Gosiutes at Government Springs on June 20, killing ten of them. Among the dead were Chief Peahnamp's wife and child. Three days later, in revenge for the deaths of his family, Peahnamp and about seventeen warriors attacked Egan Canyon Station. They caught William Riley, the station keeper, threw him in a woodpile, and set it on fire, but he managed to escape. Only four soldiers of Company E, 3rd California Infantry, were at the station. The Gosiutes killed three of them and badly wounded the fourth with a bullet in his neck.[13]

On July 6, 1863, Peahnamp was back at the station to finish the job. Not understanding that a handful of soldiers were not enough to secure the station, the military once again garrisoned the place with only four privates of the 3rd California Infantry. At sunrise, the unlucky Riley was currying a horse in front of the barn when a hidden Indian shot him dead. One soldier rushed out of a sod dugout and was killed, and the remaining three ran toward the barn. When the Indians set the barn ablaze, the privates mounted horses and made a run for it. Quickly, the Gosiutes caught up to Private Anthony Meyers and put a bullet in his back. Private Lewis Pratt rode about 50 miles and was nearly at the Willow Springs Station when the Indians mortally wounded him. An emigrant party found Pratt lying in the dirt and took him to the station where he died shortly thereafter.[14]

In mid-August, Lieutenant Josiah Hosmer, 3rd California Infantry, led Company E in search of the raiding Indians. Operating out of Camp Douglas, Utah Territory, and Fort Ruby, Nevada Territory, Hosmer marched his footsore soldiers over and across the ranges and basins. He finally located a Gosiute camp in the Steptoe Valley on the east side of the Cherry Creek Range about 25 miles north of Egan Canyon Station. Hosmer attacked, killing five Indians with no losses of his own.[15]

Soldiers were not the only ones hunting Indians. In the Boise Basin, civilians tried taking matters into their own hands. Prospectors had been killed in Boise Basin, in the Blue Mountains, and along the Snake River. Miners, including Relf Bledsoe, Jefferson Standifer, J. Marion Moore, William Tichenor, and Daniel Moffat, called for volunteers to fight the Indians. They thought that one of the Indians' hideouts was in the mountains beyond the Malheur River and figured that they would not be safe until it was cleaned out.

In March 1863, a group banded together as "independent rangers" under the tall, black-haired and black-eyed Captain Jefferson Standifer. They followed an Indian trail south to Salmon Falls, located a fortification, attacked and killed fifteen Shoshonis and wounded many more. In April, Standifer raised a company of 200 miners, scouted down the Payette River to the

Snake, and west into Oregon. They trailed up the Malheur and discovered a hilltop fortification. Standifer surrounded the place, taking a full day to maneuver into position. On the second day, the miners' rifles began taking effect, and several Indians were hit. Standifer had his men construct moveable shields made of willow rods, grass, and mud, and slowly rolled them closer to the Indians' fort. Before long the Indians sent a woman out to ask for a parley. Standifer was allowed into the fort and the Indians agreed to surrender all the property they had stolen from the miners and emigrants.

The miners, however, were in no mood to let the Indians off so easily. They poured into the fort and shot down everyone they could see, men, women, and children. The number of dead was not recorded. Only three Indian boys escaped. One 4-year-old boy was adopted by John Kelly and grew up to become an accomplished musician.

The miners returned to Boise Basin, satisfied that they had chastised the Indians. The U.S. Army and the territorial militia were not so sanguine. Brig. General Benjamin Alvord ordered Major Pinkney Lugenbeel, 9th Infantry, on an expedition to the area to disperse Standifer's rangers and prohibit any such future actions. In return, Fort Boise was established in July, to protect emigrants and the local inhabitants.[16]

The construction of Fort Boise was another point of contention for the Indians. More and more soldier forts were being built in their lands. In Nevada, Fort Churchill was built in 1860, and Fort Ruby in 1862. In Utah, Fort Crittenden was built in 1858 and Fort Douglas in 1862. In Washington, Fort Walla Walla was established in 1856. In Idaho, Fort Lapwai was constructed in 1862, and Fort Boise and Camp Connor in 1863. Fort Klamath was established in Oregon in 1863. There were also many temporary camps springing up across the countryside.

Lieutenant Colonel Reuben F. Maury, 1st Oregon Cavalry, somewhat understood the Indians' plight. "From Green River to Powder River and the Payette Valleys, and to the lakes east of the Cascades, they [Indians] were not disturbed by settlements, and only saw our people passing farther west. Now they are pressed from every direction by our settlements, and see daily the continuous approach of permanent occupation, as well as unsettled parties of more or less strength seeking location in the midst of their last hiding place."[17]

All of these factors led to an intolerable situation for the Indians of the Great Basin and Columbia Plateau. The Northwestern Shoshoni were decisively beaten at Bear River in January 1863, and the Gosiutes finally ceased fighting after their short war in the spring and summer of that year. As mentioned above, half a dozen treaties were made with the area tribes in 1863, and there appeared to be cause for optimism. When examining the physical topography, scarce resources, fragmented tribes, influx of miners, increased roads and traffic, building of forts, and more aggressive military policies, it is clearer to understand, in retrospect, why the peace treaties of 1863 ultimately failed. Indian depredations increased, and more punitive military expeditions followed. It was nearly a self-fulfilling prophecy. The Snake War was on. What began almost unobtrusively in 1864, developed into the single most destructive war, in terms of loss in human lives, of all the western Indian wars.

Chapter 3 notes

1 All these battles can be referenced in Michno, *Encyclopedia of Indian Wars*, passim.

2 Carey, *History of Oregon*, 396; McArthur, *Oregon Geographic Names*, 37-38; "Discovery of Gold in Oregon," http://www.legendsofamerica.com/OR-BlueBucket.html

3 Evans, *Powerful Rockey*, 311.

4 Greever, *Bonanza West*, 257-64, 271; Hanley, *Owyhee Trails*, 24; "The Lost Blue Bucket Mine," http://www.legendsofamerica.com/OR-BlueBucket.html

5 Jackson, *Wagon Roads West*, 85-88.

6 Bancroft, *History of Oregon* Vol. 2, 465-69.

7 Ruby and Brown, Pacific Northwest, 201; Ontko, *Thunder Over the Ochocos* III, 97; McArthur, *Oregon Geographic Names*, 686.

8 Michno, *Encyclopedia of Indian Wars*, 105.

9 Michno, *Encyclopedia of Indian Wars*, 107-08.

10 Rogers, *Soldiers of the Overland*, 69-74; Michno, *Encyclopedia of Indian Wars*, 110-11. The depiction of the Battle of Bear River as a massacre appears to be less reality than political correctness. For instance, in 1983, Brigham Madsen (*Bannock of Idaho*, 136-38) wrote that Bear River was a hard-fought battle, but two years later (*Shoshoni Frontier*, 21, 24) he wrote that the incident was a certifiable massacre, a great Indian disaster, and a national tragedy. The facts had not changed—apparently the writer did.

11 Rathbun, *Nevada Military Names*, 64-65; Angel, *History of Nevada*, 180.

12 Rathbun, *Nevada Military Names*, 55-56, 141; Orton, *Records of California Men*, 182; Angel, *History of Nevada*, 180-81.

13 Michno, *Encyclopedia of Indian Wars*, 115-16.

14 Angel, *History of Nevada*, 182; Orton, *Records of California Men*, 567, 568, 569.

15 Rathbun, *Nevada Military Names*, 41; Orton, *Records of California Men*, 521, 565.

16 Bancroft, *History of Washington, Idaho*, 407, 410-11; Greever, *Bonanza West*, 262, 264; *War of the Rebellion* (WR): V.50, 485.

17 *WR:* V.50/2, 954.

Chapter 4
THE OPENING SHOTS

"The only Indians who have committed assaults upon the frontier have been the Snakes," reported Brig. General Benjamin Alvord, commander of the District of Oregon, on October 6, 1863. "The Snakes speak the Comanche language, have the same habits, and are in fact a branch of the Comanche tribes of the region east of the Rocky Mountains," he wrote to headquarters. Since the end of the Yakima War in 1858, Alvord believed that the Snakes, as he called them, were the Indians most to blame for the new fighting. Alvord recommended the construction of Fort Boise and ordered several military parties to escort emigrants through the territory. The relative peace brought about by General Connor and Superintendent Doty in the summer and fall of 1863 seemed to be coming to an end. Alvord estimated between 10,000 and 15,000 miners had gone to the diggings in eastern Oregon and Idaho in 1863.

"It will no doubt be necessary next spring to send if possible an efficient expedition against these Indians," Alvord wrote. He was disturbed because Snakes continued to attack small parties of miners, regardless of the military presence, and, Alvord continued, "It will be our duty doubtless to give them all possible protection in the undertaking."[1]

Alvord appeared resigned to the unpleasant duty of trying to intermediate between the miners and the Indians. He doubtlessly wished the miners would stay in a safer geographic location, west of the Cascades. Citizens of the Willamette Valley had similar thoughts. Secure at his 1,000-acre fruit farm on the Pudding River east of Salem, David Newsom wrote in his journal that Oregon was divided in two classes of people—settlers and miners. The farmers, like Newsom, were a better class because they came to stay and build up the country. The miners, he said, "are *adventurers*, whose aim is to make their 'piles,' and then *leave!*" They won't work for fair wages, he complained, and their vices and bills are left behind as their only mementos. Newsom saw the latest newcomers of 1862 as merely those who wanted to escape from the Civil War in the East, and they would take to mining because they wouldn't work at any decent job. Newsom divined that the new mines on the Powder and Burnt Rivers and in the Grande Ronde, were a "mere humbug; as thousands will know in less than a year." The Salmon River finds were rich, he said, but small in extent, the Oro Fino claims paid poorly, and the Clearwater claims were taken up long ago. Anyone who is not insane, Newsom railed, should know that claims of rich strikes are false and will only lead to ruin. The state did not need the transient miners causing problems for everyone. Miners, he grumbled, say that Oregon is not their home, and "that it is only fit for coyotes and Indians."[2] Newsom wished they would leave. The Indians no doubt, felt the same way.

In early February 1864, H. Jones, of Jones & Edgar's Express, wrote a letter from Canyon City to Oregon Governor Gibbs, stating that Indians had been stealing stock and shooting at packers near Cottonwood Creek. He asked if protection could be furnished. Gibbs forwarded the request to General Alvord. Alvord had already been working on the logistics of a campaign, getting advice from Lt. Colonel Reuben F. Maury, 1st Oregon Cavalry, as to where to build a supply

A. R. Bowman Museum Crook County Historical Society, Prineville, Oregon

Brig. General Benjamin Alvord, 1864.

base. Maury learned from a guide who had been with Captain Smith in 1860, that it was impossible to take wagons up the John Day River, but that they could proceed up the Deschutes, up the Crooked, and over to a suitable location on the South Fork of the John Day. From that point, troops would be well placed between the Paiutes and the friendly Warms Springs Indians, and could fan out in all directions to scout the territory through the summer. Maury added that he did not think it a good idea to recruit a company of Indian scouts, for "Their manner of warfare is repugnant to our civilization, and they would be a constant source of anxiety and perhaps trouble to the commander of the expedition."[3]

General Alvord had a different idea about using Indians. He didn't want them as paid allies, but thought a company of twenty or thirty Indians who were hostile toward the Snakes would be useful guides. The use of Indians as scouts was not a new idea; the practice had been in use nearly since the first English colonists arrived in the seventeenth century, and they had been utilized during the entire westward march. As much as some Indians disliked the white man, enough of them felt the same about rival bands and could usually be counted on to fight against their own native enemies. Paiute hostility toward other Oregon tribes was intense, and the Warms Springs Indians in particular, relished joining the U. S. military to fight their enemies.[4]

The latest bitterness began after the creation of the Warm Springs Reservation in 1855, located on the Warm Springs River about 40 miles south of The Dalles. Friction began when Wascos, Walla Wallas, Teninos, and Wishram bands, all Plateau Culture peoples speaking different languages and more sedentary than the Paiutes, moved to an area the Paiutes considered their hunting territory. Trouble began in 1855 when Paiutes murdered two Teninos and began stealing stock from the reservation and surrounding area. The conflict had gone on for a few

A. R. Bowman Museum, Crook County Historical Society, Prineville, Oregon
Captain John M. Drake, 1865.

years before Dr. Thomas L. Fitch, the Warm Springs physician, organized fifty-three Indians, supplied with weapons from Fort Dalles, for a retaliatory raid. In April 1859, they attacked a Paiute camp near the John Day River, killed ten men and captured several women and children.

In July, Indian Agent A. P. Dennison requested that a military post be established in the area for their safety. In August, about 200 Paiute raiders swept onto Warm Springs, boldly took agency cattle and property, and flaunted a white man's scalp in Fitch's face. Fitch wrote to Dennison at The Dalles: "For God's sake send some help as soon as possible. We are surrounded with Snakes—they have killed a good many Indians, and got all our stock—don't delay a single minute."[5]

Troops moved in, retrieved some of the stolen stock, and temporarily calmed the situation. In 1859, two Paiute chiefs, Paulina of the Walpapi band, and Weahwewa of the Kidutokado band, learned something of the white man's ways. Paulina's people ranged from the upper Deschutes River to Crooked River and the upper John Day, while Weahwewa's ranged farther south and east toward the Burnt and Malheur Rivers. Both bands were the main participants in the Warm Springs raids. On one of the raids, both chiefs were captured and imprisoned by Agent Dennison. In order to get in the good graces of the whites and get out of jail, the chiefs volunteered to help guide Captain Wallen's abortive wagon road expedition. The first time they got the opportunity, the chiefs escaped, taking their horses and rifles with them. The Warms Springs Indians and the Paiutes would not pass up any chance to fight each other.[6]

In February 1864, General Alvord ordered Captain John M. Drake to take his Company D and Company G, 1st Oregon Cavalry, from Fort Dalles to the South Fork John Day River, to establish a post from which to conduct operations. With an attitude typical of many army officers untutored in Indian fighting, Alvord thought the area was home to no more than 300 or 400 Snakes, and "supposed that two companies could operate with efficiency in that region." For logistical support, Drake would take eight six-mule-team wagons and an additional 132 pack and riding mules. Company D, under Lieutenant James A. Waymire, recently promoted from sergeant, moved out first on March 1, with twenty-five men of Company D, arriving in the area on March 15, and establishing Camp Lincoln on the South Fork John Day, south of present-day Dayville. He had a number of scouts with him who agreed to participate with only subsistence rations supplied to them. They wore red headbands to distinguish themselves from the Paiutes. "The friendly Indians from the Warm Springs Reservation should be treated with kindness," read a part of Waymire's orders.[7]

A few days after Waymire arrived, Paiutes stole about forty horses and mules from the Davis Ranch near Canyon City. Mr. Davis and thirty men went in pursuit, returning to Canyon City on March 22, after determining the Indians had taken the animals to the vicinity of Harney Lake. After resupplying, Davis was going back out, and Waymire suggested that they cooperate. On March 24, Waymire took eighteen soldiers and twenty days' supplies, rode up South Fork 15 miles, and headed southeast across the snow and ice on Sugarloaf Mountain. After experiencing a snowstorm on March 27, they reached the headwaters of a stream that flowed into Silvies River and snaked their way down. Waymire had entered the Great Basin.[8]

In Harney Valley, Waymire met fifty-four citizens under command of Captain Cincinnatus H. Miller,[9] with Messrs. Davis and Bernon as lieutenants, building a depot preparatory to searching the valley. Miller assured Waymire that his men were ready to fight. On the last day of March, Miller and twenty men marched toward the upper valley to search, while Waymire followed a trail that lead to the southeast terminus of the valley, which he said was about 50 miles wide. A snowstorm delayed him another day, and Captain Miller rejoined the command, having found no Indian signs in the north. On April 2, they reached the southeast end and began climbing out of the valley. Another storm halted them for two days, and then they continued east 15 miles, crossing what Waymire called the Snow Mountains (Steens Mountain) and emerging in a long north-south trending valley with a low range of rocky, sage covered hills bordering it on the east. The valley contained three small lakes with good pasture in the mountain foothills. Waymire camped at the edge of the first lake (possibly Tencent Lake), which he estimated to be 20 miles from Harney Valley. There was evidence of an Indian camp with so many horse and mule bones lying about that Waymire concluded the Indians were stealing stock to eat.

Waymire moved about 20 miles south, following along the east side of the 60-mile long escarpment of Steens Mountain, and reached the north edge of the Alvord Desert. They saw signal fires in various portions of the valley to the south. Nearby were the remnants of another village, recently deserted, built of sagebrush, willows, and grass. Baskets, ropes, and furs lay about, with half-cooked horseflesh still roasting over dying fires. The tracks led toward the mountains. Miller's men saw two Indians, chased them, wounded one, and captured their horses.

A. R. Bowman Museum, Crook County Historical Society, Prineville, Oregon

Lt. Colonel Reuben F. Maury.

WILDHORSE CREEK, APRIL 7, 1864

They camped for the night, and at three in the morning of April 7, Waymire with 15 men and Miller with 30 men, carrying only one day's rations, moved out to fight. At dawn they saw a large smoke about three miles to the left of the trail, and Waymire sent Sergeant Robert Casteel with four men to investigate. Miller saw what he thought to be a band of horses ahead and rushed off to attack. The "horses" turned out to be a huge flock of geese, and Miller's men, said Waymire, "rendered their animals almost inefficient for the remainder of the day."

Another 15 miles took them to the northern end of the Pueblo Valley. A dry stream channel came down from the mountains, marked by a thick growth of willows, today's Wildhorse Creek. Miller and five men went to scout the area, saw two Indians about two miles ahead, and chased them. Waymire crossed what he called Willow Gulch, heard shots, and moved to Miller's support. More Indians issued from a canyon in the rocky sage hills to the west. As Waymire took position on a ridge about 300 yards from them, more Indians appeared, led by Ocheho, Egan, and Natchez, son of Winnemucca.

"I saw at once that they had chosen a strong position and could only be driven from it by a charge," Waymire said. He feigned an attack on the Indians' left, with the hopes of hitting them in front. By this time, Waymire said, Miller's men were "scattered in squads of from two to five over a plain of three or four square miles." The Indians opened fire upon Waymire's line with rifles, but with little effect. Hoping not to lose the initiative, Waymire moved his small line forward and delivered a few volleys. Mounted warriors made a dash for Waymire's right flank, trying to cut off his horses, but he shifted position in time to thwart them. A half hour was taken up by each side trying to outmaneuver the other. About twenty-five civilians gathered on the plain below, and Waymire asked for help, but Miller's lieutenant, Bernon, said he was unable to rally the men. As more Indians appeared, Waymire abandoned his position and fell back to Willow Gulch, where Miller finally got his men to form a line on Waymire's left. The Indians advanced to the plain, shouting and shooting, and at 11:45 a.m. Waymire charged. The Indian horsemen swung to the left and right, firing revolvers all the while. As Waymire approached, a band of concealed warriors on foot opened up with rifle fire. Some of Miller's men gave way, and the line fell back to its original position.

Waymire ordered a second charge, this time with drawn sabers, but Miller informed him, "this was not his way of fighting Indians," and fell back to the gulch. Waymire wanted to dismount and fight on foot, but found some of Miller's men had retreated toward a rocky sage hill half a mile to the east; one man was wounded and a physician and six men pulled out to take care of him. With Indians getting around his left flank, Waymire ordered a withdrawal to the sage hill. When warriors tried to beat them there, Waymire sent Corporal Miyers and five men to hurry and secure the hill, which he narrowly gained ahead of the Indians.

By 2 p.m. Waymire realized the Indians were too numerous, and were continually arriving with fresh horses. He decided to pull back to his camp, about 20 miles distant. Throwing out skirmishers, they advanced briskly across a flat alkali plain, while the Paiutes followed behind, harassing them on the flanks. When Waymire saw a band of about thirty-seven warriors heading north along his left, he figured they were making for his camp. The lieutenant took his cavalrymen forward at a gallop to beat them there, and after about a 12-mile ride, reached the northern terminus of the plain. The Indians had not attacked the camp and all was secure. The remainder of the command arrived late that night.

Waymire figured that, if little else, he discovered "the nature and strength of the enemy and his home." He thought he fought at least 150 Indians, but figured the entire band must be several hundred strong. For all the shooting, only one man was wounded. Several civilians' horses gave out and were abandoned. Waymire reported two horses and five warriors were seen to fall, either killed or wounded. More troubling was that Sergeant Casteel's party had not returned. When sent out on the morning of April 7, one of the men came down with measles and returned to camp. On the morning of April 8, Waymire and fourteen men went out in search of Casteel, Privates Cyrus R. Ingraham and John Himbert, and a citizen, George N. Jaquith, who owned a considerable amount of property near Canyon City. They found their tracks across the valley near the supposed smoke, which proved to be steam from a warm spring. The trail went to the pass leading into another valley, where Waymire supposed they had been cut off and killed. They searched until dark, and returned to camp about three in the morning.

Waymire waited until two in the morning of the April 9, hoping Casteel would come in, and then, on half rations, he headed back toward Canyon City, reaching there by forced marches on April 15. After being kindly treated by the townsfolk, Waymire returned to Camp Lincoln the next day, having been out twenty-four days. There he learned that on March 31, Indians attacked the camp and drove off the entire remaining herd—seven horses and one mule. The troops followed them into the mountains but could not catch up.

A. R. Bowman Museum, Crook County Historical Society, Prineville, Oregon
Major George Currey, *ca* 1865.

In addition, Indians attacked Canyon City, stole twenty-three animals, and killed two white men, named Overton and Wilson. More stock was stolen from Officer's Ranch not far from Camp Lincoln. It appeared that there were still plenty of Indians to fight on the John Day, without having to hunt them beyond Harney Valley.

Waymire reported that the roads were almost impassable, and the grass would not be good in the mountains before the middle of May. He suggested that a few howitzers would be very useful in the future. Waymire praised his men, but complained "that our defeat on the 7th instant is due to the want of organization under an efficient commander on the part of the citizen volunteers." He believed that with thirty cavalrymen he could have won. When Waymire returned to Crooked River, Captain Drake sent him west to relieve Lieutenant Stephen Watson's detachment at Warm Springs and guard the depot there. The change was made, Drake said, "in consideration of the hard service performed by Lieutenant Waymire's men in the early spring, and the jaded condition of his cavalry horses. . . ."

General Alvord, writing in his report, gently chastised Waymire, stating, "He has converted his humble task into a regular campaign into the Indian country, thus anticipating the operations which are confided to Captains Drake and Currey." Alvord believed he left too early for good grass for the horses, but said, "I forgive him for his adventurous trip, which far exceeded the programme intended for him." Drake later confided in his journal, that

Lt. Colonel Maury personally told him "that Waymire had made a mistake and had pursued the Indians too far." Maury directed Captain George B. Currey to join up with Captain Drake, take command, and conduct a more thorough operation. Maury concurred that the army force was plenty big enough to do the job.[10]

The situation was already taking the shape it would degenerate into over the next few years: citizens didn't get enough help from the military to prevent raids; soldiers wondered about the dubious help the citizens provided; line officers thought they needed more men; and field officers figured they had plenty.

Before Lieutenant Waymire made his move to Harney Valley, Captain George B. Currey left Fort Walla Walla to check Indians supposed to be harassing miners on the Palouse River in Washington Territory. Currey received his orders from Lt. Colonel Thomas C. English, now in charge of the 1st Washington Territory Infantry and commanding at Fort Walla Walla. Currey left the fort on February 16, with fifty-nine men of Companies A and E, 1st Oregon Cavalry. He marched north to the Palouse crossing of the Snake and moved upstream 20 miles. On February 21, he reached a small camp of seven wigwams of Indians who reportedly were stealing from and threatening nearby miners. Not knowing what to do after surrounding the camp, Currey had his men fire a volley toward the wigwams. Finally, thirty-one Palouse warriors and forty women and children appeared and surrendered. Currey found all the Indians' dogs with their mouths tied shut and wondered how the Indians thought they would be undiscovered in this manner. A few of the miners who had made complaints accompanied Currey. They picked out three warriors they said had driven them from their diggings. Currey arrested them, let the rest of the band go free, and marched the prisoners back to Fort Walla Walla. Unfortunately, the volley fired into the wigwams mortally wounded one man in the throat. Lt. Colonel English and General Alvord thought it was a job well done. "This expedition of Captain Currey will have a very good effect on those Indians," Alvord wrote.[11]

Captain Currey was then ordered to take his Company E, and Captain William V. Rinehart, with his Company A, 1st Oregon Cavalry, to Fort Boise. Like Drake, Currey was assigned eight six-mule wagons and 132 packmules. They were to move to a point west of the Snake River where they could "protect the whites in exploring, traveling, and mining in that country from Auburn to the California line," and not return to Fort Walla Walla until mid-October. Uma-how-lish, a Cayuse war leader, joined Currey in the Blue Mountains, ready to fight the Snakes.

On May 16, while Currey was at the mouth of the Owyhee River, he got word that 150 Snakes were fishing about 70 miles upstream. Also learning that drovers were taking 4,000 sheep from Nevada to the Owyhee Mines, he decided to move up the Owyhee, disperse the Indians, protect the drovers, and establish his main base. Currey left a temporary camp about eight miles up the Owyhee from the Snake, under Captain Edward Barry of the 1st Washington Territory Infantry, and headed upriver. The countryside, Currey reported, "presents the usual Snake River characteristics—trap rock, sage brush, dust, horned toads, long-tailed lizards, big crickets, and little grass, with an occasional rattlesnake and scorpion." On May 26, Currey established a camp about seven miles up Crooked Creek (which he called Gibb's Creek) from its junction with the Owyhee. He named it Camp Henderson, after J. H. D. Henderson, an Oregon congressional representative.[12]

From Camp Henderson, Currey sent Rinehart and twenty men back to the mouth of the Owyhee to tell Barry to come up. Rinehart, with Barry and the packmules, started back on the same trail, but because the path along the west side of the Owyhee was exceedingly rough, the supply wagons used the more-traveled miners' road up Reynolds Creek and past the Owyhee mines. While waiting for Rinehart and Barry, Currey made a short scout up Jordan Creek.

ANTELOPE CREEK, JUNE 2, 1864

On June 2, near the junction of Antelope Creek and Jordan Creek, just west of the present-day Idaho-Oregon border, Currey surprised a small camp of six Indians, attacked, and killed five of them. There were no women or children present. One of the men succeeded in escaping for a few hours, but was discovered hiding in the sage about a half mile from the trail. "I sent the Indians in chase," Currey reported. "After a two mile run they caught and shot him, making six killed in all."

Back at Camp Henderson, Currey waited for Rinehart and Barry, who arrived on the June 6 with the packmules. Receiving a letter from some miners in the Owyhee District about Indians raiding in the area, Currey moved east on Jordan Creek once again, but could find no trace of the Indians. On June 14, he had Captain Rinehart take his company to examine up the Owyhee River. Rinehart moved about 25 miles upriver from the Owyhee Crossing, finding more rough terrain and a narrow canyon with basaltic bluffs from 300 to 400 feet high. He circled back and arrived at Camp Henderson on June 16, finding Currey gone.

While Rinehart was out, the wagons arrived, and Captain Currey went on an expedition west toward Steens Mountain, arriving there on June 18, after another rough ride across dry lakebeds. The mirages were fantastic. Currey reported that some of his men "appeared to be high in the air, others sliding to the right and left like weavers' shuttles. Some of them appeared spun out to an enormous length, and the next group spindled up; thus a changeable, moveable tableau was produced."

Currey reached the eastern face of Steens Mountain in the vicinity of where Waymire fought in April. He figured that it was the central location of

31

a large number of hostile Indians and decided to move his permanent base there. The new site was named Camp Alvord, and earthworks were thrown up just south of present-day Little Alvord Creek, where there was good water and grass. Soon, Rinehart reached the new camp. While securing the depot, Currey sent the Cayuse scouts across Steens Mountain. They returned on June 21 with four captured Indian women, who said the men of their camp were in the vicinity of Harney Lake. The next day, leaving Barry's infantry and the disabled cavalry horses behind, Currey set out for Harney Lake, hoping to finally form his junction with Captain Drake. Drake, meanwhile, had already had a hard fight with the Indians.[13]

In mid-May 1864, while Currey was at the mouth of the Owyhee, Captain John M. Drake was about 170 miles out of Fort Dalles with Companies D, G, and part of B, 1st Oregon Cavalry, approaching the junction of the North and South Forks of Crooked Creek. On May 14, there occurred a harbinger of events to come. That night the horses were picketed out from the camp to graze. Lieutenant William M. Hand, as officer of the day, was in charge. He took his bed out to the herd, and as he was getting ready to sleep, he stood up to shake out his blankets, which spooked a few nearby horses tied to some small bushes. The horses yanked up the bushes and ran through the herd dragging ropes and bushes behind them, setting off a stampede. Many of the command spent the rest of the night rounding up stray horses. Most of them were caught, but Drake spent the following day on foot. The incident confirmed Drake's opinion of Hand. "He never will make an officer; it is not in him," he wrote in his journal. "God Almighty did not cut him out for it. This is the last escapade of the kind that I will pass over for his benefit. If an officer cannot under any circumstances attend to his duties; he has no right to encumber the service with himself."

Making camp on the afternoon of May 17, Drake sent out thirteen Warm Springs Indian scouts under "Cayuse George" Rundell to look for hostile Paiutes, although he doubted that Rundell would find anything, since he considered him "a worthless fellow." Even the horses were giving Drake trouble. He said, "the fitout of this expedition is miserable," and he believed that Lieutenant Jesse Robinson, the quartermaster at Fort Dalles, gave Captain David W. Porter, Drake's assistant quartermaster, "all the poor and unserviceable transportation that he had on hand." Drake saw himself being set up for failure. He learned that at headquarters, his expedition was "considered the best fit out that ever went to the plains." Drake, however, wrote, "They are most egregiously mistaken." He believed "great things are expected of us, but no means given us to accomplish them."

Regardless of Drake's qualms, at five p.m. two of Rundell's scouts returned reporting a nine-lodge village with about twenty to thirty Indians, about 13 miles to the northeast, at the head of Rabbit Valley. Drake had to make a decision. He was about to engage hostile Indians with a command led by men he had little confidence in. His Company D lieutenants were John M. McCall and James A. Waymire. Captain Henry C. Small led Company G, with his lieutenants William M. Hand and John F. Noble. Lieutenant Stephen G. Watson led a detachment of Company B. Captain David W. Porter was assistant quartermaster, and the surgeon was C. C. Dumreicher. "The officers of this command need a good deal of instruction for campaign life," Drake wrote in his journal, "particularly Hand and Noble. What can I do with such officers, they know nothing at all about their duties, and Hand I don't think wants to learn anything. Noble is willing enough, but too flighty entirely to rely upon in any contingency." Of all his men, he believed only "Watson will be a good officer to put in command" of any responsible operations.

Drake may have had a legitimate complaint with Hand, but his assessment of Noble was surprising, given that the lieutenant had served with the Regiment of Mounted Riflemen back as early as 1849, had worked in various capacities in the quartermaster department at Forts Vancouver and Dalles, and even had been an Indian Agent for Washington Territory. Noble, Small, and Hand had originally recruited the men of Company G, but Noble got the captaincy because he enrolled the most men, and Small and Hand were agreeable to the decision—at first. Noble got into trouble with General Alvord and was court-martialed, but acquitted, with the help of General Wright. Nevertheless, he was busted to second lieutenant and Small became captain, with Hand as first lieutenant. Small, formerly a grand chaplain of the Marion County Sons of Temperance, did not want Noble, with "his dissipated habits" in his command, so there was a constant friction between them, with Drake often acting as intermediary.

Drake may not have thought much of Noble's standing as an officer, but with the strained relations among officers that made many nights in camp melancholy, he kept everyone in good cheer. "If it were not for Noble I do not know what we would do," Drake wrote, "buffoon though he is, our time would frequently hang heavy but for his rollicking fun." Drake came to believe that "he will make a good officer. . .which is a good deal more than I am willing to say of some others that I have with the expedition."

Drake also had little use for Surgeon Dumreicher. The doctor once managed to get himself lost and seemed more willing to stay in the rear with the sick men than to come to the front where he might be needed during a battle. Drake called Dumreicher "a morbid, crusty, indolent old muggins and is of no account on such a campaign as this; cannot take care of himself much less take care of others." Dumreicher quarreled with Drake, and one morning, got into a shouting match with Captain Porter. Drake wrote that Dumreicher "wants half the command to wait on him and is not worth a curse for a trip of this kind."[14]

CROOKED RIVER, MAY 18, 1864

At 9:30 p.m., Drake finally decided on a course of action. He sent out Lieutenant McCall, with twenty-six men from his Company D, Lieutenant Watson, with thirteen men of Company B, and ten Indian scouts under mixed-blood Donald McKay, to join with the other scouts and surround the Paiute camp. The plan was for McCall to wait until dawn to attack. Meanwhile, Drake would leave his camp early that morning and march to McCall's support. It was after dark when McCall approached Rabbit Valley. The eleven scouts who had been watching the camp said that the Snakes were dancing, singing, and laughing most of the night, and had just quieted down. According to a soldier who later wrote to the *Weekly Oregonian* under the byline of "Hyas Cultus," McCall discovered at dawn, that "the enemy was not as accessible as had been represented and it was thought best to divide the command and charge both ends of the camp at once." McCall studied the lay of the land and decided to approach from the west, which had some tree cover. To the north and south of the camp, the ground was more

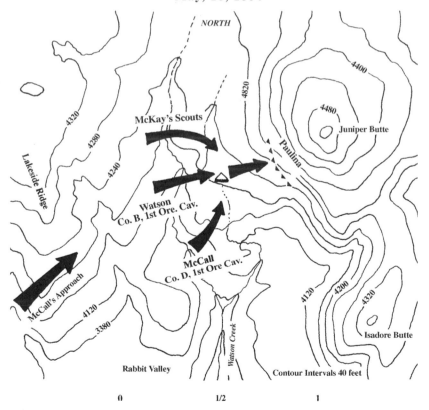

CROOKED RIVER, OREGON
May, 18, 1864

open, and to the east was a gradually ascending, juniper-covered hill leading to some rocky ledges. McCall took half the force and moved to the south side; Watson, with the other half, moved to the west; the Indian scouts took the northern sector. At dawn, Watson was to lead off slowly from the west, capturing any horses he could.

At four a.m. the plan quickly unraveled. Watson jumped off too soon and moved too rapidly, while McCall's open ground in the south turned out to be a morass. He was struggling to get clear when a herd of Indian horses ran into him, causing confusion and delay as he tried to round them up. Watson had already charged across his front and was beyond him to the east. The impetuous lieutenant charged through the camp.

A. R. Bowman Museum, Crook County Historical Society, Prineville, Oregon
Chief Ocheho, ca 1880.

"The Indians," McCall reported, "had retreated across the flat to a cliff of rocks, where they had a complete fortification. Lieutenant Watson had charged them to the edge of the cliff, where the Indians fired a volley into them."

"Hyas Cultus" wrote, "it was clearly developed that the Snakes were not taken at all by surprise, but that they were almost impregnably entrenched in a natural fortification of rocks, and although in the first part of the charge the Snakes appeared to be falling back and panic stricken, yet as the soldier's fire was becoming exhausted, they rallied and fought like devils from behind the rocks."

"Pour it into them, Boys!" Watson called out when bullets slammed into him, killing him instantly. Two Company B privates were killed with him, and five other soldiers were wounded. Unknown to McCall, civilians Richard Barker, who had arrived from Salem as the "eyes" of Governor A. C. Gibbs, and John Campbell, a reporter for the Portland *Oregonian*, were traveling with the party. Barker was severely wounded when a rifle bullet fractured his thighbone.[15]

The Paiutes—nearly seventy well-armed warriors led by Paulina and Ocheho—quickly recovered from their initial surprise. They pulled back from Watson's charge and hurried east, up a gradual slope about 250 yards to a juniper-covered ridge, where they opened fire from a rocky ledge. "This is one of their haunts," Drake later reported, "our friendly Indians say they have occupied this camp for three or four years." Apparently it was true, for the Paiutes knew just where to go and what to do. After they had blasted Watson, and the Warm Springs scouts—the fighting only took 15 minutes—they disappeared into the mountains.

McCall was caught flatfooted by the turn of events. When he saw the Paiutes were in what he considered to be an impregnable position, he decided that the only way to save the wounded men and captured horses was to retreat. He pulled back and sent a private and a scout to find Drake and ask him to hurry. Drake got the message at seven a.m. and, taking forty men of Company G, under Lieutenant Henry C. Small, rushed to the scene. They found McCall about a mile from the battle site. "The wounded had all been carried down the hill to this place;" Drake said, "the dead were in the hands of the Indians." Drake and Small hurried to the scene of the fight, but the Indians were long gone, and no tracks were found on the rocky ground.

"Our dead had been stripped and horribly mutilated," said Drake. "A Warm Springs Indian killed in the fight had been disemboweled and scalped." The mutilations were not extraordinary; treatment of captured and wounded by Warm Springs Indians and Paiutes was harsh. They would pound sticks into them, stake them to the ground, or roast them on fires. Once, when four Teninos all wanted a captured Paiute woman, they "solved" the dilemma by chopping her into four pieces.[16]

Surgeon C. C. Dumreicher cared for the wounded, and preparations were made for burial of the dead. Lieutenant Watson was killed, along with Privates James Harkinson and Bennett Kennedy, Company B. Corporal Dougherty and Privates Freeman, Henline, Level, and Weeks, all of Company B, were wounded. Indian scout, Cimmas, was shot in the head and killed, Gray Fish was shot in the throat and killed, and Simtustus was hit in the leg. Stock Whitley, a Warm Springs chief, was hit six times and dangerously wounded, as was civilian Richard Barker. Three army horses were killed and six badly wounded. Drake said he had evidence that three Paiutes were killed, but if they had any wounded, they were carried off. Lieutenant Small burned the camp, which included fifty saddles and a number of stolen items. Because McCall had captured fifty horses, Drake believed the Snakes were "without the means of committing depredations for the present."

Drake reported to General Alvord that Lieutenant McCall's management "seems to have been prudent and careful; the intended surprise was only partially successful." In his own journal, Drake wrote that McCall believed he would have risked too much by continuing the attack, but "I think he could have taken his wounded to the rear and then held the Indians in their position until assistance could arrive." Reporter Campbell's assessment of McCall was far harsher, believing Watson was killed only "by some strange mistake." He said that McCall "was never under fire," and his hasty retreat branded him a coward among many of the command. Concerning Lieutenant Watson, Drake wrote to Alvord that he "may have been precipitate and imprudent, perhaps, but his conduct on the whole was gallant and daring." Gallant or daring, Drake had just lost the only officer he had any confidence in.[17]

Drake pulled back and established Camp Maury on the southeast side of present Maury Creek near the junction with Crooked River. On a knoll south of the camp, the gallant and dead soldiers were buried. "Hyas Cultus" remarked that, "though public opinion did not so vote, it was just as deserving of praise to die here in the discharge of one's duty as it would have been to fall at Chickamauga or Gettysburg."

Lieutenant Noble described the funeral: "Poor Watson, all feel deeply and regret much his loss. He was to have been left in charge of this our Depot [Camp Maury], but the poor fellow now rests here. . .such is a soldier's lot. I thought little when I relieved him as Officer of the Day on the 17th instead that I would have to have his grave dug, and command his funeral escort. We had him and his men that were killed prepared and dressed neatly as possible, and neatly rolled in their U.S. blankets, for we had no lumber to make coffins for them. Lt. W was dressed in his blue uniform jacket (shoulder strops on it) and grey pants—I took some of his hair. They were buried about 2:00 P.M. A chapter from the Bible read by Cap. Drake. . . ."

After the ceremony, Drake sent his wagons back to Fort Dalles for supplies, and recalled Lieutenant Waymire from the Warm Springs Reservation. While Drake was at Camp Maury on June 4, a band of twelve "Snake Indians" attacked a party of whites near Mountain House along the John Day, killing Benjamin Harding and wounding a man named Rogers. On June 7, with supplies restocked and all companies present, Drake set out for Harney Lake Valley, to join with Captain Currey. So far, the two significant fights of the season had been army defeats, and the campaign intended to chastise the raiding Snakes was not off to a good start.[18]

Chapter 4 notes

1 *WR*: V.50/1, 156-58.

2 Newsom, *Western Observer,* 121-26.

3 *WR*: V.50/2, 757-58.

4 Dunlay, *Wolves for the Blue Soldiers,* 2, 13-14, 31; *Commissioner of Indian Affairs 1865,* 9-10, 589. In Oregon in 1865, there were about 759 Indians on the Umatilla Reservation; Warm Springs, 1,070; Grande Ronde, 1,144; Alsea, 530; Siletz, 2,068; Klamath, 2,000; and off-reservation "Snakes" numbered about 2,000.

5 Ruby and Brown, *Pacific Northwest,* 201.

6 Ruby and Brown, *Pacific Northwest,* 202.

7 Dunlay, *Wolves for the Blue Soldiers,* 31; *WR*: V.50/2, 764, 769, 775, 798.

8 *WR*: V.50/1, 310-11; McArthur, *Oregon Geographic Names,* 447, 605-06. Waymire said that he followed the river down to Harney Lake. From his description he probably followed Silvies River to Malheur Lake. Harney Lake lies to the west, separated from the larger Malheur Lake by a narrow point of land. Harney Lake, called Salt Lake by its discoverer, Peter Skene Ogden, in 1826, was undrinkable. Malheur, which means "bad fortune," was not much better; although it was fresh, Ogden said it "has an unpleasant taste." Occasionally, in very wet years, the lakes merge into one. The lakes lie in the flat Harney Valley, elevation about 4,100 feet, and cover about 750 square miles. Today, the area is one of the most productive waterfowl breeding places in North America.

9 Bancroft, *History of Oregon,* Vol. 2, 499. Miller, who later took the name "Joaquin," was called by some the "Poet of the Sierras." Before this foray he had been editor of the Eugene City *Democratic Register,* but it was suppressed by Colonel Wright for disloyal sentiments, and folded after about eight months. Miller moved to Canyon City with his wife and family in 1864, and served as Grant County judge from 1866 to 1870. He later wrote several political works, poems, plays, and stories. He died in 1913.

10 *WR*: V.50/1, 310-15, 336; Ontko, *Thunder Over the Ochoco III,* 158; Drake's Journal, 14. Waymire's fight, always listed as occurring in Harney Lake Valley, was actually along Wildhorse Creek in northern Pueblo Valley on the east side of Steens Mountain. Drake's Journal appears as "Cavalry in the Indian Country, 1864," Priscilla Knuth, ed., in the *Oregon Historical Quarterly,* March 1964.

11 *WR*: V.50/1, 307-09.

12 *WR*: V.50/1, 317-19; *WR*: V.50/2, 771-72; McArthur, *Oregon Geographic Names,* 147.

13 *WR*: V.50.1, 319-20, 347; Bancroft, *History of Oregon,* Vol. 2, 499-500; McArthur, *Oregon Geographic Names,* 141.

14 Drake's Journal, 13, 15-17, 22-24, 28-29, 60; *WR*: 50/2, 510-11.

15 Drake's Journal, 32-33; *Watson Meets Paulina,* 15-17.

16 *WR*: 50/1, 316, 329-30, 345-46; Ruby and Brown, *Pacific Northwest,* 202; Drake's Journal, 33-35.

17 *WR*: 50/1, 330-32; Ontko, *Thunder Over the Ochoco III,* 179.

18 Bancroft, *History of Oregon,* Vol. 2, 498; McArthur, *Oregon Geographic Names,* 148-49; *Watson Meets Paulina,* 18; *Antone Ranch and Camp Watson,* 20-21; Commissioner of Indian Affairs 1865, 473.

Chapter 5

"I AM BEING SYSTEMATICALLY SLAUGHTERED"

C aptain Currey moved his companies toward Harney Lake Valley from the southeast, and Captain Drake approached it from the northwest. Drake's experience so far had left him increasingly disillusioned of Indian campaigning. The Snakes were like willo-the wisps; "constantly lurking about our camp. . .extremely difficult to trail, always scattering out. . .never coming or going by the same route twice. I am now of opinion that it will be a harder and more difficult matter to dispose of them than I at first supposed."

In late May, Lieutenant Noble and twenty men were sent on a scout down Crooked River and to the vicinity of Sheep Rock. Lieutenant McCall and twenty-five men went on a scout up the South Fork John Day. Lieutenant Waymire arrived from Warm Springs with twenty-two more men. On the last day of the month, sixty-six more Warms Springs Indians arrived in Drake's camp, eager for revenge over the killing and mutilation of their people in the last fight. Drake had mixed feelings about the new addition to his command. "I think the first little skirmish will flatten them out;" he wrote, "they will wilt like a leaf and stampede for the Warm Springs like a herd of deer."

Drake was impatient to be on his way to hook up with Captain Currey, who, he said, "will wonder where in the devil I am at." Even so, Drake was torn between leaving the Crooked River area, where he believed most of the Paiutes were, and following Alvord's instructions to place himself under Currey in Harney Lake Valley. Still, he waited for Noble and McCall to return from their scouts, and finished putting Camp Maury together. Drake also received the services of another doctor, William H. Robertson, a civilian contracted out to the army. Drake described him as "a greenhorn, fresh from the Atlantic States; he don't seem to know anything."

On June 5, Drake's new Indian allies, who he labeled "The Chitike Cavalry," after a creek (Shitike) on the Warms Springs Reservation, returned from a scout carrying three women and eight children prisoners. It was more than his own soldiers had been able to accomplish, but Drake dismissed their effort. "They marched into camp singing a battle song as though they were returning after the accomplishment of some great feat of arms." Drake was partially right about their endurance. When their chief, Stock Whitley, ultimately died of his wounds on June 6, almost all of them gathered up his body and went home.

Finally, when Noble and McCall returned from their scouts, neither of which turned up any Indians, Drake was ready to move. Behind at Camp Maury, he left Doctor Robertson, Captain Small, and 58 men, but he quickly had second thoughts about his decision. When Drake refused to let Dumreicher take his large stack of personal gear on campaign, the surgeon blew up, reminding Drake that he was a major on the general staff, while Drake was only a captain. That was tough, said Drake, for Dumreicher didn't seem to understand that as a surgeon on the general staff, his rank was only a title, and he had no authority to command. While they were in the field, Drake was boss and Dumreicher would be treated as any of the other lieutenants, which was not saying much, since Drake didn't care much for his lieutenants either.[1]

Drake ultimately got rolling for Harney Lake Valley on June 7, worrying that he would be there about 10 days after Currey arrived. Some of the unpredictable Great Basin weather greeted them on the morning of June 11, when a snowstorm hit them for about four hours in the Silver River Valley. The next few nights it dropped below freezing. North of Harney Lake on June 14, several scouting parties went out to look for Captain Currey. "I cannot imagine where I am going to find him at," Drake wrote. Lieutenant McCall described the experience "like going to a large city to hunt up some individual, when you neither know the street he lives on nor the house he boards at." The two commands by-passed each other, with Currey on an inner circle, and Drake on a larger outer circle.[2]

As Drake moved east toward the South Fork Malheur on June 18, he camped on Crane Creek, which he described as "the most uninviting place I have seen since leaving The Dalles." The barren sage valley surrounded by rocky bluffs left Dumreicher "highly disgusted with the camp," and, almost inevitably, wrote Drake, the officers would "facetiously call it Camp Dumreicher."

The next day, Drake sent out Noble on a scout, but the lieutenant, said Drake, "made every preparation, before starting, to meet the contingency of being killed by the Indians; wrote a letter to his wife and gave. . .directions for the disposition of certain of his effects, should such an event transpire." Drake thought it was bad for morale. "I dislike to have anything to do with such men—a man who is so timid as that has no business to be in the service."

June 22 was rainy, "dull and dreary," Drake wrote, with nothing to relieve the monotony "except Noble's unremitting gas." Apparently the captain was becoming used to the lieutenant's antics. "He always has something fresh and original—true, it is not the most chaste and refined quality, but better than none, a good deal. The most versatile man I ever saw. I cannot help liking the fellow, though he is of no account as an officer, has plenty of activity and energy, but no judgment." Drake may have thought better of Noble because he and Noble shared opinions of Captain Small and Lieutenant Hand. "He thoroughly dislikes Small and Hand," Drake wrote, "for the latter he entertains the most profound contempt. Who would not, that knows him? Of all the worthless fellows that ever I saw he excels; indolent, lazy, careless, worthless. He is an encumbrance to the service."

Drake was worried that he could not find Currey or the Indians. "If I was not hampered up with instructions and orders of all kinds imaginable and unimaginable," he wrote, "I could do something with those Indians that are infesting the country."

A. R. Bowman Museum Crook County Historical Society, Prineville, Oregon
Lieutenant John M. McCall

On June 27, Drake found one of Currey's campsites that had been vacant for five days, and he was able to follow his trail north to Harney Valley. It was good and bad news to Drake. He wanted to find Currey, but he really wanted to cut loose and go after the Indians, who he figured never would be caught after the commands united. "The result of all this amounts to just this:" Drake wrote, "that General Alvord has undertaken to say for himself that the Indians are in such a place, and there the military must go. There are no Indians in Harney Valley. My campaign is spoiled and I presume Currey's also."

Finally, Cayuse George found Currey camped on Mud Lake, between Harney and Malheur Lakes. They united on July 1, on Rattlesnake Creek, which issued from the mountains on the north side of the Harney Valley. With the combined command of about 300 soldiers and Indian scouts, Currey planned to move in the direction of Canyon City, "intending to clear the region of John Day's River of Indians within the next thirty days, an undertaking presenting no great difficulty." Or, so he thought.

Headquarters at Fort Vancouver shared Currey's optimistic opinion. Assistant Adjutant Lieutenant J. W. Hopkins replied, with the bravado of one fighting from behind a desk: "If the Indians are found occupying such strongholds they can easily be dislodged by a charge on foot . . . . A charge should be made with loaded rifles. The Indians will be sure to run, and can be shot down as they run. They were never known to stand a close charge upon their hiding places."

Drake was not so sanguine. "I think he [Currey] has formed some big notions about sweeping out the Blue Mountains between here and Canyon

City," Drake wrote, "and wiping out the Indians that are doing so much stealing on the Canyon City Road during the past winter and spring." Drake figured Currey was altogether in too great a rush to do things, and might have been called hyperactive in modern terminology. Drake: "Currey is such a regular storm that I fear he'll break down our trains by his infernal rapid marches. I do not think the Snake Indians in these mountains can be hunted down in that way. They will have to be spied out and surprised, suddenly attacked wherever they make a stopping place for a few days."

Drake was correct in his assessment. The Snakes would not stand in a large, set-piece battle. A successful campaign would entail many days of trail hardship, tracking, sneaking, surprise attacks, and more chasing. It would be a war of attrition. Just how many days, or even months and years it would take was beyond anyone's guess.[3]

Currey's plan was to move the united command north into the Blue Mountains. On July 3, they moved out from Rattlesnake Camp toward upper Silvies River. On July 6, by Currey's directions, Drake sent Lieutenant Waymire with thirty men of Company D, northeast into the Aldrich Mountains and Strawberry Range, southwest of Canyon City. Rather incongruously, Currey dispatched his brother, Lieutenant James L. Currey, with twenty soldiers of Company E, to Canyon City to try to learn if the civilians had any information as to the Indians' whereabouts. Currey returned with the news that the Indians had raided the area on July 3, stealing about forty horses and killing one man, and a few days later, raided the Bridge Creek area and stole more stock. More disturbing to Drake was what he read in the newspapers that Currey brought back, which indicated the civilians' disgust with the poor job the army was doing. Their complaints made many of the soldiers feel that their efforts were unappreciated. "Judging from flying remarks I think the officers of the Cavalry will nearly all of them want to go out of service next fall," said Drake.[4]

GRINDSTONE CREEK, JULY 11, 1864

The commands marched from Bear Valley on the upper Silvies River, southwest to the headwaters of the South Fork John Day, then west and south to Grindstone Creek in the upper Crooked River watershed. In advance of the combined commands on July 11, Lieutenant Noble, with a detachment of Company G, 1st Oregon Cavalry, and some Umatilla and Nez Perce scouts, were moving along Twelvemile Table, a large, flat upland east of the Crooked River canyons. The scouts reported seeing signal fires to the north. Noble sent them to investigate and stopped to camp on Twelvemile Table. The scouts found a Snake camp and returned to tell Noble, but about 25 Snake warriors under Lame Dog, saw and chased them.

Lame Dog was operating out of Weahwewa's camp, also nearby, and had been watching Noble, along with Lieutenant David W. Porter, who had a smaller force and was roughly paralleling Noble's route. Lame Dog was about to attack Porter when Noble's scouts showed up, possibly saving Porter's command, but placing themselves in jeopardy. Lame Dog's men shot one Nez Perce in the thigh, and killed another one's horse. The dismounted scout ran for the brush near Grindstone Creek to hide. As the scouts came barreling back to Noble's camp, Lieutenant John Bowen, Company F, had slipped out of camp for an evening hunt. He happened to see some game, and shot, just about the time the exhausted scouts were approaching the camp. The shot alerted the soldiers, as well as Lame Dog's warriors, who almost blundered right into a camp full of soldiers. Lame Dog quickly halted and pulled back. When Noble learned what happened he was disappointed, because he thought he could have dealt the Snakes "a telling blow."

On July 12, couriers went out to alert Drake and Currey of the encounter. Noble marched off to look for his scouts. One was found in good shape, but the other was discovered hanging upside down from a tree limb. He was shot in the head, heart, and leg, and his body had many knife wounds and was mangled almost beyond recognition. Drake and Currey moved out, found the vacant Indian camp about six miles away, and followed the trail east and north. In advance again, Noble moved east and found Lame Dog's camp on Little Mowich Mountain, which was recently abandoned and burned. He followed the trail northeast to a good defensive position west of present-day Izee, Oregon, called Hole-In-The-Ground, which Weahwewa had also just abandoned.[5]

BLACK CANYON, JULY 15, 1864

Captains Currey and Drake retraced their steps back to the South Fork John Day, and reached the Hole-in-the-Ground area. On July 13, Currey gathered most of Companies A, D, and E, and headed down the South Fork John Day. Two days later, near the mouth of Black Canyon Creek, with surrounding walls about 1,000 feet high, Currey caught up with the Indians running their horses across the river and up Aldrich Canyon leading east. He dismounted and deployed Company A in the rocks on the west side of the canyon, Company D, to the heights on the east, and Company E in the center to cover the horses and wagons. Before Company D could gain a height advantage, the Indians fired down on them and Captain Drake had to run his men and pack animals across the creek for cover. "I noticed some few of the men getting a little shaky," Drake said, "and even indisposed to fall in at all, others manifested evident signs of being scared. I felt perfectly cool myself. . . ."

The Snakes peppered the soldiers with bullets, but all the fire seemed to be high, consistently cracking into the rocks above their heads. Only one horse was hit. Captain Rinehart was injured when thrown from his horse and he had to be taken to Camp Maury in a litter. Currey ordered Drake "to seize the spur of the mountain at all hazards," and when Company D reached the eastern rim, the Indians disappeared. A short time later, however, more warriors appeared to the rear of Company E at the bottom of the canyon. Currey turned after them but they fled upriver. By the time he consolidated his force to follow, they were gone. With the ranges many times being about 1,000 yards, Drake was not surprised few, if any, were hit. Currey's scouts followed for a time and concluded the Snakes were headed back to Harney Valley. Said Currey: "I desisted from farther pursuit, not wishing to again strike out on the plains around and beyond the lakes until I was satisfied the Indians had all been driven from this vicinity."[6]

Currey and Drake were not the only ones combing the mountains. Captain Richard S. Caldwell, with twenty men of Company B, 1st Oregon Cavalry, and Lieutenant William Wood, with nineteen men of the 1st Washington Territory Infantry, were part of the Canyon City Road Expedition. Caldwell left Fort Dalles on July 3, taking supplies to support the other ongoing campaigns. The only indications of an Indian presence were from a few shots fired at a stage near Mountain House and a reported depredation at Antelope Creek. Caldwell patrolled between Muddy, Alkali, and Rock Creek Stations and commented that "the travel on the road has been immense; cattle droves, pack trains, and families from Jackson County, Eugene, and The Dalles have passed." Caldwell set up a temporary depot on Rock Creek, which he named Camp Watson in honor of the slain lieutenant.

After Currey chased the Snakes from the South Fork of the John Day, Drake got permission to split off and he headed west to Camp Maury. "I do not like Captain Currey's way of pursuing Indians," he wrote, somewhat contradicting his earlier assessment, "he moves too slowly." He believed the large size of the combined command "was unwieldy and the whole plan was altogether impracticable. Fifty men with four days' cooked rations might perhaps have accomplished something." At Camp Maury on July 18, Drake wrote that the last forty-two days were "absolutely thrown away," and General Alvord's orders "spoiled most effectually the campaign of both expeditions." The next several days were spent abandoning Camp Maury because it was destitute of forage, and rebuilding on a new location about six miles west, to be called Camp Gibbs.[7]

Oregon's citizens looked unfavorably upon the non-productive marching to and fro across mountain and desert. Unnamed soldiers and civilians sent critical letters to the newspapers, many of which were gleefully published. On July 1, 1864, The Dalles *Mountaineer* editorialized that there "is something wrong in the management of the troops now in Indian Country." Captains Drake and Currey were "sent out for the especial purpose of protecting miners and others against Indian depredations. In view of this fact it is somewhat strange that the officers named keep clear of the scene of all the Indian outrages." It is on the Canyon City Road where all the raiding was occurring, the paper claimed, "whilst the soldiers are allowed to amuse themselves in a wild goose excursion up Crooked River."

Author's photo

Site of Camp Watson, Oregon. The marker indicates the course of Fort Creek.

Drake was frustrated and hurt. In his private journal he wrote: "By looking over the Oregon papers and private letters published I find that I am becoming an object against whom all the spleen and abuse of the country is being hurled." The people of The Dalles, he wrote, were the most abusive, "and their conduct amounts to a systematic defamation of character." Drake blamed General Alvord for much of the trouble. Alvord released his correspondence to the papers "to show how much he has done to secure the safety of the Canyon City road, but says not one word of the orders received May 10 which sent me a flanking towards Lake Harney. The fact of the matter is I am being systematically slaughtered." When Alvord told Captain Caldwell that he had given Drake the leeway to act on his own judgment, Drake called it "the damndest lie the old hoary-headed scoundrel ever told in his life."

Doctor William H. Watkins, who marched with Captain Caldwell, knew the hard campaigning they had done, and indignantly wrote a complaint to Governor Gibbs, his brother-in-law. He wanted Gibbs to tell the newspaper editors "it was unjust to publish adverse reports" from people like privates who had been sent to the guardhouse and wrote scathing comments "to get even." Watkins defended Currey, saying that he had marched 1,200 miles trying to bring the Indians to bay, that Drake has been on the move the entire time, and that Waymire's excursion was "bold and as full of danger as Sheridan's around Richmond." All the commands, said Watkins, had been campaigning extremely hard, and "then to have adverse stories published in the papers by those who know nothing about it is not agreeable."[8]

Drake and Curry, by orders of General Alvord, operated too far south to protect the Canyon City Road. He could have corrected the situation earlier

45

by directing units to move north. Instead, Alvord asked Governor Gibbs to form another company of forty mounted men with which to guard the Canyon City Road. This temporary unit, to be in service for four months, was given to Nathan Olney of The Dalles. The people of that city, whose businesses suffered because of the chaos along the road, offered to pay a bounty to the volunteers in addition to the pay they would receive from the government. The company was quickly raised, and on July 19, Lieutenant Olney left The Dalles to patrol the Canyon City Road in cooperation with Captain Caldwell.

CAMP WATSON

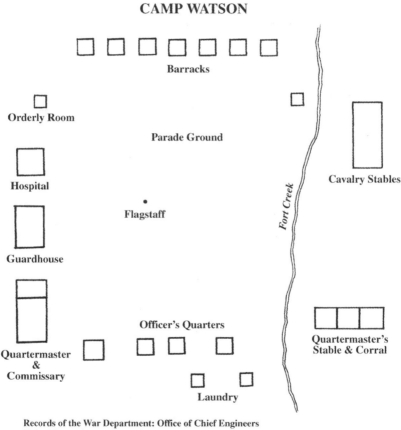

Records of the War Department: Office of Chief Engineers
United States Quartermaster's Department Barracks State of Oregon, County of Grant
Capacity: 120 men (at present)
Stable for 50 Cavalry horses and 25 Quartermaster's horses
Material: Log Roof: Shingles Condition: Good
Built from October 1864 to Present
Occupied from October 1864
Garrison of 100 troops, Cavalry & Infantry

By mid-July, however, Drake and Currey had moved into the southern Blue Mountains without Alvord's sanction, and concluded that the Indians were gone from the Canyon City area. Currey had further information that indicated it was time to leave. A courier brought word that cattle were stolen in Harney Lake Valley, and an expressman from Camp Alvord delivered news from some stock drovers that Paulina had joined up with a village at a small lake about 30 miles west of Camp Alvord. In addition, Currey was holding a letter from several civilians in the Owyhee District, signed July 13, that told of Indian depredations in the vicinity, reported a battle with the Indians, and asked for help. Currey decided to return to Camp Alvord, and concluded that since he took command, the county had been thoroughly scouted from the Malheur River to the Deschutes. He wrote to headquarters that the troops were now familiar with a region previously unknown, suggesting that he had demystified a place that was heretofore "filled by the fertile imagination of a panic-stricken people with hordes of savages strongly posted in the impregnable fastnesses of trackless mountains and yawning cañons."[9]

Why Currey seemed to make light of the settlers' fears is perplexing; the Indians may have temporarily moved out of the John Day and Crooked River region, but some were still around, and more would return. On July 20, as a result of "Currey's wishes," Drake took Lieutenant Noble and sixteen men of Company G, twelve men of Company D, ten men of Company B, and twelve men of Company E, to examine the Sheep Rock area. They marched 165 miles to the Deschutes River and back, looking for a mountain that Drake wouldn't recognize if he saw it, crossed territory that he called "utterly worthless," and found no Indians. On July 30, Drake reached Camp Gibbs on Crooked River. Currey had taken the other half of the force and scouted the Blue Mountains, arriving back at the camp on July 25. Three days later he was off, moving up Bridge Creek, across the Ochoco Mountains, and into the Crooked River watershed. There was no Indian sign. Currey returned to Camp Watson on July 30, a few hours after Drake arrived from his excursion to the Deschutes. Currey had enough in the north, packed up, and headed south to Camp Alvord.

Remaining in the Crooked River vicinity, Drake continued to have his problems. When he returned from the Deschutes, Cayuse George relayed the news from The Dalles that the captain's latest expedition was being called "Drake's fishing party." Drake again blamed his bad press on General Alvord, who he considered a scoundrel for passing personal and military business to William H. Newell, the southern-leaning Democrat editor of The Dalles *Mountaineer*.

It was true, Drake was doing a lot of marching, but the only fighting taking place was among his own men. He sent his officers out on several scouts, but with few results, and lamented, "I wish I had about two officers who could do something in the way of scouting. I have not got an officer that is worth a curse for such service." Drake disliked Small and Hand, and also wondered about Waymire and McCall's ability to perform under fire. As for Small, he was becoming something of a pariah after being observed recording discussions among officers, writing down gossip and rumors, and apparently reporting to his friend, Governor Gibbs. Drake figured that Small had "the faculty of being as mean a man as anyone I know." Small's machinations permeated to the enlisted men, who formed factions and took sides. In mid-August, when Sergeant Thomas Baker led an escort detail to take a supply train to Fort Dalles, the men mutinied near Cedar Spring and severely beat Baker. He was injured enough to require medical treatment back in camp. Drake arrested the entire detail. One of Small's men, Private John Adams, tried to explain that he and Baker had criminal records and committed robbery at The Dalles before the expedition left in April. Adams said Baker was beaten for some contretemps among thieves. Drake didn't believe it.[10]

On August 22, the depot at Camp Gibbs was moved for better forage, and for the third time since spring, reestablished on Paulina Creek three or four miles east of the battleground of May 18. It was named Camp Dahlgren, for Colonel Ulric Dahlgren, killed during the spring in a raid near Richmond, Virginia. Drake hoped there would be no need to relocate again. From Dahlgren, he continued his fruitless scouting in the mountains. In late August, Captain Richard Caldwell rode in from the John Day River to tell Captain Drake about all the trouble he was having keeping discipline among his officers and men. Nathan Olney, recently promoted to captain, gave Caldwell so much trouble that he threatened to place him under arrest and throw his company in the guardhouse. He wrote to General Alvord about disbanding Olney's volunteers because they were "utterly worthless and unmanageable." Olney was less concerned about fighting Indians and more interested in making deals with Canyon City's businessmen to raise money to "help defray the expense" of maintaining his detachment of cavalry.

There was another flare-up among Drake's officers. Surgeon Dumreicher, described as "a stiff, aristocratic old fool morbid in his sensibilities and contemptible," was thought to have wanted the campaign to fail, rather than see Drake get accolades. Dumreicher, called "Pills" by the officers, was happy to cause as many rifts between them as possible. Drake was on good terms with the quartermaster, Lieutenant David W. Porter, and that aggravated Dumreicher. On September 2, Dumreicher had Porter come to his tent and sample much of his supply of "medicinal" alcohol. Lieutenant Noble joined them and they got boisterous, staggering to Small's tent, which was sure to create a scene. The noise awoke Drake, and he stopped the gaiety and berated Noble, assuming he was the cause of the commotion. Porter stewed all night, believing Drake's comments were meant solely for him, and the next morning, said Drake, Porter "got mad as the devil." Porter remained sullen. "Pills" had succeeded in driving a wedge between the two men who had once been good friends. Drake believed the doctor had "been laboring to produce this rupture between Porter and myself." It was Noble who remained jolly and took it all in good stride. Drake came to believe that Noble was the one he could count on. Still, by the end of August, Drake was fed up and thought he would leave the service. "I am tired of it myself," he wrote.[11]

On September 9, Drake received the latest news from Fort Dalles, which included speculations that the 1st Oregon Cavalry would be filled and a new regiment of Oregon infantry would be formed, requiring about 1,500 new recruits. Drake chuckled, knowing that the news "will make the Webfoot nation squirm." It was a good portent. "I am anxious to see a few of them out here hunting Pe-li-ni," he wrote. "I think they may place a different estimate on brass buttons by the time they have worn them two or three years." Drake was tired of the "odium and reproach" that many civilians placed on the troops, and he proclaimed, "Were it not for the helpless women and children I would rejoice to see the Indians wipe out the Columbia River country one of these days, just to let the people of Portland and Dalles know what slippery ground they stand on."

On the September 11, Captain Porter went out to open a wagon road between Crooked River and the Canyon City Road. The new road went north from Camp Dahlgren, to Little Summit Prairie, and over the Ochocos to Mountain Creek just west of Camp Watson. It gave civilians and soldiers a one-day, all-weather communication and travel route between the two river valleys. The remainder of September was relatively quiet. Lieutenant Waymire went out on a ten-day scout, but, as usual, discovered no Indians. The soldiers spent much of the rest of the time in camp amusing themselves. Noble entertained the officers every night telling tales, to Drake's astonishment of the "immense fund" of stories he had. Drake found himself liking Noble more as the season advanced. "His good humor is inexhaustible," he wrote, "Always lively, always jolly. I do not know what we would do without him."

When Noble was not story-telling, the men spent their idle hours reading. It may be instructive to understand just how much frontier people read, and how informed they were about politics, economics, current events, literature, and classical studies—subjects that may appear esoteric even among some of the more crudite of the reading populace of the twenty-first century. Drake looked forward to receiving his monthly *Atlantic* and *Harpers*, but, being on campaign, his book reading was limited to "Recreations of a Country Parsons," the "Life of Jesus," "Butler in New Orleans," "Lyles Geology," and "a little poetry and a novel or two." Later in the month, Drake got hold of a *North American Review*, and voraciously read articles on "Physical Theory of the Universe" and "Philosophy of Space and Time." McCall and Rinehart were reading about Julius Caesar and spent several nights around the campfire discussing his campaigns, once trying to stump Drake with a question about the death of Pompey, but the well-read captain was up to their challenge.[12]

On September 18, orders were received to end the season's campaigning. Drake and Caldwell were to report back to Fort Dalles, and Company G was ordered to prepare to take up winter station at Camp Watson or in the vicinity. Perhaps justice prevailed in the end, for Drake had recently speculated that Captain Small was either the writer, or instigator, behind the scathing letters that had been sent to the newspapers during the summer. Now, Small was himself condemned to spend the winter in the wilderness. Noble chuckled over the situation, said Drake, "because it will be such a terrible punishment to Small and Hand." Small would remain behind with Olney's "Forty Thieves." Drake: "I think he will be the most down-hearted man in camp when he arrives. And what will Hand say? It will nearly kill him!"

Small, who had been out on a scout, returned on September 22. From Cayuse George, Drake learned that Small did not go where Drake had intended. "I never have been able to get that man to do what I wanted him to do or go where I wanted him to go," he said. As in Drake's prediction, when Small learned of his orders, he was "terribly enraged at the idea of having to remain on the Canyon City road during the winter, and Hand is almost mortified to death." Noble, who got a laugh out of it at first, changed his tune when he learned that he was to assume duties of quartermaster and stay behind also, under command of Captain Small!

On the last day of the month, Drake held an inspection and found a few dirty guns in his company. "McCall and Waymire don't attend to these things closely," he said, "they are both so anxious to get out of the service that they cannot attend to their duties properly." On October 1, Small moved and re-built Camp Watson at a better location for wood, water, and shelter, about four miles west on Fort Creek. On October 2, just before Drake started for Fort Dalles, he learned that General Alvord ordered Small to send his horses to Vancouver for the winter. "What is to be done out here in winter, by a company of cavalry without horses," Drake wondered. He even felt a little sorry for Small. "General Alvord's strategy is becoming remarkable; I am glad I am not to be made his scapegoat this time. I would hate to be in Small's predicament during the winter." No doubt happy to be done with the current season's campaign, Drake, Caldwell, McCall, Porter, Waymire, and the rest rode away, reaching Fort Dalles on October 11.

While Small was stuck at Camp Watson like Washington at Valley Forge, Drake was "glad it is ended. I am heartily sick and tired of these campaigns in the plains." He believed that his and Currey's expeditions drove the hostile Indians "out of the country near the Canyon City road far to the south." He didn't think there were any large bodies of Indians in Harney

Lake Valley. "Those Indians do not concentrate;" he wrote, "they scatter." Since the Indians raided and ran, having the soldiers concentrate "proved to be a waste of time." Drake concluded that the Indians' strength "lies in the extent and character of the country in which they live and their activity and address in availing themselves of the advantages afforded by nature." He had a poor opinion of the territory. "Of the district of country embraced within the theater of the summer's operations there is little to be said beyond the mere fact that it is worthless."[13]

Chapter 5 notes

1 Drake's Journal, 41-50.

2 Drake's Journal, 51-55; *Oregon Sentinel*, August 27, 1864.

3 Drake's Journal, 55-68; *WR*: 50/1, 320-22; *WR*: 50/2, 901.

4 Drake's Journal, 68-71.

5 Ontko, *Thunder Over the Ochoco III*, 208-10; *WR*: 50/1, 321; Drake's Journal, 72-73.

6 Ontko, *Thunder Over the Ochoco III*, 210-11; *WR*: 50/1, 321-22; Drake's Journal, 73-74.

7 *WR*: 50/1, 323-24, 332-33, 348-49; Drake's Journal, 74-76.

8 Drake's Journal, 77-78, 80.

9 *WR*: 50/1, 323-24; *WR*: 50/2, 894-98; *Oregon Sentinel*, June 26, 1864; Bancroft, *History of Oregon*, Vol. 2, 497.

10 Ontko, *Thunder Over the Ochoco III*, 217-18; Drake's Journal, 58, 80, 89, 92-93.

11 *Oregon Sentinel*, August 20, 1864; Drake's Journal, 84-89, 93-94; Ontko, *Thunder Over the Ochoco III*, 218-19, 233.

12 Drake's Journal, 95, 97, 99, 100-01, 110-11.

13 *WR*: 50/1, 341-42; *WR*: 50/2, 977; Drake's Journal, 103, 105-07, 111, 113, 116-17. Lieutenant Waymire resigned on 29 November 1864. The bodies of the enlisted men killed at the Crooked River fight were removed from Camp Maury and reburied at Camp Watson. The remains of Lieutenant Watson were taken to Fort Vancouver, where they were interred in 5W, North Side, Grave 3. A headstone was set at Camp Watson in memory of him, leading to later speculation that he was reburied there. See *Antone Ranch and Camp Watson*, 21.

Chapter 6
DREW'S EXPEDITION

W hile Drake and Currey operated in central and southeast Oregon, many of the Paiutes had cleared out of the area and had been raiding south and west along the Yreka and Canyon City Road. To cover that portion of southern Oregon, Fort Klamath was built under the supervision of Major Charles S. Drew, 1st Oregon Cavalry, and by the labor of Captain William Kelly and his men of C Company.

Kelly, born in Ireland, enlisted in the U. S. Army in 1843, and fought in the Mexican War in the 4th Infantry, leaving the army in 1853. He fought as a captain in the Washington Territory Volunteers in the Yakima War. In December 1861, he enlisted in the 1st Oregon Cavalry. Kelly was industrious, conscientious, and followed orders, as well as being able to operate independently. He constructed Fort Klamath soundly, in a well-watered and wooded area eight miles north of Upper Klamath Lake, and well situated to cover the Rogue River Road and Yreka-John Day Road, as well as being centrally located to oversee the Klamath and Modoc Tribes. In March 1864, Drew, now a lieutenant colonel, returned from San Francisco after informing General Wright of the possible benefits of opening a road east from Fort Klamath to the Owyhee country.

For some time, Drew had been under pressure from the people of southwest Oregon, to do something constructive. General Alvord had written to Governor A. C. Gibbs, recommending a movement east from Fort Klamath to act in conjunction with his two expeditions, but he couldn't directly order Drew to move, since Drew was in Wright's jurisdiction. The citizens of southwest Oregon always believed that there would be a great profit in having a road open from there to the Owyhee, to protect miners, emigrants, and travelers, and to give southwest Oregon and northern California a cut in the business markets. Even though Drew's reported expedition appeared as good news, the Jacksonville, *Oregon Sentinel* could not help but complain that Drew should have done this back in 1862. Instead, Drew, a Democrat with pro-southern leanings and labeled a "Copperhead," was accused of boondoggling, staying out of harm's way, wasting tens of thousands of dollars in the construction of Fort Klamath, and giving government contracts to his other "Copperhead" cronies. The paper named Glenn & Company as one recipient of Drew's favors, reportedly collecting thousands of dollars selling overpriced oats to feed the army horses.

The *Sentinel* compared Drew's achievements with Colonel Maury "up north." Maury, it said, "has taken his command and gone out on the plains every year, and not only aided emigrants to reach the settlements in safety, but has afforded assistance and protection to the enterprising prospectors in the Boise Country." As a result, it claimed, a new territory has been opened up to business, emigration, and prosperity. Even the mails, the *Sentinel* said, "have all already been turned to the North, leaving Jacksonville an out-of-the-way place." If Drew had been as enterprising as Maury, southern Oregon could already have been dividing up the profits of the Idaho trade. The road-opening expedition was long overdue. Send every man available, the *Sentinel* urged, so that "mines may be discovered surpassing either Boise or Washoe. That is what we say, sir. . . .You sabe, Colonel?"

Regardless of the call for action, a number of delays, including deep snow, kept the apparently reluctant Drew from his task until late June. Just before he left, he warned that a considerable number of Snakes appeared to be in the area. One of them, Howluck (Bigfoot), of the Pohoi band, he claimed was seeking to incite the Klamath and Modoc Tribes into warfare with the whites, and investigating this rumor had delayed his departure. He left Lieutenant D. C. Underwood with a detachment of Company C in charge at Fort Klamath, with orders to build two blockhouses and enclosures for the stock for additional protection. Drew and Captain Kelly, with a mountain howitzer, thirty-nine soldiers, plus guides and civilians totaling about eighty-five men, had only been on the road a few days, moving east up Sprague River, when his warning was borne out.[1]

JOHN DAY'S ROAD, JUNE 24, 1864

A wagon train of prospectors and traders from Shasta Valley, California, under John Richardson, was on the Yreka-John Day's Road near Silver Lake, about 70 miles northeast of Fort Klamath, when Indians attacked them. The eight-wagon train, with twenty-three men, two families, and about eight women, circled around in a defensive perimeter. The war party, at first thought to be either Klamaths or Modocs, severely wounded two men, stole seven cattle and destroyed 3,000 pounds of flour. The train retreated, came upon a second train under a Mr. Allen, heading out from Jacksonville with nine wagons and twenty-one men, and both trains fell back south to the John Day's Ford on Sprague River about 30 miles east of Fort Klamath, where they found Lt. Colonel Drew.

Drew delayed again while he communicated with Lieutenant Underwood as to the identity of the raiders. Underwood was satisfied that none of La Lake's Klamath band were involved because they had been around the fort the entire time. Drew was with Moshenkosket (Motcunka Sket), a half-blood Shoshoni with his mixed band of Klamaths and Shoshonis, who occupied Sprague River Valley, and he knew they were not involved. To make sure, Drew, Richardson, guide John M. Ross, and a few others, went to inspect Moshenkosket's camp. Richardson could not identify any Indians who attacked him, nor could he find any of the stolen property. Most of them concluded that the raiders were Paiutes under Howluck. On July 8, Kelly returned to Fort Klamath and Richardson and Allen changed their plans about heading toward Canyon City and decided it would be safer to accompany Drew to the Owyhee country. Drew, now shepherding two wagon trains, crawled slowly east, opening up a new road as he went.

A. R. Bowman Museum Crook County
Historical Society, Prineville, Oregon

Lt. Colonel C. S. Drew, *ca* 1863.

The expedition went into the valley north of Goose Lake, along a creek that would later bear Drew's name, an area he said was beautiful, fertile, well-watered, and with good grass and timber. Drew believed the valley was "neutral ground," not claimed by the Paiutes, Klamaths, Modocs, or Pit River Indians. All tribes fished, hunted, and gathered there—and travelers through the area might expect to be attacked by anyone. Before Drew arrived, a train owned by Tower & Company, out of Shasta County, California, had passed through the area and was attacked in the desert to the north. The Indians killed a Mr. Dean of the firm, one other employee, and stole 300 head of cattle.

On July 17, Drew's Klamath scouts found about twenty men from the Owyhee, under Charley Delaplain, who had been prospecting the upper Malheur country, but were now trying to get to Surprise Valley. The scouts escorted them to Drew's camp on the east shore of Goose Lake. They also brought in three Snakes who had come to inquire about Drew's purpose for being there. The Snakes left their horses, came in on foot, unarmed, and held a peaceful talk. Drew questioned them, got information about the country ahead, and satisfied himself that they were not hostile. He let them spend the night and sent them on their way in the morning. Some of Delaplain's party, however, had designs on the horses the Snakes had left behind. In the morning, on the pretext of going hunting, four men, led by a Mr. Parker, and including a Mr. Burton, who was said to have joined them only after taunts about being an "Indian sympathizer," went out to steal the Snakes' horses.

Later that day, two of Drew's scouts returned with the news that the party had a fight, and at least one man was dead. Drew sent ten soldiers to the scene, but they found only Burton's body. Later in the day, the other three whites straggled in and Drew learned the story. Apparently, one of the white men, who had lost some stock on the Malheur the previous year, decided he wanted the Indians' horses, and "this was their first chance to get even." They jumped the Indians and got possession of two horses just when a few more Indians happened to arrive. They killed Burton, and drove off the three other white men. Drew, noting the poor condition of the two stolen horses, concluded that the sad affair was hardly worth the effort and served only to stir up trouble. He sent the beasts back to the Indians. He then learned that a few other wagon trains of families were on the road heading east, and decided to wait for them to catch up.[2]

On July 20, several heavy wagon trains from northern California joined up, all heading to Boise. Drew and the emigrants were still in dangerous territory. Captain William H. Warner had come to this spot on an expedition seeking a railroad route across the Sierra Nevada in 1849. On September 20, east of Goose Lake, he was jumped by a band of Pit River warriors, who killed Warner and two others, and wounded a few more. Passing along the emigrant trail through the Warner Mountains, Drew gathered up his charges and continued. From near the summit, Drew could see down into the Great Basin, where the country changed drastically from timbered volcanic formations to an empty, slate gray-looking desert bounded by successive north-south trending mountain ranges. In Surprise Valley, the Allen Train left them, heading along the Black Rock route to the Humboldt River. Drew, with the remaining trains and nearly 1,300 head of livestock, swung north-east across Surprise Valley to Warner Valley, along the mostly dry, alkaline shores of Christmas Lakes, so named by explorer John C. Fremont in 1843, and to the impressive escarpment of Warner Mountain, which Drew called "the Sebastopol of the Snake Indians."[3]

Unknown to Drew, Paulina and his Paiutes watched the procession from the top of the cliffs. Drew scouted the area and believed it was unequalled for military purposes, with hundreds of square miles commanding the area and complete with good lakes, streams, grass, aspen, willow, and berries. The Paiutes thought it was a haven also, and Paulina was about to attack Drew, but was dissuaded when he saw that the soldiers had a howitzer. They remained hidden and let the wagon trains roll by. Besides, with these soldiers approaching from the west, and others soldiers (Currey) coming from the east, Paulina may have figured that it was time to lie low.

Drew slowly moved north in Warner Valley from August 1-8. He scouted around Warner Mountain and found an abandoned camp of about sixty lodges and the tracks of many horses, mules, and cattle. Drew was not in a hurry to chase the Indians. He rationalized, "Having a force of only thirty-nine enlisted men, and several families under our charge, and property to the value of perhaps one hundred and forty thousand dollars to guard. . .I deemed 'discretion the better part of valor' and avoided acting upon the offensive. . . ."

With neither side seeking a confrontation, Drew moved southeast across "the most sterile country we had yet seen," with "hardly a spot of grass. . .and no water except a small muddy alkaline lake, rendered unpalatable by being the common rendezvous of countless ducks, geese, and all other species of waterfowls common to the country." The water was "barely endurable for cooking purposes, but not at all palatable to drink. This we named, as its character suggested, Guano Lake." There were several large Indian trails in the area, most of them trending north and south through Guano Valley. Drew left Guano Lake on August 14, carrying in his ambulance a woman from one of the wagon trains, who had gotten extremely ill. They headed southeast, out of the valley and across an "interminable field of the largest and most vigorous sage we had yet seen," that clogged the wagon wheels and added to everyone's fatigue. Drew drove them a rough 28 miles, trying to reach the next spot where the guide hoped there would be water. They found the springs, flowing just enough to sustain them, coming from the east side of a table mountain with a conical top (probably today's Acty Mountain), and as a compliment to his guide, Drew named it Isaac's Springs.

From there, Drew traveled southeast, probably across today's Hawks Valley and down Long Draw just south of the border into Nevada. He circled the southern tip of the Pueblo Mountains and headed north, past today's Continental Lake, and north through Pueblo Valley. By August 21, they were back in Oregon and moving north along the east face of the Pueblo Mountains, passing the mining district, which Drew estimated to hold no more than thirty miners, and camping that night on Trout Creek, which came in to the valley from the east. The creek was nearly gone, sunk into the sand, before it reached the valley, yet it abounded with mountain trout and Drew thought it a mystery how so many fine fish could have gotten there. From where Trout Creek entered the valley, and across to the mountains, were the best grazing lands in the region. Drew stayed there three days to recuperate his animals. He had originally planned to continue east from this point to the upper Owyhee River, through a region little known, but the animals were wearing out, supplies were low, and the civilian trains still needed an escort. Drew decided to continue north where he hoped to reach Camp Alvord and perhaps obtain supplies there.

Moving north, they discovered the partial skeleton of a soldier, with scraps of his uniform still clinging to the bones; Drew guessed the remains might have been of Sergeant Casteel, lost during Waymire's expedition the previous April. Finally, on August 26, Drew connected with Currey at Camp Alvord.[4]

Currey and Drake had pestered Paulina enough in June and July that he moved south. When Currey followed to Steens Mountain, Paulina moved west to Warner Mountain, where he watched Drew march past in early August. Drew was not quite correct, Warner Mountain was not the main Paiute stronghold—that remained in the Ochoco Mountains between Crooked River and John Day River—but it was a useful base to rest, hide, obtain food and water, and send out raiding expeditions.

Currey had left Drake at Camp Watson on August 2, and headed back to Camp Alvord, which he reached on August 12, after having circled around the west and south side of Malheur Lake. On August 15, Currey sent out a courier to the mining camp that had sprung up in the Pueblo Mountains about 35 miles to the south of Camp Alvord, to search for Lt. Colonel Drew, who he assumed would have reached that point by then, but who was still back at Isaac's Springs. The next day, Currey sent Captain Barry with twenty men of the 1st Washington Territory Infantry to the southwest to hunt for Indians and Drew. Barry went to Wildhorse Creek and ascended to its headwaters. From the west side of the high point of Steens Mountains, at 9,773 feet, Barry had a commanding view, noting that even in a "dense" atmosphere he could see the mountains to the west of Harney Lake. He saw many fish in a stream that he named Trout Creek, which was actually the headwaters of Donner und Blitzen River, but he saw no Indians. Barry returned to camp on August 19. The next day, realizing the folly of chasing the mobile Indians across the country in the summer, Currey wrote to Alvord that he believed Camp Alvord could be occupied through the winter since he didn't think the weather would be too severe; it had a good supply of grass and water, there was a growing mining community at Pueblo that needed protection, and by vacating the country in the fall, "the labor of the summer will in a great measure be lost." His recommendations were ignored.[5]

The day that Barry returned from his scout, a party of twenty-five Indians, who were undoubtedly unaware of Camp Alvord, nearly rode right in among the soldiers before they turned and fled. As soon as Currey readied his horses he took detachments of Companies A and E and pursued them. The soldiers chased them south along the east face of Pueblo Mountain, until the Indians cut up Horse Creek and climbed out of the valley. Behind them they abandoned six horses, three of which they killed, and several packloads of skins and provisions. Currey gave up the chase at dusk. The months of campaigning were wearing him down. He wrote: "I am almost discouraged at the prospect of being able to accomplish anything very definite by October 1; the country is so vast and the Indians so familiar with it that until the mountain fastnesses are blocked up with snow and they are compelled to seek winter camps I can devise no means of striking an effectual blow."

Currey recruited his horses at Alvord for a few more days. On August 20, he sent out Sergeant Gates with twenty men of Company E, to scout east to the Owyhee Mountains and try to find word of Colonel Maury, who was supposed to be hunting Indians in that area. Gates went as far as Succor

Creek, saw no Indians, and heard from the settlers that Maury had already been there and returned to Fort Boise. While awaiting Gates's return, the long-delayed Drew marched in.

Currey and Drew discussed their adventures, but neither could tell the other much about finding the Indians. Currey said that Drew told him "he saw several bands of Indians in the region which I propose to visit, but as he was so encumbered with a large train of citizens, including several families, he could not pursue them into the mountains." When Sergeant Gates returned on August 30, he could not provide any helpful news about the Indians either. Both commanders went their separate ways. On August 31, Drew took a detachment of nineteen men of Company C, and escorted most of the civilian wagon trains to Jordan Creek Valley. Sergeant James Moore stayed behind with eighteen men and the most worn out stock. Assistant Surgeon Greer also remained behind, still caring for the sick woman. Her train of emigrants, completely exhausted, decided to wait and accompany Currey's quartermaster train when it returned to Fort Boise at a later date. This progression of army and emigrants from west to east runs counter to the idea of an orderly east to west wave of emigrants popularized by historian Frederick Jackson Turner in the 1890s, and today embedded in America's psyche. In reality, much of Idaho was first settled by people moving "backwards," from west to east.

Six miles from the Owyhee Crossing, the road from Camp Alvord joined up with the road coming north from the Humboldt. The crossing was by a gravelly ford on the river, 60 yards wide at that point and 14 inches deep. On Jordan Creek on September 3, Drew heard of Indian raids and the miners' retaliation and rested. He also received a special express with orders directing him to return immediately to Fort Klamath. Drew couldn't comply without first getting needed supplies at Fort Boise and letting his worn out animals rest, so he continued on to Booneville. Drew believed that a cavalry post in the area would thwart many Indian raids, and the following June, Camp Lyon was built nearby. From Booneville, some of the trains moved to Ruby City and Silver City to sell produce and flour. The cattle trains recruited for a day and continued on to Boise City. Drew, figuring the route was safe enough at this point, left most of his force camped seven miles west of Booneville, took Sergeant Garrett Crockett, Corporal Abner Biddle (or Riddle), six employees, and all the pack mules, and hurried north along Reynolds Creek 25 miles to Enoch Fruit's Ferry over the Snake River. On September 9, he reached Fort Boise and purchased enough supplies for his return journey. Yet, instead of hurrying back to Fort Klamath as ordered, Drew continued on to Idaho City. He did not pick up his supplies and get back to the Snake River until September 14. It took him another seven days to go 118 miles to Camp Alvord, reaching there on September 22.[6]

On September 2, two days after Drew left Camp Alvord for Boise, Currey headed south to the Pueblo Mountains, and southwest about 40 miles into Nevada. On September 8, he reached the vicinity of Summit Lake before many of his men came down with what he called "the bloody flux." The dysentery, which hit a number of Currey's men at Alvord before they left, now affected most of the command, but Surgeon Cochrane used "an effusion of the root of the wild geranium," which eased the men's cramps somewhat. While in camp, the ill soldiers managed to capture five Paiutes. Somehow, Currey surmised that they had been part of the band that had killed civilians in the Owhyee country, and wanted to hang them. Surprisingly, they were saved by some miners from the Pueblo District who figured that all the prospectors in the area would be safer if the Indians were freed. Currey reluctantly agreed to their wishes. Their mercy was rewarded when these same Indians later returned to murder the miners.

Currey waited in camp until September 10, and with only slight improvement in his men, decided to call off the campaign. He marched back to Camp Alvord, reaching there on September 16. Six days later, Drew came in from Boise, heading west to Fort Klamath, already about three weeks late responding to his orders to hurry back. The two met again, once more with little to discuss about finding the Indians. After recuperating for ten days, Currey left Camp Alvord for the winter, sending Barry with the infantry and baggage wagons with ten men each from companies A and E, to Fort Boise. Lieutenant Silas Pepoon, acting quartermaster, was to accompany them to Boise and then bring the wagons back to the mouth of the Malheur River to meet Currey. The captain took the remainder of the two cavalry companies north along Steens Mountain, twisted around in the forks of the Malheur, and concluded that the canyonlands of that river was no place for an emigrant road.

On October 4, three civilians visited Currey, complaining that Indians had stolen their stock, and the next morning, the soldiers awoke to find four of their own packmules missing. Currey blamed the white "rascals" running with the Indians as the thieves. After eight months of marching and fighting to prevent such thefts, the soldiers were hard pressed to protect their own property.

Currey met Pepoon on October 13, and the united command headed north to Fort Walla Walla, where on October 26, the expedition was formally dissolved. Lieutenant Charles Hobart and Company A stayed at that post, Lieutenant John Bowen with a detachment of Company F was sent to Fort Lapwai, and Currey and Company E marched to Fort Dalles.[7]

At the start of the season, General Alvord had written to Colonel Maury that his idea was to "collect and settle all these roving tribes," because "considerations of humanity and economy prompt immediate steps to remedy both evils—extermination and the cost of fitting out expeditions every summer."[8] His wishes had not been fulfilled. The expeditions based in Oregon and Washington had been in the field from March to October and had not collected, settled, or killed ten Indians. The expedition out of Nevada had even less success.

Chapter 6 notes

1 Frazer, *Forts*, 130; *Oregon Sentinel*, March 19, 1864, April 2, 1864; *WR*: V.50/2, 804, 877-78; Clark, "McKay's Journal, Part 2," 290-91.

2 Murray, *Modocs*, 39; *WR*: V.50/1, 381; *WR:* V.50/2, 900-01, 911; *Oregon Sentinel*, July 9, 1864, August 20, 1864, February 4, 1865, February 11, 1865, March 11, 1865.

3 Goetzmann, *Exploration & Empire*, 279-80; Bancroft, *History of Oregon*, Vol. 2, 504; McArthur, *Oregon Geographic Names*, 201, 449; *Oregon Sentinel*, August 20, 1864, February 11, 1865. Warner Mountain is presently known as Hart Mountain and the Christmas Lakes are now the chain of Crump, Hart, Anderson, Flagstaff, Campbell, and Bluejoint Lakes.

4 *Oregon Sentinel*, December 10, 1864, February 18, 1865, February 25, 1865.

5 Bancroft, *History of Oregon*, Vol. 2, 504; *WR*: V.50/1, 324-25, 329; *WR*: 50/2, 952; McArthur, *Oregon Geographic Names*, 297. Donner und Blitzen River was named by George Currey as he crossed it during a rainstorm in 1864. It is German for thunder and lightning.

6 *WR*: 50/1, 324-26; *Oregon Sentinel*, December 10, 1864; February 25, 1865, March 4, 1865, March 18, 1865.

7 Bancroft, *History of Oregon*, Vol. 2, 501-02; Welch, *Gold Town*, 15-16; *WR:* 50/1, 326-28.

8 *WR*: 50/2, 810.

Chapter 7

OPERATIONS IN NEVADA AND IDAHO, 1864

After the Paiute War of 1860, many of the defeated Indians who once lived near Pyramid Lake and along the Humboldt and Truckee Rivers fled to the Black Rock Desert and Smoke Creek Desert, hoping, by moving into the barren northern Nevada Territory they could avoid contact with the whites. The new mines in eastern Oregon and Idaho dispelled that hope, as miners and settlers once again streamed across the land. Three miners, Dr. H. Smeathman, W. F. White, and Frank Thompson, were prospecting west of the Pueblo Mountains just north of the Nevada border. As they looked for water on March 4, 1864, they found Indian tracks instead. Thompson suggested that they get out of the area, but the doctor objected. Soon after, Indians ambushed them and shot Smeathman off his horse. White and Thompson didn't wait around, but hightailed it south, and two days later, rode exhausted into Rabbit Hole Station to report the news.

Not learning the lesson, seven more miners entered the area two months later, traveling to the head of Kings River Valley and into the Trout Creek Mountains just south of the Oregon border. On May 3, Paiutes jumped them, killed G. W. Dodge, J. W. Burton, and two others, and captured eight animals. A man named Noble was hit in the neck, shoulder, and groin, but managed to keep firing while the two unhit miners quickly readied their horses. The three of them rode south to Star City, then a mining camp of about 1,200 people in the Humboldt Range near present-day Unionville, Nevada. The 7,781-foot mountain the miners were attacked near, took the name Disaster Peak.

The Humboldt *Register* of June 4, reported that an expedition went out to chastise the Indians. The forty-nine civilian volunteers and five Paiute scouts, self-styled as the Humboldt Rangers, secured horses and rode north. In the Disaster Peak area they found the miners' mutilated bodies and tracks heading in several directions. They split into smaller parties and searched all the trails they could follow, into the Pueblo Mountains, to Trout Creek, along Kings River, and into the mire of Quinn River. They chased off three small Paiute bands and engaged in a skirmish where one Ranger was killed and possibly three Indians. They recovered some of the dead miners' property and sixteen stolen cattle. The *Register* reported two "Bannocks" killed, one of them supposedly wearing the shirt of one of the four dead miners.[1]

Nevertheless, it was time for the military to do something about these attacks on civilians. The first large scale operation that the Nevada Cavalry participated in was called, the "Expedition to the Humboldt." It was to scout for Indians and show the citizens that the army was a viable source of protection. Company D, under Captain Almond B. Wells, left Fort Churchill June 8, 1864, crossed the 40-Mile Desert, moved up the Humboldt River and over to Star City, arriving on June 14. After several days' rest, Wells moved north to the Humboldt, crossed, and divided his command, sending twenty men west along the Applegate-Honey Lake Road to Camp Pollack in the Smoke Creek Desert. With the remaining fifty troopers, Wells moved north for two days, traveling about 80 miles over nearly waterless desert and mountain. In his report for June 21, he wrote, "Here was the scene of the late massacre."[2]

Wells marched southwest for two days to Rabbit Hole Springs on the Honey Lake Road, then west for three days across 80 miles of desert to Camp Pollack, a temporary site then located nearly on the California-Nevada border. Having seen no Indian sign, on July 8, Wells sent Lieutenant John

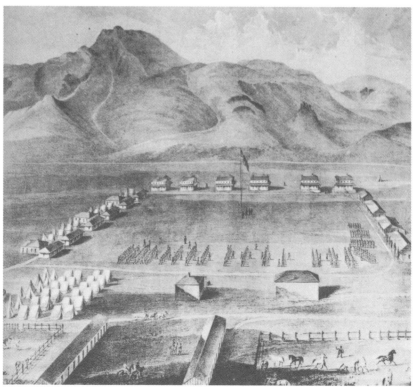

From Nevada's Black Rock Desert, *Caxton Press, courtesy Nevada State Highway Dept.*
Fort Churchill

Littlefield and ten men to Surprise Valley, about 70 miles north. Littlefield returned one week later, still without finding an Indian. While at Camp Pollack, one soldier died of disease and eight deserted. The command marched west to the Honey Lake-Susanville area. On July 22, Wells wrote to Assistant Adjutant General Richard C. Drum in San Francisco, stating that he could "see no use for troops in this portion of the country," since the Indians were quiet. If necessary, however, he believed Surprise Valley would be a good place for a fort.

In July, Nevada's Governor Nye received complaints from civilians around Star City and Unionville about a possible Confederate uprising, and Indians running off herds of horses. Nye turned the complaint over to Major Charles McDermit, 2nd California Cavalry, commanding at Fort Churchill. McDermit directed Wells to take care of it, and on July 27, Wells sent Littlefield with thirty men all the way back to Unionville, where everything proved to be quiet. Three men deserted from Littlefield's detachment before he rejoined Wells. Remaining in the Susanville area until August 24, the command finally packed up and headed south along the Sierra Nevada to Virginia City and Fort Churchill.

The expedition was the only major operation for the Nevada volunteers in their first year of service. Wells and Company D had spent eighty-four days in the field and marched about 1,200 miles.[3] They had patrolled the wagon routes and mining districts and made their presence known, at least to the whites in the area. Yet, they had not seen an Indian or fired a shot in anger. The Paiutes may have known the army was around, but the soldiers riding to and fro across the barren deserts likely had no effect on Indian plans.

In Idaho, the first serious action of the Snake War began with fighting between Indians and miners. Since the discovery of gold in the Owyhee Mountains in May 1863, the area had seen an influx of miners, businessmen, ranchers, and settlers. The first placer gold diggings along Jordan Creek quickly played out, but in October, fabulous silver-bearing quartz ledges were discovered on War Eagle and Florida Mountain, with the Poorman, Ida Elmore, and Golden Chariot Mines winning prizes during the years for the massive nuggets unearthed. The towns of Booneville (later renamed Dewey), Ruby City, and Silver City appeared. Mining activity flowed to the south in the Flint District, and ranchers took over the better water and grass areas along many creeks that headed in the Owyhees. Colonel Reuben F. Maury realized that the whites must have key areas, such as the upper Jordan River, which was known as Pleasant Valley, "for agricultural purposes, such lands on the eastern watershed of the Owyhee being remarkably scarce. In fact," Maury wrote, "so far as I have been able to judge, the Jordan Creek and Reynolds Creek Valleys are the only tracts that can be relied upon."

The influx of whites into a previously secure Indian haven naturally led to fighting. Isolated miners and travelers were killed in the region in 1863. In May 1864, Indians attacked a party near the junction of Jordan Creek and the Owyhee, one of the few places the canyon-rimmed Owyhee could be forded, and which came to be known as Owyhee Crossing. Indians also killed Porter Langdon and Thomas Renney on the dangerous trail between Warner Mountain and Harney Lake.

JORDAN'S FIGHT, JULY 12, 1864

On July 8, Indians raided near Booneville, "taking all the stock in the valley," some locals reported, "and what is still more shocking, killing and mangling one of our citizens in a most brutal manner." One of the ranchers who lost stock was Michael Jordan, one of the first discoverers of gold in the area. The civilians decided that they could not wait for military help and gathered twenty volunteers to track the marauders. They left on July 11, heading south toward the badlands of the Owyhee. The raiding Indians apparently felt no fear of being followed, for they had only gone about 40 miles from Booneville, to near the Middle Fork Owyhee. The civilians caught them in a canyon on July 12, but the Indians handled them roughly, killing Michael Jordan and wounding two others. The civilians hightailed it home, and, more sensibly, wrote a letter requesting help.[4]

The letter, dated June 13, addressed to Captain Currey, and signed by S. Skinner, J. C. Boone, H. White, R. Tregaskis, and J. Miller, reached Currey on July 23, and was one of the reasons prompting him to leave the Crooked River country and return to Camp Alvord. Word of the thefts and battle had already reached Colonel Maury at Fort Boise, and he took action. He gathered what Oregon Cavalry and Washington Territory Infantry he could spare, about 75 men under Lieutenants Funk, White, and Hobart, plus one howitzer, and headed for Booneville, reaching there July 21.

JUNIPER MOUNTAIN, JULY 20, 1864

Maury hoped that the civilians would wait for him and join his command, but although they requested help, they were too impatient to wait. This time, about 134 civilians marched out about July 15, seeking revenge. They got it, on July 20, in a canyon, probably on the slopes of Juniper Mountain near the Middle Fork Owyhee. The band they were tracking, consisting of about 120 Indians, separated, and the civilians took the trail that appeared to have more stock animals. Apparently most of the warriors had been with the other group heading southeast, for the Indians caught were nearly all women and children. The Indians fortified themselves in a canyon, but about five in the afternoon, the civilians charged in, taking two killed and two wounded, but devastating the camp and scattering the survivors. The civilians killed 35 people; reports varied from two to seven warriors, and the rest women and children. It was said that a few infants were battered to death on the rocks.

Colonel Maury later concluded that the Indians were of the same band that Captain Currey had chased away from their fishery on the Owyhee the previous spring. When he heard descriptions of the fight, he wrote, "The circumstances of our difficulties with these savages are no doubt very aggravating, but their conduct is no palliation for brutalizing our own race."

Idaho State Historical Society, 77-19.21

Silver City, Idaho, *ca* 1870s. Below, Silver City today

Author's photo

Author's photo

The Snake River near Glenns Ferry, Idaho, where Lieutenant Hobart's troopers tangled with hostiles.

Maury waited for news until July 24, and then left Booneville on his own. He marched down the Jordan 12 miles, and cut southwest. The evening of the day he left, the citizen volunteers returned, but no one thought to send a messenger to him. Maury made a wide semi-circle to the southwest, south, and southeast, roughly following the rim of the Great Basin, with the streams flowing to his west into the Basin, and to his east into the Owyhee. From the vicinity of the northern Santa Rosa Mountains on the Nevada border, he swung east and northeast. On August 4, he reached an abandoned camp that he took to be the site of Jordan's fight. Maury sent out cavalry patrols to scout the area, and then marched northeast to the head of Jordan Creek, arriving on August 8. The entire time they had only seen six Indians, but the Indians, Maury said, "succeeded in outfooting the party." At Booneville, Maury sent Lieutenant Funk and the infantry back to Fort Boise, and proceeded with Lieutenants White and Hobart and twenty-four cavalrymen to the fisheries on the Owyhee. Finding nothing there, Maury called off his expedition and headed to Fort Boise, which he reached on August 17, after an absence of twenty-eight days.[5] So far, if killing Indians was to be the measure of the summer's achievement, the white civilians could claim the only success.

THREE ISLAND CROSSING SEPTEMBER 13, 16, 1864

Army fortunes improved in September. Responding to reports of Indian thefts along the Snake River in southwest Idaho, Lieutenant Charles Hobart, with twenty-one men of Company A, 1st Oregon Cavalry, and Lieutenant Charles F. West, with twenty-eight men of Companies D and I, 1st

Washington Territory Infantry, left Fort Boise on August 27, 1864, heading for the Salmon Falls of the Snake River. Hobart, in charge of the expedition, had one mountain howitzer, 100 rounds of ammunition for each man, and forty days' rations. While en route, Hobart met Zacheus Van Ornum and his nephew Reuben. The boy had been captured by Bannocks in the vicinity in 1860, and had been recovered by his uncle in 1862. Zacheus and Reuben, familiar with the country, and perhaps hoping for some revenge, agreed to act as scouts for Hobart. They arrived at the mouth of Salmon Falls Creek on September 7.[6]

Hobart learned that Indians had stolen stock from near the ferry above Salmon Falls, and on the night before he arrived they ran off fifteen mules from a man named McFarland. Hobart sent out a party of men under Sergeant Wood, Company A, 1st Oregon Cavalry. He followed the trail of the missing stock and found the Indians on the north side of the Snake River about 25 miles above Salmon Falls. Wood killed three warriors, one of whom Hobart later learned was named Ebigon, a medicine man in one of the Snake bands. Wood recaptured a mule, a horse, and an ox.

When Wood returned, Hobart sent Lieutenant West with fifteen men of the Washington Infantry, on a scout to Shoshone Falls and Rock Creek. West left on September 13, traveled up Rock Creek into the Goose Creek Mountains, and back to the Snake River without spotting any Indians. He returned to the Salmon Falls Creek camp on September 23.

With West heading upriver, Hobart took eighteen cavalry, four infantrymen mounted on mules, and his howitzer, and headed down the Snake. Below Salmon Falls at daylight on September 13, Hobart surprised a fifteen-lodge camp of Indians he believed were from Ebigon's band. In a running fight Hobart killed six, mortally wounded one, and wounded a few more who escaped across the river. In the camp they found the stock, flour, and supplies stolen a few days earlier on the Malad River. On September 14, they continued downriver and had two slight skirmishes, killing one Indian and wounding another. They camped that night at Three Island Crossing, a frequently used emigrant ford of the Snake, located at present-day Glenns Ferry, Idaho. Early next morning, Hobart sent parties up on both sides of the Snake River to capture Indians who had been firing on them from the opposite bank. Unsuccessful in that endeavor, Hobart left at one in the morning of September 16, heading for an island about 10 miles downriver, where he understood another band was encamped.

At daylight Hobart spied the band of about thirty to forty Indians on the island. He sent men along both banks to trap them in the middle. Hobart fired a howitzer shell into the middle of the island as the signal for attack. The startled Indians fled toward both banks, and Hobart's men killed eight of them. "I had them surrounded," he reported, "and had it not been for the haste and excitement of the men sent on the east side of the river would have killed the whole party."

Hobart destroyed the camp and returned to Three Island Crossing. He made a quick scout to the Bruneau River but found nothing. Hobart was certain that most of the Indians had fled south to the Goose Creek Mountains where he believed they could raid from all winter. Receiving orders to return to Fort Boise because of a need to join Captain Currey's command, Hobart gathered up his forces, and returned to the post on October 5.[7]

Chapter 7 notes

1 Angel, *History of Nevada*, 169; Wilson, *Pioneer Nevada*, 88; *Commissioner of Indian Affairs 1865*, 473. The latter source says the Dodge-Burton killings occurred in June. Present Quinn River was usually rendered as Queens River in the 1860s.

2 *WR*: 50/1, 379-80; Smith, "Sagebrush Soldiers," 45-46. Smith said Wells crossed the Santa Rosa Mountains, but this is impossible, given Wells's recorded mileages, and the fact that it was only 73 miles to Rabbit Hole Springs from that camp. He could not have been in the Santa Rosa's and must have been in the middle of Kings River Valley, still about a dozen miles south of Disaster Peak, when he turned around to march to Rabbit Hole.

3 *WR*: 50/1, 380-82; *WR*: 50/2, 915-16; Paher, *Fort Churchill*, 37; Smith, "Sagebrush Soldiers," 46-48.

4 Greever, *Bonanza West*, 271 Hanley, *Owyhee Trails*, 26-27; *WR*: V.50/1, 323; *WR*: V.50/2, 953.

5 Bancroft, *History of Washington, Idaho*, 432; *WR*: V.50/1, 382-85; *WR*: V.50/2, 903, 913-14, 934-36.

6 *WR*: V.49/3, 386-89; *WR*: V.50, 958-59; Michno, *A Fate Worse Than Death*, 127-29.

7 *WR*: V.50/1, 387-89, 390-91.

Chapter 8

PEACE ATTEMPTS

W hen we last heard from Lt. Colonel Drew, he had escorted the emigrants across southern Oregon to the Owyhee Country and Fort Boise. Turning around, Drew marched west to Camp Alvord, reaching there on September 22, four days before Currey closed it down for the winter. Awaiting him there was another order requiring his immediate return to Fort Klamath to participate in the scheduled peace conference. Drew was somewhat faster on the return journey than on the way out, cutting off some of the winding loops in his original trail. He went straight between Steens and Warner Mountain, cutting off the southern loop around Pueblo Mountain. Even then, he stopped three days on the west slope of Steens Mountain, "explorations being necessary," he wrote. While there, Indians stole six of his horses. They then went west to Beatty's Butte, and on to Warner Mountain, seeing the first trees that they had seen in about 170 miles since leaving Jordan Creek. By cutting across between Pueblo and Steens Mountain, Drew had saved 67 miles.

Drew by-passed the southern point of Warner Mountain, found a pass across it, cut straight across the mountains northeast of Goose Lake, and then into Goose Lake Valley. This route saved another 42 miles by eliminating the dip down into Surprise Valley. From there, Drew joined his old outward route and continued along Sprague River to Fort Klamath. He believed that his return journey was about 200 miles shorter than his outward trail. It became the line of the Oregon Central Military Road, used by emigrants, traders, miners, and the military in the coming years.[1]

In 1864, Congress had appropriated $20,000 for the purpose of making a treaty with the Klamath and Modoc tribes of southwestern Oregon. After a preliminary meeting in August, in which none of the Paiutes participated, Oregon Indian Superintendent J. W. Perit Huntington set a council date for October 9. At Council Grove, 12 miles southeast of Fort Klamath, on the scheduled date, 710 Klamaths, 339 Modocs, and twenty-two "Yahuskin" Paiutes arrived.[2] With Huntington was Indian Agent for Oregon, William Logan. Captain William Kelly, with part of Company C, 1st Oregon Cavalry, Lieutenant James Halloran with a detachment of the 1st Washington Territory Infantry, and mixed-blood Dr. William C. McKay with some Warm Springs scouts, were the sole military presence. No doubt, Kelly wished that Drew was present, but the peripatetic lieutenant colonel had not yet arrived.

The treaty was standard fare, based on the assumption that all the Indians in the area were much alike and could live in harmony on the same reservation. It provided that the tribes cede all lands with the exception of part of the Klamath Range on Upper and Middle Klamath Lakes. Whites were prohibited from settling on the reservation, but the Indians were required to remain on it. Public road access was allowed through the reservation. The Indians were to receive $8,000 annually in supplies for the first five years, $5,000 for the next five years, and $3,000 for the final five years. The government also agreed to pay $35,000 for gifts provided at the time of signing and for subsistence during the first year of moving to the reservation. The tribes agreed that they would commit no depredations on U. S. citizens and cease making war upon each other or with any other tribes. The reservation was said to contain "some of the choicest country and most agreeable scenery in the state."[3]

The Klamaths were willing signers, and La Lake, Kellogue, Chiloquin, Toon-tuck-tee, Le-lu, Que-ass, Moshenkosket, and Blow were among the 20 Klamaths to sign; since they already resided on or near the reservation land, there was no problem in moving. The Modocs and Paiutes were not so sure, since they kept none of their traditional hunting grounds, but Old Schonchin and Kient-poos (Captain Jack), and two other Modocs signed, promising to keep their word. The two "Yahuskin" chiefs present, Kiletoak and Skyteocket, were also signatories, and may have participated simply to get some of the gifts. A prime reason that the Modocs and Klamaths signed was because Paulina and his Paiutes, and several other Paiute bands were raiding them as well as the Warm Springs Indians to the north. They saw a treaty as one way to get army protection against the hostile Paiutes. Huntington had wanted to get Paulina to attend. For some reason, possibly because Paulina's band was the one most often raiding Warm Springs, most of the whites believed Paulina "is well known as the head of the Snake Indians." In reality, Weahwewa and Ocheho may have "outranked" him. Those would have been the two key Paiute leaders to bring to the peace table, but, as yet undefeated, they would have nothing to do with peace at this time.

Captain Kelly's fair treatment of the Klamaths around the fort certainly helped assure them that perhaps the army could be an ally. The previous winter, when Kelly discovered the Indians were hungry, he issued them 9,921 pounds of beef, 11,401 pounds of flour, and other articles of subsistence from the military stores, and then presented a bill of $2,518 to the commissary office for payment. Kelly had no authorization to do this, but support from Huntington, who said Kelly's course "had a most salutary effect in conciliating the Indians and rendering future control of them easy and economical," kept him out of trouble. The kind-hearted captain's use

A. R. Bowman Museum, Crook County Historical Society, Prineville, Oregon
Donald McKay, center, and two Warm Springs Scouts, 1873.

of military stores extended to emigrants as well. After supplying destitute travelers with provisions, he was again in trouble. The army's response was that emigrants "should not expect the Government to supply them unless some great calamity has befallen them." Although it was Kelly's second transgression, authorities realized that it was the government's duty to assist the destitute. Thomas C. Sullivan, Captain of Commissary of Subsistence, declared that the army should try to sell supplies first, but if the party in need proved to be penniless, then free issue could be made. He warned, however, not to make this free giveaway program known, "lest poverty should be feigned." He recommended "that authority to make sales and issues of stores to indigent emigrants be obtained."[4]

The treaty was signed on October 14. A few days later, Paulina rode in to Moshenkosket's camp and tried to convince him to join the Paviotso Confederacy. Chiloquin was apparently eager to join the fight, but Moshenkosket saw wisdom in playing it neutral. By refusing Paulina's offer, Moshenkosket, who was called Moses Brown by the whites after the peace conference, became Paulina's enemy for life. Most unfortunate for the Paiutes was the continued assumption that the "Yahuskins" Kiletoak and Skyteocket, were Paiutes, and by their signatures, the Paiute people thus agreed to give up all their territory east of the Cascades and south of the Blue Mountains to the California-Nevada line. The Klamath, Waualaix, later known as Dave Hill, verified that the two signatures were those of legitimate

Paiute chiefs. It was said that Ocheho finally caught and killed Hill for his "treachery" in 1892.[5]

On October 18, Lt. Colonel Drew pulled in to the council grounds with his overdue command. Drew was glad to have nothing to do with the treaty, not because it wasn't a fair treaty, but because he didn't believe the government would live up to its provisions. Drew was tired of his military service. Like Captain Kelly, he had been accused of improprieties in the administration of his duties at Fort Klamath. The previous year, Indian sub-Agent Amos E. Rogers had complained that Drew built the fort in a bad location, was "inimical to the policy of the Indian Department," and sought to "lessen its influence, and to destroy its authority." The accusations led to an investigation by Captain James Van Voast, 9th Infantry, who concluded that Drew had not acted out of line. Still, Drew decided to call it quits. In the fall of 1864, the three-year enlistment period of many officers and men of the Oregon Cavalry was coming to an end. Drew did not wish to sign up again and was relieved of duty on November 21. In civilian life, Drew tried to make much of the route he had pioneered between Jacksonville and Owyhee, claiming that he opened up areas never before known to white men, discovered many of the "haunts" of the Paiutes, safely escorted emigrants starting a new life in Idaho, located a shorter route to connect the markets of southwest Oregon and northern California with Idaho, and, somewhat puzzlingly, believed he had contributed to peaceful relations between the Indians and the whites.[6]

PAULINA CREEK, *ca* OCTOBER 18, 1864

With the treaty signed, La Lake, acting on behalf of the government, took a peace message to try to find Paulina and induce him to stop raiding. Huntington and Logan distributed presents, left 16,000 pounds of flour to be issued to the Indians over the coming winter, and headed back to Fort Dalles the way they had come, along the eastern side of the Cascades. Their escort was a detachment of 1st Washington Territory Infantry, under Lieutenant Halloran, who commanded the Warm Springs Indian Reservation, and a party of Warm Springs Indians under Dr. William C. McKay. A few days into their journey on the upper Little Deschutes River, Huntington and Logan, riding ahead of the rest, noticed two Indians, who immediately tried to hide in the brush, but Halloran's men captured them. The two were Paiutes, Lean Man and Magpie Man. When Huntington learned from them that Paulina was nearby, he had them encamp, and Halloran sent out soldiers to find him. A several-hour search revealed another band of Indians camped east at the head of Mill-ka-ke (now Paulina) Creek, a tributary of the Little Deschutes. Halloran caught them all: three men, three women, and two children. One of the women, Falling Star, and one of the children, by a stroke of luck, were Paulina's wife and child.

They were taken to Huntington for questioning, in the hope that he could learn from Falling Star the whereabouts of her husband and talk him into surrendering. As Huntington questioned the Indians, they divined that he was going to take them all to Fort Dalles as hostages. The five warriors made an escape attempt, seizing a few guns from the soldiers and fleeing. The infantrymen chased them down, killed Magpie Man, Death Rattle, and Burning Wagon. Horse Trap and Lean Man were both wounded, but stole horses and rode away. The soldiers chased them, and realizing they could not both get away, Lean Man slowed down and led the pursuers over an easily followed path. When the soldiers caught up to him he was already dead from loss of blood. They assumed the last Indian had also died, but Horse Trap reached Paulina and told him the news. Huntington delivered the captives to Fort Vancouver on October 27.

The capture was enough to make Paulina finally sue for peace. On November 1, he sent a Paiute messenger to Fort Klamath to protest the killing and capture of his people and on November 8, he came to the fort himself. He told Captain Kelly that he was tired of war and wanted peace if he could be protected from his enemies on the Warm Springs Reservation. Huntington sent word that if Paulina wanted safety, he must "avoid the road, commit no more depredations upon whites, and not go near the Warm Springs Reservation." Huntington added: "The women which have been taken from his tribe at various times will be given up whenever he makes a treaty, and he will be expected also to give up the women and children which his people have stolen from the friendly Indians at Warm Springs." Huntington said he would visit Paulina in the spring for treaty talks.[7]

The fight on Paulina Creek closed major military operations in Oregon in 1864, and the treaty boded well for a peaceful future. Several columns had crisscrossed Oregon and Idaho, exploring many areas heretofore unknown to the military. The army had not hurt the Indians much in battle, but the hounding made it difficult for them to rest, hunt, and prepare for the winter. At Fort Dalles on November 7, Captain Currey again proposed a winter campaign to Brig. General Alvord. Although he would be mustering out the next March, Currey said "as I have no taste for garrison duty, I would take it as a great personal favor if I can be sent to the mountains." Currey said that with 50 men and one month's provisions and "starting from Captain Small's winter camp (Watson), I can find and whip the Indians." He believed that the Paiutes would be holed up at Steens Mountain. "They will be forced to winter in that vicinity," he said, "and to find them in their winter camp is equivalent to destroying them. . . I am willing to risk my reputation and life on the success of the move." Currey said the safety of the people and reputation of the army depended on punishing the Snakes.[8]

Once again, Currey's request for a winter campaign was not acted upon. True, the Indians had not received much of a chastisement, but they had been harassed. To escape the persecution, many bands left Oregon, and as a result,

Nevada would pay the price. But first, there was another flare-up along the Snake River in Idaho.

RUBY CITY RANGERS, FEBRUARY 15, 1865

In late January 1865, while the Idaho City, *Idaho World* newspaper speculated about possible trouble with the Nez Perce, the Bannocks provided immediate trouble. The snow in Boise Valley was eight inches deep, livestock were having a tough time feeding, and many died. The snows didn't seem to prevent highwaymen and Indian attacks. A Wells, Fargo & Company express was robbed on the road between Walla Walla and Umatilla, and about $7,200 in gold dust was taken. In early February, Indians raided along Jordan Creek and drove out the settlers. They killed John McComins, agent of the Humboldt Express Company, and Mr. Gregory, drove off the company's stock, 500 sheep, and burned several houses. Two companies of miners left Ruby City in pursuit, but failed to locate the Indians. Nothing was found of John McComins, except what was thought to have been his hat and a portion of his boot. They believed he had been thrown in the Owyhee River. They returned, reorganized as the "Ruby City Rangers," and about 40 of them went out again. This time, they struck a camp on February 15, "and after an hour's fighting the Indians took to the rocks, leaving between twenty and thirty dead behind them, and many wounded." A few days later, Silver City, Ruby City, and Booneville were completely cut off. The "roughest weather" of the winter dumped more than eight feet of snow on them and a correspondent wrote that they were "surrounded by a barrier of snow as formidable as the Chinese Wall."[9]

O'REGAN'S FIGHT, FEBRUARY 11, 1865

The volunteer soldiers were also in action. In late January, when residents of the Reynolds and Catherine Creek area complained that Indians had stolen their stock, Captain Frederick Seidenstriker, commander at Fort Boise, sent Captain O'Regan and twenty-five men of Company I, Washington Territory Infantry, to investigate. Supplied with thirty days' rations, O'Regan spent much of the time trying to keep warm and aiding the few persistent emigrants who still traveled the trail. On February 11, O'Regan chased down a band of Indian stock thieves, and reported killing five warriors, capturing several women and children, and recovering four stolen cattle. O'Regan wrote to Seidenstriker requesting supplies for his prisoners, but because of large demands made on the military for subsistence to destitute emigrants visiting Fort Boise nearly every day, Seidenstriker directed O'Regan to release the Indians.

While O'Regan waited in camp on Catherine Creek for his own supplies, another storm dumped an additional four inches of snow, and Seidenstriker believed that if the cold snap did not break soon, that all the citizens in the valley would lose their stock, although he believed the snow would make it easier to track the Indians. O'Regan did not have much time to sit and complain about the weather. When eight more head of cattle were stolen from the vicinity of his camp, he sent four citizens and six soldiers, under Sergeant John Storan, to track down the thieves. The trail went up the Snake River to Bruneau Valley, located near the junction of the Bruneau River and the Snake.

BRUNEAU VALLEY, FEBRUARY 15, 1865

Sergeant Storan's little group found the Indians, probably Bannocks, on February 15, in a little canyon eight miles from Bruneau Valley, dressing and curing the carcasses of the eight steers. Although there were about eighty Indians in the camp, Storan attacked, and in a tough, hour and a half fight, succeeded in driving the Indians off and gaining the field. Remarkably, with no casualties to his own party, Storan reported killing thirty Indians—and only having fired eighty-three shots. Captain O'Regan later reported that they also wounded thirty Indians. If it was true, such shooting would have been phenomenal. The fighting ended with darkness and the onset of a heavy rainstorm. Storan's men were exhausted, and since they had only three days' rations, they returned to the camp. O'Regan had not yet released his captives, and protested to Seidenstriker that it would be dangerous to set them free since they were now fully aware of the army's strength and position. Seidenstriker told O'Regan to send them to Fort Boise for imprisonment, while he wrote to his superiors of his concern about losing manpower due to many enlistments expiring soon.[10]

Chapter 8 notes

1 Bancroft, *History of Oregon*, Vol. 2, 505; *Oregon Sentinel*, December 17, 1864, March 11, 1865.

2 Bancroft, *History of Oregon*, Vol. 2, 506; Ontko, *Thunder Over the Ochoco III*, 241; Ruby & Brown, *Pacific Northwest*, 206. Although the Yahuskins appear many times in the historical record, there may have been no such tribe. Yahuskin may have been a Shoshone name for the Klamaths, and this band was possibly a wandering party of Washoes.

3 Bancroft, *History of Oregon*, Vol. 2, 506; *Commissioner of Indian Affairs 1865*, 101-03; Murray, *Modocs*, 38; Kappler, *Treaties*, 865-68.

4 Kappler, *Treaties*, 868; Ontko, *Thunder Over the Ochoco III*, 241; *Oregon Sentinel,* May 12, 1866; Murray, *Modocs*, 38-39; *WR*: 50/2, 992, 1030-31, 1115.

5 Ontko, *Thunder Over the Ochoco III*, 242-44.

6 Bancroft, *History of Oregon*, Vol. 2, 506; *WR*: 50/2, 664-668, 1067; *Oregon Sentinel*, March 11, 1865. Today, Drew's route across southern Oregon east of Goose Lake remains barren and nearly uninhabited, with few towns and fewer paved roads, arguably seeing more activity in the 1860s than in the twenty-first century.

7 Bancroft, *History of Oregon*, Vol. 2, 507-08; Ontko, *Thunder Over the Ochoco III*, 245-46; Clark, "McKay's Journal, Part I," 127; *WR*: V.50/2, 1068, 1072-73, 1115, 1143-44; *Commissioner of Indian Affairs 1865*, 103-04.

8 *WR:* 50/2, 1049-50.

9 *Idaho World*, February 11, 1865, February 15, 1865, March 4, 1865, March 18, 1865.

10 *WR*: V.50/1, 400-01; *WR*: V.50/2, 1124-25.

Chapter 9
TROUBLE SPREADS TO NEVADA

Nevada Governor James W. Nye had many of the same concerns as Oregon Governor A. C. Gibbs: miners and emigrants mixed with Indians were potential trouble. In 1864, Nye wrote to Brig. General Wright, commanding the Department of the Pacific from San Francisco, requesting help. New ore discoveries in the northern part of his state meant an influx of whites into the territory of the Bannocks, and, what he called, "the worst of the Pah Utes." Nye worried that with the mineral discoveries, "many persons will go there, and I fear the result will be to bring on an Indian war if there are not troops to protect them." Nye asked for more posts and more soldiers, and Wright agreed.

On the contrary, Commissioner of Indian Affairs, D. N. Cooley, was oddly naïve. He expected "very little difficulty with the Indians of Nevada, partly because they are a very peaceable people, and partly because of the judicious course taken by Governor Nye. . . ." Events would prove Nye's view to be the more realistic.[1]

Heightened fears of prowling Indians, and the death of prospectors near Disaster Peak, resulted in Captain Almond Wells's summer campaign, as outlined above. Fort Churchill had already been built on the Carson River as a result of the Paiute War in 1860, and Fort Ruby was constructed in 1862, east of the Ruby Mountains and south of the Humboldt River in east-central Nevada. As the ranks of the Nevada units filled, and California troops moved in, additional posts were set up. One, named Camp Nye, was built at Washoe Lake, five miles north of Carson City. A second, Camp Sadler, was also near Carson City at the mouth of King's Canyon. None of the posts helped control Indians in northern Nevada, or at the new mining district around Austin, mid-way between Forts Churchill and Ruby. The booming silver camp on the Reese River never got a permanent military presence, and relied instead on the volunteer "Lander Blues" to protect them. Austin's paper, the *Reese River Reveille*, did much complaining about the lack of troops and the seeming lack of concern of the new Department of the Pacific commander, Maj. General Irwin McDowell.

McDowell, who arrived from the Army of the Potomac in the summer of 1864, was unpopular because he "talked unguardedly" and was "given to sharp sayings." Even worse, in the West he was thought to be "soft" on Indians, and more fit to hob-nob with so-called Eastern humanitarians and philanthropists than with the rough and ready frontiersmen of Nevada. When McDowell ordered that surrendered Indians were to be fed, clothed, and given over to civil authorities, the *Reveille* wailed that the general either had "a disregard for his own race, or a deplorable ignorance of the persons with whom he deals."[2]

McDowell, who was considered a free-talker, argumentative, and usually not well liked by most of the soldiers who served with him, did little to appease the critics. Nevadans wanted more soldiers to protect them. So did McDowell. In October 1864, he wrote to Governor Nye to "please raise as soon as possible enough companies of infantry to complete, with those already in service in Nevada, a full regiment of infantry." Governor Nye had been trying, unsuccessfully, to do just that for more than two years. When Henry G. Blasdel was elected Nevada's governor in November 1864, he took up the ongoing struggle. In February 1865, Blasdel wrote to McDowell, stating that two companies were now filled, but they had no weapons. How could they fight? Blasdel was certain that soon the "sons of the forest" would be raiding and killing. Seemingly oblivious to the issues, McDowell replied one month later, "What progress is making in recruiting the Nevada volunteers? I will need them for the protection of the State."[3]

WALKER LAKE, *ca* MARCH 10, 1865

By then it was too late. Fighting had broken out across the northern half of the state. Major trouble began in early March 1865, when prospectors Isaac Stewart and Robert Rabe were murdered a few miles from the head of Walker Lake, north of present-day Hawthorne, Nevada. When word reached Fort Churchill, Captain William Wallace, with thirty-seven men of Company A, 1st Nevada Infantry, fifty men from Company E, 1st Nevada Cavalry, and twelve friendly Indians, marched to the scene. Wallace's large force overawed the local Paiutes, and Chief Josephius assisted the soldiers in catching the two murderers and turning them over. Wallace took them to Fort Churchill to stand trial. The expedition may have been an example of overkill, but it demonstrated that the white man's justice was quick and certain, and it impressed the "Diggers" to the extent that they never bothered the white population in that area again.[4]

Such was not the case in northern Nevada. The Paiutes who lived in the Pyramid Lake area were reasonably content on the reserve set up for them after the War of 1860. They liked their agent, Warren Wasson, and were left alone to fish for trout in Pyramid and Mud Lake (presently Winnemucca Lake) and live much as they had before the whites came. Things changed for the worse in the spring of 1865. Wasson had quit the agency to become a U.S. marshal, and subsequent agents were more prone to line their own pockets rather than help the Paiutes. Whites began moving on the reservation, taking up the limited grasslands, and fishing in the lakes. The Indians retaliated by stealing stock. It did not help the situation when more hostile Paiutes were driven into the area by the army operations in Oregon.

Reports came in to Governor Blasdel, of Indians raiding along the Humboldt River, along the Honey Lake Road toward Susanville, and up in Paradise Valley, an area of good grass and water, about 30 miles north of the northern bend of the Humboldt. Blasdel heard that settlers and ranchers were abandoning their homes and going to the mining camps where they would try to take matters into their own hands. He asked Major McDermit for assistance.[5]

MUD LAKE, MARCH 14, 1865

On March 12, the same day that Captain Wallace marched to Walker Lake, Captain Almond B. Wells left Fort Churchill with fifty men of Company D, 1st Nevada Cavalry. According to Sarah Winnemucca, daughter of Chief Winnemucca, Wells talked to a band of Paiutes then living "at Dayton" on the Carson River. He said, "You have been stealing cattle from the white people at Harney Lake," and claimed he would kill all men, women, and children he found.[6] Wells marched 10 miles northeast from the fort and camped. The next day the command made a long 48-mile march northwest to Pyramid Lake. Wells encountered a Paiute camp and parleyed, learning from them that a band of Smoke Creek Paiutes, camped northeast of Pyramid Lake near Mud Lake, about 11 miles from his position, were probably guilty of the thefts. Wells detached twenty-one men to stay with the Indians at hand, and left at three a.m. on March 14 for the Mud Lake camp.

With his twenty-nine troopers and civilian guides T. W. Murch and W. H. Wilson, Wells reached the camp at sunup. He divided his command into three squads under Sergeants Wadleigh and Besat, and himself, and approached the sleeping Paiutes, intending to arrest the thieves. They only got within 150 yards of the camp when the Indians began firing. "The first shot took effect in Corporal Dolan's shoulder, wounding him slightly;" Wells later reported, "the second passed through the cape of my overcoat. I then ordered a charge with sabers. The Indians fell back to the bushes on both sides of the slough. By this time the men under Sergeants Wadleigh and Besat came up and a general engagement ensued. The Indians fought like veterans."

The three squads nearly surrounded the Paiutes, and few got away. "I killed twenty-nine in all; but one escaped," Wells recounted. "I destroyed several guns, a quantity of powder, and fresh beef. I pursued and fought them for about ten miles up into the mountains. Some of my men had hand-to-hand conflicts with them. Several were beaten on the arms with the Indians' guns." The soldiers captured nine horses, but they were in so poor a condition that they let them go. Wells praised his men for being "as cool and collected as though on an ordinary skirmish drill." Wells never mentioned any female or children casualties. If this was a peaceful camp, it would likely contain women and children; if it was a war party out marauding, as reported by other Indians, there would not be any women and children involved.

After the battle, Wells said that Chief Winnemucca called on him and told him that he was highly pleased with the result. Through an interpreter, Winnemucca said that he had been admonishing the Indians all winter, "telling them not to steal the white men's cattle, and he thought that the punishment they had received would teach them a lesson."[7]

Wells's report differs drastically from the story told by Sarah Winnemucca in a book published in 1883. Her father was supposedly nowhere near the scene of battle, but was off at Carson Sink on a hunting expedition with all the men. Sarah dramatically played up the story: "Oh, it is a fearful thing to tell, but it must be told. Yes, it must be told by me. It was all old men, women and children that were killed." She continued: "After the soldiers had killed all but some little children and babies still tied up in their baskets, the soldiers took them also, and set the camp on fire and threw them into the flames to see them burn alive." Sarah said one of her baby brothers was killed there, but one of her sisters escaped by jumping on her father's best horse and fleeing.

Wells reported that the attack had met with Chief Winnemucca's approval, but Sarah claimed it resulted in the death of the chief's infant son, and which, Sarah said, "drove my poor papa away" so that he disappeared into the wilderness for two years. The two versions are irreconcilable.[8]

Sarah Winnemucca blamed most of the upcoming trouble on the deaths of Stewart and Rabe, and thought that bringing in soldiers because of it was an overreaction. "They went after my people all over Nevada," she said. Sarah was convinced that all the reports of raiding and killing were a fabrication, "and by this lying of the white settlers the trail began which is marked by the blood of my people from hill to hill and valley to valley." To Sarah, everything appeared to be one vast conspiracy. "These reports were only made by white settlers so that they could sell their grain," she wrote. "The only way cattle-men and farmers get to make money is to start an Indian war, so that the troops may come and buy their beef, cattle, horses, and grain. The settlers get fat by it."[9]

If the Indians were forced to fight because of Wells's attack at Mud Lake, the influx of soldiers, and mendacious whites, there were, nevertheless, several bands of Paiutes who weren't following Sarah's sequence of cause and effect. On March 13, the day before the Mud Lake fight, Paiutes under Black Rock Tom destroyed Granite Creek Station.[10]

GRANITE CREEK STATION, MARCH 13, 1865

Granite Creek Station was on the Noble's Cutoff or Honey Lake Road between the Humboldt River and California. The first westbound stop for fresh water after crossing the Black Rock Desert, it was situated at the mouth of Bowen Canyon at the south end of the Granite Range, about five miles north of present-day, Gerlach, Nevada. The stage and freight station consisted of a storehouse, stone corral, and sod house. Granite Creek irrigated the meadow and provided forage for stock, making it a rather pleasant location in the otherwise bleak Nevada landscape. A foolish act by "Puck" Walden may have touched off the Paiute attack, when, the month before, he reportedly murdered a Paiute without provocation. As usual, others paid the price for Walden's act.

The Paiute war party crept up to the station and took position in the stone corral; when the station employees made an appearance, they began shooting. A. J. Curry, Cyrus Creel, and Al Simmons took cover in the sod house and returned fire through the rifle ports in the sod walls. Using the storehouse as cover, the Indians got to a blind side of the soddy and set fire to the roof. The defenders held out as long as they could and then burst out. Curry waited too long and was trapped inside, dying either from bullets or flames.

Simmons and Creel took off on foot, running in opposite directions. Creel went east across the playa toward Trego Hot Springs and Simmons ran west toward Deep Hole Station. Simmons didn't get far before warriors caught and shot him, and then dragged his body across the rocks before they hacked him to death. Three mounted Paiutes caught Creel on the dry lakebed. They brought him back to the station, tied him to the ground, and burned him alive. The enraged Indians took four rifles, muskets, and several six-shooters, and then smashed the furniture and broke, hacked, or burned all the pans, dishes, and furnishings. Even the station's mongrel dog was killed, skinned, and staked out.

About the same time, Paiutes attacked the Wall Springs Station, about a dozen miles west of Granite Creek. They killed stationkeeper Lucius Arcularius and expressman George Thayer. In addition, three more people were thought to be missing: R. B. Doon, Thomas Rosse, and one other. Whether the attacks were in revenge for the murder of the Paiute, or an eruption from the growing animosity between Indians and whites is not known, but the destroyed stations and murdered men caused the scattered settlers to panic. On March 14, Judge E. F. Dunne in Star City, telegraphed Governor Blasdel: "Indian outbreak on the Honey Lake road. Three men killed; two more attacked, but escaped. Indians holding the route. Small parties dare not travel it. Last man killed at Wall Springs. Half-way station keepers on the road driven out have come here." The result was a call for more troops and the establishment of several more temporary military camps along the travel routes.[11]

At Fort Churchill, Major McDermit was hard-pressed to answer all the demands on his limited resources, and he was receiving mixed messages from his superiors. On March 14, the same day Wells killed twenty-nine Indians at Mud Lake, General Wright, commander of the District of California since McDowell took over the Department of the Pacific the previous year, cautioned the major and his officers "to be circumspect in their dealing with Indians at all disposed to be friendly, and not to permit their indiscriminate slaughter." On March 20, a wire from McDowell's office concerning the apparent uprising at Walker Lake, instructed McDermit: "If the Indians have not come to terms, take the force yourself and give them a lesson which they will not forget."[12]

On March 24, McDermit sent out Lieutenant Joseph Wolverton with forty-seven men of Company D, 1st Nevada Cavalry, to Star City, carrying along 100 extra muskets that the civilian militia was begging for. Wolverton had barely arrived when word came in of an Indian raid in Grass Valley, 28 miles northeast of Star City. Indians burned a house, wounded a settler, and stole a large number of stock. Wolverton took twenty-five men and went to investigate. On the way, he met residents from Paradise Valley, streaming south, looking for help. The Indians were in a hostile, threatening mood. Wolverton checked out Grass Valley, crossed the Humboldt and moved north.[13]

PARADISE VALLEY, APRIL 5, 1865

The land nestled south of the Santa Rosa Mountains, west of the Hot Springs Range, and east of the Bloody Run Hills was known as Paradise Valley for its comparative abundance of wood, pine nuts, birds, game, water, good soil, and grass. It was a mini-haven for the Paiutes, and naturally it was a magnet for white settlers. W. C. Gregg built the first cabin there in June 1863, and immediately cut 250 tons of wild hay, which he sold in Star City. One year later there were nearly 20 families in the valley, and by the spring of 1865, more still—and the Paiutes planned to kill them. On April 4, two friendly Indians warned Aaron Denio that in "two sleeps" a war party of Paiutes would attack. Denio, who lived on the east side of Martin Creek, took the warning seriously. He passed the word to his nearest neighbors, N. Gillelan, A. Bryant, J. T. Bryant, T. J. Fine, a Mr. Stockham, and a Mr. Rembreaux. They all decided to head down the valley to Willow Point and fort up.

They fixed up a wagon for Mr. Fine, who was prostrate with rheumatism, and for the children of several families. Mr. Stockham was at that time on his way to Star City and the camp at Dun Glen, to ask for military assistance, and neighbors helped Mrs. Stockham and her children. Another valley resident, Mark W. Haviland, was also on a similar mission, and was at Dun Glen this very day. Before they could get moving, a terrific storm set in, delaying them until morning. That night, settlers John Lackey and Thomas Byrnes joined them. On the morning of April 5, the entire party set out, but the swollen Martin and Cottonwood Creeks had fanned out into the level valley, making a mud flat about two miles wide. With the cart bogging down, the children and the sick Mr. Fine had to be carried most of the way, and it took hours to cross the flat. There were still about three miles to go to reach Hamblin's Corral, where they planned to stop. On the way, Jacob Hufford joined them, and used his horse to help pull the wagon.

They were supposed to meet up with another valley resident, Christopher Fearbourne, who was also rounding up his neighbors, a Mr. Barber and Mr. Collins. The three men were also halted by the storm. When they awoke in the morning, Indians had the place surrounded, but were not attacking. Barber suggested that they dash for their horses and make a run for it, but Fearbourne and Collins thought it was best to make a bold front, calmly saddle up, pack the wagon, and ride out as if nothing was amiss. As they went about their business the Indians approached and became belligerent. Barber said, "I am going to make the attempt to go for help, and you shut yourselves up in the cabin if there is trouble, and do the best you can till I get back."

Barber rode slowly away, followed by several Indians, one of them who questioned in broken English what he was doing. He was going out to kill a beef, he said. Surprisingly, the Indians seemed to lose interest in him and let him go. As soon as he was out of sight, Barber put spurs to the horse and sped off. He rode up to John Lackey, Tom Byrnes, the two Bryants, and 12-year-old Robert Denio, who were still struggling to get the last of their belongings across the mudflat. While Barber quickly explained what had happened, one of the listeners looked up and saw smoke rising in the valley. The cabin was aflame! The Bryants and young Denio hurried for the corral, while Barber, Byrnes, and Lackey raced back toward the burning cabin.

The three would-be rescuers only got within 300 yards of the building when twenty-two mounted Paiutes and even more dismounted Indians charged them. The "rescuers" raced their horses all the way to Hamblin's Corral, about three miles away. They reached Hamblin's about the same time as the Bryants and Denio. A smaller band of Paiutes were about to cut them off, but were foiled by the appearance of the three riders, who, with the arrival of another settler, Waldron Foster, scared the Indians off. There were now ten men, one boy, three women, and four children in the corral. By mutual consent Aaron Denio was elected captain, and he situated the force as well as he could to defend the walls.

Hamblin's house was 50 yards from the corral and Denio believed that the Indians would station sharpshooters there, so J. T. Bryant and Foster volunteered to burn it down, under a weak covering fire. More Indians were approaching and shooting, and by the time the house was ablaze, Indians were all around them. The defenders had only three rifles, one old musket, two shotguns, and six pistols. The sudden increase of Indians all around probably meant that Collins and Fearbourne were dead.

The two men had held out as long as they could, but the Paiutes set fire to the cabin. The choice came down to dying by bullets and arrows or fire.

Author's photo

Ruins of Camp Dun Glen, Nevada.

Fearbourne held a frying pan over his head with his left hand, trying to deflect the heat and burning debris that fell from the roof, while firing with his right hand. When his shoulders and arms were cooked, he broke out and ran about 150 yards before the Indians shot him in the back. He was later found still grasping the frying pan. Collins didn't get that far. He sprang out of the cabin but the Indians caught him. They tied him to some poles near the cabin, piled boards and scrap under him, mutilated him, cut out his heart, and burned him to cinders.

Back at Hamblin's, Tom Byrnes volunteered to ride for help. He galloped through the Indian lines, missed a shower of bullets and arrows, and outrode six warriors who raced after him. Byrnes reached Willow Point Station on the Little Humboldt River about 3 p.m. and found thirteen men had forted up there awaiting developments. They all agreed to return with him to Hamblin's. Although there were only twelve horses, the thirteenth man, an old-timer named Givens, would not be left behind. He seized his rifle with one hand, grabbed hold of the pommel of a saddle with the other hand, and said, "Heave ahead, boys, heave ahead, the women and children must be saved." In that manner, Givens jogged the entire 13 miles north to Hamblin's. When the rescue party approached, the Paiutes had a quick council and decided that it was time to vacate the area. They melted away and were gone. About nine that evening, the entire group at Hamblins' started south to Willow Point, reaching there at three in the morning of April 6. There they found Lieutenant Joseph Wolverton, with twenty-five men of Company D, 1st Nevada Cavalry.[14]

Wolverton left Star City to investigate reports of raids in Grass Valley. He passed through Dun Glen, a little town established in 1862 on the west slope of the East Range. In 1863 the military began to use the area as a temporary post, and Camp Dun Glen was occupied off and on, the soldiers utilizing rock-lined dugouts, tents, and rented buildings. In April 1864, Dun Glen was the nearest town where people in Paradise Valley might expect help. Wolverton passed through Dun Glen Canyon on April 4, heading to Grass Valley. The same day, Mark Haviland arrived from Paradise Valley, warning of the Indian threat, asking for help, and arguing that Paradise Valley would be a great spot for a military post. The warnings were sent to Major McDermit by Nevada legislator James A. Banks, who was in Dun Glen at the time.[15]

COTTONWOOD CREEK, APRIL 6, 1865

Lieutenant Wolverton heard of the trouble in Paradise Valley and continued beyond Grass Valley, crossed the Humboldt, and followed the Little Humboldt north. He arrived at Willow Point several hours after the party of civilians had gone back to Hamblin's. When the settlers arrived back at three in the morning, they informed Wolverton of what had transpired the previous two days. At dawn, Wolverton saddled up and rode up Cottonwood Creek, where he found the still fresh Indians' trail. The tracks led north into the Santa Rosas. The Indians' ponies were either poor or the Indians did not fear any retaliation so soon, for Wolverton caught up to them on April 6. In a quick charge, Wolverton cut through the Paiute camp and killed five warriors. The fleeing Indians hurried into the mountains, but Wolverton doggedly pursued. Before the day was over, his men killed two more Indians near Martin Creek Gap (Windy Gap), losing only one cavalry horse in the day-long affair. Wolverton returned to the burned cabin on Cottonwood Creek, buried Fearbourne and Collins, and then headed back to Willow Point.

While the rest of Wolverton's command moved north to join him, civilians from Star City and Dun Glen were moving out to provide help in Paradise Valley and along the Honey Lake Road. The requests for a permanent post in Paradise Valley were at first met with disapproval by General Wright, who believed that mobile units could better cover the area. On April 6, rancher E. F. Dunne sent a message to McDermit, albeit with some exaggeration: "Massacre in Paradise Valley. Six women and two men killed. Send cartridges, caliber .58, and revolvers, and 200 men. There are 1,000 Indians on the warpath." McDermit immediately ordered Captain Wells to collect all the men of Companies D and E, and move to the threatened area.[16] The largest Indian wars campaign in Nevada's history had begun.

Chapter 9 notes

1 Letter Secretary of War, 50th Congress, Senate Ex. Doc. 70, 222; *Commissioner of Indian Affairs 1865*, 15.

2 Smith, "Sagebrush Soldiers," 40, 42, 52-53; Edwards, "Department of the Pacific," 210.

3 Letter Secretary of War, 50th Congress, Senate Ex. Doc. 70, 248, 285, 287.

4 Angel, *History of Nevada*, 169-70; Smith, "Sagebrush Soldiers," 58-60.

5 Egan, *Sand in a Whirlwind*, 274-75; *WR*: V.50/2, 1156; Winnemucca Hopkins, *Life Among the Paiutes*, 76-77; Paher, *Fort Churchill*, 42.

6 Smith, "Sagebrush Soldiers," 61; Winnemucca Hopkins, *Life Among the Paiutes*, 77. Winnemucca's accusation is difficult to accept for several reasons: she did not hear Wells herself, he would not have told the Paiutes his plans, and Wells did not travel to Dayton, which was 18 miles west of Fort Churchill; he left the fort and headed northeast.

7 *WR*: V.50/1, 403-04; Smith, "Sagebrush Soldiers," 61-62.

8 Winnemucca Hopkins, *Life Among the Paiutes*, 77-78, 100. Another factor pointing to the unreliability of Winnemucca's recollections (p. 79) is that she said the Indians may have killed miners Stewart and Rabe at Walker Lake because of the affair at Mud Lake, but they were killed prior to the Mud Lake fight.

9 Winnemucca Hopkins, *Life Among the Paiutes*, 78

10 Angel, *History of Nevada*, 170. The exact date of the attack is unknown. Reports were received in Star City and in San Francisco on 14 March, and the survivors would have needed a day or more to spread the alarm. It is possible the attack may have occurred on the 12th.

11 Rathbun, *Nevada Military Names*, 73, 75. 153; Angel, *History of Nevada*, 170; Wilson, *Pioneer Nevada*, 105; *WR*: V.50/2, 1156, 1161-62, 1182.

12 *WR*: V.50/2, 1161, 1166; Paher, *Fort Churchill*, 42.

13 Smith, *Sagebrush Soldiers*, 63: *WR*: V.50/2, 1177-78.

14 Angel, *History of Nevada*, 170-72.

15 Rathbun, *Nevada Military Names*, 56, 58; *WR*: V.50/2, 1177-79.

16 Rathbun, *Nevada Military Names*, 47-48; Angel, *History of Nevada*, 171-72; *WR*: V.50/2, 1183, 1187. E. F. Dunne, a Paradise Valley rancher, who reported on Wolverton's fight, said that five Indians were killed in the initial attack. The report he later gave to the Gold Hill *News* on April 17, said ten Indians were killed.

Chapter 10
FIGHTING IN NEVADA, 1865

CANE SPRINGS, APRIL 15, 1865

By the middle of April, ranches and travelers as far out as 100 miles on both sides of the Humboldt River in western Nevada had reportedly been attacked, many of the raids being attributed to Paiutes under Buffalo Jim. Quickly recovering from the raid in Paradise Valley, a party of angry citizens, armed with some of the army-issued rifles, hunted for Indians. They found a band camped at Cane Springs, which was a reliable source of water and grass just west of the pass between the Bloody Run Hills and Santa Rosa Mountains, only about 15 miles from Paradise Valley. Because the Paiutes were caught unaware and so close to the valley, suggests they were not part of the raids there earlier in the month and had little idea that the whites in the area were out trying to kill them. The civilians swept into the surprised camp, as it was reported, "dealing death right and left, and brought away with them 18 scalps as trophies of their work."[1]

Amidst the fright and the fighting, a number of civilians tried to halt the killing. Although civilians during the Indian wars often have been correctly accused of fomenting trouble, there were a significant number who tried to end the madness. Some of them now stepped forward. Volunteer "Captains" Parkinson, Usher, Bonnifield, and later Arizona Territorial Governor Anson P. K. Safford, met with a Paiute delegation to talk peace. On April 23, two chiefs the whites called Captain John and Captain Soo, came in to talk. Captain Soo had already played a pivotal role in past events. Soo, a mixed-blood Bannock and Paiute whose real name was Mogoannoga, was leader of the Humboldt Meadows Band, and participated in a great council in May 1860, when the Paiute chiefs gathered at Pyramid Lake to discuss whether or not to go to war with the whites. The chiefs could not decide, so Mogoannoga took matters into his own hands. There were two versions of what happened. One was that Mogoannoga, in a hurry to start a war, took several warriors, traveled from Pyramid Lake to Williams Station, a grog shop and trading house on the Pony Express route, and killed the employees. He then rode back and defiantly told the chiefs that the war was on and they had better fight or be annihilated. The other version is that a few white ruffians at Williams Station kidnapped two Paiute girls. Mogoannoga and

Natchez, Winnemucca's son, along with several warriors, rode to the station to investigate. The white men acted alternately nervous and belligerent and when one ran, the Indians killed him. The others fought, and soon, all five white men were dead. The Paiutes searched and found the girls tied up in a trap-door cellar under the barn. They burned the station, and rode back to Pyramid Lake, naturally assuming the whites would retaliate.[2]

Now, Soo and John apparently had learned the folly of war and tried to patch up matters. The Indian and white captains agreed that the Paiutes would move all of their people who wanted no trouble away from the Humboldt River to the Carson River, to get them out of the war zone. All Indians found in the Humboldt region one week after the signing of the "treaty" would be considered to be at war. Unfortunately, the vast majority of whites and Indians never heard of the agreement, and when hundreds of Paiutes began moving into the Carson area, the whites assumed they were being invaded. On May 3, Major McDermit, with Lieutenants Daniel Vanderhoof and D. H. Pine of the 1st Nevada Infantry, and thirteen men of Company E, 1st Nevada Cavalry, left Fort Churchill to investigate. At Carson Lake they met with Indians and settlers. McDermit learned that the "excitement was caused by the peaceable Indians from the Humboldt coming to the Carson Lake to avoid trouble, and the Indians living in the vicinity, not knowing the cause of so many coming in, supposed that a general war of extermination was about to commence."

There was to be no extermination. General McDowell, concerned about reservation population and increasing numbers of Indian prisoners, knew the government had to feed and treat them well, given that "Their country has been scoured by our military parties and their food destroyed. . . ." McDowell, having retained some of those sensibilities decried by many frontier folks, declared: "Having fed refugees from slavery and prisoners of war in the East, I am at a loss to see any reason for not doing the same to the red man in the West." McDermit, also believing that fair treatment would accomplish more than coercion, tried to assuage Indian complaints. He marched to the reservation on Truckee River and learned that the agent had been leasing Indian lands to white ranchers, and that $25,000 of appropriations for the Indians had seemingly vanished without any visible improvements being made. McDermit ordered the ranchers to get off the land, and the Indians appeared satisfied. The major returned to Fort Churchill believing he had settled matters, but it was not the case.[3]

LITTLEFIELD'S ENCOUNTER, MAY 7, 1865

While McDermit was negotiating, the soldiers he had sent in the field were fighting. Lieutenant John Littlefield and thirty-five men of Company D, 1st Nevada Cavalry, were scouting east of Paradise Valley. On May 7, they ran into a large Paiute band in a small box canyon (possibly near Whiskey Springs Canyon) near the North Fork Little Humboldt.[4] The Paiutes, about

200 of them, had apparently used this location as a semi-permanent camp, for there were about fifteen rifle pits built into the rocks, each capable of holding twenty defenders. Littlefield dismounted his men and advanced only a short distance before halting to think about the situation. He was outnumbered five to one or worse, the Indians were entrenched, and they wanted the soldiers to attack. Some Paiutes showed themselves on the rock ledges and taunted them, waving bloody scalps and inviting the soldiers to come up for breakfast.

Littlefield decided to fall back. The episode produced conflicting accounts. The *Humboldt Register* insisted that Littlefield had sixty men and the Paiutes about the same number. It accused the officer of running 15 miles and making a waterless camp. It said that the men under Littlefield believed he was a coward. On the contrary, the *Reese River Reveille* claimed that almost everyone held Littlefield in high esteem, that the soldiers were greatly outnumbered, that Littlefield did not run, and charges of cowardice were "utterly false and without the slightest foundation."[5]

Littlefield returned to Paradise Valley, Captain Wells took over, and with about 65 men of Companies D and E, went after the Indians again. They marched to the site of Littlefield's encounter and took up the trail to the northeast. On May 20, near the Little Owyhee in the extreme northwest corner of today's Elko County, and just south of the Idaho border, they found the Indians in position on the side of a butte they called Table Mountain.[6]

GODFREY'S MOUNTAIN, MAY 20, 1865

The Paiutes, Bannocks, and possibly Shoshonis, nearly 500-strong under Chief Zeluawick, and probably including some of the same warriors who had taunted Littlefield, were in a formidable position on top of the butte. The Indians were in rocky rifle pits and jeered at the whites. Wells, now in a situation similar to what Littlefield was in two weeks earlier, took the bait. Wells ordered the attack at three in the afternoon, and the fight was on. There was no precipitous charge, however. The Paiute position was on a peninsula-shaped butte, with the sides nearly perpendicular, the peninsula neck with high rock ledges, and the top nearly flat. About 800 yards from the top they had to dismount and work their way up.

There were less than forty men in the assault; the rest were out scouting or holding the horses. Wells took half the men on the right and Littlefield had the other half on the left. The troopers worked their way to within 75 yards of the fortifications when the Indians fired. Surprisingly, in Wells's squad no one was hit in the first blast. One trooper thought they were in too close and the Indians shot high most of the battle. Littleton on the left was not as lucky. Isaac W. Godfrey was shot through the head in the first volley, and Lewis B. Clark was wounded in the leg, while another soldier was also hit in the leg. The Indians did not use bows and arrows, but were thought to have about sixty rifles.

The men took cover behind the rocks and waited for an Indian to stick his head over a boulder or through a loophole. One soldier said, "We fought them in this way until sundown, running from one rock to another to get a better chance." Wells got within 30 feet of the main Paiute line at one time before falling back. As Wells pulled back, the Paiutes advanced and threatened the soldiers' flanks. James Monroe was crossing an exposed point to reach the horses when some Indians caught and killed him. Since it was nearly dark, his companions could not see well enough to go after his body and left it behind. As Wells tried to retreat during the night, the Indians nearly surrounded him. He sent ten men out to scout a way through their circle and they finally broke free and made it back to Paradise Valley after losing two killed and four wounded.

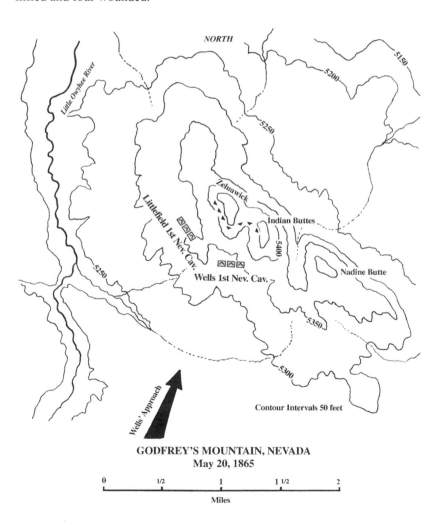

GODFREY'S MOUNTAIN, NEVADA
May 20, 1865

Major Charles McDermit and his family.

A soldier of Company D wrote a letter to a friend describing the ordeal, which was later printed in the *Carson Daily Appeal* on June 3, 1865. He said that the men did just fine, but "I will not make comment about our officers." He complained about the poor rations, poor transportation, and the stupidity of "going into the Indian country to hunt a fight without a surgeon or even a bandage." He figured it was useless to climb about in the mountains and try to surprise the Indians, and tougher yet without artillery. The Indians, he claimed, knew the territory too well and were well-armed and mounted. The battle was called Table Mountain at first, but was later changed to Godfrey's Mountain in honor of the first man slain there. The second name, however, never stuck, and to this day, few know of the actual location of the fight.[7]

While Wells operated out of Paradise Valley, the citizens of Austin were up in arms about raids in the Toiyabe Range and along the Reese River. The Paiute Buffalo Jim was believed to be the leader of the war parties in the area. A company of men called the "Lander Blues" gathered to discuss action, but their enthusiasm was curbed when they counted up only twenty muskets among them. The paper, the *Reese River Reveille*, trumpeted word of raids and thefts, and called for troops to come to their assistance. On May 4, Indians stole twelve horses in Italian Canyon, only 10 miles from the town. Finally, Captain George A. Thurston, Company B, 1st Nevada Infantry, at Fort Ruby, responded, asking how many Austin men could be counted on to join the soldiers on an expedition. Fifty, the citizens replied.

Lieutenants William G. Seamands and John U. Tolles, with forty men of Company B, 1st Nevada Infantry, ten friendly Indian scouts, and one howitzer, reached the Austin area on May 24. They camped on Silver Creek north of the town, where depredations were last reported. After purchasing sixteen horses to add to the four they had, Lieutenant Seamands took twenty men, the Indian scouts, and the howitzer to Austin to await arrival of McDermit, recently promoted to lieutenant colonel, to join him on the expedition. Tolles remained in camp with the rest of the infantry. On May 29, they chased some Indians driving stolen cattle into the mountains, fired a few shots, but could not catch them.

On June 6, Tolles, informed of more raiding toward the Humboldt River, moved north down Reese River. In the vicinity of the junction of the Reese and the Humboldt, a Mr. Klemp, who had a ranch a few miles to the east, approached Tolles for help. He said Indians had raided his ranch, shot at him, stole stock, and may have killed his hired hand. Tolles reported, "After arriving at the ranch and looking around, we found the missing man's pants, boots, and hat a short distance from the house, the pants being stiff with blood and having two ball holes in them." There was no body. Tolles concluded that it was thrown in the Humboldt. He continued up the Humboldt to Gravelly Ford, then southeast to Jacobs's Well and Fort Ruby. The entire time they saw no Indian sign except at Klemp's.[8]

Tolles's march illustrated the futility of chasing Indians with infantrymen. While he was gone, Lieutenant Seamands waited at Austin for McDermit, where the *Reese River Reveille* sarcastically noted that all the civilians who talked big about killing Indians were nowhere to be seen when the soldiers arrived. Troops were finally being siphoned into Nevada from all directions. Companies A and B, 2nd California Cavalry, moved to Fort Churchill to take over for the Nevada troops taking the field. Companies D and I, 6th California Infantry, were ordered to Nevada. Lieutenant Henry C. Penwell, with a detachment of Company I, 2nd California Cavalry, moved to Camp Dun Glen. Company A, 1st Nevada Infantry, seventy-three men under Captain William Wallace, with one howitzer, was sent to the north bend of the Humboldt River. Captain James C. Doughty was ordered to take his Company I, 2nd California Cavalry, from Smoke Creek Station to the Humboldt, and meet up with Wallace and McDermit. McDermit, on May 30, left Fort Churchill with Governor Henry Blasdel, Surgeon A. F. Meachum. Lieutenant C. C. Warner, and thirteen cavalrymen from Company E, and headed for Austin.[9]

Lieutenant Colonel McDermit arrived on June 2, and the next day, with Governor Blasdel, met with about 100 Indians to try to make the best out of the unauthorized treaty made with the citizens in April. They assured the Indians to separate themselves from the hostile bands, come to the settlements, and they would be protected. On June 4, leaving Blasdel behind, McDermit picked up Lieutenant Seamands and his twenty mounted infantrymen, scouts, and howitzer, and marched north to the Humboldt. High water delayed the crossing, but they moved downstream 18 miles to a bridge near present Winnemucca, where Captain Wallace was already waiting. Captain Doughty arrived, and then Captain Wells with eighty-two men of Company D, 1st Nevada Cavalry, and Captain Robert C. Payne with fifty men of Company E. The force, now about 240 soldiers and scouts, and two howitzers, was ready to take the fight to the Indians.

But first, McDermit wanted to see the locations of Littlefield's and Wells's encounters. They marched east 14 miles and stopped at what McDermit called Camp 12 in Littlefield Valley (south end of Eden Valley). McDermit left most of his command there, and on June 13, took fifty cavalry, Captains Wells and Payne, Lieutenant Littlefield of the cavalry, and Lieutenants Warner, McGowan, and Seamands of the infantry, Surgeon Meachum, four Indian scouts, and an interpreter, and marched northeast 25 miles. They camped near the junction of Eden Creek and the North Fork Little Humboldt. The following day, a march of 14 miles took them to what McDermit called Valley Wells, likely today's North Fork Valley between Whiskey Springs Canyon and the North Fork. Here was the site of Littlefield's May 7 encounter, and McDermit christened the place "Fort Redskin." "I visited the cañon and mountain where the Indians were posted," he wrote, "and their rifle-pits among the rocks which were ingeniously constructed, and capable of containing about 200 Indians."[10]

The command left Camp 14, "Fort Redskin," on June 14, and marched 25 miles northeast to "the foot of the Table Mountain, where Captain Wells had his fight of May 20, 1865." The place is today's Indian Buttes. Here, McDermit set up Camp 15. They found the bodies of Privates Godfrey and Monroe, scalped and mutilated. Monroe was shot in the torso and foot, and it appeared as if a fire had been built on his stomach; he had nearly bitten off his own tongue in agony before he died. McDermit wrote that he had "traveled 108 miles without seeing a stick of timber which would measure six inches, and no place suitable to establish a military post." Nevertheless, he was determined to send out scouts in all directions to find the Indians and "pursue them until I catch them or run them out of the State."

Four days later, McDermit shifted southwest to Camp 16, possibly on the west base of the Calico Mountains and east of the Santa Rosas. From there McDermit fanned out his available forces to search for Indians. He ordered Lieutenant Richard A. Osmer, with Company B, 2nd California Cavalry, to move from Dun Glen to scour the area between the Humboldt and Reese Rivers. Captain Doughty took Company I, 2nd California Cavalry, Lieutenant Seamands with his twenty mounted infantrymen, six Indians, and a howitzer, to scout the area of Gravelly Ford. McDermit took 157 men of Companies D and E, Nevada Cavalry, Captain Wallace's Nevada Infantry, Surgeon Meachum, Lieutenant Warner, three Indian scouts, a howitzer, and

20 mules, and headed east toward the headwaters of the Humboldt. Captain W. L. Knight, with part of Company D, 2nd California Cavalry, moved to Smoke Creek Station with orders to patrol between there and the Pueblo Mining District. Company D, under Captain John T. Hill, 6th California Infantry, was sent to Quinn River to protect travelers in that vicinity.[11]

The soldiers had done a lot of marching so far, but not much fighting. A Nevada soldier wrote a letter that was published in the *Virginia Union*, complaining that there was much talk, but little action. "This expedition is only a get up of officers, to keep in the service," he said. "It is the greatest boy's play that I ever saw." Referring to letters by Lieutenant C. C. Warner that the paper previously printed, the unnamed soldier said, they were "not to be relied upon. They are nothing but braggadocio, and amount to nothing; they are the laughing stock of the company."[12]

JACKSON CREEK, JULY 3, 1865

While the soldiers east of the Santa Rosa Mountains sat at the road's end in Paradise Valley and griped about a lack of action, travelers to Idaho who used the road along the west face of the Santa Rosas had plenty of action. Hill Beachey and Owen R. Johnson ran a stage line from Unionville and Star City, across the Humboldt at Gianca's Bridge (present-day Winnemucca), along the west side of the Santa Rosas, north to the Owyhee Crossing, and up Jordan Creek, to Silver City. By June 1865, the attacks and horse thefts along the line caused Beachey to suspend service until the road was made safer. With the road all but abandoned, a party of eighteen men took their chances and trekked through the nearly deserted country, heading for Boise. Beyond the headwaters of Quinn River they crossed the state line into Oregon. They were moving slowly; they had seen no Indians, and they were hauling one man in a wagon who had been accidentally shot earlier in the trip.

On July 3, about three in the afternoon, they were in an open sage plain about 20 miles from the river, riding with several horsemen in advance of the wagons, when ambushed by about fifty Indians. No one expected to be attacked in a seemingly safe, open space. The warriors were cleverly hidden behind large sagebrush along the trail. They had tied down their horses with a rope looped around the horses' necks and pulled up tight under one of their forefeet. The horses were hunched down and helpless until the rope was pulled with a jerk, and the horses sprang up. At the same time about fifty rifles barked out.

Four men were hit. P. W. Jackson, of Virginia City, Nevada, was shot off his horse and killed. Thomas Ewing was shot through the body, and Thomas Rule was pierced in several places. The two badly wounded men managed to hang on to their horses and race back toward the wagons, followed, said Thomas J. Butler, "by about thirty red devils, yelling, whooping, and shooting at their fleeing victims." Those in the rear helped the wounded into the wagon beds, covered them with blankets, and then, said Butler, "the fun began in earnest. We only had five rifles, the balance being armed with Colt's revolvers, which in an Indian fight are about as good as broom sticks."

They took cover behind the wagons. Butler had "a good Springfield government gun" and used it as well as he could, but the Indians were hidden in the sage and "their bullets were whistling about our ears as thick as bees," he said. He was sure they had killed a chief, who appeared to be rallying the warriors, and was more daring than the rest. Other Indians were hit, but it was impossible to tell how many. About five p.m. another 150 Indians joined in the fight, but they only appeared to be armed with bows and arrows. Butler watched them, "painted and with feathers in their hair," prancing

Hill Beachey fought to keep his stages running despite constant Indian attacks on coaches and stations.

around on "fine fat horses," and constantly circling, "keeping out of range of our guns, but completely surrounding us." They decided they would fight their way out of the circle and make for an adobe cabin owned by Hill Beachey Stage Line, about 22 miles back near Quinn River.

They broke out at dusk, running the horses and wagons for all they were worth. The Indians closed in, darting across the trail and firing. One of the party, thought to be a miner from Virginia City, and called a "Canadian Frenchman," was shot through the lungs with an iron arrow, the bolt going almost clear through with the tip lodging in his back. He was pulled into a wagon and they kept on going. The Indians dropped back when it became too dark to see. The fugitives reached Quinn River at one in the morning, rested a short time, and pushed on for two days. At Buffalo Creek, on the west face of the Santa Rosas, Butler and another man rode off to Paradise Valley for help. Butler wrote a quick letter to Anson Safford, dated July 5, telling him what had happened, asking for a physician, and convincing a messenger to carry it. The next day, the rest of the party pulled in to Willow Point. "Everything about the wagons was saturated in blood," Butler said, "which had began to be offensive to the smell, and we were all completely worn out and half sick, so that I think we were about the most miserable set of mortals on earth."

Butler rested a day, and then rode all the way to Unionville, trying to find a military escort to take them to Boise. The Paiutes were not finished. Within a few days they attacked parties of emigrants and miners leaving the Pueblo Mining District. In the Owyhee District, Judge C. G. Stafford and 162 others signed a petition, dated July 12, and sent it to Idaho Territorial Governor C.

D. Smith, requesting military help. Stafford described Indian attacks that killed four citizens. "The Indians took one of the men," he wrote, "cut off his head, and driving a stick through it pinioned it to the ground. They then cut off his testicles and hung them on a tree; then cut off his legs and arms and cut his body into strips and hung the pieces on the bushes. One of the men was burned to a stake. One of the men escaping, Mr. Hendricks, is now here severely wounded." It is unclear if Stafford was describing the attack north of Quinn River, and the mutilation of P. W. Jackson, or a separate incident nearer to the Pueblo mines. In any case, it is clear that McDermit's soldiers could not hope to provide protection across such a vast territory.[13]

HOT SPRINGS, *ca* JULY 15, 1865

It was July 2 before all of McDermit's detachments began spreading across northern Nevada. Captain Hill's Company D, 6th California Infantry, arrived at the head of Quinn River just after the Jackson-Butler survivors had struggled past, heading for Paradise Valley. McDermit's command, with fifteen days' rations, marched southeast, planning to link up with Doughty near the headwaters of the Humboldt after Doughty scouted the area of Gravelly Ford. About July 15, near the headwaters of the Owyhee and at a location simply called Hot Springs, McDermit surprised about 200 Indians under Zeluawick, who were still hauling some of the supplies taken from Captain Wells in May. McDermit captured seventy Indians and scattered the rest into the mountains. Zeluawick escaped, but Captain Wells and twenty-five men of Company D pursued him so relentlessly that the Indian ponies dropped in exhaustion. Wells swept in and captured the abandoned supplies, but Zeluawick and a few warriors eluded him on foot.

COTTONWOOD CANYON, JULY 31, 1865

The elusive Paiute chief only had a little longer to live. While Captain Doughty moved up the Humboldt from Gravelly Ford, Lieutenant William B. Seamands and his twenty mounted infantrymen of Company B, broke off and went south to their base at Fort Ruby to replenish supplies. After resting, Seamands mounted fifteen soldiers on the last available fresh horses remaining, and with Hank Butterfield of the Overland Express and one Indian scout, set out north to continue the search for the elusive Paiutes.

In the meantime, Captain Wells with twenty-five picked men was following Zeluawick so closely since the Hot Springs fight that they completely wore out their own horses as well as the Indians' ponies. Wells was always a step behind, but swept up Zeluawick's rabbit nets, a dried grasshopper food supply, and even the chief's gun. The beneficiary of Wells's hot pursuit was Lieutenant Seamands. At dawn on July 31, at a site reported as Cottonwood Canyon, Seamands was lucky enough to surprise Zeluawick and his band, still consisting of about 100 people, but disorganized and disheartened due to the efforts of McDermit, Doughty, and Wells. In the fight, the Nevadans killed Zeluawick and eleven of his warriors. The only soldier casualty was Sergeant Edwin D. Sherrill, seriously wounded in the neck by a barbed arrow. Zeluawick, said to be badly wounded, "was most troublesome in refusing to die," and the soldiers had to fire many bullets into him before he finally collapsed. Butterfield scalped him and sectioned off the "souvenir" to a few of his friends. It was described by newspapers as "coarse and black, and the scalp nearly as thick as sole leather."[14]

Author's photo

Pioneer graves near Gravelly Ford.

Having chased off and captured many of Zeluawick's followers and with supplies low, McDermit headed back to his base in Paradise Valley, reaching there in late July. While the soldiers were out, other bands of Indians were threatening the settlements. The people of the valley had divided into two colonies; one of them included some of the folks attacked in April, when Fearbourne and Collins were killed; the other included R. H. Scott, Edward Lyng, C. A. Nichols, Richard Brenchly, Charles Gregg, Joseph Warford, and Michael Maylen. This group resided on the east side of the valley, divided from the other colony by Martin Creek, and centered on Scott's house. They gathered at Scott's every night for protection, and worked their fields during the day. Late in July, they became worried about increased Indian signs, and Scott went to get military help.

WILLOW POINT, JULY 26, 1865

Figuring they were being watched, Scott set out after dark, but got lost and stumbled around until he unexpectedly saw a dim light. He headed toward it and walked into an outpost of Lt. Colonel McDermit, recently returned from his Indian hunt and camped near Willow Point, a watered, grassy area along the Little Humboldt River. Scott explained his concerns, and McDermit detailed Sergeant David Thomas and sixteen men from Company D, 1st Nevada Cavalry, to go with Scott. The next morning, July 26, the little band moved north from Willow Point. They stopped to graze their horses while a corporal with six men went out about four miles ahead to help Scott gather forage. Suddenly a band of Paiutes appeared, estimated to number between twenty-seven and fifty warriors. The soldiers tried to put

99

on a bold front. One man rode back to Sergeant Thomas while the remaining six tried to act unconcerned. Receiving the word, Thomas rushed forward. About the same time, a patrol of twelve men from Company I, 2nd California Cavalry, under Sergeant James F. Stephens and Corporal Charles S. Rugg, rode into the area. Several armed civilians joined them.

Now, with numbers suddenly on a more equal footing, the Paiutes raised a white flag, but Sergeant Thomas responded by charging them. The Indians retreated to a marsh adjacent to the Little Humboldt, and the Nevadans, Californians, and civilians trapped them there. The soldiers fought in skirmish line, as individuals, with nearly every man having his own plan of action. There was hand-to-hand fighting, with one soldier clubbing a warrior to death with his empty pistol and ruining his weapon. Five Paiutes got out of the marsh and took shelter in an unoccupied cabin, but the soldiers torched it and the warriors were killed as they ran outside to escape the flames. A running battle followed, covering several miles and lasting from about two p.m. until dark. Twenty-one Paiutes were killed, but they exacted a toll on their pursuers: Private Augustus Herford was killed, and Privates Thomas J. Rehill and Joshua C. Murphy were wounded, all from the 2nd California. Civilian Joseph Warfield was killed, and civilians Mark Haviland and a Mr. Travis were wounded.[15]

GRAVELLY FORD, AUGUST 4, 6, 1865

After the fight, McDermit concluded that the Indian threat to Paradise Valley was over and he moved the command to the Quinn River Valley. Down at Gravelly Ford on the Humboldt, Lieutenant Richard Osmer was still patrolling with Company B, 2nd California Cavalry, as per his July orders. He and Lieutenant W. Gibson Overend scouted the Sonoma Mountains, Golconda, and Fairbanks Station areas, down to Gravelly Ford and back. On July 17, leaving ten men to guard Fairbanks Station, Osmer took the company back to Dun Glen to refit. Having done so, he returned to the Humboldt, where Lieutenant Overend split off with a small detachment of the company and headed north to meet McDermit in Paradise Valley. Osmer continued the scout along the Humboldt. On August 2, Osmer left his camp near Gravelly Ford and traveled upstream. He crossed the Pinon Mountains and reached the Humboldt River again, about 25 miles above the ford. Finding a recently abandoned Indian camp, Osmer followed the tracks back downstream, and on August 4, surprised the Indians, killed one warrior and captured several women. Osmer returned to his Gravelly Ford camp and continued his scout downriver. Not far away, about August 6, he stumbled upon another small camp, killed two warriors and wounded several more. Osmer stayed in the area until August 12, when he received orders to repair to Camp Dun Glen.[16]

While Osmer scouted on the Humboldt, McDermit took the main command to the headwaters of Quinn River. On August 2, Lieutenant Littlefield and a detachment of troopers from Company D, had a small skirmish with a band of Paiutes, claiming to have killed five warriors. The same day, which in retrospect proved to be a fatal move, McDermit left with Captain Payne, Lieutenant Overend, twelve cavalrymen, and a mule packer, and headed west on a scout. They crossed Quinn River Valley and saw many Indian tracks, and even a series of dams and weirs to catch fish, proving the Indians had made this a primary camping ground.

McDermit took a liking to Overend as they traveled together, and confided his personal thoughts to the young second lieutenant. In a warlike mood, he told Overend that he would "make it warm" for the Indians on his return, destroying their fisheries, grass, and food supplies. Then, waxing sentimental, he indicated how he missed his family and said he had written to Mrs. McDermit and told her to have the fattest turkey ready for dinner when he returned home to her at the end of August. The next few days the little party followed the course of McDermit Creek to the west and northwest, crossing the state line. In the Oregon Canyon Mountains they discovered the area where they believed the Indians who killed Mr. Jackson had camped the previous month. Winding through mountains and valleys over the next few days, McDermit talked of his officers, two of whom, he said, "he could not trust," and one of whom failed to capture an Indian chief in a recent battle when he easily could have. He talked of death, God, and heaven, and he and Overend occasionally broke into song, one of their favorites being, "Who Will Care for Mother Now?" "How good God has been so far to us on this march," McDermit told Overend.

Many who knew McDermit remembered him as a decent man. He tried to be on friendly terms with the Indians, and tried to assure chiefs that whites who harmed any of their tribesmen would be punished. In 1863, he launched a drive against a smallpox epidemic that resulted in more than 500 Paiutes of Nevada and eastern California being vaccinated. But, McDermit could be a tough campaigner when circumstances and orders compelled him. On August 7, within half a mile of the camp at Quinn River, a few Paiutes watched the small party of soldiers ride slowly past. An Indian, later said to be the Paiute Captain John, took careful aim, squeezed off one round, and shot McDermit down. He lived only four more hours.[17]

McDermit's remains were carried to Fort Churchill for burial. His successor, Lt. Colonel Ambrose E. Hooker, 6th California Infantry, conducted a full military funeral on August 20. Flags in the entire district were flown at half-mast and all duties and operations were suspended for the day. Hooker decreed that the Quinn River camp would be known as Camp McDermit. Fighting was not over in Nevada, and the hope for peace in Oregon also proved illusory.[18]

Chapter 10 notes

1 Smith, "Sagebrush Soldiers," 64; Rathbun, *Nevada Military Names*, 36; Angel, *History of Nevada*, 172.

2 Smith, "Sagebrush Soldiers," 66; Egan, *Sand in a Whirlwind*, 91-96; Settle, *Saddles and Spurs*, 146.

3 Smith, "Sagebrush Soldiers," 66; *WR*: V.50/1, 409-10; Letter Secretary of War, 50th Congress, Senate Ex. Doc. 70, 238. In 1865, there were about 8,500 Indians on the Humboldt and Carson Valley reservations. See *Commissioner of Indian Affairs 1865*, 589.

4 The location of this encounter is discussed in footnote 7.

5 Smith, "Sagebrush Soldiers," 67.

6 The location of this encounter is discussed in footnote 7.

7 Smith, "Sagebrush Soldiers," 67-70; Angel, *History of Nevada*, 172; Rathbun, *Nevada Military Names*, 147-48. There are sixteen Table Mountains in Nevada. Smith and Rathbun incorrectly believe the fight occurred on the west face of the Tuscarora Range. One can locate the sites of Littlefield's encounter and the Godfrey/Table Mountain fight by tracing the route as discussed in Major McDermit's reports of June 15 and July 1 1865 (*WR*: V.50/1, 411-12, *WR*: V.50/2, 1274-75). McDermit visited both places, and reported his routes and mileages. His expedition is detailed later in this narrative. The Godfrey/Table Mountain fight took place on today's Indian Buttes on the divide between the Little Owyhee River and Lake Creek in extreme northwestern Elko County, about 7 miles south of the Idaho line. Even the terrain described by the Nevada cavalryman matches Indian Buttes.

8 *WR*: V.50/1, 412-14; Smith, "Sagebrush Soldiers," 70, 72-73.

9 *WR*: V.50/2, 1250-52; Smith, "Sagebrush Soldiers," 71-72.

10 *WR*: V.50/1, 410-12.

11 *WR*: V.50/1, 411-12: *WR*: V.50/2, 1274-75, 1279; Smith, "Sagebrush Soldiers," 74; Rathbun, *Nevada Military Names*, 134.

12 Smith, "Sagebrush Soldiers," 74.

13 *Idaho World*, June 17, 1865, August 12, 1865; *WR*: V.50/2, 105-06; Angel, *History of Nevada*, 172. The location of the attack on Jackson, Butler, *et al.* is near today's Jackson Creek on the west face of Battle Mountain.

14 Smith, "Sagebrush Soldiers," 74-75; Rathbun, *Nevada Military Names*, 48; Wilson, *Pioneer Nevada*, Vol. 2, 75; *Idaho World*, August 12, 1865. The sites of the Hot Springs and Cottonwood Canyon fights are not known for certain. There are dozens of Hot Springs and Cottonwood Creeks and Canyons in northern Nevada. Possible sites for Seamand's fight, within a week's march of Camp Ruby, is the Cottonwood Creek about a dozen miles north of Carlin, and the Cottonwood Creek Canyon north of Tuscarora. More detailed reports of these fights were not written because of McDermit's death on August 7.

15 Rathbun, *Nevada Military Names*, 155-56; Orton, *Records of California Men*, 185; Angel, *History of Nevada*, 173; Smith, "Sagebrush Soldiers," 75.

16 *WR*: V.50/1, 414-15; *WR*: V.50/2, 1285-86; Orton, *Records of California Men*, 184.

17 Smith, "Sagebrush Soldiers," 75, 77-78; Angel, *History of Nevada*, 173; Edwards, "Department of the Pacific," 180. Captain John, with his cousin, Captain Soo, had tried to make peace with the whites in April 1865. When the attempt failed, and Soo led the whites against his own people, John broke away and joined the hostiles, becoming his cousin's enemy.

18 Smith, "Sagebrush Soldiers," 79. Camp McDermit later became Fort McDermitt, and the Fort McDermitt Indian Reservation and town of McDermitt all sprang up in the area, all incorrectly spelled with an extra "t."

Chapter 11
THE PEACE FAILS: OREGON, 1865

With the close of the 1864 campaigns, the terms of service for the first six companies of the Oregon Cavalry expired. Not the typical frontier military unit, the 1st Oregon Cavalry was known as the "Puritan Regiment" for its supposed morality and temperance habits. One thing is certain, the regiment had far fewer desertions than almost every other Indian-fighting unit in the West: only fifty-one men in three years.[1] The 1st Oregon Cavalry was restructured in the winter of 1864-65, with some men leaving service, some reenlisting, and some new recruits joining.

In November 1864, General McDowell called for the formation of a new regiment of Oregon Infantry, and organization went on through the winter and following spring. George Currey left as captain of Company E, 1st Oregon Cavalry, and was promoted to lieutenant colonel of the new 1st Oregon Infantry; John Drake left Company G and became the regiment's major. Recruitment was slow, as it had been in building the cavalry three years earlier; the first six companies not being mustered in until June 1865. Companies went to Forts Vancouver, Klamath, Yamhill, Dalles, Steilacoom, Walla Walla, Colville, and Boise.[2]

Politics also played a part in Oregon's unpreparedness for the campaign season of 1865. There were changes in administration personnel and territories. In January, Arizona Territory was re-annexed to the Department of the Pacific; in February, Utah Territory and part of Nebraska Territory were attached to the Department of Missouri; in March, Idaho Territory was attached to the District of Oregon; and part of the District of California was added to the District of Oregon. Justus Steinberger was removed as colonel of the 1st Washington Territory Infantry, supposedly because the small size of that unit did not warrant a colonel, but also because Republican politicians believed he was a peace Democrat.

In one of the biggest surprises, General Alvord was recalled to Washington D. C. in March, and Colonel Reuben Maury assumed command of the District of Oregon. The recall startled many, including Governor Gibbs and General McDowell. Some congressmen called Alvord "a tool and plaything of disloyalists," while some senators believed he was too much of an uncompromising Unionist and accused him of meddling in state politics. The politicians told General Ulysses S. Grant that Alvord was a liability and must go, although Grant was already of a similar mind, and not averse to digging in the dirt with the rest of them. "I know Alvord well," Grant wrote to Secretary of War Edwin Stanton. "I do not think he is fit for the command, and he ought to be called East." Alvord was not the only subject of Grant's barbs. "McDowell, if I am not wrongly informed, is likely to do more harm than good where he is. I am in favor of Halleck for that department." Politics, as it often had, interfered with a smooth-running military.

As the new district commander, Maury, basing his judgment on long field experience, recommended that more troops be sent to the exposed areas of Oregon and Idaho. Because it was comparatively quiet east of the Cascades at the time, McDowell disagreed. He thought dishonest agents and increasing pressure from emigrants and miners caused most Indian problems. McDowell did not want a lot of troops on the frontier, and Brig. General George Wright, in charge of the District of California, who should have known better, advised McDowell that a few mobile cavalry units could restore order when necessary, and then retire back to the forts.[3]

The army never successfully designed a policy for Indian-fighting, and always appeared puzzled as to whether to build and staff numerous forts, cover the territory with mobile patrols, escort wagon trains, react defensively and pursue Indians only after raids, or go on a constant offensive to track down marauders and villages alike. Should the army try to force the Indians to fight in a pitched battle, in which it had the advantage, or would the Indians continue to use guerrilla tactics, striking unexpectedly, and running off into the deserts and mountains? Funding, logistics, and personnel were always issues that tended to keep responses conservative, and the military seemingly had to relearn hard lessons every time a new "war" broke out.

While Oregon restructured its forces, there was a fortunate lull in the fighting. The treaty with the Klamaths, Modocs, and part of the "Yahuskin" Paiutes in October 1864, had apparently tempered matters. With Chief Paulina's wife and child in custody, he was reluctant to continue fighting. In April 1865, he sent word to Captain Kelly at Fort Klamath that he and his 500 followers wanted peace and wished the captain to contact Superintendent Huntington to hurry and arrange a conference. The army was not convinced. Shortly before he was removed, General Alvord said that Paulina's submission "is an auspicious event if he is sincere. It was but the natural result of the activity of the troops last summer. . . . But it remains to be tested." Preparations were made for the usual summer campaigns.[4]

While all of the expeditions of 1864 had retired to winter quarters near the main forts, Captain Henry C. Small, with a portion of Company G, 1st Oregon Cavalry, maintained his frigid post at Camp Watson on Fort Creek, calling his place of exile, "Headquarters Canyon City Road Expedition." The new year had hardly begun when, on January 11, an express brought him news of an Indian raid on Cottonwood Creek Station (Cottonwood House),

Author's photo

Site of Cottonwood House, Oregon, near the junction of Cottonwood Creek and the John Day River.

about one dozen miles to the east. Small took Lieutenant William M. Hand and ten men to investigate. When they arrived they learned there was no actual raid, but Indians were "threatening" the place. Small saw six Indians and tried to trail them, but the frozen ground showed no tracks. On January 18, Hand was off again, this time pursuing Indians who stole thirteen horses six miles above Cottonwood House. Small, hampered by the removal of most of his horses, took eight men mounted on mules and rode 60 miles up the John Day River and back, without finding the thieves.[5]

JOHN DAY RIVER, MARCH 14, 1865

Back on the Canyon City Road, if Captain Small and the cavalry couldn't find the Indians, the civilians could. On March 7, a party of twenty-four settlers and ranchers met Small at Cottonwood House and told him they were going to find the Indians who had been stealing stock from the neighborhood. They trailed down John Day River, driving the Indians before them. On March 14, they induced nineteen warriors, five women, and four children to come to their camp for a parley. The citizens intended to bring in the whole band, and the chief appeared perfectly satisfied, but at the first opportunity he gave a signal and they all broke and ran. The citizens fired on them, killing twelve, including two women, and wounding nearly all the rest. They captured twenty-three horses and mules, three guns, and about fifty pounds of ammunition. None of the whites were injured. When Lieutenant Hand heard of the incident he knew there would be more trouble, and he asked Small for permission to keep his soldiers at Cottonwood House.

GARBER'S FIGHT, APRIL 17, 1865

At Camp Watson on April 13, Captain Small sent Sergeant George Garber with twenty-two men of Company G, out on a scout. They headed up Cottonwood Creek and at a timbered ridge at its headwaters, picked up an Indian trail. Garber sent the pack train back for more supplies and continued across the divide to the South Fork John Day and then upstream. At 11 a.m. on April 17, Garber discovered a camp of about twenty-five Indians on the west side of the South Fork near the upper crossing of the Yreka and Canyon City Road. Garber, in advance of the train with eight men, attacked immediately, but fell mortally wounded at the first fire. Corporal William Starkey, in charge of the train, went forward with the remainder of the detachment and joined in the fight. The troopers killed four or five Indians and wounded eight or nine, captured three horses, two guns, and large amounts of ammunition, blankets, skins, and trinkets. They set ablaze more than 5,000 pounds of dried meat. When a courier reached Camp Watson requesting a surgeon, Captain Small started immediately with a detachment of eight cavalrymen. He went as far as Cottonwood House when a fearful storm halted him, but he sent a few intrepid horsemen to ride all night and help bring in the wounded. They arrived at four p.m. the next day. The surgeon did the best he could, but Garber died of his wounds, "an honest, upright, brave, and good soldier." Small sent his remains to The Dalles for interment.[6]

On April 18, Small sent ten men to look for Lieutenant Hand, who had gone on a scout down John Day River, and then accompanied Assistant Surgeon D. Walker to Camp Watson with the wounded men. They started back for Cottonwood House in the afternoon and were about three miles from there at dusk, when Indians charged at them from the right of the road. Small and Walker sped off but ran within 40 yards of a dozen Indians who were dismounted near the road. The two men spun around. "We only escaped by a precipitous flight," Small said, "they following us some three miles." They got back to Camp Watson after dark. The next afternoon, with an escort of three troopers, they started for Cottonwood again. "When a little beyond where we saw the Indians the previous evening," Small said, "we found three citizens who had been killed, two of them scalped and horribly mutilated. The names of the unfortunate men, as far as I can learn, are a man by the name of John W. Potter, and an old man who had been staying with him at the Mountain House, name at present unknown. The other, name unknown."

Small had the victims brought to Cottonwood and buried. He sent a detachment after the killers. They rode up Cottonwood Creek to the head of the timbered ridge when they decided that the Indians had not gone that way, but must have come from the north, up the John Day, and were probably part of the band that the civilians fought with in March. The men sent out to look for Lieutenant Hand returned without finding him. Small then had to send ten more troopers out to Rock Creek to escort the Canyon City stage to Cottonwood. He was nearly overwhelmed with the duties expected of him, and was probably learning to appreciate the frustrations Captain Drake felt the previous summer. Small asked for help. Colonel Maury responded by sending Captain Loren. L. Williams and Company H, 1st Oregon Infantry, from Fort Vancouver to Camp Watson. It would help, but it wasn't enough.[7]

Although they had just mustered into service in March 1865, the men of Company H were not thrilled with marching through the snow and cold. The company "poet" wrote a song about the experience. The ten-stanza melody was titled *The Winter's Campaign. Company H*, and was sung to the tune of *Sweet Betsy From Pike*. Three of the stanzas will suffice to illustrate the men's complaints:

> *The detail was made up of thirty-five boys,*
> *As good could be found, the Captain's own choice.*
> *The weather was cold, that every one knows,*
> *For some froze their fingers and others their toes.*
> *Now this is the reason why soldiers complain,*
> *Of going a scouting on a winter's campaign.*
>
> *The Captain you know is commander-in-chief,*
> *He said unto Grant: Now where is our beef?*
> *Paulina, you know, is in a starving condition,*
> *So he sent in his men with a requisition.*
> *You may well know, and it looks very plain,*
> *If you starve out the Snakes it will end the campaign.*
>
> *If this I have written, you find it in print,*
> *I hope it will give some people a hint.*
> *When they come round with yarns and their fibs,*
> *Don't be led by old Currey nor lean belly Gibbs;*
> *But just stay at home and let them complain,*
> *And do their own scouting on a winter's campaign.*[8]

As the military tried its best to cope with a difficult situation, the civilians constantly pressured them for assistance. Nearly every concern centered on protection of the roads and making them safe for travel and commerce. Businessmen in California, Oregon, Nevada, and Idaho, wanted a military presence for commercial reasons. They clamored for army patrols and forts, insisting an intermediate post was necessary between Fort Klamath and Fort Boise, and along the Nevada routes. Commercial interests vied with each other. Those in the Willamette Valley, Portland, and The Dalles, were concerned about the new southern routes, such as the one Lt. Colonel Drew had opened, and urged more protection along the Canyon City Road, fearing competition from merchants of Red Bluff and Chico, California. Merchants in the Owyhee District had a different take on the problem; they wanted the southern routes protected so they could have easier access to California, preventing what they saw as a growing monopoly on goods and services from the Oregon merchants.[9]

While authorities talked, warming temperatures and new grass facilitated raiding. On April 27, Indians nearly captured a D. W. Douthitt & Brothers supply train bound for Idaho City. Indians ran off about 35 mules, luckily just unhitched from the wagons, while Douthitt camped at Olds Ferry on the Snake. Scraping together a posse, Douthitt followed the trail west up the Malheur River. They came upon the Indians in the rough canyons of the Malheur and a short fight ensued; the whites recovered a few animals, but the Indians prevailed and drove them away.

The Humboldt Express Company's connections along the road south of Silver City were severed and Hill Beachey withdrew his stock from the road until the line was safe. At Summit Springs, a waterhole about 18 miles north of Quinn River Station, Indians attacked three German miners, killing one of them, Henry Floder. The citizens in Idaho Territory again expressed their need for protection, and complained that the military was doing little, especially the soldiers at Fort Boise, who they saw as resting warmly in the fort all winter when they should have been out on the roads chasing Indians.[10]

On May 9, McDowell issued orders to divide the Idaho section of the District of Oregon, into the Sub-District of Boise, hopefully enabling more efficient local control. Lt. Colonel Currey became the commander. McDowell authorized a new post to be built in the area of the Owyhee mines, which the locals wanted, and more posts east of Boise to protect the emigrants, which the locals weren't as concerned about—their main focus being on the travelers and commerce coming from the west.

In May, Captain William Kelly was ordered to establish a depot in the Silver Lake area from which to patrol the roads from Fort Klamath and the Willamette Valley to Canyon City. Also in May, Captain Ephriam Palmer took his Company B, 1st Oregon Infantry, and escorted a supply train from The Dalles to Boise City. From Fort Boise, the company was divided up and sent to man three camps. Lieutenant J. W. Cullen set up Camp Reed on July 3, near the junction of Rock Creek and the Snake River near Shoshone Falls, but moved the camp downstream to the mouth of Salmon Falls Creek in August. Lieutenant Cyrus H. Walker established Camp Wallace July 12, on Soldier Creek in Camas Prairie, and on October 6, he located Camp Lander at the junction of the Salt Lake, Virginia City, and Boise Roads, three miles southeast of Fort Hall.

The camps were established to aid emigrants and keep a watch out for Indians. Since the Shoshonis and Bannocks east of Fort Boise had been fairly peaceful for the past two years, there was little for the soldiers to do. Lieutenant Walker's journal, kept for a full year, is replete with mentions of little else but weather observations, fishing, and hunting journeys. After establishing Camp Wallace, Walker took twenty-two men south to the Snake River to look for Indians, but there were none. On July 25, he met a twenty-one-wagon train, talked to the emigrants and learned that "They hung two men here a few days ago as counterfeiters." Apparently they had been caught with more than $10,000 in fake coins, gold dust, and greenbacks.

Near Big Springs, Idaho Territory, on August 7, Walker found some suspicious Indians, and not knowing quite what to do with them, he simply took away their seven guns and several pounds of powder and lead. Walker and his men spent some time at the road junction by old Fort Hall, trying to convince emigrants to take the northern road by way of Camas Prairie as being shorter, but he believed many of them "thought I was working for the ferryman, as they have been deceived so many times along the road that they don't know who to believe." On September 5, Walker met the remnants of a wagon train attacked on July 31, at Rock Creek (present-day Wyoming), where Jasper Fletcher was wounded, his wife, Mary Ann was killed, and their two daughters, Amanda and Elizabeth, were carried off into captivity.[11]

On September 14, Walker, at the easternmost station that would become Camp Lander, met a four-wagon train that had been attacked by Indians. Walker inspected the bullet holes in the canvas covers. In November, Captain Palmer visited the camp, and several Indians were seen digging roots nearby. Eager to foster good relations, the officers induced the Indians to their camp and gave them two days' rations of fresh meat. Walker spent the lonely winter at Lander with his men, and about the only travelers they met were miners heading away from the Boise and Owyhee diggings and over to try their luck at Virginia City, Montana. They expected more. Commissioner of Indian Affairs D. N. Cooley, in his 1865 report, was quite concerned about protection for "the travelers who were expected to crowd the emigrant routes from California to Idaho and Montana."

The eastward migration may appear contrary to twenty-first century conceptions of the pioneer movement, but, as one newspaper explained, the migration had reached the far shore, made its mark, and turned around for new lands to conquer. It reported that three-fourths of the trains now penetrating the forests and deserts, "with the rising sun in their eyes, are old Californians." The eastward migration, the paper claimed, had now reached back to the divide between the commercial domains of San Francisco and St. Louis. "And still the human current flows steadily to the eastward."

Company B spent one year guarding the trails across southern Idaho, without having a single Indian fight. With boredom the biggest enemy, they rejoiced when they walked back into Fort Boise on June 27, 1866, exactly one year since they marched out.[12] Very likely, the citizens of western Idaho were certain that they could have found something better for the soldiers to do.

Chapter 11 notes

1 Bancroft, *History of Oregon*, Vol 2, 508. Desertion rates for the ten U. S. Cavalry regiments in 1867-68 are as follows: 1st, 159; 2nd, 450; 3rd, 200; 4th, 105; 5th, 357; 6th, 156; 7th, 457; 8th, 481; 9th, 48; 10th, 147. See *Secretary of War 1868-69*, 768.

2 Carey, *History of Oregon*, 640; Bancroft, *History of Oregon*, Vol 2, 509; Dyer's Compendium, Pt. 3, 1556.

3 *WR*: V.50/1, 5; *WR*: V.50/2, 945; Edwards, "Department of the Pacific," 272-74, 279-82.

4 Ruby and Brown, *Pacific Northwest*, 206; *WR:* V.50/2, 1144.

5 *WR*: V.50/1, 396-99: *WR*: V.50/2, 1120.

6 *WR*: V.50/1, 396-99. Garber's fight was probably near today's Izee, Oregon. The fight is sometimes incorrectly listed as occurring 20 November 1865. Small did not send a report on the affair until November. He indicated to headquarters "that on the 20th day of November 1865 the report of a fight with Snake Indians by troops under my command was forwarded. . . ." The forwarding date later became misconstrued as the battle date. Small to AAG, January 5, 1865 [1866], RG 393, Dept. of Columbia, Letters Received, Box 3.

7 *WR*: V.50/1, 396-97; *WR*: V.50/2, 213.

8 From the collection of B. William Henry, Florence, Oregon.

9 *Idaho World*, April 6, 1865, June 17, 1865; Edwards, "Department of the Pacific," 260.

10 *Idaho World*, May 6, 1865, June 3, 1865, June 17, 1865, July 1, 1865.

11 Bancroft, *History of Oregon*, Vol. 2, 512; *WR*: V.50/2, 1224, 1227; "Idaho Military Posts," http://www.idahohistory.net/Reference; Cyrus Hamlin Walker Papers, Oregon Historical Society, MSS 264; Michno, *A Fate Worse Than Death*, 144-46.

12 Cyrus Hamlin Walker Papers, Oregon Historical Society, MSS 264; *Commissioner of Indian Affairs 1865*, 16; *Idaho World*, October 14, 1865.

Chapter 12

SUMMER AND FALL CAMPAIGN
OREGON, 1865

Major John M. Drake, 1ˢᵗ Oregon Infantry, realized the futility of sending foot soldiers east to guard the emigrant roads while they were needed to the west, and when they would be nearly useless in chasing after mounted Indians. If there was a major Indian outbreak, the lack of cavalry available while Oregon re-organized its mounted units could be critical, and by late May the Indians were becoming more active. Reports came in that about 700 horses and cattle had been run off from near the Owyhee Crossing, Jordan Creek, and along Succor Creek, which flowed north from the Owyhee Mountains to the Snake River. Paulina's people had been quiet because the government still held his family, but Howluck, Weahwewa, and others had no such restrictions. Almost as if the American soldier presence made no difference, they continued to raid other tribes as they always had.

On May 20, Snakes attacked a band of twenty-one Indians from the Umatilla Reservation while hunting on the North Fork John Day near Camas Creek. The Snakes raided their camp and stole forty-eight horses. Lieutenant Colonel Currey, commanding at Fort Walla Walla, went to the reservation and recruited forty Indians to scout the region. He also sent Captain Abner W. Waters and fifty-five men of Company F, 1ˢᵗ Oregon Infantry, to establish a temporary camp on Camas Prairie. Currey hoped to drive the Snakes away from the reservation and back south of the North Fork John Day. The Umatillas, Walla Wallas, and Cayuse who lived on the reservation planned to hold a war council to consider a retaliatory raid.[1]

In northern Nevada, Indians attacked stages and freighters along the Susanville, Smoke Creek, Granite Creek, and Pueblo roads, with two prospectors killed near the Pueblo mines. In June, John Bidwell, formerly a major in the California Volunteers in the Mexican War and a prominent California pioneer, wrote to General Wright of the necessity for a post or for army patrols on that route. With appeals for help coming in from all quarters, General McDowell ordered more protection along the roads from the Snake River to California, including a directive to construct a camp near Jordan Creek in the Owyhee District. Finally, this was more to the liking of the local miners and ranchers. In early June, Lieutenant Charles Hobart marched in to Fort Boise with elements of Companies A, B, and D, 1ˢᵗ Oregon Cavalry, and, on June 19, Drake sent him out to establish the long-anticipated post. Hobart searched the area and found a site with suitable wood, water, and grass, on Cow Creek, 24 miles from Ruby City and right on the Oregon-Idaho border. He named the post Camp Lyon.[2]

MALHEUR RIVER JULY 9, 1865

On July 2, Hobart and his forty-four cavalrymen had picked up a large trail of stock, heading northwest. They followed the tracks over the rough country bordering the Owyhee River and reached the Malheur River on July 7. There, three Indians were seen, and Hobart left a guard with the supply wagons while he hurried off to try and catch the Indians before they spread the warning. The Indians went upriver and the soldiers followed for two days, passing several hastily abandoned camps with evidence of stock trails scattered every which way into the innumerable canyons. Hobart camped on a little flat where a small creek met the Malheur, near present-day Juntura. Before dawn on July 9, the pickets reported Indians prowling nearby; Hobart called to arms, had the horses saddled, and put his howitzer in position. Detected, the warriors opened fire from all sides, with the heaviest shooting coming from a mountain ledge to the rear of the camp. A blast of canister drove Howluck and Pony Blanket's warriors from their position.

During the fighting, a dozen horses and mules in the rear broke loose and ran toward the Indians, but a party under Sergeant Wallace and Corporal Walker of Company B, rushed out to recover them. The Indians they rushed toward retreated, but they signaled to warriors on the opposite side of the camp, apparently letting them know that a significant number of soldiers had vacated the perimeter. In response, warriors in the front of the camp advanced and tried to drive the soldiers out. Private Jones of Company D was hit in the arm, but Hobart shifted his howitzer and fired more canister at the advancing warriors, driving them back over the mountain.

Sergeant Wallace was still chasing the Indians, trying to recover all the horses, and Hobart sent reinforcements to him. They rode five miles downriver, before escaping into a canyon, "leaving in our hands," Hobart said, "the body of one Indian whom they were unable to take off, his arms and ammunition, and nine horses. Three other dead Indians were carried off by them, together with their wounded; how many in number I could not say."

During the chase, Corporal Walker and Private Philips of Company B, were separated from the rest. Several warriors doubled back and came out of a canyon behind them, cutting them off from the rest of the command. A mounted warrior shot and seriously wounded Philips, and was about to tomahawk him off his horse when Walker charged in and shot him. With that, the remaining warriors disappeared into the rocks. Hobart estimated that there were seventy mounted Indians and about an equal number on foot. "I think white men must have been among them," he reported, "for they told us in good English to 'come on, you sons of bitches, we can whip you

anywhere.' They had considerable soldiers' clothing among them and appear
to have plenty of arms and ammunition." About five Indians were killed and
five wounded. Only two soldiers were wounded, but Hobart headed home,
recovering none of the stolen stock and losing three of his own animals.
They returned to Camp Lyon on July 13.[3]

OWYHEE RIVER JULY 17, 1865

Lyon was a hot spot. No sooner had Hobart returned than civilians
complained of more stock thefts. Hobart ordered out Sergeants Wallace and
Phillips with a detachment of 1st Oregon Cavalry, to take up the chase. They
headed south from Camp Lyon about 45 miles to the Three Forks area of the
Owyhee. There, on July 17, in a canyon about 800 feet below them were the
stolen animals and a camp of about fifteen Indians. Detailing a small guard
to stay with their horses on the tableland, Wallace and Phillips divided the
rest of the men and snaked their way down the steep cliffs, one on each side

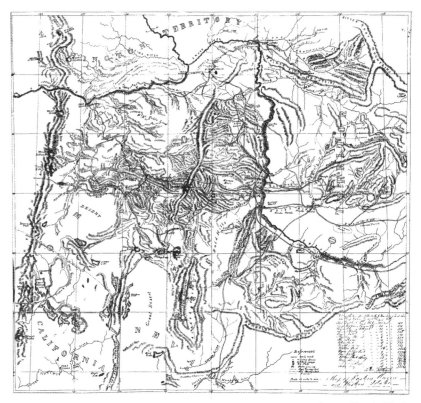

Oregon Historical Society

Lieutenant John Bowen's 1865 map of 1864 routes of the Currey and Drake
expeditions against the Indians. Bowen served in the 1st Oregon Cavalry as adjutant
for Currey's 1864 expedition.

of the camp. Phillips, who had the shorter route, was in position first. He was to hold fire until the guns of Wallace's party announced the start of the action, however, two Indians washing in the river discovered him, and the fight was on.

Phillips charged in and was met by Wallace from the other side, who had just gotten down the cliffs with his tired men. The surprised Indians put up only a token resistance and scattered, some splashing to safety across the river, although with several wounded among them. Four warriors were left dead on the field. Several of the stolen animals had been killed, and Wallace only recovered one ox and two horses, but also many bows and arrows, ammunition, a few hundred pounds of dried meat, berries, furs, blankets, trinkets, and similar trade items. They also took two revolvers and parts of a Henry Rifle. After burning nearly all of the captured items, Wallace returned to Camp Lyon on the July 18. Hearing his report, Lieutenant Hobart somehow concluded that they had killed the murderers of McComins and Gregory last winter.[4]

There were still not enough cavalry in the Owyhee sector. On July 1, Hobart had sent Lieutenant Gates with twenty-five men to patrol the road between Owyhee and Surprise Valley, California. They were to work in conjunction with troops from Camp Bidwell, or with Captain William Kelly with soldiers from Fort Klamath. The site of Camp Bidwell was temporarily occupied since 1863, but no permanent post had been erected until July 1865. The white occupants of the Owyhee Country were not alone in calling for protection; similar appeals were made in northeastern California, from Susanville, Honey Lake, Red Bluff, Shasta, and Surprise Valley. They wanted the army to patrol the roads and build a new post to guard the area. Major Robert S. Williamson surveyed the area and selected the final location in northern Surprise Valley on Bidwell Creek only two miles from the timbered mountains to the west, and four miles north of the eastern approaches to Fandango (Lassen) Pass. Williamson thought he had the perfect spot, but 300 people already occupied the valley.

Nevertheless, in an early example of eminent domain, he selected the "best for the Government without regard to the claims of the settlers." The camp was built, but not without the protests of many settlers who lost their farms and ranches as a result. One of them, Henry Miller, had already lost his farm on the Truckee River in Nevada, because the government wanted his land for a reservation. He moved to Surprise Valley, where he thought he would be far away from interference. Once again, the army took 160 acres of his land. "I am a poor man and have a family to support, and if this should be taken away from me I should not know what to do," he said. Miller, like so many others, became one of the many residual casualties of war.[5]

On June 2, George Currey was promoted to colonel of the 1st Oregon Infantry, John Drake became the lieutenant colonel, and William Rinehart the major. Drake, now as commander of the Sub-District of Boise, had several concerns. He believed that the Owyhee mines and routes to them "are more exposed to Indian raids than any other portion of the country" and the number of troops at Camp Lyon was insufficient to protect the mining settlements and patrol two California roads. He thought Camp Lyon should be made permanent and its garrison increased. Drake was certain the large mining population in the Boise District had driven all the hostile Indians

Courtesy Pilar M. Elorriaga, from Owyhee Trails, *Caxton Press*

Camp Lyon as it looked in 1866. Below, Camp Lyon site today.

Author's photo

115

south of the Snake River; as a result, he thought at least one post, Camp Wallace in Camas Prairie, could be abandoned. Most of all, Drake was worried about the lack of cavalry, which would require mounting detachments of infantry who were not trained for mounted operations. He supposed pack mules could be saddled and bridled in emergencies, so that the "infantry can be made to render efficient service in the pursuit of Indians."[6] It appeared as if the government had wasted valuable time, effort, and money to recruit and outfit a regiment of infantry, when a second regiment of cavalry would have better served the purpose.

With the end of the Civil War came more restructuring in the West, producing at least one personnel change that resulted in tragedy. On June 27, the Military Division of the Pacific was created, and General Henry W. Halleck became its commander. Its sub-divisions were the Department of California, which included California, Nevada, and New Mexico and Arizona Territories, under command of General McDowell, and the Department of Columbia, consisting of Oregon and Washington and Idaho Territories, under General Wright. On July 27, Wright and his wife boarded the steamship *Brother Jonathan* in San Francisco, to sail for department headquarters at Fort Vancouver. The next day a northwest gale began to blow, and by Sunday morning, July 29, the ship moved closer to the coast to escape the heavy seas. Seeking shelter, *Brother Jonathan* steered for Crescent City, California, when she struck a rock that knocked the keel off. One giant wave raised the bow onto a rock and another lifted her over, driving the bow underwater. Twenty minutes after first hitting the rock, it was reported, "everything had gone to eternity." Only one lifeboat made it ashore with nineteen passengers. Others were launched, but capsized in the rough seas. One of them contained Mrs. Wright. General Wright and his staff were with Captain DeWolf on the quarterdeck when the ship sank. Most of the victims were never recovered, but Wright's body was located far south near Shelter Cove, six weeks after the accident. General and Mrs. Wright were buried in Sacramento on October 21.[7]

The Malheur River area that Lieutenant Hobart penetrated looking for horse thieves was always of interest to the miners. With nearby strikes to the north in the Blue Mountains, they were certain that color could also be found in the Malheur Country, but the terrain was rough and few trails crossed it. In late August 1865, about 100 miners formed an exploration company and left the Owyhee District to prospect the South Fork Malheur and Malheur Lake. The company leaders included George Stoneroad, William Searcy, Dick Ralston, John Bennerfield, R. H. Johns, A. B. Sanders, and James Rose. In one of the Malheur's innumerable twisting canyons, one of the party, J. P. Preston, became ill, and the company halted for a few days until he could travel. While waiting, O. H. Graffan and Seth Moore started away from camp to test for color in a little creek. While ascending a hill about one and a half miles from camp, a shot rang out, a bullet tearing through Graffan's chest and out his back, and Graffan, who was walking ten yards in front of Moore, called out, "I am a dead man!"

Not knowing how many enemies were around, Moore turned and ran for about 400 yards, when he luckily met a party of fifteen mounted miners who had seen Indians and were going to investigate. By the time they got to Graffan, his shirt, rifle, revolver, and ammunition had already been stolen. They unsuccessfully searched for the culprits and returned with the body to the camp. After burying it, they carved on a nearby pine tree: "O. H. Graffan Killed by Indians, September 5, 1865." The expedition headed for home after a few more days. Far from humbling them, the experience left the miners talking about revenge.[8]

Civilian Indian-hunting expeditions had mixed results, but they were convinced that they could do better than the soldiers sent to protect them. When Lt. Colonel Drake got his hands on cavalry, he jumped at his opportunity to use them. In the summer of 1865, he sent Lieutenant James L. Currey, with a detachment of Company E, east on the Overland Trail to Rock Creek Station on the Snake River to escort the mail and deter attacks. Currey was having trouble holding on to his own stock, however, for late in July, Indians ran off four of his beef cattle along with four horses of the Overland Stage Company. Currey and twenty troopers went after the thieves and shortly caught up with them. The Indians had already killed two beeves and ran into a thicket to hide. Currey, according to the *Idaho World*'s witness, did not have the gumption to do much about it. He surrounded the brush, but would not attack, and then, "withdrew twelve men to act as his bodyguard leaving eight to guard the brush, in consequence of which the Indians escaped."

Currey returned with the four horses and remaining two cattle, but the following night, Indians were back running off more animals. On August 1, Overland Stage agents Thomas B. Fitzhugh and Joseph Douglas arrived at Rock Creek and demanded action. Currey sent a sergeant and eight privates to accompany Fitzhugh, Douglas, and two station employees, Mr. Archer and one other. They traveled far south toward the Goose Creek Mountains, but there, said Fitzhugh, the soldiers again balked, being tired, hungry, and because they "did not believe they would find any d—d Indian in the country." With that, Fitzhugh, Douglas, and their two companions, told them to go to the devil and decided to continue alone. Apparently shamed by the civilians, three soldiers joined them. They found an Indian camp of about fifteen warriors six miles ahead. Being in front of the other five men, Fitzhugh and Douglas charged first, killing the only warrior who had a rifle. Another warrior tried to grab the weapon, but Douglas rode over him and Fitzhugh shot him. The Indians ran, firing arrows as they went. The two white men chased them, killing one more in a half-mile chase. They scalped all three by the time the rest of the party caught up, and, so the story went, "were too late to take part in the dances."[9]

The sarcastic commentary was typical of how many civilians viewed army "protection." In August 1865, another newspaper joined the club as the latest "armchair general." Joseph and John Wasson learned the printer's trade in Ohio and decided to take their skills west. In 1860, Joe joined a party of gold-seekers that was attacked en route to the mines, and the experience left him with a life-long hatred of Indians. The brothers set up their paper on the upper floor of a rickety building in Ruby City, and a year later moved a few miles to Silver City. Ruby City was cramped for space and lot prices were high. The people slowly shifted up the valley where they had more room, cheaper land, and where they were nearer to the large mines. Silver City sprang up and soon had a population of 3,000, with ten general stores, four hotels, two furniture makers, two meat markets, two music stores, a stable, a photo shop, a Wells-Fargo bank, a laundry, a shoe shop, a stable, a bakery, a jewelry store, one brewery, six saloons, and a newspaper.

The *Owyhee Avalanche* became an outspoken promoter of the territory, a supporter of the army when it operated to help the civilians, and a severe critic when it did not. In one of its earliest weekly issues, the *Avalanche* reported that Lt. Colonel Drake was planning to send a company to Pueblo Valley to establish a winter camp, Captain Kelly was moving east from Fort Klamath to join up, and Company K of the 2nd California Cavalry was going to Camp Bidwell and patrol from Surprise Valley to the east. From these moves, said the *Avalanche*, the people "of Owyhee in particular, can derive much substantial satisfaction." Nevertheless, the paper continued, that was only a beginning, because sitting in camp all winter would not help at all; "One good winter's campaign against Indians is worth, as a general thing, half a dozen conducted in the summer season." It stated that the practice of "sending out parties of soldiers to scout [a]round during the warm season, to wear out their stock in wild goose chases, and to be withdrawn again into winter quarters" was not the course to take. The *Avalanche* praised the "style" of the soldiers in Nevada, who directly confronted the Indians and gave them the choice to either live in peace or be killed.[10]

Army tactics and the usefulness of the infantry were demonstrated that September. Captain Loren L. Williams, Company H, 1st Oregon Infantry, who had been guarding the Canyon City Road stationed at Camp Watson, was ordered to make a small expedition to Silvies River and Harney Lake Valley. Williams, with Lieutenant John Bowen, Company F, 1st Oregon Cavalry, and twelve men, crossed the mountains and went down Silvies River toward Malheur Lake. On September 1, about five miles beyond where the Silvies enters the valley, and where it divides into two channels, they discovered smoke coming from some willows near the river. They charged in, killed the

Author's photo

Inskip's Station near Jordan Valley, Oregon, was the target of many Indian attacks.

only Indian who was there working at the small native fishery, and destroyed ten bushels of fish. With that "victory" to their credit, they returned north.[11]

SILVER CREEK, SEPTEMBER 15, 1865

A few weeks later, Williams and Bowen were again sent into the area. On September 22, Williams, with detachments of Companies F and H, was camped on Silvies River just southeast of present-day Burns, Oregon, where he had the encounter at the fishery. A detachment of twenty-five cavalry under Lieutenant John Bowen was to meet him there. Bowen, several days behind, was on upper Silver Creek on September 15, when he ran into three Indians. Seeing the overwhelming force coming up, the Indians tried to escape. Bowen killed two of them and captured the third, but the prisoner was still dangerous. He was in custody only a short while when one of the guards relaxed his vigilance for a moment. The warrior grabbed a pistol, and shot and killed the guard before several soldiers filled him with bullets. After that sad affair, Bowen continued on to try and find Captain Williams.

SILVIES RIVER, SEPTEMBER 23, 1865

Getting a bit impatient waiting for Lieutenant Bowen, Williams took ten men of Company H, and two of Company F, to search downriver for a spot for a permanent camp. Seven miles from camp they spotted two Indians on foot heading toward Malheur Lake. Williams pursued them at double-time, but with both parties on foot, it took another seven miles just to get within rifle range. At that time, two mounted Indians rode up, put the two on their horses and all of them escaped. Frustrated and exhausted, Williams let his men rest for an hour—nearly a fatal mistake. While waiting, more Indians crossed over from the south side of the lakes at the "Narrows," where the

119

land pinched together between Mud Lake and Malheur Lake, several miles to the south of them.

They were 16 miles from camp and about to turn back, when a solitary mounted Indian rode near, circled them, fired his gun, and let out a whoop. Soon, thirteen mounted warriors were around them, constantly firing and maneuvering. Williams kept his men marching, stopping occasionally to shoot and keep the Indians back. They made directly for a "small mountain" (Wright's Point) that lay between them and their camp, hoping to climb it and save the mileage in going around. On the way, about twenty-five more horsemen and twenty-five or more warriors on foot joined in the attack and Williams was in serious trouble. The Indians fired at them from every side, but the soldiers' long-range rifles kept them back more than 250 yards. Williams hoped to make the mountain, but just before he reached it, twenty-five horsemen rode up and took position in the very spot Williams was aiming for. He turned right (east), paralleled the ridge, and made for Silvies River, about five miles away. "The men were tired," said Williams, "nearly exhausted, their lips parched with thirst, and the whole distance to the river was one level sandy sage plain."

The warriors followed alongside them at the foot of the mountain, keeping up a constant harassing fire. Corporal Johnson guarded the left flank, and Private McPherson took the rear, the two most dangerous places. Williams called the rest into single file and double-timed toward the river. The sage was thick, and Indians got in as close as 75 yards. At the river, Corporal Alexander Griffin, Company H, was severely wounded by a bullet in the left hip. The men were in desperate need of water. "My mouth was so parched that I could scarcely give command," Williams said. "I at once ordered three men through the stream without a moment's pause to protect our front. Three others were faced about to guard the rear, while the remainder took a hasty drink of water and relieved them. Our delay at the stream was not over one and one-half minutes, and at the command 'fall in on the east side,' every man was instantly at his post, and we marched at double-quick for about 300 yards from the willows along [the] stream to an open level plain."

The Indians were right behind them. Williams turned north, with the river now on his left, and stumbled forward as quickly as they could move, but the warriors easily kept pace. Private Thomas F. Smith, Company F, was wounded in the left foot. It was sundown and they had about four miles to reach their camp. Indians in front of them fired the grass in a two-mile line directly perpendicular to their path. They found a small break in the fire line and pushed through, but there was another fire ahead. Heading toward the willows near the river they were blasted by a volley of six or eight rifles from 60 yards distant. Williams turned to expect half his men had fallen, but other than hearing the whistles of the bullets, not a man was hit. Williams placed his command in a sinkhole near the river and exchanged shots until

Author's photo

Wright's Point was an obstacle for Lieutenant Loren Williams and his men during the Silvies River fight in September 1865.

it was completely dark. He kept hoping the soldiers in camp would hear the shooting and see the fire and come to their assistance, but no help arrived. Unwilling to face the fire, or the Indians in the dark, Williams doubled back four miles south, and then swung around in a semi-circle back to the north. Either they had eluded the Indians or the Indians had called off the fight. Williams and his exhausted men tramped back into camp at two in the morning on September 24. They had marched 45 miles without food or rest, and it was remarkable that only two soldiers were wounded. Williams was "certain that fifteen Indians were killed and several horses crippled." There were a number of Snakes killed in the fight; two of them, Yellow Badger and Snake Hawk, were prominent war chiefs.

Williams was justifiably proud of his men, but he was not too eager to attempt another such foolhardy reconnaissance. In his report to Colonel Currey, Williams put a positive spin on a near-disaster: "Our long-range guns and superior marksmen gave us advantages that rendered their superior numbers far less formidable than if we had been armed with common rifles." Historian Hubert H. Bancroft wrote that Williams's company "performed some of the best fighting of the season under the greatest of difficulties; being on foot, and compelled to march a long distance surrounded by Indians. . . ." True, perhaps, but Williams was the cause of his own difficulties. The civilians already knew, and the army should have known, that a small infantry force should not be sent out alone and unsupported into hostile territory.[12]

While Williams scouted around Malheur Lake, on October 6, he established Camp Wright, on Silvies River, close to the eastern point of the 250-foot "mountain" he had tried to cross while attempting to get back to his camp. The mountain, an arm of volcanic lava that protruded into the valley north of Malheur Lake, became known as Wright's Point. Williams planned to garrison the camp through the coming winter. Other camps were being built. Captain Lyman S. Scott, Company D, 4th California Infantry, patrolled east out of Surprise Valley, went to Paradise Valley for a time, and then to Oregon, where he established Camp Currey on September 30. The camp was set up on upper Silver Creek, which flowed another 35 miles southeast into Harney Lake. Companies D and I, 4th California Infantry, a detachment of Company E, 1st Washington Territory Infantry, and Company K, 1st Oregon Infantry, occupied the camp for a short time, before the volunteers were mustered out and the regulars took over in November. Camp Logan, named after Warm Springs Indian Agent William Logan, was established in September by Captain A. B. Ingram, Company K, 1st Oregon Infantry. Captain Abner W. Waters and the soldiers of Company F, 1st Oregon Infantry, constructed Camp Colfax on South Willow Creek about six miles east of Ironside Mountain in August 1865. They cut and hauled logs from the mountain to build more substantial structures for the winter, but all for naught. The company abandoned the camp, burned the buildings on December 27, and marched for Fort Boise. Camps Logan and Colfax were both on the Canyon City-Boise Road to offer more protection on that route.[13]

Camp Lyon in the Owyhee District, was being expanded for more troops and readied for a winter campaign. The *Owyhee Avalanche* was pleased. "It is beautifully situated, and just in the locality most needed," it reported. "It is designed to make a winter campaign against the Indians, when they may be more readily pursued and captured." Portions of Companies A, B, and D, 1st Oregon Cavalry were there, and some of Captain William S. Powell's Company D, 1st Oregon Infantry. Even with the increased army presence, however, raids in the area continued.

Indians raided east of the Owyhee Mountains in the summer and fall of 1865, hitting Cornelius "Con" Shea hard. Shea, for whom Sheaville, Oregon, was named, was a Canadian who moved to the Owyhee District to try his luck as a miner and blacksmith, before trying ranching on Sinker Creek. Later, in 1867, Shea and his brothers were the first to go to Texas, put together 1,000 Longhorns, and drive them to the Owyhee area. On August 15, 1865, raiders stole twenty-eight beef cattle from Shea's herd on North Sinker Creek. On September 1, they returned to run off twenty work cattle. On October 12, they hit him again, stealing sixteen workhorses, and once more on November 20, they got fifty work cattle. Shea estimated his losses at $9,900.

On September 6, Indians visited Ruby Ranch on lower Cow Creek, now the community of Danner, Oregon. The ranch, also known as Inskip's Station, after the keeper, G. W. Inskip, was first built by Hill Beachey as a way station for his Idaho Stage Company. The buildings were constructed from the native lava, which made a strong fortification and a central point for the locals to meet. The Indians ran off two horses, and the next morning seven men went after them, catching up near Cow Lake. The warriors were in position behind a lava outcrop, however, and when they let loose several volleys, the civilians, with one wounded, beat a hasty retreat to Ruby Ranch. Emboldened by their success, the Indians returned the next night and raided McWilliams's Ranch, 12 miles below Ruby, and burned up two ricks of hay, amounting to about forty tons. Soldiers from Camp Lyon arrived and found the Indians by Cow Lake. A slight skirmish ensued, but with apparently no one hit on either side. The soldiers recovered five head of stock and the Indians escaped to the north into the canyons of the Owyhee.

On October 8, the Indians again hit Inskip's, stole ten horses, and killed and ate one ox. Camp Lyon was not immune. In late October, Indians ran off fifty-seven horses and mules. The cavalry went after them and found no Indians, but on their return they happened to run into thirty-five of the animals running loose. The civilians apparently were tiring of their brief honeymoon with the army. The *Avalanche* wondered, "Whether or not the

Courtesy Violet Skinner
From Owyhee Trails, *Caxton Press*

Con Shea brought the first herd of cattle to the region and lost hundreds of animals to Indian raiders.

troops at Camp Lyon are as watchful and hostile as the circumstances require. . . ." It said that a camp of the best fighters in the world would be useless if not used properly, and hoped that the soldiers would stay all winter, if only they "were to kill a few Indians occasionally."

On November 28, a letter from G. W. Inskip was printed in the newspaper, complaining that on November 18, a squad of soldiers stayed at his station, got drunk, shot up his house, "and stole everything they could get their hands on about the ranch—flour, rice, sugar, coffee, potatoes, liquors, hay to sleep on, and robbed the corral of the fence posts and wood pile for fuel." When Inskip asked the officer to put a stop to it, he said he would "make it all right in the morning." The next morning, however, the officer said they had to leave to fight Indians, and certainly Inskip wouldn't "begrudge the soldiers a little 'straw'."

"I think these men are more to be dreaded than the native Indians of the country," Inskip wrote. The *Avalanche* concurred, stating that anyone who acted in that manner deserved censure, but soldiers and officers who acted that way "should be dismissed from the service in disgrace." The tension between the soldiers and civilians was increasing. One often repeated story that got the miners to slap their thighs in laughter over what they saw as army ineptitude, occurred on a recent army scout toward the Owyhee River. At dusk the soldiers spotted what appeared to be a village of wickiups containing at least 150 Indians. While some troops remained on lookout, the rest returned to Camp Lyon for help. They traveled all night, surrounded the village, and at dawn, commenced an attack—on a cluster of conically shaped rocks![14]

On the last day of August 1865, Major Rinehart directed Captain Franklin B. Sprague, with a detachment of Company I, 1st Oregon Infantry, and an escort of eleven cavalry, to go from Fort Klamath to Camp Alvord, examining the route Lt. Colonel Drew opened the previous year. Sprague was to find a better location for the camp, with regards to grass and water, and construct a new post. On the way east, in the vicinity of Christmas Lakes, Sprague saw a large Indian trail heading south toward Surprise Valley, which he noted, but continued his journey. Once east of Steens Mountain he located a site on Wildhorse Creek, near the place of Waymire's fight in April 1864. Sprague's new site was only about 10 miles south of the old Camp Alvord, and around a protecting spur of Steens Mountain. On October 10, he started out on his return trip, and, reaching the Indian trail he found on his way out, he realized there were no fresh tracks heading back north. Arriving at Klamath on October 17, Sprague reported to Major Rinehart about the large trail and suggested that a band of Indians was still south of Drew's Road, probably in the neighborhood of Surprise Valley. Rinehart ordered Sprague to go back to Camp Alvord again, by way of Surprise Valley, and cooperate with the command there in an expedition against the Indians.

When Sprague got to Camp Bidwell, he found that Captain Augustus W. Starr, Company F, 2nd California Cavalry, who was under Department of California jurisdiction, was already under orders to take most of his command back to Fort Crook before winter snows trapped them at Bidwell. Starr conceded to let Sprague use Lieutenant Samuel W. Backus and ten troopers as an escort, however, and Sprague headed out. The third day, they arrived at Warner Creek (Guano Creek) seven miles south of Drew's Road. Failing to find any Indians, Backus returned to Camp Bidwell, and almost immediately thereafter, the Indians found Sprague. While the soldiers walked the narrow path between Christmas Lakes (Crump Lake) and the bluffs, about 125 Indians, under Sieta (Little Rattlesnake) and Storm Cloud, appeared to the front and rear. Sprague, with Indians on two sides and a steep mountain and a lake on the other two, assessed the situation. After some long-range firing, he determined that the Indians to his front seemed to have about twenty-five rifles, while those at the rear were armed with only bows and arrows. Sprague turned his command about and charged to the rear, breaking through and making it back to Bidwell without any casualties.

At Bidwell, Starr awaited the arrival of Lieutenant Backus, but while biding his time, Pit River Indians raided the fort, killed a guard, and stole half of his mounts. There would be no more action out of Bidwell that year, but Sprague returned with the important discovery that the Christmas Lakes-Warner Mountains area appeared to be a principal rendezvous of the Oregon Paiutes.[15]

BARRY'S FIGHT,
ca NOVEMBER 19, 1865

Not all the Indians were near the southern Oregon border. On November 8, raiders identified as "Snake Indians" attacked four men within 35 miles of the Warm Springs Reservation, causing them

A. R. Bowman Museum, Crook County Historical Society, Prineville, Oregon
Major William Rinehart, *ca* 1865.

to abandon their animals, provisions, and camp equipage, and flee for their lives. On November 18, Indians drove off stock from Robinson's Ranch on the South Fork John Day. Captain Edward Barry, 1st Washington Territory Infantry, stationed at Camp Watson, took up the chase. He located the Indian camp, destroyed it, and killed five Indians.[16]

The winter campaign so much wanted by the civilians and planned for by the army was not to reach fruition. The Civil War was over and the government and the majority of people, at least east of the Mississippi, were tired of fighting. Major campaigns planned to chastise the Lakotas and Cheyennes in Wyoming, and Cheyennes, Comanches, and Kiowas in Kansas and Indian Territory, were called off. The proverbial peace feelers were being extended to many tribes. Even in Oregon, Superintendent Huntington had met with Paulina. On August 12, 1865, Huntington brought the captured women and children to the Klamath Reservation, and at Sprague River, signed a treaty with Paulina and his people, which, in effect, was an addendum to the treaty with the Klamath and Modoc the previous year.

White attendees included Huntington, Lindsay Applegate, William McKay, Captain William Kelly, and Major W. V. Rinehart. Indian signers included Paulina, Snake Hawk, Lame Dog, Black Buffalo, No Ribs, Tobacco Root, Little Lizard, and Biting Bear, mainly from the Walpapi (Mountain People), but with some Hunipui (Bear Killer) and Wahtatkin (Pony Stealer) people. They agreed to yield central Oregon lands (much of it where Ocheho's people lived) and reside on the Klamath Reservation in the

Sprague River Valley. Paulina agreed to return all his captives and said he would "endeavor to induce" other Paiutes to surrender.

If Ocheho and Weahwewa could have been induced to attend, the treaty might have had some meaning. Agent Applegate chose La Lake and Moshenkosket as peace couriers to bring in Howluck and Weahwewa, but they failed in their quest. Huntington, still not realizing that Ocheho was one of the main men, asked Paulina to bring in Howluck to settle on the reservation. Instead, next spring, it was Howluck who came to Paulina and convinced him to leave it and go back on the warpath. As evidence of the Paiutes' intention of keeping their word, shortly after the signings, Snake Hawk was on his way to alert Ocheho of Paulina's imprudence, when he joined in the September battle on Silvies River and was killed by Captain Williams's straight-shooting infantry.

None were very happy on the reservation that winter, except, possibly, for the Klamaths; it was not the Modocs home and they were dissatisfied, and neither the Modocs nor Klamaths wanted to share their reservation with the Paiutes, who they still considered as enemies. Applegate built his agency about six miles south of the fort and the Klamaths all moved down there because they did not trust Paulina. Superintendent Huntington was anxious to get the rest of the Paiutes in to sign a treaty. Their depredations were getting out of hand, and he concluded, "that it is no exaggeration to say that *ten good soldiers* are required to wage successful war *against one Indian*. Every Indian killed or captured by the military has cost the government fifty thousand dollars at least. Economy, then, indicates that it is much cheaper to feed them than to fight them."

Had Huntington been so concerned about feeding the Indians, he would have seen to it that the Paiutes received the goods they expected after signing the treaty (it was not ratified until July 1866). They did not, and as a result, they were sullen and restless by the time of the first snows. Paulina did hang around the reservation through the winter, not leaving until the raiding season started in the spring of 1866, when he pulled out with most of his band and returned to his old haunts between Summer Lake and Crooked River.[17]

By then, there were few soldiers around to bother them, for there was no winter campaign. One reason was the lack of soldiers. Oregon Governor A. C. Gibbs wrote to General Halleck, expressing his concerns that his Oregon Volunteers were being sent home while depredations continued. On November 17, Halleck responded, writing that the policy was Washington's, not his. "It is believed that the troops left in service on this coast," Halleck wrote, "and those expected from the East will be sufficient to guard the most important points on the frontiers. . . ."

After General Wright drowned, Colonel Currey took over the Department of Columbia, but when nearly all of his soldiers were mustered out of service, he retired. Drake took over, but he mustered out in December. Almost all the posts were abandoned except Camps Watson, Alvord, Lyon, and Fort Boise. Consideration was given to close Forts Lapwai and Walla Walla. As operations wound down, business suffered in Walla Walla. The army was leaving, the district judge left and the court closed down; legal matters piled up, and the people felt abandoned. The Walla Walla *Statesman* said the people were "in quite an unpleasant dilemma," and called for the annexation of Walla Walla Valley to Oregon, claiming the government at Puget Sound never gave them "due consideration" and Oregon would certainly welcome them.

The Walla Wallans were overjoyed when Colonel Currey resigned. The *Statesman* claimed that "Dirty George" Currey had something against the place all the time, and had planned to "give Walla Walla a 'highst;' that it was nothing but a d—d secesh hole anyhow and deserved no favors at the hands of Uncle Sam." The paper was thrilled when Currey, who it called "proverbially indolent," got his own "'highst' in the shape of a dismissal from the service." A byline in the paper read: "GOOD RIDDANCE—all the volunteer officers that have been stationed at the different posts in this Department are being mustered out as fast as possible."[18]

As 1865 expired, many of the commands that had been chasing Indians throughout the year were expressing their frustration. Captain Williams, who had a close call in a fight in September, wrote of the "great difficulty" that the troops operated under. "To relieve the troops in the field from great embarrassment," he wrote, "and to insure the extermination or capture of the last remnant of the hostile tribes of Oregon during the summer of 1866, I would most earnestly recommend that Bloodhounds from the Southern States be brought to this country and employed to search out the savages in their mountain fastnesses, where it is impossible for the genius of man to follow their footsteps or trace them to their rocky retreats."

As a fitting close to the year in Oregon, on an otherwise quiet Christmas Day, Paiutes raided Camp Alvord and drove off forty mules grazing in plain sight a half mile from the post. Captain Sprague, commanding the camp with men of Company I, 1st Oregon Infantry, was supplemented with a detachment of twenty-six men of Company C, 1st Oregon Cavalry, under Lieutenant Patrick McGuire. Typical of the logistics problems that they faced, they only had eleven serviceable horses for just such an incident. Sprague immediately sent several mounted soldiers after the raiders. They caught up to the Indians within four miles and wounded one of them. The raiders shot and killed the horse ridden by Sergeant Barclay of Company C, and wounded two other precious horses with arrows, but the soldiers recovered the mules. In his report, Sprague was apologetic that he was unable to kill or capture any of the raiders, because the "Indians drove off all the good horses" in a raid the previous month. He only had a few left. The frustration felt at the end of 1865 was not much different from 1864.[19]

Sprague's was one of the last remaining volunteer companies still on the frontier. The volunteers in Oregon were fast disappearing and there was less fighting during the winter of 1865-66. Whether or not the regular troops who were moving in would do better than the volunteers was yet to be seen.

Chapter 12 notes

1 *WR*: V.50/2, 1241, 1243, 1253, 1256. This Camas Prairie should not be confused with the Camas Prairie in Idaho.

2 *WR*: V.50/2, 1264; "Camp Lyon," http://www.idahohistory.net/Reference; Hanley, *Owyhee Trails*, 20-21, 54, 56. The camp was said to have been named after the Union General Nathaniel Lyon, killed in battle in 1861, and Idaho's second territorial governor, Caleb Lyon. Given the four years since Lyon's death, and since there were already several posts and forts named after the general, Caleb Lyon probably deserves the honor.

3 *WR*: V.50/1, 420-21. Hobart reported the fight took place on the Malheur about 25 miles southeast of "Pilot Rock." The reference may be to Castle Rock, which would place the fight in the vicinity of present-day Juntura.

4 *WR*: V.50/1, 424. Hobart recalled the dead men's names as McCummins and McGregor.

5 Frazer, *Forts*, 20; *WR*: V.50/1, 833, 1173, 1195, 1206, 1214, 1235-37.

6 *WR:* V.50/1, 419; *WR:* V.50/2, 1276-77, 1286.

7 *WR*: V.50/1, 6; Hunt, *Army of the Pacific*, 360-62; *Idaho World*, August 26, 1865; *Commissioner of Indian Affairs 1865*, 462. One of the passengers who perished on the *Brother Jonathan* was Warm Springs Agent William Logan.

8 *Idaho World*, September 2, 1865, September 23, 1865, September 30, 1865.

9 *Idaho World*, September 9, 1865; Bork, "History of the Pacific Northwest," http://www.usgennet. org/usa/or/county/union1/1889volumeIIpage21.

10 Knight, *Following the Indian Wars*, 32; Ontko, *Thunder Over the Ochoco III*, 305-06; *Owyhee Avalanche*, August 26, 1865.

11 Williams to Currey, October 10, 1865, RG 393, Dept. of Columbia, Letters Received, Box 2.

12 *Commissioner of Indian Affairs 1865*, 474; *WR:* V.50/1, 425-28; Bancroft, *History of Oregon*, Vol. 2, 514; Ontko, *Thunder Over the Ochoco III*, 281; Williams to Currey, October 8, 1865, RG 393, Dept. of Columbia, Letters Received, Box 2. Bancroft and others reported Williams lost one man killed and two wounded, but in his official report Williams is clear that no men were killed.

13 McArthur, *Oregon Geographic Names*, 143-45, 148, 154, 1059; Bancroft, *History of Oregon*, Vol. 2, 515.

14 Hanley, *Owyhee Trails*, 16, 18, 60-62; Cornelius Shea Depredation Claim #7644; *Owyhee Avalanche*, September 2, 1865, September 16, 1865, September 23, 1865, October 28, 1865, December, 16, 1865.

15 Bancroft, *History of Oregon*, Vol. 2, 515-17; McArthur, *Oregon Geographic Names*, 141; Ontko, *Thunder Over the Ochoco III*, 290.

16 *Commissioner of Indian Affairs, 1867*, 96.

17 Ruby and Brown, *Pacific Northwest*, 206-07; Ontko, *Thunder Over the Ochoco III*, 283-84; Kappler, *Indian Treaties*, 876-78; Murray, *Modocs*, 41; *Commissioner of Indian Affairs 1865*, 467.

18 Letter Secretary of War, 50th Congress, Senate Ex. Doc. 70, 300; Bancroft, *History of Oregon*, Vol. 2, 517-18; Walla Walla *Statesman*, October 20, 1865, December 1, 1865.

19 Williams to Currey, November 13, 1865, RG 393, Dept. of Columbia, Letters Received, Box 2; Sprague to AAG, December 31, 1865, RG 393, Dept. of Columbia, Letters Received, Box 3; Kelly to AAG, March 12, 1866, RG 393, Dept. of Columbia, Letters Received, Box 2.

Chapter 13

"THOSE. . .BOYS SOON SPOIL WITHOUT THEIR REGULAR FIGHT."

After the death of Lt. Colonel McDermit in August, the adversaries in northern Nevada seemed to step back and catch their breath, but south of the Humboldt there was still activity. Major Albert G. Brackett, 1ˢᵗ Cavalry, said that McDermit's killing "greatly incensed the California Volunteers, who were a superior body of men, utterly fearless and untiring," and from that time on they put forth their utmost efforts to defeat the Indians.[1] Camp Dun Glen had become a military supply hub for a brief time, with several expeditions radiating out from it to the Humboldt, Quinn, and Owyhee watersheds. The military activity at Dun Glen, and the mining at Unionville and Star City acted like a magnet to the Paiutes who were being harassed all across the state and unable to utilize the traditional resources of the land to sustain life.

Buffalo Jim and Black Rock Tom were leaders of a couple of bands of dissatisfied Paiutes, Shoshones, and Bannocks raiding in northern Nevada since March. Miners also felt their sting. James C. Weir had a copper and gold mining operation in the Hot Springs area of northwest Nevada, employing between twenty and twenty-five men. In late August 1865, Wier, who spent much of his time in California, got word from his mine superintendent that Indians had raided the mine. On August 14, they rode in, caught three miners in one shack, set it aflame and drove them out. The Indians, said Weir, caught them, "staked them out on the ground and set fire to the men and burned them." The rest of the miners fled the area, and the Indians destroyed much of the equipment and tools. Weir believed that his employees would have remained, had they not just gotten news that Lt. Colonel McDermit had recently been killed only about 35 miles from the mines. The news, with the increasing raids, spooked them into abandoning the region. Weir obtained a cavalry escort and returned to the mines with his superintendent "Colonel" Davis, and Irvin Hamma, but there was nothing they could do. The concentrate that had been taken out by the mill had been left on the ground and much of it was washed down the canyon and lost. No miners wanted to go back. Wier abandoned the operation.[2]

Elsewhere in Nevada, Paiutes had less reason to harass miners than they did to steal cattle, because it was becoming less of a sport for the warriors, and more of a necessity to feed their hungry families. Even though they had legitimate grievances, there were substantial numbers of Paiutes, such as those who had signed the peace agreement in April and moved to the Carson River, who wanted to stay out of the war.

TABLE MOUNTAIN, SEPTEMBER 3, 1865

Mogoannoga had once fought the whites, but was instrumental in convincing some of the Paiutes to sign the April agreement. The chief, called Captain Soo by his new white friends, had apparently come to realize that the survival of his people called for accommodation. The old ways were changing, and Soo realized his people must try to adjust to the new order. He knew that continued war would eventually antagonize all the whites, plus the peaceful Paiutes, and cause destruction to them all. It was a tough decision, but Soo realized he must aid the whites in destroying the hostile Paiutes in order to save the peaceful ones. When a rancher at Unionville named Stafford complained of thefts and said he knew where a band of Indians was hiding, word was sent to Dun Glen. There, Captain Soo teamed up with Lieutenant Henry C. Penwell, who had been promoted from corporal in Company B, 2nd California Cavalry, to a second lieutenant in Company I.

On September 30, 1865, Penwell took twenty soldiers from Company B and rode southwest to Unionville. There, Stafford, a few civilians, and Soo, with several of his band members as guides, headed across the valley toward the East Range. Stafford had discovered a rancheria at the foot of Table Mountain in the East Range, about 20 miles east of Unionville. Soo and his warriors assured Penwell that the camp contained Indians who had participated in the killings at Granite Creek Station the previous March. Table Mountain was an ancient Paiute hunting ground with steep rocky cliffs that gave natural protection to defenders on its slopes—the problem was that there were too few defenders.

Penwell divided his command into three squads at a hidden spring in a deep canyon, and then climbed after the Paiutes high above them. The going was slow, as they groped their way up during the night. Before dawn they found the camp, located on a three acre-plateau, and protected by sheer drops on almost every side. Yet, the camp was small, containing only seven men and three women. When Penwell signaled the attack at dawn of September 3, it was a case of overkill. The warriors were dispatched quickly, with most of them being killed as they slept. Unfortunately, the three women were also killed, reportedly unintentionally. The *Humboldt Register*, with commentary typical of the times, reported: "The Pah-Ute guides led the party upon the camp at daybreak this morning, so cautiously that the entire gang was taken in, and ticketed for the happy-hunting grounds before they knew what was the matter. Seven bucks bit the dust and one or two squaws were killed by accident." Penwell destroyed "a large quantity of ammunition and supplies," and the detachment returned to Dun Glen after a march of 150 miles.[3]

Back in Paradise Valley, the civilians continually pressed the army to build a post at that location, stressing an abundance of wood, water, grass, and inexpensive hay that they could sell to the army. Of course, given the military's limited resources it was probable that if a post was built in Paradise Valley, it would be less likely that another would be constructed closer to the Owyhee District. The *Avalanche* expressed its concerns, discounting the need for a post in Paradise Valley, stating that the people of the valley were "scarcely deserving." According to the paper, there were more signatures on the petition to the army than there were people in the valley, there was no timber within 60 miles, and they charged "extortionate prices for all they can spare, even down to a canteen of milk." Nevertheless, the army was considering a post in Paradise Valley, and since McDermit moved troops there in April, a military presence had boosted the local economy.

WILLOW CREEK, SEPTEMBER 12, 1865

Two units that had been in the area for much of the summer were Captain Robert C. Payne's Company E, 1st Nevada Cavalry, and Captain Albert Hahn, with Company I, 6th California Infantry. For several days in early September, campfires were seen in the Santa Rosa Mountains and west in the Quinn River Valley. On September 10, Captain Payne and Lieutenant Littlefield took eighteen troopers of Company E and went to investigate. They camped at Buffalo Station on the west face of the mountains that night, and scouted west of Quinn River the next day, returning to the Santa Rosas near Willow Creek for the night. That evening more fires were definitely seen farther up the creek toward the mountains. At one a.m. on September 12, Payne broke camp and headed out, hoping to surround the Indians and attack at daybreak. They nearly got in position when the Indians discovered them. Payne ordered Littlefield to take nine men and advance between the mountains and the camp, while Payne took the remaining nine toward the valley side.

The Indians were already scattering when Payne sounded the charge, and the ensuing fight lasted three hours and stretched out for several miles. The Indians resisted poorly, and many were shot as they ran. Occasionally, however, warriors turned about to give the others a chance to escape. One mounted Paiute brandishing a lance, charged across the plain directly at Lieutenant Littlefield. The lieutenant, who had been accused of cowardice for his lack of action at "Fort Redskin" in May, stood his ground while the warrior approached. He calmly pulled his revolver and waited, and when the Indian was almost on him and raising his lance, Littlefield squeezed off one round and dropped him from his horse.

After the fight the soldiers counted thirty-one dead Indians—in the words of the *Owyhee Avalanche*, "thirty-one *permanently* friendly Indians." No one estimated the number of wounded, but they assumed there were many. Payne captured five horses, several guns with plenty of ammunition, many bows

131

and arrows, hundreds of yards of rabbit nets, two tons of seeds and dried berries, saddles, blacksmith tools, and even dental equipment. There was also a quantity of beef liver impregnated with rattlesnake venom to be used for poisoning arrows. The supply loss was a great blow to the Indians. Only one soldier, Private Edward Billings, was severely wounded. The *Avalanche* was glad that Littlefield had proven his bravery, stating, "Good soldiers who live on sagebrush and fight Indians, should not be slandered."[4]

The Willow Creek fight was the last skirmish in their home state that the Nevada volunteers participated in, for most of the companies made their way to Fort Churchill for mustering out in December. Only four companies of Nevada cavalry were kept in service at Forts Bridger and Douglas until relieved in July 1866. The Californians would have to bring the fighting in Nevada to an end.

The summer-long hunt for renegade Indians continued into the fall. Black Rock Tom's band, the focus of several expeditions, was said to have vacated the Unionville-Dun Glen area and moved north. In early November, they were again prowling the Black Rock Desert and attacked a teamster, a Mr. Bellew, at Willow Springs. Bellew was with a party of four ox-wagons hauling freight from California to the Humboldt on the Honey Lake Road. About one dozen miles east of Rabbit Hole Springs, Bellew pulled out ahead of the other wagons when Black Rock Tom's Paiutes attacked, killed him, and plundered his wagon. When the news reached Dun Glen, Lieutenant Penwell took twenty-six troopers of Company B, 2nd California Cavalry, and headed north. Once again, his guide was the Paiute-Bannock Captain Soo.

Soo helped Penwell defeat his quarry in September, but not this time. Black Rock Tom was watching them as they marched north from Cedar Springs, Rabbit Hole, and up Quinn River east of the Black Rock Range. On November 9, Penwell's force trailed up Paiute Creek and west of Paiute Meadows deep into the mountains to a point where the canyon narrowed and the steep rock walls were easily defended. Suddenly the Indians attacked, pouring down a heavy fire on the surprised soldiers. With bullets seeming to come from every direction and the assailants almost invisible, Penwell ordered a withdrawal seven miles into the Black Rock Desert to regroup and camp for the night. Knowing he faced a large, alert, and well-armed force, the lieutenant called it quits and returned to Dun Glen for reinforcements.[5]

Adhering to its statement that "Nearly every issue of our paper has contained an account of Indian depredations," the *Owyhee Avalanche* didn't fail to disappoint on November 11, reporting a "BIG FIGHT IN NEVADA!" The paper claimed that during the battle, seventy Indian scalps were taken. "We've been expecting this item," it continued, "for those Nevada and California boys soon spoil without their regular fight, and when things get a little nauseous they *hunt* and *force* the murderous savages to fight, and what's better, clean them out." Then, engaging in a bit more vitriol than

From Nevada's Black Rock Desert, *Caxton Press, 1978*

Paiute Creek Canyon provided cover for Black Rock Tom's warriors when Lieutenant Penwell's troopers approached the Indian camp.

usual even for the *Avalanche*, the paper continued: "Here's seventy more reasons for those safely-located, chicken-hearted, high-toned-mealy-moral-suasion philanthropists to generally wail about, and we're glad of it." It is not known what "big fight" the *Avalanche* was talking about. It may have been expounding on a rumor, but if so, it was prescient, for six days later, the "boys" south of the state line performed almost exactly as the paper had reported.[6]

LEONARD CREEK, NOVEMBER 17, 1865

Lieutenant Penwell returned to Dun Glen and reported his repulse on Paiute Creek, and on November 13, Lieutenant Richard A. Osmer, Company H, 2nd California Cavalry, led sixty men of Company B and one mountain howitzer back to the scene. Four troopers deserted on the way, but joining them at Willow Creek were seven enlisted men on detached service, Captain Soo with about ten Paiute warriors, and several civilians, including Tom Rule and Tom Ewing, who were both badly wounded in the Jackson Creek fight the previous July. Rule had a new Henry Rifle and wanted to join up for revenge.

Captain Soo took the command north through the Black Rock Desert. At two a.m. on November 17, Osmer dropped his wagons and baggage at a swampy area near Quinn River under a guard of fourteen men, and continued on. At first light, Soo declared that he could see smoke from the Indian camp nine miles away; they were within five miles of the camp before the soldiers saw the smoke. The trail led along the east face of the Black Rock

Range and toward the southern edge of the Pine Forest Range, pointing to Fish Creek (now Leonard Creek), about 20 miles northeast of the site of Penwell's repulse.

Black Rock Tom and his people did not see the soldiers approaching until they were within two miles of his camp. Osmer yelled, "Come on boys, we can't go around, and the best man will get there first." The entire force ran for the camp in what was called a "go as you please style," two-mile charge. Captain Soo, striving to be first, reached down with a knife, cut the girth, threw his saddle away while at full speed, and was the first man in. The Indians scattered and tried to escape, but the soldiers chased them up into the rocks and ravines, killing many. The fight and chase lasted four hours and covered several square miles.

The Indians did not all run without putting up a fight; Private David W. O'Connell was killed, and two enlisted men, Sergeant Alexander Lansdon, and a private, were wounded. Osmer placed the number of dead Indians at 120, with eighty of them warriors. The bodies of fifty-five Paiutes were definitely found, and likely a significant number of others were killed or mortally wounded. A substantial number of women and children were killed; some inadvertently, but many by Soo's Paiutes who felt little compassion for the hostile bands that were making their own life hell. Only one woman was taken prisoner, and only about ten Indians escaped, including Black Rock Tom.

The army report indicated it was very difficult to distinguish between male and female during the heat of the battle, but that the unrestrained allied Paiutes did most of the slaughter. The civilians, however, did some of the killing. Two soldiers, a corporal and a private, captured a wounded woman and her two young children.

"Let's take her down to the camp," the private said, "it's a pity to leave her here to die, and the little fellows to starve."

The corporal, engaged in other duty, noticed a civilian approaching, and said, "Call --- --- and he will help you, I must hurry down." After reaching the foot of the hill, the corporal heard several pistol shots, and saw the private coming down alone.

"Where is your squaw?" the corporal asked.

"That was a fine specimen you called to help," he answered. "The d--n bushwacker shot the whole lot of them, babies and all, before I knew what he was up to."

Tom Rule later talked to the editor of the *Avalanche* and said he took a "special hand" in the fight, "and thinks he made a good beginning in getting even." The boys out there, he said, "fight Indians in their own way."

After the battle, Osmer gathered up the plunder, which included supplies from Mr. Bellew's wagon, the man killed east of Rabbit Hole Springs earlier in the month. A number of guns, ammunition, seeds, supplies, and five horses

Nevada Historical Society, MIL-164

Camp McDermit

were captured; the friendly Paiutes were given all they could pack out, plus the five horses. The remainder was burned. Osmer returned to Dun Glen on November 20, after marching 250 miles.[7]

Black Rock Tom had survived the battle at Leonard Creek, but he realized that resistance was futile. Soldiers and civilians had seen him in battle many times, riding a large "white horse of extraordinary qualities," and forever dallying provokingly just out of rifle range. In mid-December he gave up, went south to Big Meadows (near present Lovelock) and surrendered to Captain Soo, who turned him over to the Nevada citizens. One of them, Thomas Stark, wrote to Lieutenant Osmer that he had the chief and two of his tribesmen, who had "sued for peace, and want to form some treaty." Osmer contacted Fort Churchill for instructions. In the meantime, Captain Harlow L. Street and nineteen men of Company K, 2nd California Cavalry, had left Fort Churchill on December 21, to head for Dun Glen. On Christmas Day, while at Blake's Station at Big Meadows, the civilians handed Black Rock Tom over to Captain Street. Captain Soo warned Street that Tom would not honor his word and his peace gesture was just talk to buy time. Tom, meanwhile, was having second thoughts about what he had gotten himself into; the civilians had convinced him that the soldiers would hang him at Fort Churchill. Tom decided to make a break for it, and Street succinctly recorded his end: "After being put in charge of the guard, he tried to escape, and was shot dead by some of the command." The *Owyhee Avalanche* noted Tom's passing: "He has quit this vale of tears; but the horse has not been taken."[8]

With the hostile Paiutes seeming to congregate in northwestern Nevada, and the civilians calling for more protection on the route from Susanville and Honey Lake, north to the Pueblo and Owyhee Districts, soldiers finally moved in to build another camp. Captain Hahn left Paradise Valley, where the situation appeared to have quieted down, and took elements of Companies D and I, 6th California Infantry, west to the Black Rock Mountains. Hahn

135

searched the area for a good location, and six days after the Leonard Creek fight, selected a place by Mahogany Creek a few miles northeast of Summit Lake. The site, later named Camp McGarry, was first called Camp Summit Lake. It was never intended to be a permanent facility, and usually consisted of tents, improvised huts, and stables made of willow branches. It was, however, a useful depot to assemble troops and supplies for the continued hunt for hostile Paiutes.[9] Although the Department of Columbia lost most of its troops when the Oregon and Washington volunteers began mustering out, the Department of California retained its California troops longer, and was able to continue operations into the winter.

BATTLE CREEK, JANUARY 12, 1866

Soldiers fanned out across northern Nevada, keeping constant pressure on the harassed Paiutes. Some of Black Rock Tom's people joined with Captain John and his discontented Warner Lake band. In mid-winter they were less concerned about fighting, and more worried about surviving. On January 8, 1866, Captain George D. Conrad took thirty-seven men of Company B, 2nd California Cavalry, out from Camp Dun Glen on a scout. With them rode nine civilian volunteers and twelve friendly Paiutes under Captain Soo. They traveled north to Cane Springs, at the north edge of Bloody Run Hills about midway between present-day Winnemucca and Camp McDermit, where Lieutenant Robert L. Duncan and twenty-five men of Company I, 2nd California Cavalry, joined them. The combined forces headed west into the Quinn River Valley. A heavy snow fell, which concealed their move, but made the going miserable.

As they ascended each mountain range, they carefully scoured the far horizons for sign of smoke from campfires. Finally, on January 11, Conrad, civilian W. K. Parkinson, four soldiers, and Captain Soo, went in advance seven miles to a hill that overlooked the Black Rock Desert. Smoke was issuing from the edge of the mountains across the desert, perhaps a dozen miles southwest of the site of the Leonard Creek fight the previous November. Preparations were made to move out by 11:30 p.m. They had about 20 miles of desert to cross before dawn.

The long, single file column moved across the desert rapidly, despite the snow, fog, darkness, and eerie, disorienting steam clouds caused by innumerable hot springs. By three a.m. they were as close to the Indian camp as they dared to move without giving away their position. While waiting for dawn, and to keep from freezing in the bitter cold, Conrad had the men dismount and run in circles for the next few hours. This extraordinary effort undoubtedly saved some men from frostbite and even death, yet twenty soldiers still suffered frozen hands, feet, and faces. The horses had been kept saddled and huddled together for warmth; they were covered with a white frost mantle and seemed almost frozen together.

From Nevada's Black Rock Desert, *Caxton Press, 1978*
Captain Conrad had his men march in a circle to keep from freezing while waiting to
make a dawn attack on the Indian camp.

When the eastern horizon finally turned gray, and Indian campfires began
to appear, Conrad had the soldiers rest, make a weapon check, and creep
closer. Lieutenant Duncan took Company I to the right flank. Sergeant Louis
Korble took a detachment of men from Company B to the left flank, and
Conrad advanced in the center with the remainder of the soldiers, plus the
civilians and Indian scouts. The camp was in a three-mile wide basin in the
foothills of the Black Rock Range along a cattail-lined stream that would be
called Battle Creek. Many gullies and tall grasses provided excellent local
cover.

Despite all their preparations, the soldiers were discovered about one
mile from the camp. Conrad charged, but the Indians had a couple of minutes to grab weapons and break off in defensive clusters along the creek
banks. The surround was almost perfect, however, and Conrad advanced
in a tightening circle. Korble's men fired first, which distracted the Indians
and allowed Conrad and Duncan to get in close before firing began in their
sectors. Having no escape route, the outnumbered Indians fought with great
desperation, and the fight lasted two and a half hours. At one strong point,
Captain John fought to the end, making no attempt to escape. A volunteer
named Rapley felled him with a bullet in the head.

When the fighting ended, thirty-five Indian bodies were found, including
two women. Three more warriors were badly wounded, but crawled off in
the gullies to die. Several women survived. Conrad gave them provisions,
allowed them to tend to their dead, and gave them their freedom. Indians
later said that only one wounded warrior escaped and survived. Corporal

137

Author's photo

The Guano Vally, near the Oregon-Nevada border.

Henry Biswell (arrow in the head) and Private Allen (arrow in the leg) of Company I, and Privates Thomas A. Duffield (bullet in the arm), John Riley (arrow in the arm), and Bernard Schulte (arrow in the shoulder) of Company B, were wounded. One of the Paiute scouts, Jim Dunne, was wounded in the back by an arrow. Two horses were killed and nine wounded. Conrad returned to Dun Glen on January 15, after a march of 220 miles.[10]

Several western papers printed news of the battle, all with the usual frontier slant. The *Avalanche* referenced thirty-five Indians sent to "the Happy Hunting Grounds," and lamented that the soldiers on their end never could seem to get the job done. "Those Humboldters *go after* them, and never let up—especially in the winter time. Had the Idaho end of this route shown the hand of Humboldt for the last nine months, there would be all of three hundred Indians less. . . ."

When the *Humboldt Register* praised the troops, it came under criticism for citing "brave" soldiers armed with Maynard rifles, fighting half their number armed with bows and arrows. The *Register* answered, explaining that fog and poor visibility meant that the soldiers had to go up within very close range of the Indians to see them, and the Indians then had the advantage being close-up with bows and arrows that they could discharge many times faster.[11]

The reported death of Captain John is questionable. A civilian was said to have killed him, and reportedly, beside his body was the rifle he used to slay Lt. Colonel McDermit. How anyone could determine that the rifle was used to kill McDermit is a mystery. Besides that, the Paiutes said John survived the fight. Later, Captain Soo reportedly went to find his cousin, Captain John, and see if the war could be brought to an end. John wanted nothing to do with Soo, saying that he had betrayed his people; he should abdicate as chief, and let John take over. Both men argued so vehemently

138

that Soo's brother proposed to shoot both of them, and the one with the stronger medicine would live and be the chief. The crafty younger sibling shot Soo down, killing him, and proving him to be "no good medicine." Before he could perform the test again, John "blazed away" himself and badly wounded the would-be arbitrator. Soo was dead, and the fighting went on.[12]

GUANO VALLEY, FEBRUARY 15, 1866

Pressed from the south, the Paiutes moved north into an isolated area in the canyons at the edge of the Guano Rim, with its abrupt 1,000-foot ledge above Guano Valley below, and running perpendicular to the Oregon-Nevada line. The hungry Indians raided across the state line into Surprise Valley, California, stealing livestock and other property, and stirring up troops from the California forts as well as those in Nevada. Several columns of cavalry combed the area looking for the raiders. A nineteen-man

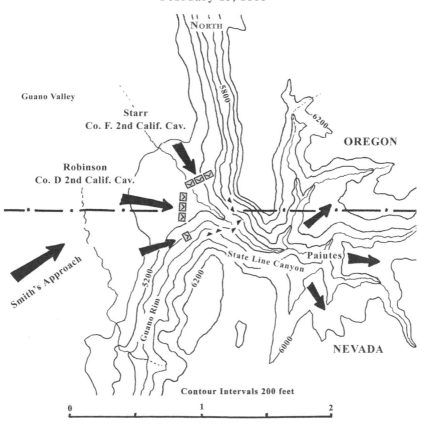

GUANO VALLEY, NEVADA
February 15, 1866

NORTH

Guano Valley

Starr
Co. F. 2nd Calif. Cav.

OREGON

Robinson
Co. D 2nd Calif. Cav.

Smith's Approach

Guano Rim

State Line Canyon

Paiutes

NEVADA

Contour Intervals 200 feet

0   1   2

139

detachment of Company F, 2nd California Cavalry, under Captain Augustus W. Starr, marched east from Fort Crook, California, and joined thirty-two men under Lieutenant George H. Robinson of Company D, 2nd California Cavalry, out of Camp Smoke Creek, Nevada. The combined force consisted of about fifty-three soldiers and thirty civilians, and was under command of Major Samuel P. Smith. Riding with them was Major Henry B. Mellen, also of the 2nd California Cavalry.

Smith marched northeast for five days, discovering the Indian camp in the valley below the Guano Rim, just south of the Oregon-Nevada border and about 80 miles east of Camp Bidwell, California. On February 15, scouts reported Indians camped near the mouth of Rock Canyon (now State Line Canyon), and Smith attacked at 9:30 a.m. Captain Starr took twenty men to the left. Major Mellen, Lieutenant Robinson, twenty-one soldiers, and nineteen civilians from Surprise Valley were the main force in the center, and six civilians took the extreme right. Smoke Creek Jim, leading his conglomeration of Paiutes, Shoshonis, and Bannocks, was killed during the initial charge. Nineteen women and children were captured while the rest of the Indians retreated up Rock Canyon, hiding in the tumble of boulders and in several caves. The soldiers and civilians followed the Indians into the rocks, killing many as they went. At one point, a detachment was nearly cut off by the Indians, but was extricated by the courageous acts of Majors Smith and Mellen. Isolated groups of Indians fought tenaciously, but they no longer had a leader and could not offer any organized resistance. Fifteen women and children were inadvertently killed in the valley and rocks along with eighty-one warriors, the report stating, "it being impossible to distinguish one sex from the other." The battle lasted six hours. About fifteen wounded warriors escaped.

The next morning, the captured women and children were given provisions and allowed to leave. About seventy-five horses stolen from Surprise Valley settlers were recovered. Smith had the thirty-five Indian wickiups burned, along with equipage and supplies, including about three tons of dried beef. Major Smith was wounded during the fight, as were Privates Edward Resler, Henrich Ruhmann, and Frank Belto of Company D and Privates Alexander Mills and Charles H. Smith of Company F. Private Charles Austin of Company D, was killed. The fights at Leonard Creek in November 1865, and this one in Guano Valley, were the most destructive to the Indians in all the years of fighting in Nevada.

PARADISE VALLEY, MARCH 7, 1866

Guano Valley was the last, large contest between Civil War volunteers and Indians in Nevada. On March 7, 1866, Sergeant James T. Edwards, with eight troopers of Company I, 2nd California Cavalry, battled with Paiutes making a last raid in Paradise Valley. Edwards killed six of them with no loss of his own. After that, Nevada experienced nearly a full year of comparative peace.[13]

The big fight in Guano Valley may have benefited Nevada, but its repercussions were felt back in Oregon. Some of the people killed belonged to Howluck's band, and the enraged chief wanted vengeance. One of his responses was to contact Paulina on the Klamath Reservation. Paulina, dissatisfied over the poor rations and itching for the spring raiding season, needed little incentive to leave. On April 22, he and his people fled the reservation. Moshenkosket reported the news to Major Rinehart at Fort Klamath, and Rinehart wrote to Superintendent Huntington that Paulina left "in obedience to a summons from 'Howlock' who has declared that in consequence of the killing of a number of his people a short time ago near Surprise Valley by the California troops he is now very angry and determined to take the war-path for revenge." By the spring of 1866, all the major Indian leaders were still out fighting.[14]

Chapter 13 notes

1 Brackett, "Fighting in the Sierras," in Cozzens, *Eyewitnesses*, 2

2 James C. Weir Depredation Claim #6866.

3 Rathbun, *Nevada Military Names*, 59-60; Orton, *Records of California Men*, 185; Wilson, *Pioneer Nevada*, Vol. 2, 74; Angel, *History of Nevada*, 173-74. The *Humboldt Register* is quoted in Angel. This Table Mountain should not be confused with the Godfrey/Table Mountain fight in May 1865.

4 Rathbun, *Nevada Military Names*, 156-57; Smith, "Sagebrush Soldiers," 79-80, 83; Wilson, *Pioneer Nevada*, Vol. 2, 76; Angel, *History of Nevada*, 174; *Owyhee Avalanche*, September 30, 1865, October 7, 1865. Angel lists the fight as occurring on 13 September. Captain Payne, after mustering out of service, put his knowledge of the terrain to use when he became a noted cattle rustler in northern Nevada.

5 Smith, "Sagebrush Soldiers," 82-83; Rathbun, *Nevada Military Names*, 104, 156; Angel, *History of Nevada*, 174.

6 *Owyhee Avalanche*, November 11, 1865.

7 Rathbun, *Nevada Military Names*, 30, 86-88, 156; Orton, *Records of California Men*, 185-86; Angel, *History of Nevada*, 174; *Owyhee Avalanche*, December 16, 1865.

8 Rathbun, *Nevada Military Names*, 29-30; Orton, *Records of California Men*, 186; Wilson, *Pioneer Nevada*, 103; Angel, *History of Nevada*, 175; *Owyhee Avalanche*, February 10, 1866.

9 Rathbun, *Nevada Military Names*, 93.

10 Rathbun, *Nevada Military Names*, 23-27; Orton, *Records of California Men*, 186-87; Angel, *History of Nevada*, 175; Bancroft, *History of Nevada*, 220.

11 *Owyhee Avalanche*, February 10, 1866; *Humboldt Register*, January 27, 1866, cited in Rathbun, *Nevada Military Names*, 27.

12 *Idaho World*, February 24, 1866; Angel, *History of Nevada*, 150-51. In a story told two years later (*Owyhee Avalanche*, February 1, 1868), the *Humboldt Register* reported that Captain Soo was poisoned by a Paiute "medicine man."

13 Rathbun, *Nevada Military Names*, 79-80; Orton, *Records of California Men*, 186-87, 190-91; Brackett, "Fighting in the Sierras," in Cozzens, *Eyewitnesses*, 4; *Owyhee Avalanche*, April 7, 1866.

14 Rinehart to Huntington, April 24, 1866, RG 393, Dept. of Columbia, Letters Received, Box 3.

Chapter 14

THE REGULARS ARRIVE: OREGON, 1866

With the Civil War over and the regular army freed from duty in the East, the Western volunteers could be sent home. War-weary and eager to save money, Congress was busy cutting the military, and the War Department was in no hurry to build up troops on the other side of the continent. Nearly all of the regular army units fought in the East, and only the 5th and 9th Infantry, and 3rd Artillery remained in the West, with some companies scattered across the frontier, but most of them guarding the Pacific coastal regions. The first regulars to be sent west after the war were from the 14th Infantry. The 14th was organized not as a standard regiment, but in three battalions. When the volunteers disbanded, it was said that many wild characters found their way into the regular units, with the idea that since the war was over, discipline could be relaxed and they should be permitted to have a "high old time." The 14th was said to have gotten more than its share of "Bacchanalian warriors."

In the last week of July 1865, the 2nd Battalion, 14th Infantry, assembled at Hart's Island, New York, preparing to sail to California via Panama. In the two weeks' wait, 221 men deserted. After arriving in San Francisco in September, the 2nd Battalion was sent to the Department of Columbia headquarters at Fort Vancouver, and Colonel Charles S. Lovell arrived with his staff on December 1. Lovell had joined the army as a private in 1830, and had served in the 2nd Artillery, 6th, 10th, and 18th Infantry. He was cited for gallantry at Gaines Mill, Malvern Hill, and Antietam, and appointed colonel of the 14th Infantry in February 1865.

In command of the 2nd Battalion, which would move to the frontier and do the fighting, was Major Louis H. Marshall. Marshall, born in 1827, was the son of Anne Lee Marshall, Robert E. Lee's sister, and received an at-large appointment to the Military Academy in 1845. He served in the 3rd and 10th Infantry, but saw little fighting in the Civil War, spending most of his time as aide-de-camp. In that position under General John Pope in Virginia, Marshall was involved in a controversy, in which his misconstrued verbal orders to General Nathaniel Banks led to the Union defeat at the Battle of Cedar Mountain on August 9, 1862. General Lee was not pleased with his nephew's loyalties or politics. "I could forgive [him] fighting against us," he told his daughter, "if he had not joined such a miscreant as Pope." Now, Marshall would see how his battalion would fight against the Indians.[1]

The 1st Battalion, 14th, sailed in October, arrived in San Francisco in November, and temporarily took station at the Presidio. The 3rd Battalion arrived in December, and promptly exhibited its enthusiasm by running wild in Chinatown, "cutting off the pigtails off the Pagans." The battalion was quickly shifted to Fort Goodwin, Arizona Territory. After a short stint at Fort Drum, most of the 1st Battalion was transferred to Fort Yuma, California. General Halleck was ordered to disband the rest of the volunteers upon the arrival of the 3rd Battalion. Halleck wanted to comply, but on October 19, 1865, he replied to Washington D. C., urging a regiment of regular cavalry be sent to the coast as soon as possible. "The services of mounted troops are absolutely necessary," he stated, and the little remaining cavalry could not be dismissed until "some other comes to take its place." General Grant replied that no regular cavalry regiment could be sent until the spring of 1866.[2]

Two companies of the 2nd Battalion, 14th Infantry, under Captain John H. Walker, were sent out to Fort Boise in the late fall of 1865, where they soon discovered what Indian campaigning would be like. In November, a man named Clark was shot near the mouth of the Owyhee River while he camped with a party of freighters; Indians stole five government mules from McWilliams's Ranch on Jordan Creek; and Indians drove off three cattle and seven horses from Baxter's Ranch. It was reported that, "two red gentry were killed and scalped in good style."

In December, the civilians of the Owyhee District began organizing another expedition, recruiting men to hunt gold and Indians in the Malheur Country. The weather was up to its usual unpredictable tricks. In early January 1866, it was so mild and spring-like that people could go out in shirtsleeves and "a band of Snake Indians" drove off four cattle from a ranch on John Day River; later in the month there was three feet of snow on the ground and D. A. O'Donnell froze to death at Oregon Gulch. In early February, Indians went to Babington's Ranch, only three miles from Ruby City, and stole ten horses. They next hit Parson's Ranch on Reynolds Creek, stole two more horses, and finally attacked Cold Spring Station, halfway between Ruby City and the Snake River, drove out the stationkeeper, took three more horses and all the provisions at the station. The same month, a band of Indians attacked Brownlee's Ferry on the Snake below the mouth of Powder River and killed four horses. More Indians, identified as "the Malheur band of Snakes," drove off all the cattle from Miller's Ranch near the lower Burnt River.[3]

OWYHEE RIVER, FEBRUARY 16, 1866

In early February, a detachment of Company C, 14th Infantry, moved from Fort Boise to Camp Lyon, where some of the last remaining Oregon cavalry was still stationed, in charge of a few officers not yet mustered out. Captain

F. B. White, who had been the regimental adjutant for much of the time, and Lieutenant Silas Pepoon, who had been acting assistant quartermaster and commissary for expeditions under Currey and others, were finally getting their chance to command troops in battle. Pepoon had earlier met the Wasson Brothers in Ruby City, and they found him a "jovial gentleman" who was "slightly barefooted on the top of the head," rather mild-mannered, and "specially fitted for bucking against scalp-taking."

On February 13, about thirty Indians attacked Andrew Hall's Ranch in Jordan Valley. Hall had temporarily left his wife, Amanda, near Marysville, California, in 1862, because, as she explained it, "He was broke." Four years later, Hall was still struggling to make his fortune. There were several men with Hall that evening, a few passing through and a few neighbors, including packer John G. Clark, Bill Bartlett, Sam Marks, a man named Kelly, and two men named Killingsworth and Blakey, who lived a half a mile from Hall, but came there at night to fort up.

About 10 p.m. there was a commotion outside. Hall, hearing gunfire and his dog barking, got his rifle and went outside to find his dog dead at the door and an Indian leading away one of his horses. He ran toward the corral and shot the Indian, but was also shot by a warrior hiding between the haystacks, wounding him badly in the abdomen. Mr. Blakey helped Hall into the house, while Killingsworth shot and killed one warrior who was trying to set the house on fire. Inside, the men took positions at several portholes cut specifically for this very situation. The Indians could not get close enough to the house to burn them out. The structure itself was built of a combination of rocks and timber, but the roof was thatched. The Indians rolled a wagon with burning hay secured to the tongue, up against the house; the flaming tongue was high enough to reach the roof and set it ablaze. One of the men inside poked a shovel through the burning roof and pushed the tongue away. Even so, the roof was partially consumed and collapsed in places, burning and destroying some of Hall's property. The flames, however, were not enough to drive the defenders out in the open. Through the portholes the men saw other warriors with burning torches, setting the corral, barn, and haystacks on fire. The Indians stayed until three in the morning, and rode off with thirty-seven cattle and nine horses. They then went to Cow Creek, shot a man in the arm, and stole his mule team.

More neighbors arrived in the morning, including hay cutter, Eli Rogers. While some rode to Camp Lyon to ask for help, Rogers tried to nurse Hall. "I had him as much as I could turn over on his stomach," he said, "for fear it would bleed inwardly." The missile made a large hole. John Clark said he was "confident that Mr. Hall was struck with a bolt fired out of a gun." Sometimes the Indians used iron bolts, "they broke them some kind of a way and put them in the guns," he said. The two men helped Hall until a doctor arrived and took him to Booneville.[4]

At Camp Lyon, Captain White promised to assist. He sent Lieutenant Pepoon to find the marauders with thirty-five Oregon cavalrymen and 14th Infantrymen of Company C. Pepoon rode to Andrew Hall's Ranch and found a trail leading six miles up Jordan Creek, where it crossed over and ran south for five miles. There, the Indians had killed and eaten a cow. The trail turned west; Pepoon followed it for 10 more miles and camped. On February 16, they continued west eight miles and saw four head of cattle that had fallen behind. Pepoon pulled out his "glass," saw the Indians about five miles ahead, and told his men to prepare for a chase. One trooper, Private John McCourt, said they started at a gallop and kept it up for the whole distance. When the Indians saw the dust approaching, they abandoned the stock and ran. At that point they were about two miles from the Owyhee River, north of the Three Forks. The pursuit continued to the riverbank.

At the river, McCourt counted ten mounted Indians and several more on foot. He saw three warriors dismount; one shot his horse, and they all joined the others on foot, hiding in the willows and brush along the banks. Half the troopers chased the mounted Indians across the river. Said McCourt: "They ran them from the river about four miles, and fired on them all the way." When they returned, they joined the other soldiers hunting the warriors hidden in the willows. The action was close-up and deadly. Soldiers flushed out one warrior who was lying in the sagebrush; he popped up, shot Pat Raney's horse through the neck and killed it. Ed Miller rode up, fired, and hit the Indian, who turned to shoot an arrow into Miller's side. "Another man rode up to the Indian," said McCourt, "and cut his bowstring in two; on seeing this the latter gave a look towards the men and fell dead."

By that time it was dusk and Pepoon made camp on the battleground. About ten p.m. the Indians returned and fired into the camp. The pickets blazed away at them and there were scores of rifle flashes in the dark, but no certainty that anyone was hit. About three in the morning, said McCourt, "the squaws came down and had a — of a time over the dead Indian." On Saturday, February 17, they scouted up the Middle Fork Owyhee six miles, locating more abandoned stock. Pepoon figured he did not have enough men to protect the recovered animals and fight Indians, so he drove them back to Hall's Ranch.[5]

DRY CREEK, FEBRUARY 23, 1866

Recently arrived at Fort Boise were Captain John H. Walker, now the commander of the Sub-District of Boise, and Lieutenant Thomas F. Tobey, with men of the 14th Infantry. Walker left Boise with Lieutenant Tobey on February 12, with thirty-four enlisted men of Companies C and D, to join up with a civilian expedition to the Malheur Country. The civilian force of twenty-five men included the leaders John Holgate and Charles Gassett, and Jim Beard, Thomas B. Cason, Aaron Winters, William Younger, Wash Waltermire, and Charles Webster. They crossed the Snake River, when on

February 15, four troopers from Camp Lyon delivered a message to Walker from Captain White; Lieutenant Pepoon could not join him because he was engaged chasing raiders south of Camp Lyon. Walker continued up the Malheur, finding recently abandoned Indian camps, but no Indians. On February 20, he stopped near the forks of the Malheur, where Lieutenant Hobart had his fight in July 1865.

Walker then turned southeast across country toward the Owyhee. About four p.m. on February 23, between the Malheur and Owyhee, probably on Dry Creek, they came upon a twelve-lodge rancheria under Yellow Jacket. The camp was in a canyon and the Indians could not flee without losing their plunder. The soldiers came in from the north and the civilians from the south. "The Indians fought with desperation," Walker reported, "asking no quarter." They barricaded themselves in the rocks and the soldiers had no choice but to charge and drive them out. They fought until nightfall ended the action. Eighteen Indians were killed, and only three got away, including Yellow Jacket and two wounded warriors. In the charge, Corporal William Burke, Company D, who had survived twenty-one Civil War battles, was shot and killed, and Musician Vrooman was wounded. Walker lost twelve horses to bullets and hard use, but captured nineteen others. He destroyed Indian blankets, guns, ten pounds of powder, twenty pounds of balls, knives, files, tools, canned goods, and 300 pounds of jerked meat. In the camp they found a U.S. saddle blanket and a soldier's blouse. Later, Walker reportedly told the *Idaho Statesman* that he wanted "no better sport" than to set out on a similar expedition.

Having used up much of his rations and exhausting his horses, Walker first went to Camp Lyon to recruit the horses, and then back to Fort Boise. The *Idaho World* praised the expedition, saying that Walker successfully treated the Indians "to lead backed up by powder," but it was concerned that by treating the Indians "in true military style," Walker was liable to dismissal. Apparently, the paper "surmised that Captain Walker is removed or will be." Many civilians believed there was a conspiracy against them. "Now that we have finally got a fighting man of sense on this end of the route," the paper figured he would be taken away, and it wished that whoever caused his removal "may be forced into the Indian haunts and be removed from earth by Indian bullets or arrows."[6]

The *Idaho World's* concerns were borne out, but the change, however, was not a dark plot, but an attempt to achieve administrative efficiency and more local troop control. On February 24, the Department of Columbia got another commander, when Major General Frederick Steele took over. Steele graduated from West Point in 1843, and served in the 2nd, 3rd, and 11th Infantry, as a colonel of the 8th Iowa Infantry, and a brigadier and major general of volunteers. He was cited for gallantry at Contreras and Chapultepec in the Mexican War, and at Vicksburg and Little Rock in the Civil War. The young wife of an army officer described him as "a pleasant affable gentleman." Steele went to Fort Vancouver. On March 2, the Sub-District of Boise became a full military district under Major Louis H. Marshall. Marshall moved to Fort Boise on March 20, and immediately requisitioned Steele for three more companies, some of which included the long-awaited cavalry.

After the 14th Infantry, the next veteran regular unit to arrive was the 1st Cavalry. With the end of the Civil War, the regiment was ordered to Louisiana to help in Reconstruction of the South. It remained there until sailing for California on December 29, and arrived at the Presidio in San Francisco, on January 22, 1866. Companies A, G, and K went to Drum Barracks, and Companies C, D, and E joined them there the following month. The other companies followed, and as usual, they were scattered among various western posts from Washington to Arizona. By April, six companies had been sent to Arizona, two to Nevada, and four to Oregon. Company I, under Captain Eugene M. Baker, went to Camp Watson in April.

General Steele's first action was to abandon most of the camps and concentrate troops under Marshall at Fort Boise. Captain Walker had already called for the abandonment of Camp Alvord and its removal to a better location about 20 miles southeast on Whitehorse Creek, later to be named Camp C. F. Smith. In April, Captain James B. Sinclair, Company H, 14th Infantry, left Camp Currey and moved the soldiers to Fort Boise. The same month, Major Albert G. Brackett, 1st Cavalry, took command of Fort Churchill. About this time, 14th Infantry companies under Captain John J. Coppinger and Captain James Henton, coming from The Dalles and from the mouth of the Columbia respectively, arrived at Boise. Captain James C. Hunt brought his Company M, 1st Cavalry, up the Humboldt route to Camp Lyon, joining Captain Patrick Collins with a company of the 14th Infantry, and some of the last Oregon Infantry still in service, under Captain Franklin B. Sprague. Captain David Perry marched his Company F, 1st Cavalry, to Camp C. F. Smith by way of Chico, California. In June, 1st Cavalry regimental headquarters assembled at Fort Vancouver.[7]

Depredations continued while the new troops were moving in and Captain Walker was returning to Fort Boise. On February 28, a band of about twenty-five Paiutes attacked Ruby Ranch. Six men were there: proprietor G. W. Inskip, and travelers Frank Osgood, R. B. Gibb, H. B. Carter, J. D. Osborne, and a man named Thomas. The fight started at 8 p.m. and the men were besieged until eight the next morning. Bullets flew all night, but harmlessly bounced off the stone walls. One commanding Indian voice was heard through most of the night, but when one of the defenders blasted a double-charged shotgun toward the voice, his calling ceased, and the men inside figured they had killed a chief. The raiders butchered a horse, cooked it, and ate it within sight of the men defending the ranch. After midnight, Osborne crept out the back and made his way to Camp Lyon for help.

148

Osborne reached Lyon and Captain White and thirty soldiers rode toward Ruby Ranch, but got lost in the dark. The Indians set the hay and a wagon on fire and took four horses before they left. White arrived later that morning, too late to do anything.

If the men at Inskip's did kill a chief, the warriors soon got revenge. On March 1, David P. Brown and Moses Mott were heading to the mines from the Owyhee Ferry with two yoke of cattle and a wagon. Indians jumped and killed them about eight miles from Inskip's. They scalped Brown's whiskers and smashed his head with a rock. "Mott's head was beaten into a jelly, and his heart cut out and carried off—" reported the *Avalanche*, "we presume to Boise City, to be presented to the High Priest of this sort of sacrifice, as an earnest of fidelity to the cause." Citizens and four soldiers recovered the bodies and buried them at Lockwood's Ranch in Jordan Valley. "Can it be that we are much longer to record the humiliating facts that the Government will not protect her pioneer citizens?" the *Avalanche* lamented. "How long?"[8]

The civilians soon had an answer. In early March, the Ada Volunteers of Boise City and the surrounding valley, marched to the Snake River to "clean it up to the mouth of Bruneau, thence up it and kill all Indians found." The Bruneau bands, Bannocks, and Shoshonis for the most part, were said by some to have been at peace since the Soda Springs Treaty in 1863; others insisted they continued to depredate. The Ada Volunteers were certain of their guilt, but when Governor Caleb Lyon found out about the expedition, he sent runners with instructions "not to molest those Indians, as he was about to make a treaty with them." The story went, that an unnamed "executive lickspittle" concocted a story that the miners of the Owyhee District had also made a separate peace, and had remonstrated against killing the Bruneau Indians. Confused, the Ada Volunteers retraced their steps and went home. When the folks at Owyhee found out, the *Avalanche*, as could be expected, howled in protest. Not only did the citizens not make any peace with the Bruneau tribes, they wished the citizens had gone in and killed all the Indians. "The volunteers have been outraged," the paper said; the people of Boise have been "robbed of their money," and the Owyheeans were liable to take matters into their own hands "and rid the earth of not only the Indians but their infernal protectors." The *Avalanche* hoped to discover "the motives of certain parties connected with his excellency and his lambs."[9]

Immediately caught up in the controversy upon his arrival at Fort Boise, Major Marshall, apparently trying to show that he meant business, quickly organized an expedition. The *Idaho Statesman* reported that Marshall hoped to get the extra troops he called for, "but if he does not he intends to chastise the Indians with the men he now has." Marshall left the fort on March 28, traveled to the Bruneau River, found only 150 unarmed young and old "Snakes" peacefully encamped, and returned to Boise after a march of 110 miles. Apparently the Indians he located were not the ones he planned to "chastise." On April 18, Marshall sent Captain Collins with ten 14th Infantrymen of Company D, and ten troopers of Company B, 1st Oregon Cavalry, one of only four Oregon companies left in service, south to Squaw Creek, which entered the Snake about seven miles below the mouth of Reynolds Creek. There were reports of Indian and white bandits hiding out there and robbing travelers, and Collins was under orders to find and hang them without ceremony. Collins searched up Squaw Creek and back, but found nothing. Collins next was sent to investigate the theft of 40 horses on Burnt River in Oregon, but was again unsuccessful.[10]

The tentative honeymoon between the new military regime and the locals was eroded a bit after two soldiers, one a volunteer and one a regular, broke in to Osborne's Ranch on Cow Creek on March 21. The soldiers stormed into the house and demanded liquor from Messrs. Stewart and Williams. To prevent violence, they gave the soldiers a canteen of whiskey. The soldiers left, drank up the contents, and returned later in the night, took an ax to several boxes of supplies stored outside the house, broke them open and stole about $1,000 worth of goods. Mr. Stewart and a companion rode to see Captain White at Camp Lyon, but while they consulted with him, their horses were cut loose and saddles and bridles stolen. The outraged civilians went to Silver City and obtained a warrant for the arrest of the guilty men. Deputy Sheriff Springer took a posse of five men to Camp Lyon, but when they arrived, Captains Sprague and Walker intervened. They promised the deputy "to have the scoundrels arrested and sent to Fort Boise for court-martial." Springer and the complainants agreed to drop the matter, but goodwill between the parties had been tested.[11]

By May, Captain White was pouring out his frustration to headquarters at Fort Boise. Small parties of Indians were "committing depredations at so many different points at the same time," he wrote, "that it is impossible with the available force at this camp, to give protection on all the roads leading to the Owyhee mines." He said that 100 mules had been stolen on Jordan and Reynolds Creeks during the past two weeks. "I have sent small detachments after them in every instance, but without recovering any of the stolen stock, except fifteen or twenty of the mules stolen at Inskip's ranch about ten days ago." The Indians seemed to head northwest for the Owyhee and Malheur Rivers, but White could never catch them because they crossed the Owyhee, which he claimed "is very high and cannot be crossed on the Indian trail without swimming it."[12]

Why White viewed the river as a barrier when Indians could easily cross it is debatable, but Marshall and his men had an excellent opportunity to salvage their tarnished reputation after a tragedy in May. The incident began with an influx of Chinese miners to the Idaho and Montana diggings. The arrival of groups of Chinese miners in the area unfortunately coincided with an increased Indian presence.

In the spring of 1866, large roaming bands of Paiutes seemed to be making their way north along the Humboldt Road, striking at Beachey and Johnson's stage stations as they went. The first one they hit was at Cane Springs. The station was on the Humboldt Road at the summit of the pass between the Santa Rosa Mountains on the north and Bloody Run Hills on the south, and Paradise Valley on the east and Quinn River Valley on the west. It consisted of a station house and barn, wagons, mowers, thirty tons of hay, ten tons of barley, eleven stage horses, and all the assorted harnesses, blankets, buckets, combs, pitchforks, axes, and so on, associated with running a stage station, plus assorted furniture and weapons. Co-owner Owen Johnson evaluated the property at $5,755. On 7 May, Paiutes wrecked the station, destroying or carrying off nearly everything.

The large war band moved north about 10 miles, coming upon the next station at Buffalo Springs the following day. The station consisted of a house and corral, but Beachey and Johnson had more supplies stored there than at Cane Springs, including fifty tons of hay, fifteen tons of barley, and nineteen stage horses. The Indians hit Buffalo Springs and again caused havoc. Johnson estimated losses at $7,660. The war party moved north to the Owyhee Crossing. There they destroyed Chauncey Bacheler's ferryboat, stole three horses, and shot him in the arm. Possibly satiated with the large hauls, the war party holed up near the crossing to lie in wait of another opportune target.[13]

The unsuspecting victims were the Chinese miners. The Chinese had a tough time in a number of ways. They were just as anxious to stake rich claims in the mining regions of the West as the EuroAmericans, but generally were excluded because of various discriminatory mining practices. In 1866, the first federal mining law was enacted, and Chinese were forbidden to file mining claims on public lands; they circumvented that by purchasing old claims rather than filing new ones. There was even a "Chinese tax" passed in 1864 and 1866, to make money on those who managed to obtain claims. The Owyhee and Boise Districts didn't start to see significant numbers of Chinese until the fall of 1865. Although the white miners weren't happy about the competition, the merchants and politicians of the area realized that increasing the "Chinese tax" and inducing Chinese immigration, would be one way to get revenue in a cash-strapped, isolated economy. The local papers ran contradictory stories both verifying and denying that promoters were "dispatched to California to encourage Mongolian emigration." In any event, a few groups of several hundred Chinese made the journey; some had wagons and supplies, some walked with few possessions, others hired teamsters to transport them and their equipment. Some unscrupulous freighters took the money, but only carried them half way before abandoning them.

The Chinese were in very short supply of one important item: weaponry. It was reported that one unscrupulous promoter outfitted several large groups of Chinese with wooden rifles to "scare away the Indians." It didn't work.[14]

Reports of what happened to the various parties are confused. There were several groups that went east from California, and the Indians destroyed at least two, and possibly three of them. There were three practical routes: one went from Chico, California, clipped the northwestern corner of Nevada, and then northeast to the Owyhee Crossing near the mouth of Jordan Creek, and east to Silver City; one followed from the Comstock District, up the Humboldt to present-day Winnemucca, Nevada, and then north, meeting the Chico route at Owyhee Crossing; a third, less used, followed up the Humboldt to its headwaters, and then north to the Bruneau River and down to the Snake. The southern edge of the Columbia Plateau, with its lava flows and deep canyons, was nearly impossible to cross except in a few places—one accessible spot was Owyhee Crossing.

CHINESE MASSACRES, MAY 19-21, 1866

The Indians, now with several additional Henry Rifles, Colt revolvers, carbines, and muskets recently stolen from Beachey and Johnson's stage stations, had been watching several columns of Chinese cross their country, apparently unarmed and unwary. One of the bands reportedly following them was under Chief Pony Blanket (Egan), born a Cayuse, but taken as a young boy by a Paiute family after his parents were killed. He married a Paiute and led them on many war raids. Indians attacked one Chinese party of fifty or more men on the Humboldt route in Oregon, just north of Camp McDermit. Exactly when or how many were killed is unknown. On May 19, another party of fifty Chinese neared Owyhee Crossing when more than 200 of Pony Blanket's Paiutes struck. The *Avalanche* reported all but one Chinese was murdered, and "Their bodies were mutilated in the most shocking manner." They only had thirteen horses, and all were stolen. Their equipment was carried off or destroyed, except "the picks, were stuck through the bodies and the heads of the victims." The Chinese were reportedly recent arrivals brought directly from China by a man named Cue Long, and unfamiliar with the dangers of the trip. When the Paiutes struck, Cue Long dropped everything and ran as fast as he could, going a few miles to the banks of the Owyhee when an Indian caught up to him. They struggled, fell off a cliff into the river, and the warrior disappeared. Cue Long climbed out on the opposite bank and made it to Sheep Ranch on the Jordan River, the only survivor.

A third attack occurred between May 19 and 21, on a party of about 300 Chinese miners and two white men using the upper Humboldt road and Bruneau River route. From the upper Bruneau they branched northwest toward the Owyhee mines and were in Battle Creek Canyon when Indians, reportedly Paiutes under Chief Winnemucca, but more likely Bannocks, attacked them. About fifty were slaughtered without quarter along a line of about 200 yards. Many carried sluice forks, umbrellas, and bamboo poles, seemingly oblivious to the dangers awaiting them. A few reportedly had pistols, but barely knew how to use them. The Indians apparently scalped the unresisting Chinese with ease; their hair was "considered a choice article...on account of the tails."[15]

In early May, Major Marshall had taken the field, going from Fort Boise to Camp Lyon, and toward the Owyhee with thirty-five men of Companies A and C, 2nd Battalion, 14th Infantry. They went down Jordan Creek to the Owyhee, and upriver, where they waited for cavalry reinforcements.

When word reached Camp Lyon about the massacre at Owyhee Crossing, Lieutenant Pepoon with his Oregon Cavalrymen "dashed to the spot and found the dead bodies spread along the road for six miles." In one place, five or six bodies were piled together. Pepoon tried to pursue the Indians, but they had too much of a head start. He returned to bury the bodies. Chinese miners in Idaho went to the Battle Creek site to bury their own people, placing the remains in a large, deep grave about 12 feet square.[16]

THREE FORKS, MAY 27-28, 1866

When Pepoon finished the burials, he took his forty-nine cavalrymen and went to find Major Marshall. They combined forces about May 23, and Pepoon related news of the massacre. The next day Marshall struck a trail of the Indians he believed had "murdered a large party of Chinese." They marched southeast up the Owyhee, but at Three Forks, found more than they bargained for. On May 27, Marshall met many warriors well-posted along the east bank of the main Owyhee, probably on the sides of present Three Forks Dome, while he was on the west bank. The canyon was steep, with few trails down, and fewer places to cross. When the soldiers began moving toward the river, about 500 Indians including women and children, began driving their stock over the divide behind them to the Middle Fork Owyhee. Before Marshall could get to the water, he reported more than 300 armed warriors had taken position in the rocks above them on the opposite shore, making a crossing extremely hazardous. Only four Indians exposed themselves in front, said Marshall, "one, the chief, giving his directions. These were instantly shot, two of them killed—one being the chief—and two badly wounded."

The adversaries blasted away at each other for almost four hours. The howitzer lobbed five shells over the ridge into the camp beyond, with unknown effect. On the front side, however, Marshall said "we could see them pack their dead and wounded over the hills and bring fresh men to take their places." He estimated that seven Indians were killed and twelve wounded. As yet, no soldiers were hit.

Finally, Marshall moved downstream to try to cross over below the forks and flank the Indians, but daylight was running out. He only had half his men across to the east shore when his raft sank in the river, taking down

Author's photo

Three Forks, Oregon, on the Owyhee River.

the howitzer with it. When night fell, Marshall was in an extremely bad spot, with his small force split on two sides of the river. Had the Indians attacked, they probably could have annihilated his command. At first light, the soldiers built a makeshift raft, and the rest of the men and supplies were ferried across. They were on the east bank, but they still had to ascend the cliffs. Marshall sent scouts up to find a path when the Indians attacked and killed Corporal William Philips, Company B, 1st Oregon Cavalry. It looked like 100 rifles blazed at the trooper directly behind Philips; his horse was killed, but somehow he danced his way double-time down the cliff and safely to camp. The Indians roped Philips's body and dragged it away. Horrified, Lieutenant Pepoon volunteered to take a detail and attempt a rescue, but Marshall denied his request as too dangerous. The Indians kept Marshall pinned down by the shore until evening. Marshall decided to retreat. "The country is so difficult," he wrote, "that only one man at a time can climb these Indian trails. Ten men can hold a hundred in check and prevent their ascent."

The Oregon cavalrymen, angered at having to abandon one of their men, became even more incensed when Marshall left four more behind. "At night I deemed it best to get back to the west side for fear I might be hemmed in," Marshall said. They made a hazardous river crossing in the darkness, going up and back many times on their poor raft. By morning they were safe—except for the four soldiers who apparently missed the orders to pull out and were left behind. Sorely pressed and with depleted ammunition, Marshall pulled out, vowing to return again and recover his gun. Marshall's beaten command was back at Camp Lyon about June 1.[17]

154

The *Idaho World* had high hopes for Marshall's expedition. "Major Marshall is now making a raid after the Chinese murderers on the west side of the Owyhee," it announced. "If the major overtakes them and is not overpowered, may the Lord have mercy on their miserable souls—if they have any—for the troops will have none." The *World,* farther from the point of action and with the slow communications, was not aware that Marshall had already returned. The *Owyhee Avalanche* was ready to print its June 2 issue, when it discovered Marshall was back, and a reporter rushed over to get the news. Marshall announced that about ninety-five Chinese were killed in massacres at two places the previous week, and in his attempt to find the

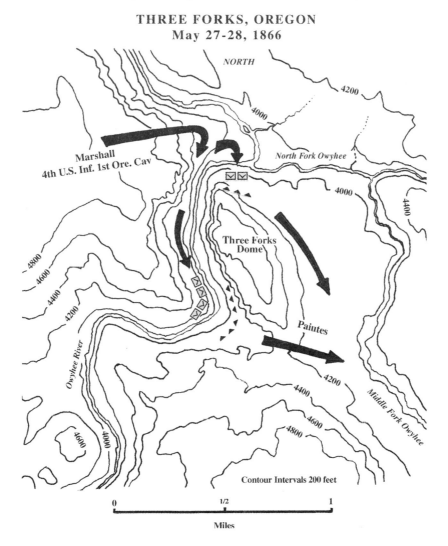

THREE FORKS, OREGON
May 27-28, 1866

murderers, he ran into 500 Indians with at least 250 armed warriors, and it would have been "madness and murder" to have attempted to attack them. The major, the paper reported, "Says he'll go after them continually, if he can't wipe them out this Summer, will go after them in the Winter and keep doing so till the job is completed."[18]

As the days passed and more news trickled in about the soldiers' poor showing, public opinion soured again. Marshall's expedition seemed to have sparked more raids. In May, Indians murdered John Witner, a settler on the John Day River. About May 25, teamsters Jim Beard and Joe Miller, on their way from Chico to Idaho, lost 421 out of 460 cattle. On May 30, Indians raided near Booneville and stole sixty-five head of cattle and horses. On June 1, raiders again hit Con Shea on Sinker Creek and stole fifty-seven beef steers that he valued at $3,420. In early June, "Snake Indians" attacked a pack train near the Buttermilk Ranch by Weiser River. About June 10, a large war party, possibly the same band that had attacked Beachey's stations in May, hit his Willow Creek Station, 12 miles north of Buffalo Station, and destroyed the house, barn, corral, forty tons of hay, twenty tons of barley, and assorted items. They stole eight horses, two Henry Rifles, two carbines, and two Colt pistols. Owen Johnson valued the losses at $7,110.

On June 12, Indians crept into the Flint District and murdered Charles C. Gassett outside his tent only half a mile from the miners' camp. He was shot and hacked with a shovel and ax, the shovel being "bent nearly double from the blows." Fifteen miners pursued the raiders to South Mountain, found a butchered ox, and lost the trail. On the last day of June, the Paiutes, probably enthralled about the easy pickings they seemed to have at Beachey and Johnson's stations, were back again. This time they hit Summit Springs Station, located about 18 miles north of Camp McDermit. The usual destruction and theft followed, this time to the tune of $4,935. The Indians were not done. A few days later, Rattlesnake Station, one stop south of the Owyhee Crossing, was next on the list. The raiders got away with the station's weapons, 18 horses, and caused about $6,810 in losses.

The white civilians were outraged, and the newspapers began to lecture the army on how to do its job. It was useless to send a handful of soldiers out every week or two on short punitive scouts, when "A continual three, four or more months' war must be made." The supplies had to follow the troops so they didn't have to keep stopping and returning to base. The army only wore out its horses and men marching to and fro without fighting. As a better example, the *Avalanche* cited "a few earnest men" who conducted "the Humboldt war of 1865," where only a few companies "killed four hundred savages in a few months. They never waited for theft or massacre, but went after the Indians day and night." Why couldn't Idaho troops accomplish the same, it asked. There were enough soldiers in the area to keep 200 in the field constantly, and if they used friendly Indian scouts like they ought to, the

Indians could be beaten.[19] The *Avalanche* had the right prescription, but the army could not seem to get its act together.

When Marshall went back to Fort Boise, the *Avalanche* stepped up its sarcasm. Marshall and Captain Collins, were apparently "spending a few quiet days in Idaho," resting from their recent exertions, while stock was being stolen and people murdered. After all, the paper said, "It is dangerous over this way and great captains should not imprudently expose themselves." The major showed how prudent he was "in one of those celebrated retreats from the Owyhee, leaving a portion of his men and baggage behind" while the Indians went the other way. Even Lieutenant Pepoon, "in one of his military inspirations, was imprudent enough to want to go after the retreating savages." But, the major's main design, the paper mimicked in baby talk, was to "find the woad into the Indian country," and he had done that. "The howitzer was

Nevada Historical Society ETH-59
Numaga "Young Winnemucca"

safe in the bottom of the Owyhee River; could get that anytime." The paper supposed the men who had been abandoned could find their way out again too.

At this time, General Halleck made an inspection tour of his department, with an entourage of enough staff and escorts to have run his own campaign. About June 20, he arrived at Fort Churchill, where a great number of Paiutes from the Truckee and Walker River Reservations visited with him. Numaga, a nephew of Winnemucca and often called Young Winnemucca, led the speech-making, airing grievances, but professing eternal friendship. His warriors put on a fine martial display of horsemanship for Halleck, and almost all of them wanted to shake his hand. Numaga agreed to take all the Indian prisoners who had been brought in, and watch them on the Truckee Reservation. When Halleck left, he was suitably impressed, and directed that a supply of rations be distributed to them.

Traveling north up the Humboldt route, Halleck arrived at Camp Lyon on June 26. The general had taken a tough stance, having no patience with intractable Indians, and believing force was necessary to keep them at peace. "Let them fully understand," he wrote, "depredations upon our people must entirely cease, or they must be exterminated." That was something the fron-

157

tier people could understand. Civilians went to see him at Camp Lyon to pay their respects and to "make true representations concerning the defenseless condition of Owyhee and the importance of immediate protection." Halleck and his staff went to Ruby City and Silver City and stayed at the Idaho Hotel. They were shown the mines and mills and were wined and dined. Halleck could not be induced to give a speech, but he made several toasts, and he left the next day to continue his inspection, heading for Fort Boise. The citizens were favorably impressed, especially with his seeming seriousness and lack of ostentation. Maybe the army would begin to operate the way they thought it should.[20]

JENNINGS'S FIGHT, JULY 2-7, 1866

Some civilians would wait to see what the soldiers would do, but others, in one of their periodical bursts of impatience and energy, again decided to take matters into their own hands. Marshall cautioned them, but they would not listen. The civilians of the Owyhee District organized another Indian-hunting party. About thirty Chinese wanted to join up to avenge the loss of their countrymen, but the white residents dismissed their help. "The expedition is well supplied with arms and express a determination to make a few Los [Indians] bite the dust," the paper reported.[21]

Anxious to get moving, on June 22, Isaac Jennings, an ex-Civil War soldier, led about thirty-six men south toward Juniper Mountain to hunt Indians. In the Flint District they picked up more men. If any of them were looking for omens, they may have noted that they followed in the wake of millions of locusts. The previous year, the pests traveled in a northerly direction through the Owyhee area; this year they swarmed south, having cleared the area north of War Eagle Mountain a few weeks before, and were now devouring everything green in the Jordan Valley. Jennings's hunters passed beyond the swarm and settled in to hunt down Red Canyon south of Juniper Mountain toward the Owyhee River. Other civilians got ready when they could and headed out in small parties to join Jennings on the way south. A party of nine under George W. Hill, ran into a small band of Indians near Jordan Creek, killed two, and captured eight horses, but swung east to Catherine Creek and missed the expedition. Jennings could have used the reinforcements.

The Paiutes were camped in a box canyon near the junction of the main Owyhee and the South Fork, in a place they called Sihwiyo, "Willows Growing all in a Row." On July 2, they were resting, repairing equipment, and digging potatoes, when the volunteers appeared over a hill to the west, and then came in shooting. The warriors fought while the others moved to the rimrock on the east. They battled until nightfall, when the Paiutes held a council and decided they would shift position into a nearby canyon, and leave a plain trail so the whites would follow them in. The next morning, Jennings saw the Indians were gone, picked up the trail, and walked into a box canyon, but not before five men deserted him before going into what they perceived was an obvious trap. The Paiutes surrounded Jennings in a spot where they had no water and would have to fight through the Indians to get it. The miners built small defensive positions out of rocks and brush and fought all during the hot day. Thomas B. Cason, cut off from the main group, built a rock shelter and held out all day, reportedly killing fifteen Indians before he was shot dead. Bullets struck Aaron Winters in the neck and Charles Webster in the side. George Green was also wounded. One Indian present commented that they would have killed all the whites, except they had old, broken-down rifles and most of the warriors were poor shots.

On the night of July 2, if they had not known it before, the civilians realized that they were in a bad spot. They couldn't get out, couldn't reach the creek, and were almost out of ammunition. Dave Pickett and S. E. McCanless volunteered to ride for help. They broke out of the ring under Indian fire and made their way north, reaching the Flint District about two in the morning, where they first met Captain James Henton with sixty soldiers of Company B, 14th Infantry, who had set up a temporary camp in the District only two weeks earlier. Jennings's written message briefly indicated that they were surrounded by 250 Indians and asked for plenty of "Henry rifle cartridges and lead." "Now, gentlemen," he wrote, "in the name of Heaven, send us assistance within 36 hours—if possible. There are but thirty-two of us all told. We have killed and wounded at least twenty Indians. . . .Unless you can send the force required, not one of us can escape."

At the mines, the mills' steam whistles began blowing up valley and over mountain, until the entire area was aroused. By 8 a.m. almost 200 men had assembled, armed themselves, gathered five days' provisions, and moved out. In Flint, they divided into two companies, under William Wallace and A. M. McMillan, and guided by Pickett and McCanless. They had more than 60 miles to go. After 18 miles, McMillan camped for the night, but Wallace marched on. The night march served only to get them lost, while McMillan took a different route in the daylight and passed them by.

The volunteers, meanwhile, withdrew to a lava crater and kept shooting, but picking their targets carefully to preserve ammunition. At night, men crept out to get water, but one, Frank Curier, was wounded in the hip, and they retreated back to the crater. The desperate civilians finally expanded their perimeter with rock breastworks to include a flat shaded by some willows and a portion of the creek. Now they and their surviving horses had access to water. Still, they could not break free. By Saturday evening, July 7, it looked like time had run out, when suddenly the Paiutes began to leave. Up the canyon came McMillan's Company, followed directly by Wallace's.[22]

The rescuers were ready to fight, but the Indians were gone. They took stock of the situation. Jennings had one killed and three wounded, but they estimated that they had killed anywhere from twenty-eight to forty Indians.

Jennings had several horses killed, but there was a net gain, when sixteen Indian horses wandered in to the civilian lines. A new supply of horseshoes and nails allowed the stock to be re-shoed. One of the horses that came in to the civilian lines looked familiar. It once belonged to James Perry, a native of New York who had lived in Michigan most of his life, mined in the Washoe District for a few years, and was a pioneer in Owyhee. About June 27, Indians jumped him near the head of Sinker Creek, five miles from Silver City, shot him, chopped off his arms and legs, and pinned him to the ground. On the horse was Perry's saddle and bags, ten pounds of ammunition and two of Perry's jacks.

The volunteers, about 250 of them, considered their options and reorganized on Sunday. More supplies came in, and about 150 of them vowed to "remain and see the thing through." Jennings, Owen Johnson, of the Beachey-Johnson stage line, and men named Hill, Cutler, and Anderson were the captains. They prepared for a twenty-five-day expedition. Captain Wallace, who had caught a fever upon arrival and was carried in on a litter, recovered enough to return to the mines with 100 men. On Sunday night, July 8, Captains Henton and White arrived with fifty soldiers. The volunteers thought they would join them, but to their disgust, they discovered that the soldiers, "having *only three days rations*, had to return next day, without making a single scout of the country."

The volunteers sent out their own scouts and picked up a large trail heading west, "satisfied that Lo had from 800 to 1,000 head of stock." Jennings set out Monday morning. "The boys are in the best of spirits," it was reported. They moved down toward the Three Forks area, believing they were chasing Winnemucca's Paiutes. Said Owen Johnson: "We are cooking by Winnemucca's fires. We have invited him to fight us and let him choose the ground, but we have not been able to bring him to a stand yet. He would not stand on the famous Marshall field. We run him over it and he is going towards Queen River Mountains, and throwing away everything that they can go without."

On July 14, Jennings, Johnson, and a few others left the command 20 miles back, and rode to Camp McDermit. Having "lived on raw bacon and cold bread for a week," they hoped to obtain succor at McDermit. Captain John P. Baker, Company L, 1st Cavalry, in command at the post, was happy to help them. Baker, Johnson said, "is a brick; he has rendered us all the assistance in his power and filled our requisitions in one hour's time, and is going with us with twenty-five of his command mounted." Johnson thought they had all the Owyhee Indians in their front, and were pushing them west toward Steens Mountain. The volunteers moved to Summit Springs and then to the new Camp C. F. Smith. Along the way there was serious dissension in the ranks, with some volunteers wanting to give up the chase and others wanting to push ahead. A few volunteers, it was said, "experienced a weakness in the abdominal regions which resulted in giving their garments anything but a rose-water perfume." There was an "unfortunate shooting affray" among several of Jennings's command. An army surgeon at Camp Smith treated the wounded, and with that, the expedition dissolved. Jennings and most of the command returned to the Owyhee District on July 27.[23]

STEENS MOUNTAIN, JULY 17, 1866

About the time the civilians broke up, Captain John H. Walker went on a scout toward Harney Lake Valley. Walker left Camp C. F. Smith with thirty men of Company C, 14th Infantry, accompanied by Dr. W. A. Tompkins, who had served at Camp Wright the previous winter. They marched over Steens Mountain, in what Tompkins called, "some of the roughest country I ever saw." They found a trail through a mountain pass that looked like it was made by 300 Indians; Tompkins thought they were heading to Harney Valley "to recruit after the race Col. Jennings and party gave them some time ago." Walker never made it to the valley, for he was "only rationed for a few days." Nevertheless, the soldiers fought a rear-guard of Indians in the mountains, killed three and wounded five, with the loss of only one soldier wounded, although several later discovered bullet holes through their clothing. Captain Walker's horse was shot from underneath him.[24]

When General Halleck left Ruby City he went to Fort Boise, and on July 4, issued directions to General Steele. He said that Boise was useless as a military post, being too far from the hostile Indians and off the military supply line. He wanted Major Marshall to take the field and establish a camp on the Bruneau River, closer to the Indians and more easily supplied by steamer on the Snake River. He ordered another camp to be built near the Three Forks, and those two posts were to be the centers of operations unless poor winter forage forced the soldiers to return to Lyon and Boise. He wanted ten mounted men permanently stationed at the Owyhee Ferry to escort trains on the Chico and Fort Klamath routes, and wanted Captain John Baker to escort trains coming from the Humboldt.

Halleck was disturbed by Marshall's performance. "The failure of Major Marshall's recent campaign to the Forks of the Owyhee, I am satisfied in my intercourse with the civil authorities. . .has caused great dissatisfaction and has emboldened the Indians to commit new outrages." He ordered Marshall to go to the Bruneau Indians, raise 100 scouts from that supposedly friendly tribe to assist his soldiers, and punish the Snakes, driving them out of the Owyhee Mountains. "If old Winnemucca or Paulina should be captured," Halleck wrote, "they will be placed in close confinement for having violated their engagements and run away from the reservations."[25]

RATTLESNAKE CREEK, JULY 18, 1866

The Indians Jennings and Walker chased over Steens Mountain, moved into Harney Valley and northwest to the John Day and Crooked Rivers.

Paulina's people, who had left the Klamath Reservation, went to the area between the John Day and Crooked Rivers and east toward Harney Valley. As a result, the area that had been partially cleared of Indians by the army campaigns of 1864, was filling back up, and stock thefts were increasing. In the summer of 1866, Camp Watson was home to Company I, 1st Cavalry, under Captain Eugene M. Baker. Baker's right-hand man was Lieutenant Reuben F. Bernard. Bernard, born in Hawkins County, Tennessee, in 1834, joined the 1st Dragoons as a private in 1855, and participated in 15 fights before the Civil War took his regiment east. During the war, he fought in 65 more engagements. By the time Bernard reached Oregon in 1866, he was ready for his eighty-first battle. He got the opportunity in July.

On the nation's 90th birthday, Bernard was sent out from Camp Watson with forty-five men of Company I, to "pursue and punish" the Indians who were hiding out in the wilds of south central Oregon. He marched to Silvies River, to Harney Lake, around Malheur Lake and up the main fork of the Malheur River to the vicinity of present-day Drewsey, Oregon. From their camp on the Malheur, Lieutenant Bernard and fifteen men scouted to the north and west, returning the next morning. Upon return, he rested his detachment and sent out Sergeant Thomas W. Connor, in command of nineteen troopers, and guided by A. J. Boyd, to scout to the south and west. On the morning of July 18, Conner ran into a large camp of about 300 Paiutes under Weahwewa on upper Rattlesnake Creek, near the divide of the Malheur River and Harney Lake Valley. About eighty warriors protected the camp, but Connor barreled into them and drove them into the hills, killing thirteen, wounding many, including war chief Broken Knife, and capturing four horses and mules. Corporal William B. Lord was killed by a bullet in the chest.

Connor returned to the Malheur camp, and Bernard saddled up the whole command and returned to the battle site, accompanied by a party of forty-seven citizens from the Powder River settlements who were looking for the same Indians. Bernard left them at the abandoned campsite to destroy it, and continued hunting the Indians. He found them only a mile from where Connor had fought them, fortified in a deep canyon, but they fled as Bernard approached. He chased them west to the Silvies River, and captured two women, two children, and eleven horses and mules. A civilian cook, "became delirious and ran off," Bernard reported. The cavalrymen marched back to Camp Watson, concluding a scout that lasted twenty-six days and traveled about 630 miles. The official report noted that the operation "furnishes an example well worthy of imitation." On July 28, Bernard received his captaincy. In August, he was sent to Carlisle Barracks in Pennsylvania, and began two years of recruiting duty. He would not see battle again until posted to Arizona in 1869.[26]

Chapter 14 notes

1 Anderson, "Fourteenth Infantry," http://www.army.mil/cmh-pg/books/R&H/R&H-14IN.htm; Heitman, *Historical Register*, Vol. I, 643, 691; Freeman, *Lee's Lieutenants*, Vol. 2, 21; Hennessey, *Bull Run*, 21.

2 Letter Secretary of War, 50th Congress, Senate Ex. Doc. 70, 298; Anderson, "Fourteenth Infantry," http://www.army.mil/cmh-pg/books/R&H/R&H-14IN.htm.

3 Bancroft, *History of Oregon*, Vol. 2, 518; *Commissioner of Indian Affairs 1867*, 96; *Owyhee Avalanche*, November 11, 1865, February 24, 1866; *Idaho World*, December 2, 1865, February 24, 1866.

4 *Owyhee Avalanche*, December 2, 1865, February 17, 1866; *Commissioner of Indian Affairs 1867*, 96; Amanda Hall Depredation Claim #6762. Ontko, *Thunder Over the Ochoco III*, 298-304, tells an elaborate story of Andrew Hall trying to escape Indians in the wilderness, fighting a duel with Gray Head, in which both men died, and scout Archie McIntosh carrying Hall's body into Ruby City. It didn't happen. Hall recovered, returned to California in early 1867, and died there in 1891.

5 *Owyhee Avalanche*, February 17, 1866, March 3, 1866; Webb, *List of Engagements*, 24; *Idaho World*, February 24, 1866.

6 Bancroft, *History of Oregon*, Vol. 2, 518; Ontko, *Thunder Over the Ochoco III*, 308-09; *Commissioner of Indian Affairs 1866*, 187-88; Madsen, *Northern Shoshoni*, 44; *Idaho World*, March 3, 1866; *Owyhee Avalanche*, March 3, 1866.

7 Heitman, *Historical Register*, Vol. 1, 918; Gilliss, *So Far From Home*, 91; Wainwright, "First Regiment Cavalry," http://www.army.mil/cmh-pg/books/R&H/R&H-1CV.htm; Russell, *One Hundred and Three Fights*, 59; Letter Secretary of War, 50th Congress, Senate Ex. Doc. 70, 314; Bancroft, *History of Oregon*, Vol. 2, 519; *Owyhee Avalanche*, March 3, 1866.

8 *Oregon Sentinel*, March 31, 1866; *Owyhee Avalanche*, March 10, 1866; Hanley, *Owyhee Trails*, 67-68.

9 *Owyhee Avalanche*, March 10, 1866, March 17, 1866.

10 Bancroft, *History of Oregon*, Vol. 2, 520; *Idaho Statesman*, March 24, 1866; *Owyhee Avalanche*, March 28, 1866, May 5, 1866; *Commissioner of Indian Affairs 1867*, 97.

11 *Owyhee Avalanche*, March 31, 1866.

12 White to Marshall, May 4, 1866, RG 393, Dept. of Columbia. Letters Received, Box 3.

13 Owen R. Johnson Depredation Claim #10289; Chauncey D. Bacheler Depredation Claim #7239. Hill Beachey died in 1875. His only child, a daughter, Gray Beachey, who married Lt. Robert E. Lee Michie, 2nd Cavalry, co-filed a depredation claim with Owen Johnson in 1893.

14 *Idaho World*, June 2, 1866; Rusco, "Chinese Massacres," 3-4, 11; Hanley, *Owyhee Trails*, 212.

15 Hanley, *Owyhee Trails*, 53-54; Bancroft, *History of Oregon*, Vol. 2, 521; Rusco, "Chinese Massacres," 5-11; *Owyhee Avalanche*, May 26, 1866; *Oregon Sentinel*, June 16, 1866; Brackett, "Fighting in the Sierras," in Cozzens, *Eyewitnesses*, 5-6.

16 Rusco, "Chinese Massacres," 11, 13; *Commissioner of Indian Affairs 1867*, 97.

17 *Commissioner of Indian affairs 1867*, 97; Bork, *History of the Pacific Northwest*, http://www.usgennet.org/usa/or/coounty/union1/1889vol2/volumeIIpage21-31.htm; "Battle of Three Forks," Idaho State Historical Society, http://www.idahohistory.net/Reference%20Series/0239.doc. "The Snake War, 1864-1868," Idaho State Historical Society, http://www.idahohistory.net/Reference%20Series/0236.doc; Rusco, "Chinese Massacres," 13-14. The Philips killed in the battle may have been the same Philips badly wounded in Hobart's fight on the Malheur in July 1865.

18 Bancroft, *History of Oregon*, Vol. 2, 523; *Idaho World*, June 9, 1866; *Owyhee Avalanche*, June 2, 1866.

19 Cornelius Shea Depredation Claim #7644; Owen R. Johnson Depredation Claim #10289; *Owyhee Avalanche*, June 16, 1866; *Commissioner of Indian Affairs 1867*, 97.

20 Marszalek, *Lincoln's Armies*, 240; *Owyhee Avalanche*, June 23, 1866, June 30, 1866; Brackett, "Fighting in the Sierras," in Cozzens, *Eyewitnesses*, 5.

21 *Owyhee Avalanche*, June 23, 1866. The paper's use of the word "Lo" was quite common in the nineteenth century. It came from Alexander Pope's 1711, *Essay on Criticism*: "Lo! The poor Indian, whose untutored mind sees God in clouds, or hears him in the wind." Many early "politically incorrect" people found the phrase, "Lo! The poor Indian" funny or facetious, because they used it countless times on the frontier, with "Mr. Lo" sarcastically referring to Indians. The useage illustrates a bit of racial stereotyping and frontier humor, as well as showing that a good number of supposed country bumpkins were exposed to a classical education.

22 *Owyhee Avalanche*, June 23, 1866, June 30, 1866, July 7, 1866, July 14, 1866; *Oregon Sentinel*, July 21, 1866; *Commissioner of Indian Affairs 1867*, 97; Hanley, *Owyhee Trails*, 73-77. Dave Pickett is sometimes called Dan Pickett.

23 *Owyhee Avalanche*, July 7, 1866, July 14, 1866, July 21, 1866, July 28, 1866; *Commissioner of Indian Affairs 1867*, 97;

24 Webb, *List of Engagements*, 25; *Owyhee Avalanche*, August 11, 1866; *Oregon Sentinel*, August 25, 1866.

25 Letter Secretary of War, 50th Congress, Senate Ex. Doc. 70, 315-16.

26 Russell, *One Hundred and Three Fights*, 59-61; Ontko, *Thunder Over the Ochoco III*, 322; Webb, *List of Engagements*, 25; Letter Secretary of War, 50th Congress, Senate Ex. Doc. 70, 319-20; Bork, *History of the Pacific Northwest*, http://www.usgennet.org/usa/or/coounty/union1/1889vol2/volumeIIpage21-31.htm. There are two Rattlesnake Creeks in the area. Russell has incorrectly mapped the fight in the southeastern Oregon location.

Chapter 15
HIDE AND SEEK, 1866

The Snake War had been on for more than two years and it didn't appear that any progress had been made. Oregon and Washington volunteers had chased many Indians out of Oregon to northern Nevada in 1864. Nevada and California volunteers chased the Indians back into Oregon in 1865. Indians in the Owyhee Mountains of Idaho, ranged through portions of all three states and territories. When things got too hot, they moved farther west into Oregon. When Paulina's Paiutes abandoned the reservation, they moved farther east into Oregon. Dozens of Paiute bands crisscrossed the area, seeking food and shelter, and responding to military pressures. In the long term, the Indians were taking more casualties than the whites, and the soldiers in Nevada seemed to obtain better battle results—the people of Oregon and Idaho opined for similar efforts and effects.

The regulars had replaced the volunteers, but they did not appear to be an improvement. The civilians blew hot and cold on a whim; they praised or condemned the volunteers, depending on how much service they had done for the local communities, and they did the same with the regulars. Officers could be heroes one day and villains the next. Californians believed army policies favored Oregonians, while those of the mining districts of Boise, Owyhee, and Burnt River, accused General Halleck of favoring California, by distributing his troops to protect the Chico route. Halleck had visited the area, but had seen no Indians and met with few obstacles. He had heard many civilian complaints, and, other than trying to fine-tune General Steele's department, probably saw nothing to dissuade him from the thought that his administration had been efficient.

Halleck's interference only led to more opprobrium for Major Marshall. After being directed to strip Fort Boise of all but a skeleton force and establish a new post, Marshall left on July 16, and commenced building Camp Buford on the Bruneau River near the junction with the Snake. The people of Boise Valley did not like the idea that there would be less protection and less army business in their area; the people of Owyhee didn't see the Bruneau Shoshonis as a great threat, and the Bruneaus were themselves terrified of the hostile Paiutes and Bannocks. On August 3, while Marshall was preparing to leave on an expedition looking for Indians, he reported to General Steele that he would leave Captain Sinclair behind with his Company H, 14th

Infantry, to continue construction of Camp Buford. "He is making adobes at the rate of three thousand (3,000) per day," Marshall proudly reported, while Captain Coppinger was cutting lumber for a new post at the Three Forks of the Owyhee. Marshall said he would be taking thirty days' rations and would expect to get more at Camp C. F. Smith. "I go to the Goose Creek Mountains," he wrote, "where I expect to meet them in force." He asked for permission to have two pieces of artillery sent to each new camp, and asked if Captain Patrick Collins and his Company D could be shifted from Camp Warner to the Three Forks, where he expected the action to be. Marshall appeared satisfied with his progress, but apparently he had not fully followed Halleck's directive that the soldiers were to build posts from material found locally, and not contract out for supplies and laborers without authorization. When Marshall spent several thousand dollars erecting Camp Buford, a post that was only meant to be temporary, orders came to immediately suspend construction.[1]

HUNT'S FIGHTS, AUGUST 21, 26, 1866

No doubt frustrated, but with a fresh chance to prove his military prowess, Marshall gathered about 200 men with thirteen Bruneau guides, and on August 4, took the field looking for hostile Indians. He marched up the Bruneau, southeast toward the Goose Creek Mountains, but reports of hostile Indians in those mountains proved inaccurate. After skirting the northern fringe of the Goose Creeks, Marshall cut southwest, camping on August 10, in Duck Valley, inside the Nevada border. They then turned back north into Idaho Territory, going to the main Owyhee, to the South Fork, to Red Mountain, and to the North Fork. On August 21, Captain James C. Hunt, with Company M, 1st Cavalry, routed a small band of Indians and killed five, in Pleasant Valley, near the Oregon-Idaho line.[2]

Five days later, Hunt, with his 1st Cavalry, and remnants of Company B, 1st Oregon Cavalry, while on the Owyhee River south of the Three Forks area, came "upon seven Indians, all of which were killed." Hunt reported the fight was on the South Fork. The next day they turned about and marched 35 miles back toward the North Fork. Marshall doggedly followed the Indians' trails, but his marching and counter-marching apparently did little but drive his quarry out of the territory. Several more days of marching to every point on the compass brought them back to the Three Forks, where they camped on the last day of August. On the final leg to Camp C. F. Smith on September 3, two horses dropped dead of exhaustion.

Operating out of Camp C. F. Smith prior to Marshall's arrival, Captain Walker with fifteen men of the 14th Infantry, went up Steens Mountain pursuing Indians they believed were with Paulina. On August 10, Walker's abortive attack resulted only in his horse being shot dead underneath him. After that, Walker awaited Marshall's arrival and further instructions. Marshall's summer campaign received little publicity, likely because it was nearly devoid of results. The major allegedly told General Steele that, "while scouting on the south fork of the Owyhee, his command killed 35 Indians." In publications, such as the Yreka *Union*, the story was that Marshall had killed 30 Indians in the Goose Creek Mountains and won a battle in the vicinity of the Three Forks, after which he avenged his earlier failures by "hanging thirty-five captured savages to the limbs of trees."

The *Owyhee Avalanche* printed a similar story on September 8, stating that Marshall had killed thirty Indians in the Goose Creek Mountains, and captured two women, one horse, and two tons of provisions. Immediately following, it added a postscript that indicated several passengers had just arrived in Silver City, who had passed through Camp C. F. Smith three days earlier. While at the camp, they saw Marshall, Hunt, and 200 men resting before continuing the campaign. They talked freely with several members of Marshall's command, "and heard no mention made of any fight with the Indians or the killing of any," the *Avalanche* reported, "from which we conclude that the whole story was a fabrication to bolster the old hulk—Marshall." Captain Hunt, who accompanied Marshall the entire time, and whose command participated in the two skirmishes accounting for the deaths of twelve Indians, wrote absolutely nothing about any other large fights in the Goose Creek Mountains, or anywhere else, and nothing about capturing or killing thirty or more Indians.[3]

Poor Major Marshall apparently had no support from his own superior. General Steele had made four inspections of his department in 1866. The first trip took him around Puget Sound. In April, Steele went to Camp Watson, and with Company H, 1st Cavalry, under Lieutenant Edward Myers, and proceeded to Camp Currey and Malheur Lake, where Snakes drove off fifty-two packmules. Steele then went to Camp Lyon, Fort Boise, and returned to The Dalles, leaving Myers's company at Boise, which brought more complaints from the citizens of eastern Oregon. Steele, with Halleck, next inspected the forts along the lower Columbia River. In August, Steele was back at Fort Boise, then off to the Bruneau River, and over to the Owyhee mines. He passed through Ruby and Silver City about September 1. There, Steele "freely stated" to the Wasson Brothers that he could see no use for a post on the Bruneau where Marshall had begun construction, either forgetting, or omitting the fact that Halleck had ordered it. The Wassons inferred that Steele "does not approve of the general course of the present District Commander, and that a different policy must be adopted." Done muddying the water, Steele was off to look for a site for a new post in the Three Forks area.[4] Marshall was taking hits from all sides.

Regardless of the army operations taking place, depredations continued almost uninterrupted. In late July, two men, named Fisher and Drake, drove four-horse teams on the Chico route to Idaho, when Indians ambushed them six miles from Camp McGarry (Summit Lake), Nevada. Both men were badly wounded, but rescued by soldiers from the post. On August 9, Indians stole thirty-five head of work cattle from Shea's Ranch. On August 12, warriors killed Samuel Leonard, a miner from Mormon Basin, on Canyon Creek, a tributary of the Malheur River. Indians shot teamster James Grett on August 17, while he drove along Jordan Creek between Wagontown and Baxter's Ranch. On August 20, Indians attacked the Hay Ranch on Burnt River while the men were out in the field mowing, stealing supplies and food worth $300. The same day, more warriors attacked a party of prospectors camped, supposedly in safety, near Canyon City. Matthew Wilson was killed instantly and David Graham was severely wounded. Miners asked for help at Camp Watson, but the troopers were already out looking for other raiders. Camp Watson was hit on August 25, with the Indians stealing fifty-four army mules and eighteen beef cattle. The Indians then stole stock from Rock Creek Station, and attacked prospectors at Dixie Creek near Canyon City, killing one man.

In late August, Indians killed a station keeper at Summit Springs Station on the Humboldt Road, stole Hill Beachey's stock, and kept the keeper at Rebel Creek pinned down in his station, while unsuccessfully trying to burn him out. The loss of men and animals forced Beachey to temporarily close down his line the previous year, but this time he doggedly kept the stages running. On September 5, William J. Hill, current owner of the Owyhee Ferry, lost a horse and assumed travelers heading from the Owyhee mines to Virginia City, Nevada, had taken it. He overtook them at Summit Springs, 45 miles south of the ferry, but did not find his horse. On his return, only three miles from the ferry, Indians attacked him from behind a rye grass-covered bank. A bullet went through his right shoulder, but Hill slid off his horse and used it as a barrier. A swarm of arrows hit the horse, and one pierced Hill's left shoulder. Regardless, Hill kept firing his Henry Rifle, hit many warriors, left his horse, and ran to the ferry. The next day, a search party found the bodies of two Indians. Also in September, Indians stole horses from Clark Creek and Burnt River. In the last few days of the month, Indians, thought to be the Malheur Band of Snakes, raided Clarksville, a mining camp near Burnt River, and stole six horses. More horses were taken from California House on Burnt River, and from Glover's Ferry on the Snake at the mouth of the Powder.[5]

On September 13, Indians under Paulina attacked the Canyon City & Dalles Stage west of Mountain House. On board were $10,000 in greenbacks, 1,200 ounces of gold dust, $300 in gold coins, and a number of diamond rings. Bullets hit Henry C. Paige, a Wells Fargo messenger, in the side, and Henry Wheeler, the driver, in the face, tearing out his tongue. Although both badly wounded, the men managed to climb down and cut loose the lead horses to make their escape. Tall Man rode in quickly to stop them. He got within point blank range of Paige and pulled the trigger, but the pistol misfired. With the tables suddenly turned, Tall Man peered down the barrel of Paige's .38 Colt revolver. His pistol worked fine, and Tall Man fell dead with a shot to the head. Paige and Wheeler got on the two lead horses, but Paige was bucked off. Wheeler stopped to pull him aboard his horse, and the two men escaped. Paulina got the diamonds, greenbacks, coins, and horses. The gold dust was blowing to the winds.[6]

CLARK'S FIGHT, SEPTEMBER 15, 1866

James N. Clark was among the first men to settle in what was then Wasco County, when he built a house near the junction of Bridge Creek and the John Day River, which functioned as a stage station. Because of Indian trouble, and because his wife wanted to see her parents, Clark had recently sent his family

Author's photo

Site of Indian attack on Henry Wheeler and the Wells Fargo stage, Canyon City Road, Oregon.

to safety in the Willamette Valley. A short time later, Indians raided along the Canyon City Road and on September 13, as described above, attacked the Canyon City & Dalles Stage east of Clark's Ranch. The following day, Clark and his 18-year-old brother-in-law, George Masterson, were working in the fields and had just forded the John Day to gather firewood from a large tangle of driftwood that gathered at a sharp bend in river. They carried their firearms with them every day—except this one. Just when they crossed the river they saw about fourteen Indians riding toward the house, but were powerless to do anything. The Indians burned the house, stables, forty tons of hay, 1,000 bushels of barley and oats, and ran off two horses and a cow. Clark later estimated the losses at $6,494, and the remains of the house thus received the name it bears today—Burnt Ranch.

The raiders saw the two white men and chased them. Clark tried to tell young Masterson to rein in his horse and save him, for they might have a long ride, but George lashed him at full speed. Clark went just fast enough to keep out of range of the Indian arrows, and could see Masterson, who was ahead by a quarter-mile or more, but was slowly dropping back as his horse tired. Soon, Clark was even with Masterson and a warrior on a black horse was within ten yards of them. When the Indian raised his gun to fire, George jumped from his horse, called "O, Lord," and ran for Bridge Creek only a short distance away. The rest of the Indians were 50 yards behind, so the lead warrior continued after Clark, probably figuring that the other warriors would take care of the foolish man who jumped from his horse. Clark, however, who had saved his horse, soon outdistanced his pursuer, and Masterson made it to the creek, saw an overhanging bank draped with matted roots, dove in, and crawled underneath. "I was compelled to hide and secret myself in a creek," he said. He found a deep hole and tried to keep only his nose above water. The Indians "were very near me but did not discover me," Masterson said.

Clark rode eight more miles until finding a party of Canyon City packers with an escort of Warm Springs Scouts under Private Skanewa. At Clark's request, they joined forces and returned to look for Masterson, whom they found, nearly in a state of shock, but still alive.[7]

The Warm Springs Scouts returned to Camp Watson and Clark convinced the packers to join him to look for the Indians and try to recover some of his property. The eight men, including Clark, Perry Maupin, John Atterbury, John Bonham, William Thompson, and a shaken George Masterson, trailed the Paiutes, led by Ocheho, west up Cherry Creek and over to Trout Creek. About the same time, Weahwewa and Howluck were in the area raiding the Warm Springs Agency. They found the Wasco Chief Postaminie and his brother Quepama, with seven other Wascos and their families who had left the agency to hunt. Postaminie waved a white flag and tried to talk, but was gunned down. The other Wascos fled and Weahwewa stole seventy-seven horses. At dawn on September 15, Clark's party ran into Quepama's camp. Figuring they had caught Ocheho's raiders, they charged in, but some of the Wascos saw the attackers were white men and shouted out, "Warm Springs! Warm Springs! Wascos, Wascos!" Clark and Maupin recognized them and yelled, "For God's sake, boys, don't shoot!"

"We halted among them without firing a shot," Thompson said. The two parties exchanged stories and learned there were at least two raiding bands in the area, Ocheho's and Weahwewa's. That morning the Scott Brothers and five other men rode into the camp, also looking for stolen horses. Clark got Scott and his men and several Wascos to join him. Some of the Wascos believed Paulina was bullet-proof and could not be killed, but figured that maybe by going with the white men, who had "good medicine," they could kill him. Now there were about twenty well-armed men to take up the trail. The tracks they picked up were not Ocheho's, who was long gone, but that of Weahwewa, who did not expect the Wascos to follow him. Clark's party trailed south up Trout Creek into the Ochoco Mountains and over the divide down Little McKay Creek. About three in the afternoon, they found Weahwewa's camp at the junction of McKay and Allen Creeks. There looked to be about sixteen warriors. Clark and his men discussed if they should wait until the next morning, and take a chance on being discovered or the Indians pulling away in the night. The Wascos wanted to attack immediately, and

Clark thought the same, but added, "we might bite off more than we can chew." Regardless, they divided in two, with the Wascos going around to the west side to stampede the Snakes' horses.

The Wascos were nearly into the Snake horse herd before they were seen, and at that time, let out their war whoops and charged in. The whites burst in from the other side, shouting and shooting. The Wascos quickly drove off the horses and the Snakes were left on foot, running for the thick

A. R. Bowman Museum Crook County Historical Society, Prineville, Oregon
Burnt Ranch, ca. 1880

Author's photo
Burnt Ranch, Oregon, 2006.

woods nearby. Bill Thompson, with a bit of braggadocio, said this was his first Indian fight, but "I felt no fear and not so much excitement as when stalking my first buck." He dropped to his knee, took careful aim, and hit a great "big fellow" who "sprang into the air and fell, and I then knew I had made one 'good siwash,'" Thompson said. He later came to believe he had killed Bigfoot. Thompson then took his Colt pistol and, with the other whites, chased the Snakes into the timber. There, the Indians quickly regrouped and got in a good defensive position, where, to pursue them, Thompson claimed, "would have been madness." Clark called a halt to the attack and the Snakes crept through the trees and escaped. Two Wascos were wounded and four Snakes were dead, or soon to be. The Wascos caught one wounded Snake and scalped him alive. Thompson watched the process of running a knife around the head just above the ears and peeling the skin back. "That was the first I ever saw," he said, "and I had no desire to see the operation repeated."

After the fight, the Scott Brothers went back to looking for stolen livestock, the Wascos headed for Warm Springs, and Clark and his volunteers returned to Bridge Creek where he fully assessed the losses to his property. The ruins of "Burnt Ranch" smoldered until late September.[8]

At times it appeared that the civilians had better luck tracking down the Snakes than did the army. In August, Captain Richard F. O'Beirne, with Company E, 14th Infantry, marched from The Dalles along the Canyon City Road to Fort Boise, scouting the country along the way, but finding no Indians. From Boise, O'Beirne scouted the Burnt and Powder River regions, again with no result. In September, Captain Perry left the Three Forks area with fifty-three men of Company F, 1st Cavalry, and marched to Camp Lyon. He then went northwest to the Owyhee, found and destroyed a native fishery, and crossed over to the Malheur River. He trekked along the main and South Fork, across to the Silvies River, to Pilot Rock, over to Willow Creek and Burnt River, and back to Fort Boise. Five hundred miles and thirty-seven days later, he reported, "I saw no fresh signs." O'Beirne and Perry returned to Boise to the usual civilian scorn of unsuccessful army commanders.[9]

CAMP WATSON, SEPTEMBER 14, 1866

The army finally scored two small successes. On August 22, Indians ran off a number of mules from Camp Watson. The next day, Captain Eugene M. Baker, with thirty-five men of Company I, 1st Cavalry, chased the thieves 175 miles before catching up. They charged in, and the Indians saw them coming and fled, but not before shooting most of the mules with arrows to prevent their use by the army. Baker captured one woman, two children, and 13 mules, most of them pincusioned with arrows. "I also found where they had killed 17 of the animals," Baker reported. He returned to Camp Watson on September 2. After resting only a few days, Baker was back on the trail.

Author's photo

Donner und Blitzen River Valley.

On September 14, Baker ran into a small band of Snakes, killing one and capturing one.[10]

DONNER UND BLITZEN RIVER, SEPTEMBER 28, 1866

In early September, Major Marshall rested and refitted at Camp C. F. Smith while Jennings's civilian expedition broke up from internal discord. On September 10, Marshall marched out with three 1st Cavalry companies and stopped at old Camp Alvord the first night. The next morning, Marshall ordered Captain Hunt to take Company M and proceed across Steens Mountain to Donner und Blitzen River and wait for him there. The major took two companies west to newly established Camp Warner on the east side of Hart Mountain, reconnoitered, and headed back east. He never went to Donner und Blitzen River to meet Captain Hunt.

After leaving Marshall, Hunt marched along Steens Mountain, exploring for seven days before crossing over and selecting a campsite on the creek about 30 miles south of Malheur Lake. Then he waited. Running low of supplies, on September 25, Hunt sent a sergeant and twenty men back to Camp C. F. Smith, retaining twenty-eight men himself. Two nights after they left, about 100 Paiutes, under Winnemucca, surrounded Hunt. They did not attack, but cautiously watched the soldiers, probably to ascertain their numbers and see what they would do. They pulled back, but remained menacingly within striking distance. On September 28, an orderly and a guide, recently discharged from the 1st Oregon Cavalry, went out to scout the Indian position. About five miles from camp, warriors chased after them, but Lieutenant James Patton heard the firing and he and ten troopers rushed to their assistance.

The Indians fired and wounded Corporal Cooke and four horses. Patton dismounted in a well-suited defensive position and made a stand for three hours. They believed they had killed six Indians and wounded many more. When their ammunition supply dwindled, Patton had them all mount up and make a run for Hunt's camp, which they reached without further casualties. With few men and not knowing if and when his men and supplies would return, Hunt fortified his position and prepared for a siege, but the Indians did not attack. On October 5, the soldiers arrived with a pack train, and two days later, Hunt moved to the foot of Steens Mountain. The next day he moved eight more miles higher up the mountain to get a good view of the surrounding countryside. He moved to new camps several more days, searching for the major, but still, Marshall did not arrive. On October 12, he gave up and marched 28 miles back to Camp C. F. Smith. It goes without saying that many of the soldiers were extremely unhappy that their commander did not support them as he had promised.[11]

All the while these skirmishes occurred, the government and military tried to find a way to end the conflict. After the Civil War, Americans were tired of fighting, and by late spring of 1866, nearly one million men were mustered out of the volunteer services and the regular army consisted of about 33,000 men. Congress desired to trim the army and cut costs, but with the Western volunteers now out of the service, more regulars had to be recruited. On July 28, 1866, President Andrew Johnson signed an "Act to increase and fix the Military Peace establishment of the United States." While the artillery remained at five regiments, the infantry was increased from 19 to 45 regiments, and the cavalry regiments went from six to ten. The result was to increase the army strength by the summer of 1867, to nearly 57,000 men.[12]

The act had a special significance in the West, where the white population always clamored for more troops and protection. On August 2, 1866, General Halleck sent a telegraph to Washington that read: "Indian hostilities in the Owyhee country very serious. General Steele asks for reinforcements, but I have none to give. Can not authority be given to raise a regiment of cavalry, under recent law, on this coast?" Five days later, Halleck received orders to recruit one of the new regiments, the 8th Cavalry, wholly on the Pacific coast. The arrangement allowed many of the mustered out Californians and Oregonians to reenlist, and the 8th Cavalry received a significant number of officers and men with Indian-fighting experience. In addition, the act allowed the recruitment of 1,000 Indian scouts; 100 were allotted to the Department of Columbia.

All this took time. Oregon papers complained that General Steele was not doing enough. "As usual in such emergencies," stated the *Oregon Sentinel*, "assistance is not forthcoming, and it appears that the Government has scarcely enough here to garrison the posts, and none for active operations in the field. It is the old story over again." The papers called for Oregon Governor George L. Woods to call up state forces, and on October 7, Woods met with the legislature to pass a resolution that stated that if the federal government did not send troops to protect eastern Oregon within thirty days, Woods would call out state volunteers. Soon after Woods made General Steele aware of his intent, army recruiters came to the Willamette Valley, and men began to sign up in the 8th Cavalry.

Another facet of the reorganization affected the 14th Infantry. The 1st Battalion received a few more companies and retained its 14th Infantry designation. The 3rd Battalion, posted in Arizona, became the 32nd Infantry. The 2nd Battalion stayed in the Department of Columbia and became the 23rd Infantry. Officers were also shuffled around, with Captains Samuel Ross, Henry deB. Clay, John J. Coppinger, John H. Walker, George K. Brady, James B. Sinclair, James Henton, George L. Browning, and Major Marshall assigned to the 23rd.[13]

General Steele could not get troops to the danger areas fast enough for the civilians, and even those already posted could not avoid reproach. The Dalles *Mountaineer* suggested that citizens of eastern Oregon organize their own "volunteer companies to protect the soldiers and animals at Camp Watson from the Indians." Lampooning the apparent uselessness of the troops there, the paper said that "the indolent or cowardly loons permit the red rascals not only to steal the animals from the Government corrals close by the fort, but either decline to, or dare not, sally out to rescue white settlers and travelers near there from murderous attack of savages who infest the road."

The *Owyhee Avalanche* continued its attacks on the army, blaming Major Marshall for not joining up with Captain Hunt, leaving him alone in the middle of Indian country, and not participating in the fight on Donner und Blitzen River. It believed that the military was "never properly managed" and questioned if the government would continue in service such men as Marshall.

The *Idaho World*, on the other hand, more or less defended Marshall, and believed the dismissed volunteer officers were the worst of the lot. For instance, the paper claimed that Lieutenant Henry Small "was as arrant a coward as ever quaked at the sight of an Indian. It said that Small once saw a scarecrow, thought it was an Indian, and "ran his horse for ten miles to escape." The *World* thought the regular army was much better officered than the volunteers. Nevertheless, it found a bugaboo in General Halleck. Ever since he inspected the territory, it reported, "there have been more and worse Indian outrages. . . ." Halleck, described as "the redoubtable hero of the failure of Shiloh," was said to have "made a so-called tour of observation through the country. . .accompanied by his aids, his black servants, and his wine and liquor cases. He rode in a covered wagon, so cleverly arranged that neither could he see any of the country. . .nor could anybody see him." As a result, the paper declared, Halleck returned to California with the conviction that there were already too many troops in the country and that more posts needed to be dismantled. What was needed, it preached, were more soldiers and winter campaigns to kill the Indians' stock and destroy their provisions. To fight Indians "by treaties and presents, and in short, unimportant summer campaigns, will never do."[14]

LONG VALLEY, OCTOBER 3, 1866

Hoping to end such verbal abuse, plans were made to expand the military campaigns into the fall and winter. Operating out of Camp Bidwell, Lieutenant John F. Small moved 25 miles east into Long Valley, Nevada, with a detachment of Company A, 1st Cavalry. On October 3, Small hit a Paiute camp and reported killing eight Indians with no loss of his own.[15]

SPRAGUE RIVER, OCTOBER 5, 1866

The last surviving unit of the 1st Oregon Infantry, Company I, under Captain F. B. Sprague, was still in service and based at Fort Klamath in the fall of 1866. The area was comparatively peaceful, but the Klamaths and Modocs felt somewhat threatened ever since Howluck talked Paulina into leaving the reservation back in April 1866. Occasionally, Paiutes approached the Klamath Reservation looking for stock to steal or putting out peace feelers, depending on circumstances. On October 3, Agent Lindsay Applegate met with a band of Paiutes that had come in to talk.

Prior to the council, Applegate said he had little confidence in their professions of friendship, believing they only wished a truce so that they could camp within 40 miles of the agency in Sprague River Valley where they could secure winter supplies and communicate with hostile bands east of them. He had little reason to trust them, for several of them, including Biting Bear, Lame Dog, and Black Buffalo, had already signed one treaty back in the summer of 1865. This time, Pony Blanket (Egan), of the Togwingani band, and Biting Bear met with Applegate and again insisted that they wanted peace. Applegate countered that they must come to the Council Grove at the agency where they could be cared for and protected. The Paiutes agreed, came in, talked, got supplies, and assured the agent that they talked with a "straight tongue." They stayed one day, and the following night, they ran off, stealing horses and guns belonging to the "Yahuskins" and Klamaths. Captain Sprague had sent out a wagon train to bring in the Paiute property to the agency, but he recalled it. Instead, he sent out Lieutenant Harrison B. Oatman with a detachment of Company I, on a scout to Sprague River to try and round up the Paiutes and recover the stolen property. On October 5, Oatman caught up with a rear guard of Paiutes on Sprague River and killed four, but the rest got away with the stolen items.[16]

Depredations continued as usual. On October 1, Indians again hit Con Shea's place on Sinker Creek, stealing sixteen head of work horses and mules, and twenty pack mules, valued at $3,900. On October 3, Paulina's warriors unsuccessfully tried to run off stock from Alkali House on the Canyon City Road, but were warded off by some straight-shooting teamsters. The next day they hit Pennington's Ranch 12 miles farther down the road, but were driven off by a party of soldiers who had stopped there for the night. In October, either Bruneau Indians or the Paiutes they claimed to be so afraid of, stole eleven horses from prospectors on Rock Creek, near the Snake River.

On October 7, John Dixon and Frank Osgood were hunting ducks on Cow Creek, not far from Inskip's Station. They saw plenty of Indian tracks and decided they had better get out quick, when their dog began to bark. The men tried to escape, but the Indians were on them and firing, and Dixon fell with a bullet through his heart. Osgood ran to the creek and hid in some large tules on the bank. A bold warrior entered the tangle, and Osgood watched him part the vegetation with his bow just ten feet away, when he fired his load of birdshot right into the Indian's breast. He shifted position, but the Indians kept trying to ferret him out. When another warrior parted the tules right near Osgood, he let him have a full load of shot, much as the first time. After this, the Indians backed off, and Osgood half crawled and swam his way four miles to Inskip's. He made it inside, "wet up to his armpits, and pale, and when he related what happened he wept like a child." The Indians attacked Inskip's that night, but were driven off.[17]

HARNEY LAKE VALLEY, OCTOBER 14, 1866

In another small success that hardly seemed to compensate for all the Indian raids, Captain Eugene Baker defeated some Paiutes, probably from Weahwewa's band. At the time Paulina ranged from the upper Deschutes River, across Crooked River, and to the upper John Day. Weahwewa, half-brother of Paulina, generally ranged along the Malheur and Burnt Rivers and around Harney Lake. Howluck covered the territory between Goose Lake in the west, the Owyhee River in the east, and as far as the Humboldt River in the south. Winnemucca ranged across northern Nevada to the Owyhee River in the east, and across southeast Oregon. With men of Company I, 1st Cavalry, Baker scouted out of Camp Watson, and on October 14, hit a Paiute camp in Harney Lake Valley, killing three and wounding eight warriors, with a loss of one trooper wounded.[18]

LAKE ABERT, OCTOBER 26, 1866

As Lieutenant Colonel Drew and Captain Sprague discovered in 1865, the area around Warner Mountain and Christmas Lakes appeared to be a prime rendezvous for many Snake bands. When Camp Warner was built there, the Indians lost one of their last refuges. On October 15, Captain Sprague sent an expedition to reconnoiter the area. Utilizing three Klamath scouts under Chief Blow, as authorized by the July 1866 act, Lieutenant

Author's photo

Abert Rim, Oregon.

Harrison Oatman and twenty-two men of Company I, 1st Oregon Infantry, with hospital steward George A. Summers, left Fort Klamath for the 153-mile march to Camp Bidwell, California. They reached the post, joined up with Lieutenant John F. Small, with twenty-five men of Company A, 1st Cavalry, and on the October 22, marched out to find the Indians.

In overall command, Small led them north into Oregon, guided by Chief Blow. They searched Warner Valley and the Christmas Lakes in vain for two days, when they decided to head west across the mountains. They traversed twisting canyons for about 12 miles, crossing over Abert Rim and into the valley of the Chewaucan River by a route thought never before traveled by white men. In front of them was Lake Abert, a high Great Basin lake, at 4,255 feet in elevation, one of only a handful of Basin lakes that is full of water year round.

About 11 a.m. on October 26, the command saw Indians ahead, about two and a half miles beyond the point they entered the valley. The Paiutes, from Tecolote's (Ground Owl) Band, saw them too, and ran for the mountains where they had chosen a good defensive position up on Abert Rim. Small's command passed through the hastily abandoned camp of about fifteen lodges and moved uphill. Small dismounted his cavalry and joined Oatman's foot soldiers to climb up the rocky slopes to attack. Leaving the horses behind with a guard, Small took one squad to the right and Oatman took one to the left, and they advanced on two sides of a canyon that about seventy-five Paiutes had entered. The fight began at noon and lasted three hours. The soldiers slowly worked their way up, dodging and shooting from behind rocks, while the Indians, "well supplied with firearms" according to Oatman, returned fire and slowly fell back. Chief Blow (Oatman spelled it "Blogue") and his Klamaths were conspicuous, a fact noted by the Paiutes,

Author's photo

Soldier Creek, Oregon.

who were angry that Indians they were somewhat friendly with, would guide white soldiers to their hideout. When several Paiutes hid in a cave, Blow was in the forefront trying to root them out, and the Oregon Volunteers commented on his bravery. John Sargent of the 1st Oregon, and another soldier were wounded, along with one Klamath scout when a rifle bullet grazed his chin. Small and Oatman routed the Indians, killed fourteen warriors, wounded about twenty-eight, and captured three women and four children.

After the fight, the soldiers destroyed the Indian lodges, which Oatman believed to have been recently stocked as a winter quarters. They marched about two miles from the fight scene that evening and camped. That night, in what Oatman called "pitchy darkness," the Paiutes returned and fired into their camp, causing a commotion and forcing Small to opt for a night move to a new camp location with better natural defenses. The next morning, figuring they had accomplished their goal, the command returned to Bidwell, reaching there on October 29. Tecolote was badly wounded, captured, and killed by the Klamaths. The Paiutes vowed revenge.[19]

Back in July, General Halleck had ordered the construction of two new posts in the Owyhee District. Major Marshall began construction on Camp Buford on the Bruneau, which turned out to be an ill-advised location. The second was finally begun in September, by Captain John J. Coppinger, of the newly formed 23rd Infantry. Coppinger, born in Ireland, moved to New York, and joined the 14th Infantry in 1861. He served in that regiment throughout most of the Civil War, until becoming colonel of the 15th New York Cavalry in January 1865. He received brevets for gallant and meritorious service at the Battles of Trevilian Station and Cedar Creek, and would also be cited for "zeal and energy" in the upcoming Indian battles he would participate in. Coppinger later became a major general of volunteers in the Spanish

American War before retiring in 1898. In late summer of 1866, however, Coppinger was given the task of selecting and building that long-awaited second post in the Owyhee country.

The main road from the Humboldt went north to Owyhee Ferry and east up Jordan Creek. Seeking to cut the distance, travelers and stages were trying a shorter, but more dangerous route that left the main road north of Camp McDermit and cut northeast across country, roughly following Big Antelope Creek, to the Three Forks area, one of the few places that the Owyhee could be forded.

General Steele ordered Coppinger to establish a winter camp in the area and "to build a block house at the Three Forks." On September 26, Coppinger established Camp Winthrop on Soldier Creek at the southwestern base of South Mountain, just inside the Idaho border. He never got around to building the blockhouse at the Three Forks, about 16 miles southwest, but since the road through that area was seldom used, few people were affected. The demand for a post at Three Forks was solved the next April, simply by renaming Camp Winthrop as Camp Three Forks. The single post was confusingly known as Camp Soldier Creek, Camp Winthrop, and Camp Three Forks. The situation was no less confusing to many civilians. Julia Gilliss, wife of Captain James Gilliss, 5th Artillery, wrote from Fort Stevens to her sister in Washington D. C., "I never saw such a mixed up Department; they don't seem to know what to do. All the summer they have been busy breaking up and abandoning posts, selling off at sacrifices, and transporting property at great costs and now they are refitting the same places. . . ."[20]

O'BEIRNE'S FIGHT, MALHEUR COUNTRY, OCTOBER 30, 1866

After the army reorganization, Captain Richard F. O'Beirne, who was with the 14th Infantry, became a captain in the 32nd Infantry in September 1866. While much of his newly constituted regiment was serving in Arizona, O'Beirne was still posted to Idaho Territory. On October 13, O'Beirne left Camp Three Forks with a mounted detachment of Company E, 23rd Infantry, in search of hostile "Snake" Indians.

The scout took him into what was reported as "the Malheur country" of western Malheur County and eastern Harney County, Oregon. O'Beirne, heading northwest from Three Forks, got twisted around in the lava beds just beyond the western bend of the Owyhee River. The sojourn proved beneficial, however, for they captured an old Indian who had been left behind by the band as being too old and infirm to keep up. Instead of stoically accepting his fate, the old man sought revenge against those who had abandoned him and volunteered to guide the soldiers to their rendezvous. Heading toward the Malheur River on October 30, the mounted infantrymen found and attacked the unsuspecting camp. They killed two Paiutes, probably of Weahwewa's band, wounded eight, and captured one man, three women, and

Near the site of the Owyhee Ferry, at the mouth of Jordan Creek, Oregon.

four children. The soldiers also rounded up thirty-eight horses, two mules, an ox, and a large amount of camp supplies and ammunition. Two soldiers had minor wounds, and one civilian, S. C. Thompson, was fatally wounded. No word was reported of what became of the turncoat Paiute.[21]

TROUT CREEK CANYON, NOVEMBER 1, 1866

Captain John Walker apparently was one of the few officers that the *Owyhee Avalanche* spoke well of, one reason likely being that the gregarious captain frequently communicated news of army operations with the Wasson Brothers, often visiting them in Silver City on his way to and from Fort Boise. For the past few months, Walker was in command at Camp C. F. Smith on Whitehorse Creek, and was one of those transferred to the 23rd Infantry with the reorganization. Walker visited the Wassons on September 20, and told them that five days earlier he had been in the Trout Creek Mountains and destroyed an Indian camp and a large amount of provisions. He lamented, however, that he could not do as thorough a job as he would have liked. Soon, however, he expected to have a full company of cavalry, "and then he will be enabled to punish Lo for past depredations." Walker said there was no trouble in finding Indians, "but his command has been composed of poorly mounted infantry, and not enough of them for post and field duty."

Walker returned to Camp C. F. Smith after obtaining supplies at Fort Boise, and by late October, he had his cavalry. On October 30, with Walker's soldiers now well-mounted, the Paiutes chose a bad time to raid the post granary. The next day, Walker took a detachment of Company C, 23rd Infantry, with all the horses available, and with a detachment of Company H, 1st Cavalry, led them south into the Trout Creek Mountains. On November 1, working his way up Trout Creek east of Mahogany Ridge, Walker had nearly reached the Nevada border when he found sign of another Paiute camp, not far from the site he destroyed in September. Leaving the main body at the canyon entrance, Walker took Private Robinson of Company H, Messrs. Reid and Griffith of the quartermaster department, and a civilian guide named Drake, up the narrow canyon to scout the Paiute position. They twisted up the canyon about three miles and suddenly came upon about thirty Indians. With no time to return for help or plan a maneuver, Walker and his small party charged. Eleven warriors immediately counter-attacked, but Walker's men shot and killed four in the first few seconds. The remaining Indians fled, but not before three more were wounded. With no loss of his own, Walker was victorious. He destroyed the camp equipage and rode back to Camp C. F. Smith. In General Orders No. 1, on January 1, 1867, General Steele cited Walker for gallantry. For the dispossessed Paiute band, it would be a cold, hard winter.[22]

How drastically different cross-country trips through Indian country could be is illustrated by two stages that ran between Ruby City, Idaho, and Virginia City, Nevada, only weeks apart. If a traveler went unscathed or was killed was merely a matter of chance. J. W. Hadlock paid his $60 fare to ride Hill Beachey's stage from Ruby City to Hunter's Station, east of Virginia City, where he picked up the Pioneer Stage Company coach to continue his journey west. Along the route he paid 75 cents to one dollar for meals at the various stations. The road, he said, "was good, hard, and was comparatively free from dust." Safe in San Francisco in mid-October, Hadlock said, "I consider the route a safe and good one." He concluded: "I saw no Indians on the route, and I think the danger exists more in imagination and rumors than in fact." It was the kind of letter the stage companies wanted to publicize to attest to the safety of using their routes.

On November 8, another stage pulled out of Silver City on its way to Virginia City. At 10 a.m. Indians attacked the coach about four miles east of Owyhee Ferry. The warriors fired a volley while concealed behind a rock wall they had built near the road. One bullet tore into passenger W. Wilcox's chest.

"Oh my God, I'm killed!" he cried out, and his head slumped onto George Harrington's knee. Seconds later, Harrington caught a bullet in the left hip. One bullet tore through the carriage and clipped driver Wash Waltermire in the side, causing a minor wound. Waltermire whipped the horses into a run, but galloped right into a mounted party of Indians who were waiting down the road. He tried to go around them, but was soon caught by the band that had first fired on the stage. Now, two groups of warriors were on both sides, trying to catch the stage in between. As Wash whipped the horses, guard James McRae fired his carbine, keeping the Indians at bay for about two miles. A bullet hit one of the wheel horses and it fell, dragging the stage to a halt. Two other horses were wounded. While Wash unhitched the horses,

McRae kept firing, and Harrington got out of the coach, assisted by the last two passengers, J. M. Holland and P. Casey.

They tried to get on the horses, but the spooked animals bolted; one ran off and the other two were unmanageable. The men stumbled and ran the last two miles to the ferry. As they approached, the employees and soldiers stationed there heard the firing and prepared for action. When the breathless survivors came in, a Sergeant Brown, eleven soldiers, and four station men, hurried back to the stage. The Indians were already gone, but not before they had cut out Wilcox's heart, scalped him, and stripped his clothes. They cut up the mail sacks and tossed the mail to the wind, but did not have enough time to destroy the coach. The soldiers buried Wilcox, pulled the stage to the station and repaired it. Harrington was cared for, and by that evening, with a fresh team of horses, the stage continued its journey.[23]

Given such disparate examples, it would be almost impossible to make generalizations about a typical stage trip. Certainly, most travelers got through unscathed, but the significant numbers who were attacked illustrate the very real dangers of travel through Indian country.

On the last day of October 1866, Paiutes attacked Frederick P. Brougham as he drove a herd of cattle from Silver City to Camp McDermit, running off twelve work cattle valued at $100 each. On November 12, Indians raided Walter's Ferry on the Snake River on the Silver City to Boise road. Chauncey Bacheler, who had lost his ferryboat and horses to the Paiutes the previous May at Owyhee Crossing, moved to a "safer" spot closer to Fort Boise. This time the Indians got two more of his horses. It was not the first time Indians have "cleaned him out," reported the *Avalanche*. "We sympathize with the losers," the paper said, "but are truly glad that these pets are coming in to denser settlements." The reason being, the editor hoped, was that if more raids were made closer to Fort Boise, it might "put a taste in the mouths of the people and teach the editor of the *World* that Major Marshall's Summer campaign was not a success but a miserable failure. . . ."

According to the *World*, however, the *Avalanche* was just angry about Major Marshall "preferring to attend to his military duties, instead of making his soldiers vote as the *Avalanche* would like them to." The *World* insisted Marshall was a real soldier, and not a politician.[24]

The ongoing feud between the two papers was a microcosm of a broader, but similar disagreement in public opinion between the West and the East. The farther removed geographically, the less the Indians appeared to be a problem, and the more the military appeared to be the cause of all the troubles. The perception was the reality.

FORT KLAMATH, ca NOVEMBER 17, 1866

In November 1866, Paiutes under Paulina threatened to attack the Indians at the Klamath Reservation in revenge for Klamath scouts assisting the soldiers in the battle the previous month at Lake Abert. Modocs who had been in communication with the Snakes, brought word to Agent Applegate that a large Snake force was near Goose Lake and about to move on the agency. Paulina's warriors invaded the Sprague River Valley, where lived the Modoc, Schonchin, who was friendly to the whites. The Paiutes stole some of his horses, but the 70-year-old man and some of his warriors pursued the raiders and captured two "Snake" women. Agent Applegate was certain there would be fighting, commenced building fortifications around the agency, and asked for enlisted men from Fort Klamath to help defend it.

When Applegate reported the news to the fort commander, Captain Sprague, 1st Oregon Infantry, Sprague reported to headquarters at Fort Vancouver that he did not have enough men to defend the reservation and pursue the Indians. In the middle of November, Paulina's warriors advanced down the Sprague River, approaching within a few miles of Fort Klamath before confronting a force of Company I, 1st Oregon Infantry, under Lieutenant Harrison B. Oatman, and friendly Klamath and Modoc Indians. Paulina's men were no match for them. At a cost of two enlisted men wounded, the Oregonians and their Indian allies killed thirteen Paiutes and wounded about twenty more. Paulina retreated to southeastern Oregon to plan his next moves.[25]

The men of Company I, the last of the Oregon Volunteer Infantry still left in service, waited in anticipation for their release. The men, according to the *Sentinel*, "are heartily tired of camp duty, and desirous to quit the service," where they could take up "more useful" avocations in life. "There was no reason, whatever, for continuing them in service," said the paper, "when there were plenty of regulars to take their place." Plans were made several times for them to be relieved at Fort Klamath, by a company of the 1st or 8th U.S. Cavalry, but something always happened to delay the move. In fact, Company C, 8th Cavalry, was a prime candidate to replace it, which would have brought back a familiar face to Fort Klamath. Captain William Kelly, who had been in Company C, 1st Oregon Cavalry, during the Civil War and spent much of his time at Fort Klamath, mustered out on July 28, 1866. On the same day he enlisted as a captain in the 8th Cavalry. Coincidentally, he was assigned a captaincy in Company C, and, in December 1866, found himself again on the road to Fort Klamath.

Kelly marched from Fort Vancouver to Oakland, Oregon, about two-thirds of the way to Fort Klamath, when he received orders to turn around and march back, reportedly by order of General Halleck, because the roads and weather were bad. The *Oregon Sentinel* picked up on this questionable action and, like many other newspapers, ridiculed the army for mismanagement. Halleck's order to turn Kelly around was an excuse of "trifling balderdash," and his reasoning was said to be "doubtless, a piece of consummate strategy, such as he displayed when he didn't capture Beauregard at Corinth." The paper called him an "old fossil," and said if he "had the sense he was born with, he would have known that the journey of Kelly's company back to Vancouver, from Oakland, was as severe as from Oakland to Fort Klamath, and no less expensive; and their relief of Captain Sprague's company would have saved the Government thousands of dollars." The *Sentinel* went on to sarcastically say that Company I, and Jacksonville, owe "'Old Brains' an india rubber medal for his last brilliant strategic movement."[26]

Neither the Indians nor the civilians showed the military much respect.

JOHN DAY RIVER, NOVEMBER 18, 1866

Skirmishes occurred all across Oregon. When Paiutes, possibly of Weahwewa's band, stole three head of cattle from Fields's Ranch on the South Fork John Day, civilians reported the theft to Captain Baker at Camp Watson. Baker sent out Lieutenant John Barry with ten men of Company I, 1st Cavalry, to find the thieves. On the upper John Day on November 18, they found a camp where the hungry Indians were drying the beef they had just killed. Barry charged in, killed three warriors and wounded one. The Indians never got to finish their supper. In the camp, Barry captured three horses, one of them recently stolen from the stage company. He burned the camp and returned to the post.[27]

The increased troop presence and continuous scouting did not seem to deter the raiding. On November 15, Indians ran off cattle from Dean and Bayley's Ranch on Dixie Creek, Idaho Territory, but the cattle were recovered. On November 20, a dozen of Ocheho's warriors attacked a party of hunters on Canyon Creek, about six miles from Canyon City, killing J. Kester. On November 23, Indians attacked Fruit's Ferry on the Snake River and cut loose the boat. Two miles away they crept up on two men, C. G. Waltse and a Mr. Walsh, who were camped on an island in the Snake. About one in the morning their dog barked and alerted them that something was up. Believing coyotes were around, Walsh got his gun and went to drive them off, receiving a bullet in his groin for his efforts. He and Waltse hid in the bushes until dawn, and then went to the ferry for help. Indians stole four of their mules.

The same day, Indians attacked four men on the Boise Road. Frank McCoy, R. Hall, and J. C. Adams were each driving a four-mule team laden with freight, while a man named Sims was riding horseback with them. About two in the afternoon, while they were doubling teams to ascend a hill in the canyon near Reynolds Creek, Indians opened fire on them. Bullets hit McCoy in the wrist, mouth and heart, killing him instantly. Sims escaped north to the ferry. Adams was shot in the hand, but he and Hall ran into the rocks and kept up a return fire with the few rounds they had—the rest was packed away in a wagon they could not reach. After a short time, Levi H. Mays rode up from Reynolds Creek, counted 11 Indians shooting at men in the rocks, fired three times at them, and rode for help, reaching another train two miles south on Reynolds Creek.

The Indians ransacked the freight wagons, which were the property of Hall. They stole all the mules, the entire load of flour and oats from one wagon, and ripped up several other sacks before other white men began arriving. Hall's losses amounted to about $3,000. McCoy had a wife and three children in Walla Walla, and he had just sold out his business in Owyhee with the intention of taking his money, gathering his family, and returning to the States. Rescuers found his body "stripped of clothing and his head mashed." He was buried near Fruit's Ferry on the Snake.

About the same time, Indians stole fourteen cattle from upper Sinker Creek, which heads near War Eagle Mountain and flows northeast to the Snake. Between there and the site of McCoy's murder, they jumped a lone Chinese miner, killed him, and chopped off his arms and legs. Also on or about November 23, warriors attacked a cabin on Sinker Creek owned by two Frenchmen. They tried to force the men out by throwing small logs down the chimney, and in broken English, cursing at them, threatening to burn them out, and daring them to come out and fight. In terror, the men waited for the assault that never came. The Indians left after doing some minor damage to the surrounding structures.[28]

CAMP WATSON, DECEMBER 3, 1866

Posted at Camp Watson for much of 1866, Captain Baker with Company I, 1st Cavalry, and Lieutenant Amandus C. Kistler, with Company F, 14th (now 23rd) Infantry, were among the few units to guard The Dalles to Canyon City Road. Baker's right-hand man was Sergeant Thomas W. Connor, who was instrumental in Lieutenant Bernard's victory over the Paiutes at Rattlesnake Creek in July. On December 1, Paiutes drove off a civilian packmule train on the Canyon City Road. When notified, Baker ordered Sergeant Connor and nineteen cavalrymen to pursue them. As they followed the trail, snow began to fall, dropping temperatures, but making for easier tracking. Connor finally overtook the Indians on December 3, "during a violent snowstorm, 70 miles from the post."

In the frigid dawn, Connor noticed the Indians were already up and preparing to break camp and he had to act fast. His troopers dismounted and moved in from two sides, but when they tried to shoot, most of the weapons, which had gotten wet and frozen, snapped and missed fire. Connor quickly called for all to mount up, draw sabers, and charge. The Snakes were caught by surprise, but many tried to hold their ground and fire at the charging troopers. They, however, were plagued by the same problem as the soldiers—their guns popped and fizzled. In seconds, Connor's men were upon them, slashing with sabers and running down individual Indians as they fled into the blizzard.

In a short time, fourteen Indians were dead and five women and children captured. Connor recovered all the stolen mules except two that had been killed and eaten. An additional seventeen mules were taken, along with eleven horses, and a large amount of dried meat and camp equipage was destroyed. Connor returned to Camp Watson after a march of 180 miles. The hungry Indians were deprived of their sustenance, but instead of teaching them a lesson, it only served to make them more needy, and more likely to commit further thefts.[29]

On December 5, Sergeant J. T. Buckley and a detachment of Company A, 1st Cavalry, had a skirmish with a small band of Paiutes near Surprise Valley, California, but no Indian loss could be determined. At 3 a.m. on December 16, twenty Indians again attacked Ruby Ranch in Jordan Valley, Oregon, capturing the corral and stables before the occupants of the house awoke. They drove the stock out and set the stable ablaze before the whites began firing at the marauders, outlined by the flames. George Barry claimed that they killed one Indian and wounded others. The shooting kept up until dawn, when the Indians rode away, leaving the rock and log house riddled with bullet holes and stuck with arrows. The raiders got all the cattle, but after daylight, the civilians pursued them and recovered all the stock. "Where are the soldiers?" the *Oregon Sentinel* asked.[30]

When the snowstorms began in December, the raiding slackened. The Indians sought shelter, and the soldiers, if events followed their usual course, probably thought they would cease campaigning and go into winter quarters. This time, however, it would be different.

Chapter 15 notes

1 Bancroft, *History of Oregon*, Vol. 2, 522; *Owyhee Avalanche*, August 18, 1866; Bork, "History of the Pacific Northwest," http://www.usgennet.org/usa/or/county/union1/1889volumellpage24; Marshall to AAG, August 3, 1866, RG 393, Dept. of Columbia, Letters Received, Box 2; Letter Secretary of War, 50th Congress, Senate Ex. Doc. 70, 316; *Commissioner of Indian Affairs 1866*, 38, 188-89.

2 *Owyhee Avalanche*, September 8, 1866; *Commissioner of Indian Affairs 1866*, 189; Hunt to McGregor, November 25, 1866, RG 393, Dept of Columbia, Letters Received, Box 2; Webb, *List of Engagements*, 26. Hunt said the fight was in Paradise Valley, and Webb listed the fight at "Paradise Valley, Ore." There is no Paradise Valley in this section of the state; Hunt probably meant Pleasant Valley.

3 Bancroft, *History of Oregon*, Vol. 2, 522; *Adjutant General's Office*, 24; *Commissioner of Indian Affairs 1867*, 98; Rusco, "Chinese Massacres," 14; *Owyhee Avalanche*, September 8, 1866; Hunt to McGregor, November 25, 1866, RG 393, Dept. of Columbia, Letters Received, Box 2. Ontko, *Thunder Over the Ochoco III*, 327, says the 35 Indians killed were from Black Eagle's camp near Yreka Butte in present southeast Deschutes County.

4 Bancroft, *History of Oregon*, Vol. 2, 526-27; *Owyhee Avalanche*, September 8, 1866.

5 *Commissioner of Indian Affairs 1867*, 98; Cornelius Shea Depredation Claim #7644; Bancroft, *History of Oregon*, Vol. 2, 523; *Owyhee Avalanche*, September 8, 1866, September 15, 1866.

6 Bancroft, *History of Oregon*, Vol. 2, 523; *Idaho World*, September 29, 1866; Ontko, *Thunder Over the Ochoco III*, 332-33. Ontko states the attack on the stage took place on 9 September, the *World* reported the attack was on September 12, but James N. Clark, who was directly involved, reports it occurring on the 13th, as he found one of the stolen mail bags on his property the following day. See James N. Clark Depredation Claim #1721.

7 James N. Clark Depredation Claim #1721; Thompson, *Reminiscences of a Pioneer*, 48-51.

8 Clark, "McKay's Journal, Part I," 125; Ontko, *Thunder Over the Ochoco III*, 333-37; Thompson, *Reminiscences of a Pioneer*, 51-57; James N. Clark Depredation Claim #1721.

9 Bancroft, *History of Oregon*, Vol. 2, 525; Perry to McGregor, October 22, 1866, RG 393, Dept. of Columbia, Letters Received, Box 3.

10 Webb, *List of Engagements*, 26; Baker to AAG, September 4, 1866, RG 393, Dept. of Columbia, Letters Received, Box 2.

11 Webb, *List of Engagements*, 26; *Adjutant General's Office*, 24; *Commissioner of Indian Affairs 1867*, 98; *Owyhee Avalanche*, October 27, 1866; Hunt to McGregor, November 25, 1866, RG 393, Dept. of Columbia, Letters Received, Box 2. The CIA and *Avalanche* both report Lieutenant Patton conducting the fight, but Heitman, *Historical Register*, lists no Patton in the 1st Cavalry.

12 Utley, *Frontier Regulars*, 12; Heitman, *Historical Register,* Vol. 2, 626.

13 Letter Secretary of War, 50th Congress, Senate Ex. Doc. 70, 320-21; Dunlay, *Wolves for the Blue Soldiers*, 44-45; Bancroft, *History of Oregon*, Vol. 2, 526-27; *Oregon Sentinel*, September 29, 1866; Anderson, "Fourteenth Infantry," http://www2.army.mil/cmh-pg/books/R&H/R&H-14IN.htm.

14 *Owyhee Avalanche*, October 27, 1866; *Idaho World*, October 6, 1866, October 13, 1866, November 3, 1866.

15 Webb, *List of Engagements*, 26; *Adjutant General's Office*, 24. John Small should not be confused with Henry Small of the Oregon Cavalry.

16 Letter Secretary of War, 50th Congress, Senate Ex. Doc. 70, 325; Ruby and Brown, *Pacific Northwest*, 207; *Commissioner of Indian Affairs 1867*, 91-92; Ontko, *Thunder Over the Ochoco III*, 342; Webb, *List of Engagements*, 26. Lieutenant Oatman was the cousin of Olive Oatman, who was captured by Indians in 1851.

17 *Idaho World*, October 20, 1866; *Owyhee Avalanche*, October 18, 1866, November 3, 1866; Cornelius Shea Depredation Claim #7644; Bancroft, *History of Oregon*, Vol. 2, 523.

18 Clark, "McKay's Journal, Part I," 139; Webb, *List of Engagements*, 26; *Adjutant General's Office*, 25. The former source lists eight Indians wounded; the latter lists eight captured.

19 Bancroft, *History of Oregon*, 528-29; Ontko, *Thunder Over the Ochoco III*, 344; *Commissioner of Indian Affairs 1867*, 99-100; Oatman to Sprague, October 31, 1866, RG 393, Dept. of Columbia, Letters Received, Box 2; *Oregon Sentinel*, December 1, 1866; *Adjutant General's Office*, 25; "First Regiment of Cavalry," http://www2.army.mil/cmh-pg/books/R&H/R&H-1CV.htm; *Owyhee Avalanche*, December 8, 1866.

20 Heitman, *Historical Register*, Vol. 1, 327; "Camp Three Forks," Idaho State Historical Society, http://www.idahohistory.net/Reference%20Series/0358.doc; Gilliss, *So Far From Home*, 105.

21 *Secretary of War 1868-69*, 770; Anderson, "Fourteenth Infantry," http://www2.army.mil/cmh-pg/books/R&H/R&H-14IN.htm; *Adjutant General's Office*, 25; *Owyhee Avalanche*, November 10, 1866.

22 *Owyhee Avalanche*, September 22, 1866; *Oregon Sentinel*, February 9, 1867; *Adjutant General's Office*, 25; Heitman, *Historical Register*, Vol. 2, 427. The latter source says the fight occurred on 31 October.

23 *Owyhee Avalanche*, November 17, 1866; *Idaho World*, November 3, 1866, November 24, 1866.

24 Frederick P. Brougham Depredation Claim #7988; Chauncey D. Bacheler Depredation Claim #7239; *Owyhee Avalanche*, November 17, 1866; *Idaho World*, November 24, 1866. This was not Bacheler's last confrontation with Indian raiders. In February 1867, they stole two more of his horses near Cow Creek, just inside the Idaho border.

25 Bancroft, *History of Oregon*, 529-30; Applegate to Sprague, November 11, 1866, RG 393, Dept. of Columbia, Letters Received, Box 3; *Commissioner of Indian Affairs 1867*, 92, 100; Murray, *Modocs*, 40; *Adjutant General's Office*, 25. The latter source lists the fight as occurring on 15 October.

26 *Oregon Sentinel*, December 15, 1866, January 5, 1867; Heitman, *Historical Register*, Vol. 1, 590; Letter Secretary of War, 50th Congress, Senate Ex. Doc. 70, 325. Company I was the last of the Oregon volunteer companies to leave service, not mustering out until July 19, 1867.

27 *Commissioner of Indian Affairs, 1867*, 99; Webb, *List of Engagements*, 27; *Adjutant General's Office*, 25.

28 *Commissioner of Indian Affairs, 1867*, 99-100; *Owyhee Avalanche*, December 1, 1866; *Idaho World*, December 1, 1866. Reports sometimes confuse Sinker Creek with Succor Creek, streams that both head in the Owyhee Mountains, and Succor Creek is often spelled Sucker.

29 *Secretary of War 1868-69*, 770; *Commissioner of Indian Affairs 1867*, 100; *Owyhee Avalanche*, January 5, 1867; *Oregon Sentinel*, February 9, 1867; Webb, *List of Engagements*, 27.

30 Webb, *List of Engagements*, 27; *Commissioner of Indian Affairs 1867*, 100; *Owyhee Avalanche*, December 22, 1866; *Oregon Sentinel*, January 19, 1867.

Chapter 16
CROOK TAKES OVER

Born September 23, 1829, near Taylorsville, Ohio, George Crook attended West Point, and graduated in 1852, thirty-eighth out of a class of forty-three. He became a second lieutenant in the 4th Infantry, and was posted in California, where he took part in several campaigns and Indian fights. On June 10, 1857, in a fight at Pit River Canyon, Crook took an arrow in his right hip. His men thought the arrow was poisoned, for Crook became very ill. A surgeon checked him, but thought it would be better to leave the embedded arrowhead alone, and it remained there for the rest of his life. Crook went east to fight in the Civil War, where he was once captured and exchanged, and rose to the rank of brevet major general of volunteers.

After the War, with the drastic cutbacks, Crook was made major of the 3rd Infantry for a short time, before being promoted to lieutenant colonel of the newly formed 23rd Infantry on July 28, 1866. The lowering in status rankled many officers in the post-war years, including the likes of once-Maj. General George A. Custer, who had to settle for a lieutenant-colonelcy in the 7th Cavalry. Crook also felt the sting. While he once commanded a division, two of Crook's subordinate brigade commanders, Charles H. Smith and John I. Gregg, became colonels.

Crook was sour about what he saw as unfair. "I regret to say that I learned too late that it was not what a person did, but it was what he got the credit of doing that gave him a reputation and at the close of the war gave him position."[1]

Crook sailed on the *Ocean Queen* from New York for San Francisco on November 1, 1866. On the voyage he became acquainted with fellow Ohioan, Lieutenant Azor H. Nickerson, and the two hit it off well. Nickerson was going to what he assumed was the 14th Infantry in Arizona, but because no specific battalion was mentioned in his orders, Crook talked to General Halleck upon his arrival in San Francisco, and arranged for Nickerson to be Crook's adjutant and go with him to Idaho instead of Arizona. Nickerson described Crook as being between 40 and 45 years old (he was 38), because of his almost white hair, beard, and "grizzled" countenance. At six feet tall and weighing about 170 pounds, Crook had a square jaw, broad shoulders, a short neck, blue-gray eyes, and a Roman nose, by which Nickerson saw a firmness of character that approached stubbornness. He noted that Crook

A. R. Bowman Museum, Crook County Historical Society, Prineville, Oregon
George Crook, ca. 1860.

rarely wore clothes that distinguished his military rank, but had a penchant for wearing an old, military, black slouch Burnside hat. Nickerson was drawn to Crook, not only because of his past achievements, but also "by reason of his genial, modest and unassuming personality, his warm sympathy and interest. . . ."

From the time of Crook's arrival in California, Major Marshall's days were numbered. Complaints from civilians and dissatisfaction with the major's performance by his superiors forced them to remove Marshall from command of the district and name Captain David Perry, Company F, 1st Cavalry, as interim commander. Crook and Nickerson took the Central Pacific rails to Cisco, California, where they caught the Overland stage

190

across the mountains to Truckee Valley, and transferred to a springless, comfortless, "dead-axe" Idaho Stage Company vehicle for the ride north. The trip took six days, with stops only for quick meals of bread, bacon, and tea, and short rests. Nickerson noticed that Crook, normally a fastidious, clean person, did not wash. When Nickerson asked why, Crook told him the water was impregnated with alkali, and combined with the alkali dust, it would become a "powerful lye," burn his eyes, and take the skin off his face. Nickerson also quit washing. They traveled through what Nickerson called "about as desolate a portion of our country as any I had ever yet seen."

After crossing Owyhee Ferry, the stage driver mentioned the Chinese massacre that had occurred in the area earlier in the year. It was there, the driver said, "the Snakes and Paiutes held 'A Mongolian Picnic'" When Nickerson asked what that was, the driver told him about the Chinese miners who, after walking hundreds of miles, saw no Indians and put their weapons away in their wagons. The Indians had been following them, saw that the strange men with long black pigtails were unarmed, and the "picnic" commenced. The driver, although he could not have known, assured his passengers that the Chinese even offered their guns to the Indians, saying, "Me good Chinaman; me no hurt um Ingin." The Indians of course, gladly accepted the gifts, and then shot down the Chinese. Their long pigtails facilitated the scalping that followed.

"Taking it all in all," Nickerson wrote, "they must have considered a Mongolian picnic superior to any other class of entertainment in their bloody reperatory." After that, when the stage came to dangerous ground, Crook and Nickerson would get out and walk alongside, with rifles ready. "We intended that," said Nickerson, "if the Indians purposed adding a Buckeye picnic to their list of entertainments, we would endeavor to furnish part of the music."

Once in Silver City, Nickerson wondered why such "small groups of slab-fronted shanties" all seemed to take the name of cities, "as Vienna City, Paris City, and the like," and always have a run-down boarding house called "The Palace Hotel." He figured it was because "if the inhabitants had failed to designate them as cities, strangers who happened to pass that way would certainly never have suspected them."[2]

News of Crook's arrival set off a new round of speculations in the newspapers. The Wasson Brothers learned from Crook's personal acquaintances that the lieutenant colonel was "a splendid Indian exterminator, and if he will only do half as well as a General as he did as a Lieutenant, the Lo family may expect much trouble." After that praise, they toned down their hopes: "He can't fail to be an improvement on his predecessor; however, we shall await performance." The *Idaho World*, which had always been pro-Marshall, wrote, "While we accord ample credit to the retiring commander for having performed his duty well and faithfully, and to the full extent of his means, we join in welcoming the new commander to the post."[3]

One factor that would greatly facilitate Crook's upcoming campaign was the July 1866 Act that called for the recruitment of Indian scouts to assist the soldiers. Using Indians to scout and fight for the military was not a new idea; it had been in practice since the earliest colonial days, and had been tried off and on ever since. Although seemingly a good idea in retrospect, contemporaries gave it a mixed reception. Many civilians saw it as economical and a way to save white lives, while the military resisted because of cost

Idaho Historical Society 76-138.96

Silver City, Idaho, *ca* 1870s. Below, The Idaho Hotel, Silver City today.

Author's photo

and control concerns, and, as Lt. Colonel Maury said in 1864, the Indian way of war was "repugnant," and they would be nothing but trouble for their commanders. Oregon Governor George L. Woods was enthusiastic, and he applied to General Steele to have two companies of fifty men each organized under lieutenants of his choice, to begin immediate service and take the field independently of the army, but acting in conjunction with them. Steele rejected the proposal, stating that the army bill meant for Indians to act as scouts only, and in numbers of ten to fifteen per command.

Woods next took his plan to General Halleck, but "Old Brains" concurred with Steele, and rather rudely declined. Angry now, Woods telegraphed to Secretary of War Stanton and explained his proposal. Stanton ordered Halleck to conform to Governor Woods's wishes, and the authorization grudgingly was issued. Within a year, both Steele and Halleck would change their tunes.[4]

Crook and Nickerson reached Boise on December 11, and Crook took over as commander of the district. The locals were glad to see him, for conditions were tense, with Indian troubles and lawlessness so bad that vigilance committees had taken over, organizing companies to fight Indians and deal with troublemakers. In the months before Crook's arrival, the vigilantes had reportedly lynched about sixty men, including the crooked Sheriff Dave Opdyke. When he arrived, Crook said, "affairs in that country could not well have been worse." He believed the whole area from northern California to Montana was in "a state of siege." Indians dealt death and destruction everywhere. "People were afraid to go outside of their own doors without protection. There was scarcely a day that reports of Indian depredations were not coming in."

Crook quickly learned that the feeling against Major Marshall "and many of his officers was very bitter." There was no progress being made, and among the officers he found "a general apathy" and "indifference to the proper discharge of duty." Within a week of Crook's arrival, word of an Indian raid near the mouth of the Boise River energized Crook to see if he could achieve some better results than had his predecessors. He phrased the beginning of what would turn out to be a long, hard campaign in simple terms: "So I took Capt. Perry's company of the 1st Cavalry and left with one change of underclothes, toothbrush, etc., and went to investigate matters, intending to be gone a week. But I got interested after the Indians and did not return there [to Boise] again for over two years."[5]

Captain Perry and forty-five men of his Company F were Crook's main force, along with about ten Paiute Indians and two civilian guides: Sinora Hicks and Archie McIntosh. Little is known about Hicks, except that he was said to be half Cherokee and familiar with several Indian languages. McIntosh was born in 1834, to Scotsman John McIntosh, who worked for the Hudson's Bay Company, and a full-blood Chippewa woman. After

Indians killed his father, Archie, his mother, three sisters and three brothers, were cared for by Dr. John McLoughlin at Fort Vancouver. Archie received good schooling, including two years in Edinburgh, Scotland. He was a clerk for Hudson's Bay Company, served as a scout in the Pacific Northwest beginning in 1855, and participated in several military expeditions, including scouting for Major Rinearson. He was described as "tall, slender. . .a good drinking man and a hell of a talker. He always had an audience."[6]

OWYHEE RIVER, DECEMBER 26, 1866

Unfortunately, Crook had not given his complete trust to McIntosh yet. The expedition proceeded down the Boise River to the Snake and then turned south up the Owyhee. The weather was bad and getting worse, and Crook commented that, "Everybody was opposed to it." Crook said that Marshall's old Indian scouts, particularly "Cayuse George" Rundell, "was utterly worthless and demoralized. I had not proceeded far before I caught him in a lie, but, not discouraged by that, we went on until we found the rancheria." Crook was learning to have more faith in McIntosh and Hicks.

The winter march caused many complaints. Nickerson: "Much of this march was made in a violent snowstorm, men and officers alike being without tents and with only a meager supply of blankets to keep us from freezing." They trailed up the rough canyons until December 26, when they found an Indian camp in the area between the Owyhee Breaks and Diamond Butte, about 20 miles west of Camp Lyon.

At daylight, Crook left ten men behind to guard the horses, and moved in to attack with his remaining soldiers and scouts. Uncharacteristically, the Paiutes did not flee at first fire. Howluck (Bigfoot), who was a bold, defiant chief, was in charge, and perhaps seeing that he outnumbered the attackers about two-to-one, he made a stand. Warriors gestured and shouted for the soldiers to come on. After every mounted Indian was shot down, the remaining adversaries dodged and clambered among the rocks for several hours, but the Paiutes were taking much the worst of it, and they finally vacated the field at mid-day. We "had a good time killing Indians," mixed-blood Sinora Hicks said. "Big Foot made his escape," he reported, and then enigmatically added, "but we got Little Foot and the Gray Horse." Crook was caught up in the moment himself, rather prematurely announcing, "That ended any more depredations from that band."

The casualties were far out of proportion to the numbers engaged. Sergeant Lawrence O'Toole, said to have engaged Howluck himself, was mortally wounded by two arrows and died two nights later. He had survived twenty-eight Civil War battles. Howluck lost about twenty-five warriors killed, plus his wife, Running Deer, and nine women and children captured. It was his first major defeat. The soldiers rounded up thirty horses, two belonging to Hill Beachey, and found a Wells, Fargo & Company mail-bag that was taken from the stage during the November attack that killed passenger Wilcox. About twenty-five wickiups and large amounts of Indian stores were destroyed.[7]

To almost everyone's surprise, Crook did not immediately head back to Boise; he wanted to continue tracking the Indians. The *Avalanche* soon got word of the battle. "The old Humboldt style of fighting is being inaugurated here and in Oregon," it trumpeted. Crook "sent to Fort Boise for more supplies and all the spare troops, and *stays in the field* and don't wear out his men and animals and fritter away his time running back and forth."[8]

The part about not wearing out his men and animals may have been contested by Crook's soldiers. The tired and cold command trailed back down the Owyhee that afternoon and one more day, reaching a good place to camp that Crook had seen on the way up, probably in the vicinity of the mouth of Dry Creek. The commander noticed some sheep sign in the bluffs, and, as was his habit, sent his animal to camp, and wandered off alone with his hunting rifle. Crook got up on "sheer precipices" about 1,000 feet above the river when "a thick fog set in." He tried to go back down the cliff, but he said, "by the time I had reached the trail, night had set in, and that, combined with the fog, made it so dark that I could not see my hand before me, let alone the trail." Had one of Crook's subordinates pulled such a bonehead stunt, he would certainly have felt his commander's wrath. It began to sleet; Crook only had a thin coat, had no matches, and was soon thoroughly soaked. As he tried to make his way down the smaller canyons that cut perpendicularly across toward the river, he tumbled and fell on several occasions. He tried to take shelter under a bank, but when a nearby section of the wall caved in, he decided he had better keep moving.

Down in the river bottom, Captain Perry grew concerned about his commander, built several fires on high points in the valley, and had soldiers discharge their rifles, but Crook neither saw nor heard anything. About midnight, fearful of passing the camp in the darkness, Crook sat down to rest, tucking his hands inside his blouse, and "knocking my knees together" to keep up circulation. About two in the morning the sky cleared and the moon came out, and Crook saw the camp below him. "I was not long in reaching my blanket," he nonchalantly reported.[9]

They moved down to the Snake River to the mouth of the Boise River, and Crook sent couriers to Boise for more Indian scouts and supplies. When they arrived on January 3, Crook marched to the Malheur River. They traveled 40 miles upstream when they discovered another Indian camp ahead, but failed to surprise it, because of what Crook described as "the misbehavior of the chief of scouts." Whether or not Cayuse George purposely gave away their position is unknown, but Crook was through with him, and increasingly leaned on McIntosh for advice.

MALHEUR RIVER, JANUARY 9, 1867

Crook followed the fleeing Indians upriver into Malheur Canyon, locating them again on January 9, "collected on the North Fork some three miles from its junction with the other branch," which would be near present-day Juntura. Crook watched "some half a dozen mounted Indians bantering us for a fight," and could not help but accept their offer. The bottom was a half-mile wide, choked with willows and rose bushes and cut up by sloughs alternating with sand ridges. "[W]e made a charge on them," Crook said, "when we came close to them, the most of this number ran into the brush while some fled up the caãon on the river and as the men charged up they were fired into from the brush." Crook had attacked the Indian stronghold against a willow and rose bramble that eyesight could not penetrate more than 10 feet. Perry's dismounted troopers ran upon "an almost impenetrable thicket of willows and briers," said Crook, and he called them back. Firing from concealment, the Indians hit one soldier in the chest, but the bullet was deflected by a horseshoe that he kept in his shirt pocket, saving his life. "In all of my experience in campaigns against Indians," Crook wrote, "this was the only time I could have used artillery to advantage."

Instead of attacking the stronghold, Crook sent Perry up the canyon, but he could locate no Indians there. When he returned, it was nearly dark. Crook placed his men around the stronghold, planning to attack the next morning, but that night, the scouts established contact with the Paiutes, a band under war chief Storm Cloud, who wanted to talk. Crook did not want to negotiate, but said, "Knowing that if I was to make an attack I would get but few of them, I consented to their coming in provided they would give up their horses and go to Boise." That was highly unlikely. Storm Cloud said he wanted peace, but Crook did not believe him. "I didn't like their tone," he said, "they were too independent and saucy." Even so, a truce was declared, and in the morning the soldiers and warriors mingled. Crook fed the Indians, but neither side trusted the other. Crook was outnumbered and felt the Indians might "commit some act of treachery on us." Perhaps not seeing the irony of the situation and his intended duplicity, Crook said, "I was strongly urged to take the initiative and kill them while in my camp."

Crook and some soldiers were allowed in the Indian camp. "When I came to inspect their stronghold afterwards," Crook wrote, "I was very thankful that the affair terminated as it had, for the brush extends along the banks of the river varying from one quarter to half a mile in width, the willows are so thick that a rabbit could scarcely get through it, matted with the worst kind of briers." The camp was a quarter-mile into the thicket, "with but one serpentine path approaching it, over which the men would have to march single file, this ground again was intersected by almost impenetrable sloughs, the Indians were behind those sloughs burrowed in the ground with stockades of willows." Crook realized that in a battle, "our loss would have

196

been very severe." He said, "I thanked my stars" that there was no further fighting. Storm Cloud had out-bluffed Crook.

Crook did get Storm Cloud's word that he would follow him back to Boise, however, the next morning when they prepared to move out, "some of the Indians took alarm and slipped away." Still, Crook had the majority of Indians under guard and riding with him. They moved upstream on the Malheur toward the South Fork for about 20 miles, and then cut across the high plateau toward the Owyhee. On the way, Storm Cloud and the rest of his people absconded with some of Crook's horses and rode away; it was the first of many times that Indians would steal Crook's horses. Crook did not wish to chase the Indians, he said, because he knew "about where their camp is" and could get a fresh company and attack them later. He never did.[10]

As Crook crossed the plateau, a series of great storms blew in from the Pacific Ocean, dumping eight or more inches of rain in northern California, causing severe flooding, and dropping heavy snows in the Sierras, Cascades, and east into the Great Basin. East of the Malheur River, the system swept across the plateau, covering Crook's command in what he called "a frightful snowstorm." They couldn't see 50 yards ahead of them, but had to make for a certain landmark a dozen miles ahead, or risk being caught in some of the Owyhee's impassible canyons. Crook trusted to Archie McIntosh, who guided them unerringly to their destination. The wind, meanwhile, threw Crook forward against the pommel of his saddle and sifted through his clothes to wet him to the bone. That night they camped in the open with nothing but sagebrush for fuel. They pitched the only "A" frame (Sibley) tent they had, built wing barricades of snow and brush out from the sides, and managed to start a fire on the lee side.

The blizzard continued through the next morning, but the command reached the Owyhee and snaked down into the canyon where the snow had stopped, the sun appeared, and the temperature rose. "I actually saw grasshoppers jumping about this 24th [14th] day of January," Crook wrote. They next traveled to Camp Lyon, where Crook found Captain Hunt secure at the post. Without knowing, Crook assumed Hunt and his men had been doing nothing. "From appearance and information the normal condition of the officers there was drunkenness," Crook said. "They didn't seem to do much else but get drunk and lie around doing nothing."

OWYHEE RIVER, JANUARY 8, 1867

The assessment was unfair. The troopers had recently returned from a scout that produced more results than had Crook's jaunt up the Malheur. On the morning of January 3, when the temperature was four degrees above zero, Lieutenant Moses Harris, who was brevetted captain for his service at the 1864 Battle of Winchester, and received a Medal of Honor for "distinguished gallantry in action" at the Battle of Smithfield, West Virginia, took a detachment of Company M, 1st Cavalry, on a scout. Accompanying him were four friendly Indian guides, interpreter Dave Pickett, Jim Beebe, and a Mr. Phillips. They traveled west from Camp Lyon until they struck the Owyhee at its westernmost big bend, then turned downriver about 25 miles.

On the evening of January 8, at a spot downriver from where Crook had his December 26 fight, Lieutenant Harris discovered twelve Indians with six horses. The soldiers and scouts barreled into them, killing and wounding five, and chasing the survivors across the icy river. They captured two horses and destroyed several bushels of seeds. With that accomplished, Harris returned to Camp Lyon, later to meet a somewhat testy Lt. Colonel Crook returning from his march in the blizzard.[11]

On the morning of Harris's fight, 200 miles to the west, an earthquake shook the soldiers and Indians around Fort Klamath. The quake was followed by a cloud of black and brown smoke and ash that covered the area, accompanied by a sulphurous smell. As the men sat down to breakfast in the mess-room, they had to light candles to see, when a greater tremor followed, described as "the earth seemed rolling like waves upon the ocean." Timbers cracked, dishes rattled, and windows broke. As the men ran outside, "The tall pines around the fort seemed lashing themselves into fury." Dogs howled, cattle fell to the ground, and the Klamath Indians uttered "unearthly yells." The sutler's store moved about 20 feet. Men were bruised and shaken, but there was no loss of life. L. Tennyson, the quartermaster-clerk, believed "that a volcano has broken loose near the Klamath Marsh, as a continuous dark volume of smoke is ascending in that direction." Word of the quake was sent out by express as "singular if not serious news."[12] There were many, white as well as Indian, who saw the event as a foreboding omen, but of what, no one could say.

While the ground shook in the Cascades, another expedition was battling Paulina's band on Crooked River. The upshot of Oregon Governor Woods's disagreement with Halleck was the eventual approval to enlist two scout companies from the Warm Springs Reservation. The Warm Springs warriors needed little persuasion to join up. They had been battling the Paiutes for years, and in September 1866, after Weahwewa's warriors killed Wasco Chief Postaminie and stole seventy-seven horses they wanted revenge. When Lieutenant William Borrowe, 2nd Artillery, came to the reservation the next month seeking scouts, they were eager to sign up. Within a week, he had seventy-four men. Considering that there were only 394 male Tyghs, John Days, Deschutes, and Wascos (Walla Wallas) of all ages, enrolled at the reservation, Borrowe had recruited almost one out of every five.

The scouts were ready to go, but another hold-up resulted from confusion as to what set of orders they would be operating under. When Major Marshall first made a call for scouts, Steele figured they could be paid with the plunder they took, but Agent Huntington protested that plundering would set a bad example for the friendly Indians, and the plunder they took may

Author's photo

In January 1867, troops surprised a Paiute village on Crooked River, near Prineville, Oregon.

have turned out to be property initially stolen from the whites. Huntington said he would allow his Indians to enlist, but only if they were paid by the government as scouts. In August, Steele reportedly issued an "extermination" order, indicating that enlisted scouts were to take no prisoners, regardless of age or sex. Governor Woods concurred, stating that the Snake women were some of the most brutal murderers of all, citing the 1854 Ward Massacre in Idaho, when Indian women assisted in torturing some of the white captives taken by the warriors.

It was finally decided that the scouts would receive pay equivalent to cavalry soldiers, they could keep stock taken from the Snakes, except for animals branded as "U.S.," and get a two-week furlough in the spring and fall to tend their farms. Lieutenant Borrowe, during his recruiting speeches, was also said to have stated that the Warm Springs scouts were to take no prisoners. If Borrowe thought that would encourage the Indians to enlist, he was mistaken. The Indians figured they would be better off if they did not slaughter everyone, but not because of humanitarian reasons. First, they desired to take more captives as slaves, and second, they were certain that the Snakes would retaliate by murdering their own wives and children. Regardless, when Huntington was absent from Oregon on business, Borrowe recruited all the scouts he wanted.[13]

The commanders of the two scout companies were Dr. William C. McKay and John Darragh.

Darragh, born in New York in 1830, arrived in Oregon in 1851, and married Mary Jane Gates, daughter of Nathaniel Gates, later a prominent attorney who served in the state legislature. Darragh was an intelligent, ver-

199

satile man, working at several occupations, including school superintendent of Wasco County. He returned to New York in 1884, where he was engaged in building the city's first skyscraper, plus the Vanderbilt Mansion and the Waldorf-Astoria.

McKay, son of the famous trapper Thomas McKay and his Chinook Indian wife, was born in Astoria about 1824. He received his primary education from many employees of the Hudson's Bay Company. Missionary Dr. Marcus Whitman convinced Thomas McKay to send his son to Fairfield, New York, where Whitman had gone to school, to "make an American of him." William studied in New York and Ohio, but returned to Oregon before getting his diploma, but with a license to practice medicine. McKay was a clerk, miner, trader, coroner, soldier, and eventually a "doctor." In appearance, he was dark-skinned, short and stocky, and always dressed well, preferring silk hats and Prince Albert coats. McKay worked as interpreter and secretary to Isaac Stevens and Joel Palmer, Washington and Oregon's superintendents of Indian affairs. President Lincoln appointed McKay as the Warm Springs physician in 1861.

With General Halleck's authorization, General Steele was told to offer scout company positions to McKay and Darragh, with the same pay as a second lieutenant of cavalry. They were referred to as lieutenants and later as captains, but were officially paid as "interpreters."[14]

CROOKED RIVER, JANUARY 7, 20, 1867

By early December 1866, the companies were ready to move. Darragh had about thirty-six Wascos and McKay had about thirty-eight Deschutes; McKay also reported having nine civilian employees and fifty-four pack-mules. The scouts were issued government horses, clothing, and equipment, down to the cavalry hat, which McKay and Darragh insisted were necessary to distinguish them from the friendly Paiute scouts that Crook was using. The scouts even got relatively new and desirable Maynard Carbines. They slowly moved up the Deschutes River from The Dalles, establishing daily routines and polishing up their tactics.

In mid-December they were searching south of Crooked River in the Maury Mountains, and then moved northwest to the western side of the Ochoco Mountains. McKay returned to Warm Springs for a few days, and was back with his men on January 4, where they built a camp on Cottonwood (now McKay) Creek, north of today's Prineville. On January 6, a small scouting party discovered the tracks of a single Indian in the snow about eight miles from their camp. About five p.m., McKay and Darragh, with twenty men each, hurried to the spot, and in deteriorating weather conditions, followed the tracks until 11 p.m. when they had to stop to wait for daylight. In the morning they picked up the trail and went another eight miles before coming to the brink of a steep canyon, about 1,200 feet above a bend of the Crooked River, southeast of Prineville.

They saw a small camp on the river below, and the scouts snaked down the bluffs, hoping to surprise it. The descent was steep and rocky, and the Paiutes heard them before they could completely encircle the camp. Nevertheless, Darragh and McKay attacked, killed three Paiutes, captured two children, two mules, one horse, and much ammunition and skins. On the valley floor, they saw Paiutes across the river moving to a high point formed by the confluence of Crooked River and another small stream coming in from the south. After some hard climbing, the Warm Springs warriors engaged about forty to fifty Snakes, who were in a position, said Darragh, "so well chosen and fortified, that it was equal, in strength, to the best block-house." It was one of Paulina's strongest "forts." The scouts had to approach across a smooth tableland and Darragh and McKay concluded that a direct assault would be too costly. They fought from long range until dark. "The Indians claim," said Darragh, "and I think with truth, that they shot three at this place—McKay saw one fall himself." One of Darragh's and one of McKay's scouts were wounded, as were five horses. That evening they pulled out and returned to camp on Cottonwood Creek, which they reached at two in the morning.

While in camp for the next several days, a large Tygh hunting party visited them, and McKay reported "they had a jolly time of it by War song and Dances." On January 18, with ten days' rations, they were ready for another extended Snake hunt, and they left that afternoon toward the site of the previous battle. They traveled that night for 20 miles through a terrific snowstorm on the highlands, which changed into rain and sleet in the Crooked River Valley by morning. With the weather so bad, McKay made camp on the river and sent out several small parties to fan out and look for signs. Many tracks were found four miles downstream, and at midnight, McKay and Darragh sent out fifteen men from each company, under William Chinook, John Mission, and Mashampella, to take up the trail.

On the morning of January 20, McKay, Darragh, and the rest of the command, crossed south of Crooked River and headed downstream to catch up. Shortly thereafter, a messenger rode in and declared that the scouts had attacked one camp, demolished it, and took nine scalps. The camp was that of Wahi (Fox), and among the dead was Wahi's wife, the daughter of Oytes (Left Hand), of the Lohim band. When Wahi later found her, with her head smashed by a Wasco war club, he reported the news to his father-in-law, and both vowed vengeance.

McKay and Darragh caught and joined the others, and moved quickly on, hitting and destroying several more small Paiute camps in the area. The weather was very bad, said Darragh, "we all wet as rats and nearly frozen," but it "was just the thing for gobbling up Snakes." With snow from 14 to 20 inches deep, and some of the horses failing, the scouts still devastated the Snake camps before turning back to the Crooked River Valley. In one camp they killed one man, one woman, and one child, and in another, they killed six women and children. The fights on January 7 and 20 resulted in twenty-eight dead Paiutes and eight captured, along with three horses, five rifles, three pounds of powder, and many robes and skins. One of the captured weapons, McKay later testified, was "a rifle gun belonging to James N. Clark," and he asserted "that I verily believe that the said band of Indians are the identical same Indians that destroyed the property of said James N. Clark." The scouts made a great display of the eighteen scalps they took. Most demoralizing for Ocheho and Paulina, they realized that some of their camps had been found and that they were no longer immune from attack during the harsh Oregon winter.

McKay and Darragh returned to a warm camp on the Cottonwood on January 23. There were mixed reactions over the killed women and children. Huntington and others condemned the killing of non-combatants. The scouts did not kill all the prisoners, as they claim their orders had intended them to do. They did, however, keep all the captured Indians as slaves. The affair may have angered the Snakes to further resistance, but learning that they now had organized Indian enemies hunting them as well as white soldiers, certainly was a psychological burden that further wore down their will to resist.[15]

STEENS MOUNTAIN, JANUARY 29, 1867

While McKay and Darragh's scouts chased Paulina along Crooked River, Crook was preparing for the second leg of his winter campaign in eastern Oregon. After recuperating from his scout up the Malheur and his battle with the elements, Crook released Captain David Perry and Company F to return to Fort Boise. On January 21, he took Captain Hunt's Company M, 1st Cavalry, twelve Indians, and four civilians, including George W. Hill, John Manning, and Rufus Hanson, to continue the search for Indians. They returned to the area where Crook had crossed the Owyhee on the way to Camp Lyon, and picked up another Indian trail heading southwest. About 15 miles west of Owyhee Ferry, the scouts brought word of a Paiute village farther west near the eastern edge of Steens Mountain.

Crook marched through the evening and stopped about midnight, while the scouts continued ahead to pinpoint the camp's exact location. When they returned, Crook moved out slowly, hoping to time his arrival at the rancheria at daybreak. Dawn, January 29, found Crook and Hunt's Company in line of battle on a sagebrush plain, close to some low foothills, only 200 yards from the village, thought to be Howluck's. Scouts were sent around the flanks to cover any escape routes.

Crook intended to remain in the rear to observe, but when he ordered the charge, his horse bolted and he found himself leading the command, with bullets whistling by and in more danger from his men firing behind him than from the Indians in front. Crook's unmanageable steed carried him through the village, but his men followed right behind him. Crook jumped off his horse and ran back to the rancheria. Warriors approached him, with one very brave one in particular, stoically loosing a dozen arrows while singing his death song. "He must have been shot through and through a half dozen times before he fell," Crook said.

Crook and Rufus Hanson, who lived in Silver City, approached a wickiup. Hanson boldly went up to the front, where sagebrush covered the entrance. Crook cautioned him "not to be so venturesome, but either he was reckless or else didn't appreciate the danger." An Indian popped out of the entrance and shot Hanson through the heart. Rather than go in after the warrior, troopers blasted a volley into the wickiup and killed him. The men of Company M were deadly efficient. They killed sixty Indians and captured twenty-seven more, plus thirty-seven horses. Only two males and two women escaped. In addition to Hanson's death, civilian John Manning and three soldiers were wounded.

Shortly after the battle, which was called "Tearass Plain" in some newspaper accounts, Crook's scouts discovered a small camp of seventeen Indians. They attacked, killed five, and took several more prisoners. One of the captured men was recognized as having been taken prisoner before, but was released under oath not to fight against the white men again. The soldiers shot him. Crook headed for Camp C. F. Smith, where he deposited the prisoners. Unlike some other officers, Crook was indignant that women and children had been killed—inadvertently, he hoped. Crook sent a detachment to escort the prisoners back to Fort Boise; on the way, they buried Hanson's remains at Owyhee Ferry. Of the prisoners, at least two ended up in Silver City homes; Reverend Sterling Hill took a three-year-old girl and his brother took a five-year old boy.[16]

On January 26, 1867, a few days before the Battle of "Tearass Plain," James R. Doolittle signed his name to the Report of the Joint Special Committee on the Condition of the Indian Tribes. Doolittle, a senator from Wisconsin, was chairman of the Senate Indian Affairs Committee. The report was the culmination of a two-year investigation into "the condition of the Indian tribes and their treatment by the civil and military authorities of the United States." The study, initiated largely because of the Sand Creek incident in Colorado Territory in November 1864, took up much time and money over the next two years. The committee, largely on a witch hunt, had not even heard the evidence yet, when it announced it would be investigating "a wholesale massacre of Indians in Colorado for no just cause. . . ."

Doolittle's seven-man committee was divided into three geographical areas: Doolittle and two other members went to the Central Plains, New Mexico and Utah; two other members went to Minnesota, Nebraska, and the Dakotas; and two more were assigned California and the Pacific Northwest. Doolittle concluded that the army was dealing too harshly with the Indians—

he believed Indians should be offered the carrot instead of the stick. He recommended that Indian affairs be removed from military control and he wanted to depoliticize the system by turning administration of Indian affairs over to churchmen. The committee concluded that the Indians were dying out because of white aggression, railroads, and gold rushes. It recommended a board of Indian Commissioners be formed to supervise Indian affairs to reduce fraud and violence. Doolittle's report was laced with condemnations, such as "cruel treatment on the part of the whites," "encroachments of the white emigration," and "aggressions of lawless white men." It was a particularly one-sided report because of the leanings of Senator Doolittle.

On the contrary, Oregon Senator James W. Nesmith, former superintendent of Indian affairs for Oregon Territory, took a very different stance, but his sub-report did not receive the publicity of Doolittle's. After making his study in the Pacific Northwest, Nesmith concluded that the Indians were very much to blame for the constant warfare in his region of investigation, particularly the Snakes. Nesmith called them "natural thieves and murderers," who "have taken many valuable lives and destroyed hundreds of thousands of dollars' worth of property." Nesmith said, "They infest all the routes of inland travel east of the Cascade mountains and south of the Columbia River, and pay their respects alike and simultaneously to the stage stations, the ranch men, the farmers, and the miners. They respect neither age, sex, nor condition, and seem to live solely for blood and plunder." Nesmith hoped the Indians would live up to past treaties, and that the government would negotiate new ones with the still hostile bands, yet he had little hope that any treaty would bring about peace. The Snakes, according to the senator, would never submit because of "their constitutional and ingrained tendency to rob and murder."

Nesmith's view was just as biased as Doolittle's—the former's villains were Indians, and the latter's were whites. Westerners and Easterners continued to see the same facts through different lenses.[17]

Chapter 16 notes

1 Thrapp, *Frontier Biography*, Vol. 1, 348; Robinson, *Crook and the Western Frontier*, 7, 83; Michno, *Encyclopedia of Indian Wars*, 54-55; Schmitt, ed., *Crook Autobiography*, 141.

2 Nickerson, "George Crook and the Indians," 1-9; Bancroft, *History of Oregon*, Vol. 2, 532.

3 *Owyhee Avalanche*, December 8, 1866; *Idaho World*, December 15, 1866.

4 Bancroft, *History of Oregon*, Vol. 2, 531-32; Dunlay, *Wolves for the Blue Soldiers*, 44-45.

5 Schmitt, ed., *Crook Autobiography*, 142-44; Robinson, *Crook and the Western Frontier*, 87, 89;

6 Thrapp, *Frontier Biography*, Vol. 2, 908-09. Sinora Hicks's name is sometimes spelled Senora. One of Archie's younger brothers, Donald McIntosh, was acting captain of Company G, 7th Cavalry, when he died at the Little Bighorn on June 25, 1876.

7 Schmitt, ed., *Crook Autobiography*, 144; Robinson, *Crook and the Western Frontier*, 90; *Commissioner of Indian Affairs 1867*, 100; Ontko, *Thunder Over the Ochoco III*, 358; *Adjutant General's Office*, 25; *Owyhee Avalanche*, January 5, 1867, January 12, 1867.

8 *Owyhee Avalanche*, January 5, 1867.

9 Schmitt, ed., *Crook Autobiography*, 144-45.

10 Schmitt, ed., *Crook Autobiography*, 145-46; Ontko, *Thunder Over the Ochoco III*, 359; Crook to McGregor, January 20, 1867, RG 393, Dept. of Columbia, Letters Received, Box 3; Webb, *List of Engagements*, 28; *Adjutant General's Office*, 25; *Secretary of War 1868-69*, 770. The latter three sources report that Crook captured 30 Indians in this engagement, but he makes no mention of any captures in his autobiography.

11 Schmitt, ed., *Crook Autobiography*, 147-48; Webb, *List of Engagements*, 28; Heitman, *Historical Register*, Vol. 1, 503; *Idaho World*, January 12, 1867; *Owyhee Avalanche*, January 19, 1867, February 2, 1867.

12 *Owyhee Avalanche*, February 2, 1867.

13 Bancroft, *History of Oregon*, Vol. 2, 531; *Commissioner of Indian Affairs 1867*, 70, 85; Dunlay, *Wolves for the Blue Soldiers*, 47; Clark, "McKay's Journal, Part I," 132, 149n98; Clark, "McKay's Journal, Part II," 329-30. Clark tried to find a copy of Steele's reported "extermination" order, but it could not be located.

14 Dunlay, *Wolves for the Blue Soldiers*, 45-46; Clark, "McKay's Journal, Part I," 133-37.

15 *Commissioner of Indian Affairs 1867*, 100-01; Clark, "McKay's Journal, Part I," 138-53; Darragh to Borrowe, January 31, 1867, RG 393, Dept. of Columbia, Letters Received, Box 3; Ontko, *Thunder Over the Ochoco III*, 362-63; James N. Clark Depredation Claim #1721. On 27 January, one of the scouts, Skanewa, died of consumption brought about by his hard winter service. The scouts returned to the agency on March 29.

16 Schmitt, ed., *Crook Autobiography*, 148-49; *Commissioner of Indian Affairs 1867*, 101; *Secretary of War 1868-69*, 770; *Owyhee Avalanche*, February 9, 1867; *Idaho World*, February 9, 1867, February 16, 1867.

17 Michno, *Battle at Sand Creek*, 259, 264, 277; *Condition of the Indian Tribes*, 1-10, Appendix, 4-5.

From Nevada's Black Rock Desert, *Caxton Press, 1978*
Surprise attack.

Chapter 17

MORE FIGHTING IN NEVADA

While raids and battles had been flaring off and on in Oregon and Idaho for the full year of 1866, Nevada had been remarkably peaceful since the hard fight in Guano Valley in February 1866. The district, under Major Albert G. Brackett, was not devoid of incidents. Companies of the 1st Cavalry and 9th Infantry garrisoned the posts, and elements of the newly formed 8th Cavalry began arriving. District headquarters was moved from Fort Churchill to Camp McGarry in August 1866.

On August 8, eleven miners of the Pueblo District signed a letter to General McDowell complaining about Indians destroying and stealing their equipment, tools, and shooting their horses. The letter, with E. Schappmann the lead signatory, claimed the army had never done anything for them, and they wanted a military post, or at least troops to patrol the area. Brackett sent Lieutenant Alfred Morton, 9th Infantry, on a scout to what Morton called the "Hot Springs Mining District," to investigate the claims. Morton could do little but verify the destruction, but could not tell when it might have occurred. His opinion was that it was "unsafe for a small party to remain in that vicinity without some military protection."

That was the response the miners hoped for, but no help was forthcoming. Brackett studied the matter and somehow determined that the destruction was done "long before Mr. Schappmann went there," and that Schappmann was represented to Brackett "as a most unreliable person, and one who will do anything to get soldiers stationed at his mine. . . ."

In the fall, Indians attacked a wagon train coming from Susanville, California. One teamster was badly wounded, and one warrior was killed. Paiutes hovered on the outskirts of Camp McGarry into the winter months, occasionally running off a horse or two, and once, boldly robbing the blacksmith's shop.

Searches were made, but no Indians could be found except a few tracks and a torch constructed from "the inner fibers of a sagebrush, by which fire could be preserved and carried for a long time." Brackett couldn't figure how the Indians survived. "With snow covering the country for many miles around," he said, "it was a mystery how these people eked out a living."

Brackett unwittingly touched on an ironical reason for the continuing warfare, and a nineteenth century version of "Catch 22"; the Indians couldn't

Author's photo

Site of Camp Winfield Scott, Nevada,

eke out a living without stealing from the people whose presence contributed to their destitute condition. On January 1, 1867, Paiutes captured and killed a Mr. Westover, the mail carrier who rode between Camp McGarry and Trout Creek in the Pueblo Valley.[1]

EDEN VALLEY, JANUARY 18, 1867

Paradise Valley, the scene of much activity in 1865, was also fairly quiet in 1866. Indians began reappearing in the area in late 1866, as a result of Marshall's and Crook's campaigning to the north. The confrontations generally followed a north-south cyclical track, as the Indians were pushed from one location to the other by alternating military expeditions. Settlers in Paradise Valley, who had been clamoring for a fort in that area for years, finally got their wish on December 12, 1866, when Captain Murray Davis, and men of Company A, 8th Cavalry, arrived to erect Camp Winfield Scott. It was built of adobe, rock, and lumber in the northern end of Paradise Valley on Cottonwood Creek near where it issues from the east side of the Santa Rosa Mountains.

The 8th Cavalry was composed of Californians, most of whom styled themselves as "Forty-niners," and had worked as miners. Its colonel was John I. Gregg, once one of Crook's subordinates. The lieutenant colonel was Thomas C. Devin, and the majors were William Gamble and William R. Price. Headquarters of the regiment went to Camp Whipple, Arizona Territory, where Gregg joined it in December 1866. In early 1867, Companies B, I, K and L went to Arizona Territory; Company C went to Fort Vancouver; D went to Fort Walla Walla; E to Fort Lapwai; F to Camp Logan; and G, H, and M were stationed for a time in California. Company M later went to Camp McDermit. Company A was organized at the Presidio of San Francisco, and Camp Winfield Scott was its first post outside of the state. After a few weeks of construction, the camp was in good enough shape to allow the soldiers to shift from the manual labor mode and try to make themselves into horse soldiers.

Second in command, Lieutenant John Lafferty, who had spent two years in Company B, 1st Battalion California Native Cavalry, took fourteen men of Company A on a short scout. On January 18, they came upon a rancheria of Paiutes in barren Eden Valley, near the junction of Eden Creek and the Little Humboldt, only about 18 miles southeast of Camp Scott. Lafferty attacked, killed two Indians and scattered the rest, but Sergeant John Kelly took an arrow through the palm of his right hand. Lafferty destroyed the rancheria and a large quantity of provisions.[2]

VICKSBURG MINES FEBRUARY 7, 1867

Patrols had been sent from Camp McGarry without much luck, looking for the killers of mail rider Westover. The last week in January saw the heaviest snowfall of the winter in the three-corner area of Oregon, Idaho, and Nevada, when about two and a half feet fell. The weather was miserable to campaign in, but the soldiers persevered. In early February, twenty men of Company B, 1st Cavalry, in command of Lieutenant George F. Foote, 9th Infantry, were scouting in the northern reaches of the Pine Forest Range near the Oregon border. Miners from the Pueblo District had filtered south and staked a number of claims in the Pine Forest Range, with some of them surrounding Vicksburg Canyon and adjacent gulches, about nine miles southwest of present-day Denio Junction, Nevada. As Foote followed a trail up Vicksburg Canyon, he stumbled upon an abandoned mine that was being used as an Indian hideout. The Paiutes saw him coming and attacked first, severely wounding Private William Hill, while Private Samuel Hollister was badly hurt in an accident during the resultant scramble. Foote drove the Indians off and returned to find the cave where they had holed up, and a small rancheria outside. They burned the wickiups and returned to Camp McGarry.[3]

BLACK SLATE MOUNTAIN, FEBRUARY 15, 1867

At Camp Winfield Scott, Nevada, Captain Murray Davis knew he could rely on the services of the aggressive Lieutenant John Lafferty. Following up the successful action in January, Davis sent Lafferty out on another scout to search for Indians reported to be in Eden Valley and further to the south. Lafferty, Sergeant John Kelly, and thirteen soldiers of Company A, 8th Cavalry, rode out of the camp on February 11, with six days' rations.

They camped on the Little Humboldt River and moved down to the Humboldt, scouting two days with no luck. Lafferty moved east and on February 15, on his way back to Camp Scott he encountered fifteen Indians on the slopes of Black Slate Mountain, now known as Golconda Butte, about eight miles north of present-day Golconda, Nevada. Lafferty sent Sergeant

Kelly and five troopers around to cover the most likely escape route, but the trap sprung before Kelly could get in place. Nevertheless, Lafferty charged.

"There were only two rifles and a pistol in the party;" Lafferty reported, "one fired his rifle, but missed his aim, and then succeeded in making good his escape. The other attempted to fire, but his gun missed, when he received a bullet through the head, killing him instantly." Lafferty pursued the Indians until sundown, killing five. When they returned to the rancheria they found two large kettles in which the Indians were melting snow. The soldiers destroyed the camp, which had plenty of stored winter food, grass seeds, fish and rabbit nets, and assorted knives and hatchets, plus several articles they described as "belonging to the whites." Lafferty destroyed the camp and marched back to Camp Scott.[4]

SURPRISE VALLEY, FEBRUARY 16, 1867

One day after Lafferty fought the Paiutes, Captain Samuel Munson, who had fought in the 5th Maine Infantry in the Civil War, had a battle in Surprise Valley, California. Munson, now a captain in the 9th Infantry, took a detachment of Company C, 9th Infantry, and Company A, 1st Cavalry, out of Camp Bidwell. Not far from the post they fought a band of Paiutes, with possibly some of their Pit River allies. Munson was victorious, killing five and capturing two.[5] The increasing action in northeast California aroused Lt. Colonel Crook's suspicions that the Paiutes were being supplied with weapons and horses from the Pit River Indians.

PUEBLO MOUNTAIN, FEBRUARY 25-26, 1867

After the fight near Steens Mountain in January, Crook rested for a time at Camp C. F. Smith. On February 22, he took Company M and the other 1st Cavalry troop at the post, H Company, and moved out toward Camp Warner. On the march, McIntosh's scouts picked up Indian sign farther south in the Pueblo Mountains, and Crook moved his column toward the Nevada border. In deteriorating weather near the state line, Captain Hunt ran into a small camp of Paiutes, killed a warrior and captured three women and children. Captain Edward Myers of Company H, on his last assignment before transferring to the 7th Cavalry, swung south to Warm Springs (Bog Hot Valley), Nevada, killed one warrior and captured two women. They rejoined and angled northwest, aiming toward the Warner Mountains. Crook, in his usual low-key manner, said, "Several small bands of a few Indians each were cleaned up on the way."[6]

As they moved across southeast Oregon, the weather worsened. They stopped in northern Guano Valley about 14 miles from Camp Warner, in most inhospitable country. Explorer and trapper Peter Skene Ogden traveled through this part of Oregon several times, none of which he enjoyed. Back in 1827, he wrote, "I may say without exaggeration Man in this Country is

Author's photo

Jackass Flat, about 10 miles from Denio, Nevada, is near the site of the Vicksburg Mines. Indians sometimes used abandoned diggings as hide outs.

deprived of every comfort that can tend to make existence desirable if I can escape this year I trust I shall not be doomed to endure another."

Nothing had improved in forty years. Crook's command awoke in the morning to a raging blizzard. McIntosh did not approve of moving, but Crook set the men in motion, an action he later regretted. Crook: "I should have remained in camp that day. But we started in a storm that obscured everything, sun, landmarks, and even one part of the column from the other." The snow piled in drifts from 15 to 20 feet deep and animals would sometimes go out of sight. No trail could be followed, for as soon as an animal would raise its foot up, the roaring wind would fill in the hole with snow. "It was almost like traveling in the dark," said Crook. In mid-afternoon a gust of wind swept his hat away. "From there on my hair and whiskers were one mass of sleet and snow," he said.

It was almost sundown when they finally approached Camp Warner. Crook let his horse go ahead and waited to shepherd in the rest of the troops, but he found "I never in my life was so nearly exhausted." He sat down on a snow bank and waited. Luckily a saddled mule came along with no rider. It was so deep in the snow, Crook merely had to slide off the bank and into the saddle, where he was carried in safely to the post. The snowdrifts were level with the roofs of Camp Warner's huts and it was with great difficulty that they dug out the haystacks to allow the animals to feed.

A few days after the storm abated, Crook continued to the Warner (Christmas) Lakes, west of Camp Warner, and into a valley where the blizzards did not blow. The series of lakes were at high water level, connected, and nearly 70 miles long. Crook sent McIntosh with some scouts to investigate the area around Goose Lake. With the rest of the command, Crook found a place where the lakes pinched together in a neck only about

211

400 yards across. He had a stone causeway built across the shallowest part, but the spots of cane-covered "land" that they tried to connect proved to be no better than bogs that sank under the weight of the stones. "It seemed this ground was simply floating," Crook said. Lacking engineering skills, they simply piled tons of rocks into the holes to build up a solid crossing. Even so, they could not repair it enough to bring across McIntosh's party dry-shod. Only with more days of labor were enough rocks thrown in to make a reasonably safe causeway that saved many travel miles.

McIntosh had been gone several days longer than his allotted time, and Crook interrogated him about what he had found: "He made some cock and bull report, but I was satisfied he was drunk the greater part of the time, and the hostiles he saw and slayed were mostly in his mind."[7]

SOUTH FORK OWYHEE, MARCH 23, 1867

While Crook waited for better weather at Camp Warner, Captain Davis and Lieutenant Lafferty were keeping busy in Paradise Valley, Nevada.

They had responded to several civilian reports of stolen stock and gone on scouts with little luck in catching the thieves. On the last day of February, Captain Davis was transferred out of Camp Winfield Scott, leaving Lieutenant Lafferty in charge.

On March 13, Paiutes ran off stock from Charles Gregg's Ranch about eight miles south of the post. The next day Lafferty took fourteen men of Company A, 8th Cavalry, and went in pursuit. The Indian trail headed east. Notwithstanding the fierce snowstorm that obliterated the tracks, part of the same series of storms that were buffeting Crook's command farther northwest, Lafferty continued his search. Nine days later Lafferty caught up to the band near the South Owyhee River, north of present-day Tuscarora, Nevada. In a short, sharp fight the troopers killed six Indians, captured their weapons, and destroyed their camp.[8]

Chapter 17 notes

1 Schappmann to McDowell, August 8, 1866, RG 393, Dept. of Columbia, Letters Received, Box 2; Morton to Brackett, September 4, 1866, RG 393, Dept. of Columbia, Letters Received, Box 2; Brackett to AAG, October 14, 1866, RG 393, Dept. of Columbia, Letters Received, Box 2; Brackett, "Fighting in the Sierras," in Cozzens, *Eyewitnesses*, 6.

2 Rathbun, *Nevada Military Names*, 60-61, 127, 199; *Adjutant General's Office*, 26; Angel, *History of Nevada*, 175; O'Connor, "Eighth Cavalry," http://www2.army.mil/cmh-pg/books/R&H/R&H-8CV.htm.

3 *Adjutant General's Office*, 26; Brackett, "Fighting in the Sierras," in Cozzens, *Eyewitnesses*, 6; *Owyhee Avalanche*, January 26, 1867.

4 Rathbun, *Nevada Military Names*, 31-32; *Adjutant General's Office*, 26; O'Connor, "Eighth Cavalry," http://www2.army.mil/cmh-pg/books/R&H/R&H-8CV.htm.

5 Heitman, *Historical Register*, Vol. 1, 736; Webb, *List of Engagements*, 28; *Adjutant General's Office*, 26.

6 Schmitt, ed., *Crook Autobiography*, 149, 151-52; *Adjutant General's Office*, 26; Webb, *List of Engagements*, 28.

7 Cline, *Great Basin*, 110; Schmitt, ed., *Crook Autobiography*, 149-51.

8 Angel, *History of Nevada*, 175; Rathbun, *Nevada Military Names*, 128, 177.

Chapter 18
THE DEATH OF PAULINA

It took some time before the blizzards of January and February 1867, blew themselves out and the first signs of spring appeared in the northern Great Basin. Camp Warner, at nearly 5,000 feet in elevation, was in terrain too harsh and exposed. A sergeant left the post in a storm, got lost, and was later found frozen to death. Several nights the men had to be marched around in a circle for hours on end, to prevent them from freezing. Crook planned to abandon the post and build a new Camp Warner in a spot with a milder climate.

The winter was little better at Camp C. F. Smith. To curb drunkenness among his 23rd Infantrymen, post commander Captain Walker issued orders that no liquor be kept for sale or use within the encampment. The sutler, having a full barrel and unwilling to destroy it, half-buried it, while the drifting snow concealed it completely. A mail rider on the Chico route somehow stumbled across it, let a few soldiers in on the secret, and they dug up the treasure and emptied it into several kettles, which they took back to their quarters. About February 12, they spent the entire evening indulging in "an immense drunk." The corporal of the guard discovered them. He did not want to get the men into serious trouble, but he insisted that the remaining liquor be disposed of, and got the brilliant idea to pour it onto the hot embers in the fireplace. When the spirits hit the coals, flames shot out and ignited the wooden barracks. The soldiers tried in vain to extinguish the fire, but barely escaped "without being roasted alive. The floors and roofs of several tenements were soon consumed, besides blankets, clothing, arms, ammunitions, provisions, etc. . . . ." The mail rider and a number of soldiers went to the guardhouse. In the confusion, two soldiers stole two horses, the private property of Captain Myers, and deserted. They were heading for the mines when caught several days later at the Snake River by former captain, now a civilian, George Conrad, and interpreter Dave Pickett.

While Crook campaigned during the winter, the Department of the Pacific received yet another restructuring. Orders of January 29, 1867, abolished the old District of Boise, reconstituting it as the District of Owyhee, and including Fort Boise, and Camps Lyon, Winthrop (Three Forks), C. F. Smith, and Warner. Camps McDermit and Winfield Scott, without being taken from the District of California, were placed under orders of the commanding officer of the Owyhee District. The new commander was George Crook, who was not even aware of the changes for some time. Regardless, Crook didn't go to headquarters at Fort Boise, but remained in the field. As the first wildflowers appeared on the harsh volcanic plains, Crook moved north, hoping to find the Paiutes in the Harney Lake region. In mid-March they traveled to what Crook called the "Dunder and Blixen" country.[1]

While camped on that river, about thirty Paiutes crept up to the horses and mules about two in the morning of March 23. Crook said he "made the usual dispositions and took the usual precautions," putting the stock in a picketed circle, but the Indians stampeded them by shooting arrows into the herd and waving blankets so that ninety spooked animals ran off, including almost all of the mounts of Company H. The troopers managed to recover thirty-five head, but the loss, said Crook, "weakened my strength so much. . . that I was compelled to return" to Camp Warner. They just had enough animals left to pack out. Crook sent some men back to Camp Warner to re-stock and re-provision. "By making two loads we got back all right," he said.

On April 2, Crook was in a temporary camp on Warner Lake, writing to General Steele about his predicament and blaming others for his loss, stating a "want of knowledge of Indians and gross stupidity was the cause of the stampede." Crook at times did not seem to grasp the incongruities of his pronouncements; "gross stupidity" may have been the cause of the stampede, but it was a result of his own orders to provide only the "usual dispositions" and "usual precautions" that opened the door for the successful raid. The Indians were beginning to look to Crook as their commissary.

Back at Camp Warner, Captain Collins could do little to assist Crook, because Indians ran off some of his own stock, and killed one of his soldiers during the unsuccessful pursuit. Crook tried to put on a bold front, saying that he believed all the Indian troubles in the district emanated from the Warner area, and "I can with what troops I have soon rid this country of hostile Indians." The problem was, he concluded, "I can do nothing until I get the transportation. . . ."

Shortly after, Crook and some of the troops traveled back near Malheur Lake, but remained "powerless to operate against the Indians until we could have our stock replenished." While waiting, Crook, as was his custom, easily shifted from Indian hunter to game hunter. He had a pine-log canoe constructed and paddled around, noting the depth to be very shallow, with only a few places being from four to six feet deep. The lake was ringed with tule and bulrushes and teeming with wildfowl. When the ice froze or thawed, Crook said the resultant cracking sounded like the discharge of artillery. In the open water between ice floes, swans gathered in great numbers, and Crook said he could get in many shots before they would fly, believing the birds mistook the gunfire for cracking ice. Crook collected sixty-seven dozen cormorant and coot eggs on one excursion; a coot egg was good eating, he said, but the cormorant egg was bitter and unhealthy.[2]

While Crook idled his time away, filling his diary with bird observations more than Indian matters, the bands avoided him and got to work elsewhere. In January 1867, warriors shot a man named Glass, while hunting with two companions between the Boise and Snake Rivers. On The Dalles and Canyon City Road in February, Indians stole Charles Breymer's packmules and destroyed his saddles. They took one horse from Frank Thompson's (or Tompkin's) Ranch, and 13 miles from Canyon City, Indians ran off a number of cattle from Riley's Ranch. About March 5, Indians stole thirteen head of cattle from Miller's Ranch on the Boise and Umatilla Road. The owners of the Straw Ranch, on the same road,

A. R. Bowman Museum, Crook County Historical Society, Prineville, Oregon
Chief Paulina, ca 1865

decided to abandon their place because of previous raids that left them destitute of stock and moveable property.

In mid-March, Indians drove off stock from Officer's Ranch on the South Fork John Day, and from Brackett's Ranch on the Cottonwood. They raided Current Creek on The Dalles and Canyon City Road and stole eleven mules and two horses from C. M. Lockwood's packtrain, plus a number of cattle from Alkali Ranch. About March 19, a party of white hunters in Baker County, Oregon, surprised a small band of Indians near the junction of Eagle Creek and Powder River. They ambushed the Indians, killing six, with no losses of their own. On March 22, marauders ran off about twenty-five mules from a packtrain camped near Snake River at the Weiser Ferry, and drove the animals in the direction of Malheur River. On the same day, Indians killed a cow on Ray's Ranch on Reynolds Creek north of Silver City, and three days later returned to drive off twenty-two head of his cattle.

The same raiders who hit Ray's went north along Reynolds Creek and on Monday, March 19, jumped the Boise and Owyhee Stage. Just before noon, eight warriors opened fire from ambush 60 yards to the right of the road, blasting the four-horse coach driven by William Younger while it was in a small canyon one mile past the summit of the divide between Reynolds Creek and the Snake. Riding beside Younger was former packer, F. C. Pomeroy. Younger had just mentioned to Pomeroy that they were in almost the exact location where driver Frank McCoy was killed four months before.

Just then, the first shotgun blast hit Younger in the side and he fell into the stage's boot, moaning, "Oh, Oh, I'm shot!"

Pomeroy grabbed the reins and whipped the horses into a run. There were three passengers inside: B. V. Reichenberg, a partner in the merchant firm of Hyman & Reichenberg in Idaho City; James Ullman, a miner, clerk and musician; and Frank Bennett, who was recently a stage driver for Hill Beachey. Bennett climbed out to help and they drove the stage far enough away to stop and quickly carry Younger inside. Pomeroy had a pistol, but it was packed away in his carpetbag.

When the Indians reappeared, Pomeroy lashed the team for one more mile before the breast-strap on one of the wheel horses broke and the horse fell beneath the tongue, dragging the coach to a halt. Pomeroy and Ullman cut loose the leaders, but one broke free and ran toward the ferry. Pomeroy hopped on the other horse and went after the runaway. Ullman ran after him. Bennett found Reichenberg's unused pistol in the coach and took it. He and Reichenberg freed the remaining unhurt wheel horse and Bennett said he would try to ride Younger to safety. Reichenberg ran off. After getting Younger on the horse, Bennett mounted and tried to ride while holding the mortally wounded man in the saddle. He fired back a few times with Reichenberg's pistol, and kept the Indians at a reasonable distance. Finally, Younger said he could no longer hold on and asked to be left hidden in the sagebrush. Bennett found a dry ravine and dropped him off there, unobserved by the Indians.

Bennett overtook Reichenberg and helped him up, and the two rode on. They caught up with Ullman, who had been hiding in the rocks until they approached. He exited his hiding place, but when he discovered they could not help him, he ran back to the rocks, but too late, for the Indians had seen him. The horsemen reached Fruit's Ferry, spread the alarm, and immediately seven mounted men went back to help. They were too late. Ullman was already dead, shot through the right shoulder and breast. The Indians had only gotten his coat, boots, and one sock before the rescuers rode up. Younger had died in the ravine. The stage was ransacked and the mail bags split open, with letters being blown with the winds.

Just then, another rider approached, telling the posse that he had just seen another body in the road. They went south two miles up the canyon and found the body of a Mr. Bouchet, a resident of Owyhee, who was traveling alone and on foot a few hours behind the stage. Bouchet had left Ray's Ranch that morning and was warned to take some weapons, but inexplicably, he went unarmed. The Indians had come upon him after ransacking the stage. They killed, scalped, stripped, and mutilated him. The posse took the three bodies to the ferry, where Bouchet was buried. They carried the remains of Younger and Ullman to Boise City for burial.[3]

With the nearly constant raiding, it was only a matter of time until an Indian chief would meet the same fate as a high-ranking officer, such as Lt. Colonel McDermit. The incident began as had hundreds of others. Many of Paulina's people, who had been hard hit by McKay and Darragh on Crooked River, had moved north of the Ochoco Mountains to an area that had been comparatively free from raids for a while, among the last being the September 1866 attack on James Clark's house, later called Burnt Ranch. After his place was destroyed, Clark got a job as a mail carrier and stage driver on The Dalles and Canyon City Road. The route kept to the high ground between the steep canyons of the lower Deschutes and John Day Rivers, swinging southeast at the head of John Day Canyon, and following the river a short way before heading up Bridge Creek.

LITTLE TROUT CREEK, APRIL 25, 1867

Near the head of the John Day Canyon were a small number of ranches, including Clarno's and Cooper's. The story went, that when stockman Andrew Clarno first settled in the area in the vicinity of present-day Clarno, Oregon, there were no neighbors. When he learned that a friend had built a ranch 20 miles to the east of him, Clarno rode over and asked, "Bill, don't you think you're crowding me a little?" On April 25, Clarno and the others probably wished there were a few more settlers in the area for better protection, for the nearest settler was still 12 miles away. On that day, Chief Paulina and seven warriors swept down on Clarno's and Cooper's Ranches. Like the majority of raids, its purpose was simply to steal stock animals. Paulina got thirty horses and thirty-one cattle from Clarno—every animal he owned save the one horse he was riding while hunting stray cattle. Clarno figured it was useless to seek help at Camp Watson, which was 80 miles away. He estimated his loss at $3,540. Paulina then headed west and hit Antelope House, between Antelope Creek and Trout Creek, a station run by Howard Maupin, and relieved Maupin of his stock.

Passing along the Canyon City Road at the time was the driver for Hank Wheeler's Dalles and Canyon City Stage, James Clark, and Howard Maupin. Only one passenger, William Ragan, rode with them. Clark and Maupin's son, Perry, had been in the fight with Weahwewa's band in September 1866, after Clark's Ranch was burned. When the stage approached Antelope House, the men saw the dying flames of the burned station. An angry Maupin immediately wanted to go after the Indians, and Clark, finding himself in a reminiscent situation, agreed to help him. Ragan wanted to join them.

"It's your funeral," said Maupin, "but come on, the more the merrier."

It is unclear what happened after this time, but apparently Clark and Maupin had completed their shift and turned the stage over to another driver. A few other civilians, John Atterbury among them, may have joined the three men, but it was a small posse, perhaps foolhardy as well as brave, that rode after the Indians. The tracks were easily followed to the junction of

Trout Creek and Little Trout Creek in Degner Canyon, just north of present-day Ashwood, Oregon. Ragan, perhaps believing he had made a bad choice, began lagging farther behind, and Maupin and Clark continued on. The Paiutes, perhaps believing that no one had followed them, or too hungry to wait any longer, had stopped to butcher a beef. They had made camp and were enjoying their ox roast when Maupin peered over a rock wall and saw them. He was certain they were dining on his favorite milk cow. Maupin and Clark opened up on them with a Henry and a Spencer Rifle. The repeaters devastated the surprised Paiutes. Paulina, who had just walked up to the fire, went down first, his right hip shattered. Horse Trap, who had been away scouting the area, just rode in when the firing started. He saw Paulina go down, and charged at the whites who were shooting his people. He took a .44 slug to the chest that knocked him off his horse and into a rocky depression. Within minutes, four were dead, and the remaining four unceremoniously fled. Clark and Maupin ran up and blasted the dead or dying Snakes. Clark saw one Indian still alive and reportedly recognized him "as the same Indian that chased me all over Bridge Creek and burned my house and barn!" He was wrong. It was Ocheho's band that burned him out, but Clark was not to be denied his revenge, and he shot five more bullets into the dying Indian. Remarkably, the tough warrior was still alive. Maupin finally shot him in the face with his .36 caliber Colt and took his scalp. They recovered the remaining cattle. The four dead Paiutes were left for the coyotes and buzzards.

Four days later at The Dalles, Clark and Maupin showed the army officers and Wasco scouts the scalp, warbonnet, rifle, and hunting knife they had taken from the Indian. They were immediately identified as belonging to Paulina, and Clark and Maupin became instant celebrities. By killing Paulina, they had done the job that Lieutenant Borrowe had fervently wished that McKay and his scouts would do. Back in February, Borrowe wrote for McKay to "get your horses up as fast as possible so that you can make another dash at your old friend Paulina before you come in. I am particularly anxious to have you kill this man. It would pay for the whole expedition."[4]

Chapter 18 notes

1 *Owyhee Avalanche*, February 16, 1867, February 23, 1867, April 6, 1867; Schmitt, ed., *Crook Autobiography*, 151.

2 Crook to AAG, April 2, 1867, RG 393, Dept. of Columbia, Letters Received, Box 3; *Commissioner of Indian Affairs 1867*, 101; Schmitt, ed., *Crook Autobiography*, 152; *Owyhee Avalanche*, April 20, 1867.

3 *Idaho World*, February 2, 1867, March 9, 1867, March 30, 1867, April 6, 1867, April 27, 1867; *Owyhee Avalanche*, March 30, 1867; *Commissioner of Indian Affairs 1867*, 101.

4 McArthur, *Oregon Geographic Names*, 206; Andrew Clarno Depredation Claim # 1738; Clark, "McKay's Journal, Part I," 170-71; Clark, "McKay's Journal, Part II," 272-73; *Commissioner of Indian Affairs 1867*, 101; Ontko, *Thunder Over the Ochoco III*, 377-80; Ruby and Brown, *Pacific Northwest*, 209; Thompson, *Reminiscences of a Pioneer*, 62-63. Clarno, filing his depredation claim in 1891, mistakenly recorded the year of the incident as 1866. The fight has been said to have occurred on 25 and 28 April 1867. Thompson tells the story a little differently, with Howard and Perry Maupin at the station, and Clark and Atterbury arriving on the stage.

Chapter 19
"It Was No Easy Task"

While activity in the Harney Lake Valley slowed as Lt. Colonel Crook duck-hunted and waited to get more horses and mules, the surrounding area continued to see action, some of which was fought in the newspapers. The *Avalanche* and the *World* kept up their feud, with the former accusing the latter of wanting Fort Boise built up, to the detriment of Owyhee. The "Government leeches having their permanent headquarters round Fort Boise, have been. . .urging the abandonment of Camps Winthrop and Lyon for the further pleasure and profit of Boise," the *Avalanche* moaned. It was a shame that while "Crook and men have been fighting and freezing through this winter," those folks "who never suffered from depredations" were doing their best to nullify the gains of the past six months.[1]

At this time rumor spread, apparently from some captured Paiute women, that Paiute Chief Howluck (Bigfoot) had been killed in January at Crook's battle on "Tearass Plain." The story was challenged by rancher George Hill, who had been at the battle, where no dead warrior of such size as the giant Bigfoot was found. In addition, Hill recently had been searching for stolen stock in the vicinity of Owyhee Ferry, where he "discovered the unmistakable mammoth foot-tracks which bore evidence of having been impressed by something more substantial than Bigfoot's ghost."

Bigfoot was legendary in the area, and was known by several names, including Oulux, Qualuck, Howlark, Howlash, and Nampuh, from which the city of Nampa, Idaho, reportedly took its name. Bigfoot was supposedly six-feet nine inches tall, weighed 300 pounds, was 59-inches around the chest, left a 17 ½-inch long footprint, and could run down jackrabbits and kill them with a club. A mountaineer named Reid, who occasionally scouted for Crook, and who had a personal encounter with Bigfoot, attested to his dimensions and prowess. He was first reported living in the Boise Valley area, where he had murdered emigrants along the Oregon Trail, but Bigfoot and his band ranged from Idaho to the Klamath Lake region. At one time he had a $1,000 reward on his head, but no one could seemingly bring the elusive Bigfoot to justice.[2]

Crook had nearly got him in January 1867, at "Tearass Plain," but since then, Crook had been fighting the weather and lack of horses more than the

Indians. Other commands may not have had much more luck, but at least they were actively campaigning. Lieutenant John Barry, with men of Company I, 1st Cavalry, left Camp Watson on April 6, when the snows in the Ochoco Mountains were still deep. He traveled to Bridge Creek and Muddy Creek, crossed the mountains southwest to Dead Indian Creek, then southeast to Cottonwood Creek. He went along Ochoco Creek and south to Crooked River where much of the valley was flooded. Moving east, Barry reached the North Fork, went upstream, and then over to old Camp Dahlgren, which was abandoned when Captain Drake left the area in 1864. From there he moved north and tried to recross the mountains, but snow from two to four feet deep stopped him. He returned to Dahlgren Creek and sarcastically reported, "Wood and grass very scarce. Water very plenty." He waited until his men extricated many pack animals that had bogged down in the snow and mud.

On the morning of April 16, Barry moved out, but could not find a place to cross the swollen creek. "Horses and mules all mired," he wrote. "Had to unpack and unsaddle to cross the swamp. Most of the mules had to be hauled out with ropes." The men had to pack and carry all the supplies on their own backs. They only made four miles that day. Barry wrote, "it is almost impossible to travel this country at this season of the year, the country is so flooded from the snow melting on the hills." That night, back on the North Fork Crooked River, there was plenty of wood and water, but no grass. Barry had to empty his aparejos to find the last of the grain to feed the animals. On April 17, they headed west, and while crossing the North Fork, said Barry, "had four men and horses washed away in the current—Private Snell was drowned. I saved the other three men and all the horses."

By now, with supplies nearly exhausted, Barry left behind the pack animals, nine soldiers, and four packers with the remaining provisions. With eighteen men and horses, he made an emergency ride for Camp Watson, but unable to cut directly north over the snowbound mountains, he had to nearly retrace his outward route. They marched 52, 48, and 64 miles on three successive days, and finally reached Camp Watson on April 22, after a scout of about 440 miles—and then had to go back to rescue the men left behind. They saw no Indian sign. Barry's trip was more typical of the numerous scouts made into the wilderness—with no results other than exhausted men, horses, supplies, accident, and injury—than the comparatively rare expedition that resulted in an Indian battle.[3]

At Malheur Lake, when Crook finally replaced his animals, he was nevertheless stymied—he did not know where the Indians had gone. His long wait in Harney Valley gave the Indians plenty of time to disperse. Not knowing where to go, Crook had little alternative other than to split up his companies and send them back to their posts while he continued moving from camp to camp, hoping for a lead. Captain Hunt, with scouts Dave Pickett and Jim Beebe, returned with Company M, 1st Cavalry, to Camp Lyon. Hunt rather lamely told the newspaper that there were "plenty of Indians in the vicinity of Warner Lake, but says that he could not find them together in sufficient numbers to obtain a fight."

While Hunt waited at Lyon, Crook and Captain Walker went down the Malheur River and over to Silver City, arriving on April 13. To the approval of the Owyhee citizens, Crook indicated he would not go back to Fort Boise, but would re-fit, gather up his companies, and head south to Camp McDermit and then over to Camp Warner, which he believed to be "right in the heart of an Indian country. . . ." On April 22, Captain Walker left Silver City for Camp C. F. Smith, to go "after the Lo family."[4]

Crook intended to go to McDermit, but first he went back to Camp Warner to pick up his scouts and soldiers. On May 1, the command marched to Camp C. F. Smith, and then south to Camp McDermit. It would be well that Crook would visit the Nevada post, for the soldiers there could not seem to get their act together. There were the usual civilian complaints that they did nothing but stay close to the shelter of their tents and collect their pay. Posted there at the time was Lieutenant Harrison Moulton. Born in New Hampshire, Moulton joined the 1st Dragoons/Cavalry in 1857, and was cited for gallantry at the June 21, 1863, action at Upperville, Virginia. Some may have wondered about his gallantry in early April 1867. Moulton took a scout of Company C, 1st Cavalry, out from Camp McDermit. From the Montana Mountains above King's River Valley they saw a band of Paiutes. Moulton approached, but there were more Indians than he first anticipated. The Paiutes, not at all threatened by the small force, reportedly "applied most vulgar and insulting language to the soldiers and defied them to come on." Moulton, to the disgust of several men, unceremoniously rode back to the post.

Crook reached McDermit on May 7, and rested for a few days, but there is no record of what he may have discussed with Lieutenant Moulton. On May 10, however, Crook saddled up to take his own brand of warfare to the Indians of the Quinn River Valley. Unfortunately, the Indians would not cooperate. Crook said that he "scoured the country west of Queens River valley from opposite Camp McGarry to the Chico road and north" to Camp C. F. Smith, "but only found one band of poor foot Indians, some 8 bucks, the rest having gone west of Steins Mountain."

By May 24, Crook was back at Camp C. F. Smith, writing to General Steele. He said that all the depredations in the McDermit area were committed by Indians who had since vacated the region and had gone west to Warner Lakes, "because they think themselves safe there." Crook extrapolated on the Indians he was facing. He found two classes: "the higher order" was mounted and included the ones committing the depredations; the lower order included the "poor local foot Indians." He likened them to rich whites and poor whites, who kept separated and had different aspirations and abilities. As for the Indians, the mounted ones were the stock thieves and fighters, while the foot Indians "would give us no trouble," but for "stealing a lame or eating a dead animal left along the road." When Crook finished with his ethnography lesson to General Steele, he said he would commence his campaign against the Indians west of Steens Mountain, but only "as soon as the animals and supplies arrive here from San Francisco." Crook also asked for more scouts. "I would very much like to have the company of scouts you speak of," he wrote to Steele, "please send them to Fort Boise via Umatilla and the old Emigrant road, as the Indians are very vigilant and have got their spies all over the country...." Want of horseflesh and provisions always seemed to hamper Crook's ability to carry out his plans. Now he was becoming so dependent on his scouts that he was reluctant to move without them.[5]

In his autobiography, Crook made a lackadaisical summary of his time spent along the Oregon-Nevada border. "I made a scout from Camp McDermit in the Quinn River country, but beyond my hard work, nothing was accomplished."[6]

SILVIES RIVER, APRIL 27, 1867

While Crook was preparing to move to Camp McDermit, Indians filtered back into now vacant Harney Lake Valley. The soldiers at Camp Logan picked up the slack. While most of the 14th Infantry had transferred to Arizona months ago, a few officers remained in the Pacific Northwest waiting for orders to join their units. Lieutenant Charles B. Western remained in command of Camp Logan, located east of Canyon City and six miles up Strawberry Creek from its junction with the John Day River. On March 28, Lieutenant Western, with a detachment of seven men of Company F, 8th Cavalry, attacked a camp of Paiutes high on the divide above Murderers Creek, captured three oxen, 2,000 pounds of jerked beef, and destroyed the camp. Western chased the fleeing Indians the next day and due to the "gallantry" of Privates Stott and Jackson, captured eight horses. The remaining warriors got away on foot high in the snowy peaks. Western returned to Camp Logan on April 2.

Having resupplied, on April 20, Western and thirteen men of Company F, went on another scout in search of reported Indian marauders a dozen miles farther down the John Day River at Canyon City. He found the Indian trail on April 24, but it led south into the Aldrich Mountains. They followed the tracks for two days until the pack train could advance no farther in the rough country. Western cut loose from his train, taking twelve men and three days' rations. On April 27, they found about fifty Indians, including twenty or more warriors, on the upper Silvies River north of present-day Burns, Oregon.

The river was running high, but Western left three men to guard the horses, and with the remaining troopers, waded neck deep in the water to the opposite bank. The Indians did not expect an attack from the river, and Western charged into the camp shooting. The Indians put up only a token defense, and then fled. Six were killed and left on the ground in the camp. Others were wounded and carried off by their comrades. "A number of wounded were also drowned in attempting to cross the river," the after-action report stated. Western captured 32 horses and the camp equipage, including one and a half tons of camas root, which was destroyed.[7]

Crook was only gone from Silver City a few days when Indians again struck the area. The maddening situation could have been likened to a man standing in the midst of a prairie dog town; as he approached one hole, the prairie dog would disappear, only to bark at him from a hole he had just left. The residents of the Owyhee District tried to take solace in the apparent shrinkage in the size of the Indian bands that raided the area. Whereas, previous to the fall of 1866, bands of scores of Indians came close to town, but since then no parties of more than a half-dozen were reported nearer than 30 miles. It was small compensation, for civilians were now more likely to go out in small numbers or unarmed, while lesser number of Indians could more easily sneak in to ambush them.

That very scenario was enacted on April 26 and 27. Four men, James Fraser, William Slack, and Messrs. Reed and Smith, were prospecting in a gulch just below Wagontown, a small village named for the numerous wagons parked there in the days before the road was built up to Silver City. While the men worked, Slack and Fraser walked a mile back to Fraser's cabin to get some blankets and gum boots. On the return, Fraser stopped off at Thomas Wall's cabin to talk and buy some bacon. In the evening, Slack went to Wagontown and Reed and Smith went to Smith's cabin for the night. Fraser never showed up. At Wall's, men heard gunfire in the direction Fraser had gone.

The next morning, the three men showed up to work and wondered where Fraser was. Nevertheless, they toiled until about lunchtime, when Slack took a break to go back to the cabin to find some grub. When Smith got hungry, he took his pick and walked toward the cabin. Only a short distance down the trail he saw Fraser—or at least he thought it was Fraser. A few steps farther and Smith discovered it was an Indian wearing Fraser's coat. He ran back to Reed, told him what he had seen, and the two men ran to Wall's. When they all went back to investigate, they found Fraser shot in the right breast and Slack in the left side. Both were scalped, but Fraser, killed the previous night, was the more horribly mutilated; his chin whiskers were cut off, his thighs split open, bowels cut out, and much of his flesh peeled away. Slack's gut was slit open and slices around his shoulders looked as if the Indians tried to sever his arms from his torso.

The Indians—only three were seen—chased B. F. Flathers's pack train from Wall's to Hill's Ranch in Jordan Valley, before disappearing into the mountains. The murdered men's bodies, being so close to town, were seen by a large number of curious citizens, including Lieutenant James A. Waymire, who had hung up his saber in the Oregon Cavalry in November 1864, and in January 1867, signed up with the 1st Cavalry. Waymire was on his way to join Captain Hunt at Camp Lyon. The uproar in Ruby City and Silver City commenced again. Where was the army? How could anyone help from Camp Lyon when there were only half a dozen soldiers there? Why couldn't more men be sent down from Fort Boise? There was talk of organizing another volunteer expedition to look for the Indians, but by now, the majority of the locals had the attitude, "I haven't lost any Indians."[8]

In late April, a Mr. Kirkpatrick, who ranched on Catherine Creek, unearthed a skeleton, which was reportedly that of a "white woman who had been scalped." On Sunday, May 5, Indians hit several ranches along Catherine and Sinker Creeks, including those of Con Shea, John McMahon, H. B. Eastman, Ben Parker, and Mr. Enos. They got many horses and cattle from these places, Shea alone losing about 150, and were moving them west up Sinker Creek. On Monday, McMahon, Catlow, Johnson, Enos, and four others followed the thieves, one trail heading over the divide between Sinker Creek on the east and Reynolds Creek on the west. The ranchers caught up to the Indians about four miles from Ray's Ranch on upper Reynolds Creek. The Indians watched McMahon and Enos, who were scouting ahead, and opened fire on them. The ranchers returned fire and headed back for help. When all eight of them were together, their numbers matched what McMahon and Enos figured the Indian strength to be, and they charged back to the ambush site. Upon their arrival, the Indians had moved on, and were firing at something else in the distance.

When ranchers on Reynolds Creek heard about the raid on Sinker Creek, a few of them got together to see if they could help. The night before, Indians shot at Robert Dorning as he rode home from a visit to Babington's Ranch. Monday morning, Cyrus Polk and a Mr. McKnight got their weapons and rode over the divide from Reynolds to Sinker Creek. About noon, they ran into the same Indians who had just chased off McMahon and Enos from the opposite direction. The warriors, possibly believing they had fallen into some clever trap, decided they had better fight their way out, and Polk and McKnight were in the path of least resistance. As the two ranchers peered over the rocks to see what the firing was about, a volley blasted them from above. A bullet tore through Polk's arm. They returned fire, but more bullets ricocheted among the rocks, with one or more going through both of McKnight's legs below the knees. Polk kept firing and was certain he killed at least one Indian. A few warriors kept them pinned until nightfall, by gunfire and by rolling rocks down on them. When things quieted down, Polk gave McKnight his pistol, told the older man he was going for help, and ordered that he kill himself before letting the Indians capture him.

224

The Indians were gone, however. Most had headed northwest, where the Sinker Creek ranchers had followed their trail over to Reynolds Creek, not far from the place where the stage was hit in March. Losing the track, they returned up Reynolds Creek to learn of Polk's and McKnight's fight. Polk, meanwhile, had gotten help, and the next morning recovered McKnight and took the critically injured man to Babington's. "The bones in one leg are badly mashed," reported the newspaper. "Owing to his age such wounds will go very hard with him." They did. McKnight died two weeks later.[9]

CAMP WATSON, MAY 5, 1867

There was a little action around Camp Watson. In April, Captain Eugene Baker, with twenty men of Company I, 1st Cavalry, made an unsuccessful scout along the John Day, looking for stolen mules. Lieutenant John Barry made a similar scout in the other direction, detailed above, to the North Fork John Day, finding "plenty of Indian signs," but no Indians. It was left to Sergeant J. H. Jones, with a detachment of Company I, to achieve a minor victory, when he chased down a small band of Paiutes near Camp Watson on May 5, killing one warrior.[10]

SUMMIT SPRINGS STATION, MAY 18, 1867

While George Crook marched west of Quinn River, finding little Indian sign and concluding that they had all gone west of Steens Mountain, there were still plenty of Indians around Camp McDermit, and they apparently didn't know or care about the increased troop presence. On May 16, they raided Brougham's Ranch on Flat Creek at the foot of the Santa Rosa Mountains, about 16 miles south of McDermit. Brougham had already lost twelve cattle to Indians the previous October. This time the Indians drove off twenty mules and ten horses that Brougham claimed were worth about $4,500. They hit his ranch again on the last day of April 1868, getting two cattle, and again on May 6, running off another fifteen mules and eight horses.

On Saturday, May 18, Paiutes hit Summit Springs Station, about 18 miles north of McDermit. In a daring mid-afternoon raid, the warriors watched as a number of Hill Beachey's stage horses and several from another team that had been resting at the station were turned out to graze. The warriors saw their chance, but a station employee had just picked that inopportune moment to go out to hunt—right in the Indians' chosen attack path.

Regardless, twenty-four warriors burst out from cover and came charging in. The unnamed station hand probably looked in astonishment at the Indians barreling toward him across an open sage plain. Quickly weighing his chances, he decided to use his Henry Rifle and stand his ground. The horsemen came in a single line to about 80 yards from him, when they split in two files and thundered by on both sides, firing as they went. As bullets kicked sand around him, the station hand spun right and left, getting off twelve shots with his repeater. In seconds, the Indians were gone; the station hand was unhit, but he was certain that a few of his bullets struck home. He decided not to wait around to see what the Indians would do next, but ran for cover.

The warriors were not interested in him—they wanted the horses at the station. The employees and a handful of soldiers posted there heard the firing and war whoops coming closer. They immediately realized the Indians were going for the grazing stock and tried to get there first, but were too late. The Paiutes were in and driving the horses away. The owner of the team who had just turned his animals loose fired five shots from his wagon. Corporal Clancy and another soldier got close enough to fire a few times. The combined shooting wounded two Indians and one of their horses—animals described as being splendid stolen U. S. cavalry horses. The Paiutes ran off twenty-one horses, sixteen of them belonging to Hill Beachey, four to the teamster, and one to a man named Clark.

The Indians rode off northwest, ignoring the station hand hiding in the sage with his Henry. A half hour after the raid, six men from Brougham's Ranch at Flat Creek rode up, on the trail of these same Indians that raided Brougham's two days earlier. Two men from the station joined them, and they rode after the Indians, but their horses were so jaded they gave up after nine miles. Two days later, station hands found a horse with a rawhide Indian saddle, all spotted with dried blood, giving them assurance that at least one of the raiders had been killed or severely wounded. The loss of horses was another blow to Beachey, who could barely keep his struggling stage company out of the red ink.[11]

STEENS MOUNTAIN, JUNE 19, 1867

While Crook waited at Camp C. F. Smith, Archie McIntosh and his mixed bag of fourteen Cayuse and friendly Shoshoni and Paiute scouts were busy scouring the area for hostile "Snakes." On June 19, they surprised a camp near Steens Mountain. McIntosh's scouts killed twelve Indians, wounded one and captured two more. In a day they were back celebrating at Camp C. F. Smith.[12]

DONNER UND BLITZEN RIVER, JUNE 22, 1867

Ever since William McKay and John Darragh's successful campaign against Paulina's band along Crooked River in January, they had been in camp or at the Warm Springs Reservation, waiting for further orders. John Darragh got his first, being directed to join with Crook at Camp C. F. Smith. The scout company moved up Crooked River and across to Camp Currey on upper Silver Creek, where they found "fresh signs of Snakes" heading in a "straight wake" for Harney Lake and then to the south end of Steens Mountain. On June 21, they discovered more Indian tracks about 15 miles south of Harney Lake near Jackass Creek, and the next day near

Donner und Blitzen River they caught "a few napping—killed five—captured two—besides four good horses, bows and arrows &c." Darragh trailed more fresh signs to old Camp Alvord, before heading to Camp C. F. Smith, where he reported to Crook on June 28.[13]

MALHEUR RIVER, JULY 8, 19, 1867

Captain Eugene M. Baker and Company I, 1st Cavalry, had been stationed at Camp Watson on the Canyon City Road for the past year. He and his lieutenants had gone on numerous scouts, many in response to civilian complaints about Indians stealing stock. On June 24, 1867, Baker supplied his company with thirty days' rations and went on an extended hunt. Baker crossed

A. R. Bowman Museum, Crook County
Historical Society, Prineville, Oregon
William McKay, 1875.

the Ochoco Mountains, went up the South Fork John Day, and down Silvies River into Harney Lake Valley. After scouting around Malheur Lake, he headed northeast to investigate the headwaters of the Malheur River. On July 8, Baker attacked a village of Indians, probably Weahwewa's Paiutes, killed two warriors, captured fourteen women and children and two horses. Moving southeast into what was reported as the "Malheur country," Baker jumped another rancheria on July 19, this time killing two warriors and capturing eight women and children. With supplies low, and the horses rapidly wearing down, Baker circled back to Camp Watson on July 24, after a march of about 700 miles.[14]

There were other expeditions crisscrossing the same terrain as Baker, giving the Paiutes little rest. William McKay and his scouts had been waiting near Warm Springs Reservation for orders. On May 22, Lieutenant Borrowe wrote to McKay that he was to wait for Superintendent Huntington and escort him and a supply of Indian treaty goods to Fort Klamath, after which, he was to proceed to Camp C. F. Smith and report to Crook. McKay moved to Trout Creek on June 5, where he waited for Huntington, not realizing he had established camp only a few miles from the spot his adversary, Paulina, had been killed in April.

William McKay bided his time, but the superintendent never arrived. His scouts were all back from their spring planting and were "becoming very impatient and uneasy at being detained in camp." McKay asked to be relieved of escort duty and allowed to take the field. On June 22, orders finally arrived for McKay to start for Camp C. F. Smith immediately, by way of Harney Valley. McKay didn't take the same route as Darragh, but went up the John Day to Canyon City, making a side trip to look for cattle stolen from Hamlin's Ranch near Mountain House. On Independence Day, McKay and his scouts were invited by residents of Canyon City to join in their July Fourth celebration. McKay wrote in his diary: "Went home today and brot the boys to make a 4 July demonstration. They were quite well received. It was quite satisfactory to all the parties concerned. Indians had a regular blow out. . . ." Apparently the frontier settlers could get along quite well with the Indians—as long as they were both fighting on the same side.

With the singing, dancing, and drinking over, McKay took his company south to the upper reaches of Silvies River in a mountain dell, "a very pretty and muddy valley," McKay wrote. "Had very hard times in getting across it." By July 11, they had moved down to "Rattlesnake Camp," which had been a temporary site on Rattlesnake Creek where it issued from the mountains in the north, about two miles from present-day Harney, Oregon. The site had been occasionally used by troops since 1864, and would become "official" on August 16, 1867, when it was established as Camp Steele. The name only lasted one month, when General Halleck wrote to Crook that he disapproved of the name, and suggested the name Camp Harney be used. On July 12, from the future site of Harney, McKay wrote to Lieutenant Goodale, who was also in the area, inquiring about his plans.[15]

Lieutenant Greenleaf A. Goodale, Company K, 23rd Infantry, had fought as an enlisted man in the 6th Maine Infantry during the Civil War. Cited for gallantry at the 1863 Battle of Gettysburg, he became a lieutenant in the 23rd Infantry during the army reorganization of July 1866. Company K had been stationed at Fort Vancouver before being ordered to Camp Wright to wait there for Crook. Goodale was absent at the time, acting as a guide for new recruits of Company F, 8th Cavalry, delivering them to Camp Logan.

With the task completed, Goodale transported five enlisted men prisoners back to face courts martial at Fort Vancouver. On the way, he met up with his company, in command of Lieutenant William F. Rice, who was going to Camp C. F. Smith. Rice, also a veteran, fought in several Massachusetts and New York regiments in the Civil War, before joining the 23rd Infantry at the same time as Goodale. When Goodale learned the company had been reassigned, he hurried the prisoners to The Dalles, went to Portland for one day on business, and overtook Rice one day's march beyond Fort Dalles. In their hurry, one soldier's foot was crushed in an accident and several came down with dysentery. Goodale wished a surgeon and an ambulance had accompanied them. "I have been badly poisoned with poison oak," he wrote. "Several of the men are afflicted in the same manner."[16]

Goodale reached Camp Watson on June 13, where he hired civilian guide A. J. Boyd, whom he thought boasted a little too much, and packmaster Aaron Hewey. Goodale was surprised when he found that Hewey was the son of one of the Heweys he knew back in Bucksport, Maine, and was considered one of the best packers in the country. The train they organized was large, with 210 mules, 180 packs, thirty saddles, and divided into three outfits. They first traveled east to Camp Logan, then back to Camp Currey on Silver Creek, and Goodale commented on Boyd as a guide, saying he was "helpful in getting us through the Blue Mountains." From Currey they went down to Harney Lake and east to Camp Wright, the location of which, according to Goodale, "was known only to Mr. Boyd."

Goodale bivouacked at Camp Wright on the lower Silvies River for forty-three days, waiting for either Crook's arrival, or instructions as to where to proceed. While waiting, Lieutenant Rice made one trip back to Camp Watson for supplies, and Goodale scouted on the headwaters of the Malheur. Several other scouting parties went looking for Indians, and one of them captured four Snakes, one of whom was reported to be Weahwewa's daughter, who

A. R. Bowman Museum, Crook County Historical Society, Prineville, Oregon

Camp Harney, 1872. Below, Camp Harney site today.

Author's photo

229

passed on important news: Chief Paulina had been killed in a fight with some civilians a few months ago. While Goodale and Rice waited at Camp Wright, they received a letter from McKay that he had been at Rattlesnake Camp and was moving southeast to the east end of Malheur Lake. On July 12, Goodale quickly sent off a note, carried by one of McKay's scouts, telling McKay to wait for him so they could join forces. With the letter came word of Paulina's death, and McKay commented, "It was quite a rejoicing amongst the scouts."

SOUTH FORK MALHEUR, JULY 15, 1867

Goodale joined McKay about noon on July 13. The next day, the combined force traveled east toward the South Fork Malheur. Goodale went ahead with six soldiers and six scouts on mules, figuring to investigate the area west of Steens Mountain. On the South Fork Malheur he found Indian sign, plus the tracks of Captain Baker's cavalrymen who were currently hunting Paiutes in between the main and South Fork Malheur. Goodale returned to the camp that evening and he and McKay made a plan. On July 15, they left at six a.m. and moved to the South Fork Malheur in the vicinity of present-day Venator. At four in the afternoon, McKay, Goodale, Boyd, Hewey, twenty-four scouts and eight soldiers, all mounted, (Goodale said there were twenty soldiers and ten scouts) started down the South Fork to look for Weahwewa and his Paiutes. The search didn't take long, for about twilight the scouts noticed a cave in the mountains and evidence of a camp. The Paiutes saw them coming and made the first charge, but when the rest of the scouts and soldiers came up, they turned and fled. A few Indians were seen running into the cave.

Scouts took position around the entrance and exchanged fire with those inside. In front, Boyd took one side, while the 30-year-old Warm Springs scout, Squalth, took the other side. It was already dark when a Paiute shot Squalth dead. Boyd fired at the gunflash and killed the Paiute, and in a final charge, they entered the cave but found no one left alive. Goodale reported killing six Indians, wounding one, and capturing two, plus three horses and one mule. With the Warm Springs Indians carrying Squalth's body, they traveled back to camp in the dark, arriving after midnight. The Indians buried Squalth in the morning, according to Goodale, with their own "peculiar and interesting rites." They then trampled over the grave and built a fire on it to remove any trace.

On July 16, they moved upstream to the junctions of Camp Creek, Indian Creek, and the South Fork Malheur, and stopped in the early afternoon when it turned cold and began to rain. The next morning, Goodale returned northwest to Camp Wright and McKay turned southeast to cross Steens Mountain. About two in the morning on July 19, McKay's two Paiute prisoners escaped during a freezing windstorm. By mid-morning the command finally arrived at Camp C. F. Smith.[17]

230

After all the waiting and preparations, Lt. Colonel Crook was almost ready to begin the next phase of his campaign. He had been gathering men, animals, and supplies for weeks. Lieutenant Moses Harris left Camp Lyon with forty men of Company M, 1st Cavalry, on June 12, heading to Camp C. F. Smith. On a sad note, before Harris left Camp Lyon, the post sutler, George D. Conrad, died. Conrad, who commanded the troops at the January 1866 fight at Battle Creek, mustered out of the California Cavalry in June 1866, moved to Silver City, and became sutler at Camp Lyon. Seemingly healthy just a few days earlier, Conrad caught what the physician called "brain fever," and died suddenly.

John Darragh's scout company arrived at C. F. Smith on June 28. Lieutenant William R. Parnell, who had been on temporary recruiting duty with the 8th Cavalry in California, was sent back to his own Company H, 1st Cavalry, which was also gathering at Camp C. F. Smith. A detachment of Company D, 23rd Infantry arrived. William McKay and his scouts came in on July 19, and the captain met his younger half-brother, Donald McKay, with his own small command of eight Cayuse Indians. Archie McIntosh and his mixed company of friendly Shoshones and Bannocks, sometimes called the "Boise Scouts," were there.

Owyhee businessmen and half-owner of the Beachey Stage Line, Owen R. Johnson, knew a good opportunity when he saw it, and he and Alf Mix went to California to buy horses. They rode in from Chico in mid-July with more than 500 horses, which were badly needed by the army. The valley of Whitehorse Creek was filled with about 200 soldiers, 100 Indian scouts, and nearly 1,000 cattle and horses. One of the last additions was Joe Wasson, co-owner of the *Avalanche*, whose health was being drained by the daily grind of newspaper work. He explained his situation: "To stand up to the metal-rack like a beast to stake-oats and die by inches had become my lot. . . ." Wasson joined Crook's expedition as one of the West's first Indian war correspondents, to regain his health, to seek adventure, and get a first-hand scoop of the fighting. Wasson, who arrived earlier in the same day as McKay, noted the appearance of his men, who paraded into camp displaying the scalps they had taken. Wasson commented: "Their war songs may be music to them. Together with the Boise Indians here, they made the camp howl last night."[18]

Born in Ireland in 1836, Lieutenant Parnell had served with the British 4th Hussars, and later was with the Lancers during the famous charge of the Six Hundred at Balaclava in the Crimean War. He fought in the Civil War in the 4th New York Cavalry, rising to the rank of lieutenant colonel before mustering out in December 1864. He joined the 1st Cavalry in February 1866. Although he had seen plenty of action, Indian fighting was new to Parnell. "It was no easy task that General Crook had before him," he wrote. The Indians did not fight like the Confederates in the manner he was familiar with. "Were it possible for him to concentrate those scattered bands and with his troops give them battle, the problem would soon be solved; but for hundreds of miles the country had to be thoroughly scouted to find—after, perhaps, weeks of hard and tedious marching—but a small band of warriors, who would scatter to the four winds at the approach of troops. It was only when they had every advantage in position and numbers that they would show any disposition to fight. . ."[19]

Parnell verbalized what almost everyone on the frontier knew, and had known ever since the first colonists had arrived: Indian warfare was guerrilla warfare. Yet, the army seemed to have to constantly relearn those non-textbook rules decade after decade—a process that continues today.

Chapter 19 notes

1 *Owyhee Avalanche*, April 6, 1867.

2 Hanley, *Owyhee Trails*, 152-60; "Bigfoot," http://www.idahohistory.net/reference%20series/0040. doc; *Owyhee Avalanche*, April 13, 1867. Bigfoot grew into a local legend in his own time, becoming the bogeyman for white, as well as Indian children. Today, Bigfoot tales have evolved as the legendary giant, hairy creature called sasquatch, said to inhabit the northwestern forests.

3 Barry to Baker, May 10, 1867, RG 393, Dept. of Columbia, Letters Received, Box 3.

4 *Owyhee Avalanche*, April 6, 1867, April 20, 1867, April 27, 1867.

5 Heitman, *Historical Register*, Vol. 1, 732; *Idaho World*, April 13, 1867; Crook to AAG, May 24, 1867, and May 25, 1867, RG 393, Dept. of Columbia, Letters Received, Box 3.

6 Schmitt, ed., *Crook Autobiography*, 153.

7 *Adjutant General's Office*, 26, 27; *Secretary of War 1868-69*, 770-71; Western to AAG, April 2, 1867, RG 393, Dept. of Columbia, Letters Received, Box 4; O'Connor, "Eighth Cavalry," http://www.army.mil/cmh-pg/books/R&H/R&H-8CV.htm.

8 *Owyhee Avalanche*, May 4, 1867.

9 Hanley, *Owyhee Trails*, 79-80, 82; Cornelius Shea Depredation Claim #7644; *Commissioner of Indian Affairs 1867*, 102; *Owyhee Avalanche*, May 4, 1867, May 11, 1867.

10 *Idaho World*, April 6, 1867; Heitman, *Historical Register*, Vol. 2, 428; *Adjutant General's Office*, 27; Webb, *List of Engagements*, 29. Heitman and *Adjutant General* list Jones's action on 5 May; Webb lists it on 22 May.

11 Frederick P. Brougham Depredation Claim #7988; *Idaho World*, May 29, 1867; *Owyhee Avalanche*, May 18, 1867, May 25, 1867.

12 *Secretary of War 1868-69*, 771; Webb, *List of Engagements*, 30; *Adjutant General's Office*, 27.

13 Clark, "McKay's Journal, Part II," 270.

14 *Secretary of War 1868-69*, 69; *Commissioner of Indian Affairs 1867*, 102; Heitman, *Historical Register*, Vol. 2, 428; *Adjutant General's Office*, 28; Webb, *List of Engagements*, 31. Webb indicates the first fight occurred on 7 July. *CIA* indicates 12 Indians were killed.

15 Clark, "McKay's Journal, Part I," 163, 167-71; Clark, "McKay's Journal, Part 2," 270-72; McArthur, *Oregon Geographic Names*, 367.

16 Heitman, *Historical Register*, Vol. 1, 462, 827-28; Clark, "McKay's Journal, Part 1," 165.

17 Clark, "McKay's Journal, Part II," 272-75; *Commissioner of Indian Affairs 1867*, 102; *Secretary of War 1868-69*, 771; Webb, *List of Engagements*, 31. Webb lists the action as occurring on the 13th, but McKay's journal indicates the fight was on the 15th.

18 *Secretary of War 1868-69*, 68; *Owyhee Avalanche*, June 1, 1867, July 27, 1867; Parnell, "Operations with Crook," 482-83; Clark, "McKay's Journal, Part 2," 275; Knight, *Following the Indian Wars*, 34.

19 Heitman, *Historical Register*, Vol. 1, 771; Clark, "McKay's Journal, Part 2," 283; Parnell, "Operations with Crook," 482-83.

Chapter 20
SUMMER, 1867

On July 20, the expedition finally got under way, with Crook leading Captain Perry's Company F (forty-five men) and Lieutenant Harris and Company M (thirty-seven men), 1ˢᵗ Cavalry, and three companies under McIntosh (twenty-five scouts), McKay (thirty-five scouts and eleven packers), and Darragh (thirty-seven scouts and eleven packers). Captain Walker, with Company C, 23ʳᵈ Infantry, remained in camp, and Captain Coppinger, 23ʳᵈ Infantry, came over from Camp Winthrop (Three Forks) to claim his share of the newly acquired horses. Donald McKay and his scouts accompanied Coppinger back to Camp Winthrop.

Crook moved 20 miles southwest to Trout Creek the first day's march, and already the command lost nine mules and their packs. Searching for the lost animals delayed their start the next morning. It had been Crook's intention to head north into the Malheur Country, but at Captain Darragh's suggestion that the Indians had moved south and were getting weapons and horses from their Pit River allies in northern California, Crook decided to head south and west. As Wasson heard the story, the Indians "like the whites down there better than those residing up this way—they can get all sorts of materials for war. Which is a good joke on the whites up this way." Wasson heard that Weahwewa was "a terrible creature—bearing a charmed life; has white hair so long that he can sit on it—very handy, I should think, for a cushion or for scalping."

Crook: "We marched mostly after night, lying by in secret places in the day time. . . ." It was a good start in beginning to fight like the guerrillas he was chasing. The second day, they marched south 18 miles, to the Nevada line, and camped near the now-abandoned Pueblo Mines in the vicinity of present-day Denio. The view embraced much of the Pueblo Valley, which Wasson described as "a billiard table stripped of its green." McIntosh's scouts picked up a trail of four Paiutes early in the morning and tracked them west for 12 miles before catching and killing them. They jubilantly returned to camp at 8:30 p.m.

On July 23, they traveled generally southwest to Bog Hot Valley, almost to the southern tip of the Pueblo Mountains, then cut northwest and up the valley of Rincon Creek. No marching orders were issued until July 25, when the command moved northwest about 20 miles to Isaac's Spring on the northern flank of today's Acty Mountain, where Drew had camped in 1864—a point that could be seen from Warner Peak, about 50 miles away. This evening, McKay's scouts came in after killing one Paiute and taking six children prisoners, about 12 miles to the southwest. Crook detailed two Wasco scouts to check out the area ahead at Beatty's Butte and Guano Lake, and some of McIntosh's scouts to cover Warner Lakes, while the command rested again.[1]

Leaving Camp C. F. Smith two days after Crook, Lieutenants Parnell and John Madigan with Company H, 1st Cavalry, and a mounted detachment of Company D, 23rd Infantry, under Lieutenant Henry Bacon, headed straight for Camp Warner, about 100 miles to the west. Accompanying them was Lieutenant Richard I. Eskridge, acting quartermaster of the 23rd Infantry, who would work to outfit and supply them when all converged at Camp Warner. They marched across Steens Mountain through Skull Creek Canyon, where Parnell described basalt church spires and arched windows carved "almost as perfect as if done by the skillful hand of the architect." Thirty miles farther, he called Beatty's Butte a "perfect amphitheatre" of earth surmounted by towers from 50 to 60 feet in height, and walls 10 feet thick. Parnell and others apparently paid more attention to the grandeur of the land than to the inhabitants who watched them go by. Just before Parnell marched in, Paiutes killed one and wounded another 23rd Infantryman only 200 yards from Camp Warner. Even after the reinforcements arrived, Indians constantly crept up to the stockade and either stampeded animals or killed them with arrows. On one occasion they ran off thirteen mules, but there was no cavalry at the post to chase after them. At Warner, they anxiously awaited Crook's arrival.

CAMP WARNER, JULY 27, 1867

On July 26, Crook's command moved northwest, heading for Lone Grave Butte, just southwest of Beatty's Butte. After losing their way in the dark, they waited for morning to correct their course, continued, made a dry camp from 7 to 10 a.m. and headed out again. About noon, only 7 or 8 miles from Camp Warner, fresh moccasin and pony tracks were discovered crossing the path heading south. Darragh's scouts followed the trail, which led over a lava bed less than 2 miles and then went down onto a grassy flat that surprisingly held a large rancheria. McKay and Darragh followed, saw what was ahead, and motioned for the rest of the command to come on. Half way across the lava, Crook got the notion that they were only chasing a lone horseman, and called the cavalry off. The resultant fight, therefore, was between the Warm Springs scouts, the packers, and Joe Wasson on one end, and the Snakes on the other. Lava rocks bordered the rancheria, and the surprised Paiutes, many of them of Winnemucca's band from the Pyramid Lake country, tried to take shelter in them. Most of the scouts bounded in from the west side, while a number of packers, who had been in the rear of the train, attacked

234

from the east. Wasson, who was near McKay and Darragh and riding a fast horse, got in with the first charge and fired into "the nest with a Henry rifle." The two captains, Wasson, and another scout all shot at one warrior hiding in the sage about 200 yards away; after two rounds apiece the warrior was killed, but by whose bullet no one could tell.

After the first heavy shooting, the scouts scattered to chase individual Snakes to and fro among the rocks, and Wasson remarked how strange the battle seemed with more shouting than shooting. The fight rolled across half a mile of sagebrush and rocks before the Paiutes, armed with only bows and arrows, holed up in a boulder field and fought for a half hour. Packers Tom

A. R. Bowman Museum Crook County Historical Society, Prineville, Oregon
Chief Winnemucca, ca 1880

McKay and Frank Cunningham each killed an Indian. A number of Paiutes who could not escape, hid themselves in the jagged lava, and fires were set around them.

"Three hostile Indians had to be literally burned out of the rocks," wrote Wasson, "one being cooked almost white; they would not yield on more tolerable terms. One of the besieged Snakes made a defiant speech from his position in the rocks." Surrender was an option, however. Not all the Paiutes were killed, as General Steele and Governor Woods may have preferred. The Paiutes lost eleven warriors killed and eleven women and children captured. Only two of the scouts' horses were wounded. They recovered six "Paiute" horses, all bearing the "U. S." brand. "The Columbia Indians went through the spoils for everything they could find," said Wasson, "and it appeared to me were more inclined to look after the spoils than follow up. . . ." Wasson thought that McIntosh's scouts were the best of the three companies: "The Snakes are the superior Indian every way in this outfit for 'fighting the devil with fire.'"[2]

Upon reaching Camp Warner, Crook was welcomed by Lieutenant Parnell, as well as Captain Patrick Collins, Company D, and Captain James Henton, Company B, 23rd Infantry, who were stationed at Warner. The next day, Crook sent Captain Perry and twenty-six men of Company F, with ten of McKay's scouts and guide Isaac Wilson, on a trip southwest toward Goose Lake to look for Indian sign. He detailed Darragh's scouts to head to the north end of the Warner Valley to do the same.

Crook, in the meantime, made good on a promise he made to himself the previous winter, which was to abandon the camp and move it to a more sheltered area. Camp Warner was on an unsheltered plain with Warner (Hart) Mountain running north-south just to the west; it once had a fine grove of pine trees, but the trees were cut to build a number of low log structures. Joe Wasson said it appeared to be a good location for a post and was in some of the finest country he had seen since leaving Jordan Valley, but the post was good only in the summer and fall. "It is entirely out of favor with Colonel Crook," Wasson said, "who came near losing his own life and endangered his men in getting to and from it last winter. . . . This is a terrible place for snow in winter, and so swampy for several months afterwards that its removal on that score is imperative."

While the scouts were out, Crook took Lieutenant Harris and Company M, with five Snake scouts, and headed west to look for a new site for the post. They circled around the southern end of Warner Mountain and crossed the chain of lakes at a narrow point, probably where Crook had filled the channel with rocks the previous winter. This time Captain Henton performed the task, and soon the command crossed over and headed west. They moved to a timbered, north-south trending mountain range (the northern end of today's Warner Mountains) about 20 miles west of Hart Mountain, which ended in Abert Rim and Lake Abert, where Lieutenant Small had his fight in October 1866.

On the last day of July, on the east side of a 7,834-foot elevation that they called Crook's Peak, they began building the new post. According to Crook, since it was not in the Warner Mountains, it should have a new name, and, in an uncharacteristic attempt at humor, Crook wrote, "I respectfully recommend that the new station be called Camp Wood, in honor of the present Governor of Oregon and also that it is the only *Woods* in all the country." When General Halleck got word of it, he wrote to Crook that a military post should not be named after a civilian, and suggested he keep the name Camp Warner; thus, the new post became Camp Warner, and the other post that would be abandoned became known as Old Camp Warner. In any case, Crook suggested that since the new camp had easier access to Camp Bidwell, all communications and supplies should be channeled through there, "thereby avoiding the terrible road between Camp C. F. Smith and this place, which in winter, can only be traveled at the imminent risk of life."

On August 1, while Henton remained to construct the post, Crook returned to Old Camp Warner. The day was so hot that Wasson was reminded of the story of a soldier who died of sunstroke in the desert, went to purgatory, and immediately returned to his camp to get a blanket. While Crook was out, Perry returned to Old Camp Warner without finding any Indian sign. Archie McIntosh's scouts came in after killing two warriors and capturing eleven

Paiute women and children, and McKay's scouts came in with six prisoners and one horse.

There was a developing rivalry between the scout units as each sought to come in with the most "trophies." Wasson reported that McIntosh could have killed more on his last excursion, except he had only four of his "Snakes," while the rest of the force were Warm Springs Indians, and the latter were more concerned about plundering than fighting. It was illuminating to Wasson that the Snakes fought harder against their own people than the Wascos, their supposed enemies. Wasson said McIntosh could not dislodge the remaining Paiutes with his handful of men while the others were looting the camp. "He is considerably disgruntled," Wasson said, and supposed there would be a "pretty sharp talk" to the Warm Springs bunch before the next expedition. Wasson may have only gotten one side of the story, for McKay's and Darragh's scouts had already proven themselves capable fighters on several occasions earlier in the season.[3]

While Camp Warner was being constructed, Crook wrote a three-page letter to General Steele, lobbying for a new district. According to Crook, all the Indians east of Steens Mountain were now in the Owyhee Country and could be controlled from the District of Boise, while all bands west of Steens Mountain were caught between Camp Watson on the north, Camp Bidwell on the south, Steens Mountain on the east, and Fort Klamath on the west, with Camp Warner in the middle. Thus, Crook recommended that a "District of the Lakes" be created, with all the above posts in the new district, because it is "difficult for one District Commander to attend properly to such an extent of country with Steens Mountain intervening."

Crook may have seen Steens Mountain as an administrative and communications barrier to army operations, but his belief that it was a physical barrier to the Indians is incomprehensible. "I have little fear of these Indians crossing Steens Mountain should we push them too hard here," Crook wrote, "and if they do they cannot winter there." His assessment was already proven to be fallible countless times. The Snakes traveled, and wintered, wherever they wanted. To them, mountains were less a barrier than a safe haven, and should the bands be currently divided in eastern and western segments, that did not mean they would not be in different regions days later, completely obviating Crook's intended administrative boundaries.

Crook closed his letter to Steele with a familiar refrain. "The Indian war here is of a greater magnitude than the country have any idea of, and I have been so much embarrassed by the want of, and the non arrival of animals, supplies, etc in time that I have not been able to accomplish much so far." He said he would be leaving for Camp Wright the next day to see that the troops began construction of a new post in Harney Valley, "and especially to get part of their pack train," because the mules recently sent to him from California "are so young—two years and little over—that they are of no more use than suckling colts would be." Crook forever seemed to be plagued with transportation problems.[4]

On August 3, Crook took twenty-five men of Company F, Lieutenant Alexander H. Stanton commanding, and McIntosh with fifteen of his Indians, on a scout to Harney Valley. They reached the west side of Harney Lake after two hard marches of 25 and 40 miles, with one water stop at noon on the second day, in what Wasson called "a puddle of warm alkali, equally as palatable as secondhand soapsuds." The next day they traveled along the north side of the lake, heading east, over alkali flats spotted with greasewood and sagebrush. Swarms of large flies covered them, biting the horses, and, said Wasson, "rendering riding about as pleasant as trying to run a race over a mixture of hedge and picket fence." On August 6, they reached Camp Wright on the lower Silvies River, which had been occupied by Lieutenant Goodale for the past six weeks, waiting word from Crook.

Wasson did not like Camp Wright, with its adobe ruins, lack of wood, and bad water. He noticed an old flatboat and heard the story that Captain Currey's subordinates had built it, wanted to place a mountain howitzer in it, and sail the lake to blast any Indians near the shore. Since Silvies River did not reach Malheur Lake at more than a few inches depth, and was frequently blocked by beaver dams, Wasson concluded that this "terminated the most brilliant naval exploit of modern times."

Crook, as he did whenever he had an opportunity, went hunting, with Goodale, Wasson, and entourage, along the northern shore of Malheur Lake. They blasted away at the waterfowl from 5 p.m. to sunset, until, according to Wasson, "Henry cartridges began to look bigger in value than the birds, and further operations were postponed." Back at Camp Wright, McIntosh's scouts questioned the Paiutes captured by Captain Baker in his campaign in the Malheur country in mid-July. The women could not, or would not, tell anything except that there were only a few Indians in the entire country and Weahwewa was still leading them. Because everyone talked of Weahwewa, but apparently no one had ever seen him, Wasson said, "I am beginning to believe there is no such animal," and that he was perhaps only a phantom made up to fool the soldiers.

On August 7, Crook went north to Camp Rattlesnake/Steele/Harney; he didn't approve its location because of it being in a narrow canyon with a south face open to the prevailing winds, but he did nothing to change it. Two days later they marched south and then west, going around the promontory near Camp Wright—the "mountain" that Lieutenant Loren Williams tried to reach during his fight in September 1865. From there they headed up Silver Creek and some of the command inspected abandoned Camp Currey. Wasson pronounced Silver Creek, with its red top grass, wild pea vine, and clover, as being a better section of land than around Silvies River.

On August 12, the command marched southwest to Wagontire Springs, and over the next few days, to Mount Juniper north of Lake Abert, southeast to Warner Lakes, and east to old Camp Warner, arriving on August 17. Wasson said that the entire return journey from Camp Currey was over a high, bleak, barren waste of bedrock. "I don't wonder that there is no Indian sign," he wrote, "as there are but few places on which they could make an impression with a cold chisel." Still, it was a comparatively smooth road, and with the new posts being built, Wasson thought that with continuing campaigning, "southern Oregon east of the Cascade range must, by next summer, be made pretty safe for citizens in any civil pursuit."[5] His prediction was surprisingly accurate.

While Crook went to Harney Valley, those remaining at Old Camp Warner bided their time. On August 3, one of McKay's female prisoners escaped, but was recaptured, and three days later another one escaped in the morning and was caught in the evening. The following day, yet another one escaped. While the soldiers chased captives, they found the time to run several horse races. In one, Captain Perry's horse beat Lieutenant Joseph L. Jack's mount by a narrow margin, which McKay called "a bad race," and implied something was not quite fair. McKay's horse, Slapjack, lost to Perry's horse in another race; in all, McKay lost $25 in bets.

The last week in August was taken up by the gradual removal of all salvageable items from Old Camp Warner to the new post. Wasson expected that when the move was complete, they would learn about a new expedition. The only orders he said he got in the meantime were at the dinner table, when Crook grunted to "help myself," which Wasson willingly followed. Wasson "foraged" with Captain Perry, and slept in Captain Hunt's tent. Captain Collins had been transferred to Arizona, which Wasson called "one step this side of purgatory." Wasson said he was still friends with Captains Darragh and McKay, and hoped that anything he wrote would not be viewed by anyone in a bad light. When Crook ordered preparations to extend the upcoming expedition to late October, Wasson wrote, that since no one ordered him to leave camp, "I expect to make the round trip."[6]

The constant grinding campaigning of troops through the northern Great Basin appeared to be having some effect. Nevada was comparatively quiet, and raids in Oregon and Idaho tapered off slightly. In late May, Indians were in the Burnt River area near some settlements. Lum Davis and another man were hunting in the valley about 12 miles from Miller's Ranch, when they spotted two Indians prowling about. They trailed them and caught up just as the warriors "were preparing to cook a piece of a horse they had stolen and killed." They jumped up to flee and were in a straight line when Davis fired his Henry; both men fell. Davis and his partner were certain they were "playing possum" and cautiously approached. Incredibly, the single bullet appeared to have been fatal to them both, but just in case, they pumped several more rounds into the prostrate bodies.

In June, Indians burned a house and barn on Jordan River near Inskip's Station; cattle were driven off, but recovered by the soldiers at Camp Lyon. The same month, Indians attacked a man named Richardson on Burnt River, but he escaped. In July, Indians attacked a teamster near Straw Ranch on Burnt River; the volley of bullets only perforated his hat. On the night of July 10, Indians drove off forty cattle from Sinker Creek in Idaho; only fifteen were recovered. In late July, an unidentified Irishman stole a wagon and harness from Big Camas Prairie in Idaho, and was making his way to Lemhi, when he "was killed by three Snake Indians," who destroyed the wagon and all the property they could not carry away. "Bannock Jim" reported the killing to Idaho Special Indian Agent Charles F. Powell, "to assure you that they were not any of his tribe." Another Indian, "Bannock John," said his band was "anxious to go against the Snakes."[7]

In Nevada, where there had been no fighting since Lieutenant Lafferty's skirmishes in the winter of 1867, the latest raid caught the settlers' attention. With things quieter in the spring and summer, folks let their guard down. James A. Banks, the Speaker of the House in the Nevada Legislature, was visiting Paradise Valley. Banks, a Pennsylvania native, immigrated to California in 1852, and spent several terms as a member of the legislature before moving to Nevada in 1863, where he helped write the state constitution. Banks was at the time a resident of Dun Glen, but with the Rev. Mr. Temple, was visiting Camp Winfield Scott.

On August 1, they took a break to go fishing up Cottonwood Creek north of the post. Lieutenant Lafferty joined them for a time, and then he and Temple strolled back toward camp while Banks moved a little farther north for a few minutes more fishing. When Banks did not arrive after another hour, Lafferty instituted a search. They found Banks, shot through the breast, stripped, and mutilated. Two days later, Temple officiated at the funeral, and the remains were buried in the post cemetery.

The Indians who killed Banks were thought to be of Howluck's band, for his presence had been reported in the area. In a scenario that had been played out many times in the past, pressure from Crook to the north drove the wild bands back into Nevada. A detail of Company A, 8th Cavalry, tried to catch the murderers, but was unsuccessful.[8]

On August 9, four Indians jumped Jack Mangin and J. K. Belk at Charley Brooks's Ranch in lower Jordan Valley. An arrow punctured Mangin's side, but the two men rapidly fired back and drove the attackers away. When they went to a neighbor for help, the Indians returned and sacked Brooks's house of all the cash, clothing, and portable property. Belk gathered a posse and chased down the raiders, catching three. H. J. Hill shot one of the warriors and Belk scalped him; the other two escaped. About August 10, twelve horses were stolen from Briggs's and Boyles's Ranches in the heavily settled Grande Ronde Valley in Oregon. Soon after, the horse thieves came upon three prospectors in Mormon Basin and killed them all while they unsuspectingly worked their claim. About August 13, teamsters A. C. King and a Mr. Haggert were killed by Indians in Rye Valley, while driving between Burnt River and Mormon Basin.[9]

Of course, for those who still experienced raids in the Burnt River area, the situation had not improved. The Walla Walla *Statesman* wondered why the military was so negligent in putting a stop to depredations along the road from Grande Ronde to the Snake River, and how they could let "insolent" Indians continue to steal and destroy property. The army tried to appease everyone it could. Captain Seth Weldy was ordered to move with his Company I, 23rd Infantry, leave a detachment at Auburn, Oregon, and establish a temporary camp between the Burnt and Powder Rivers. Lieutenant Simon E. Chamberlain took Company D, 8th Cavalry, by way of Uniontown and Miller's Ranch, to set up a temporary camp near the Washoe Ferry on Snake River.

The *Idaho World*, which previously had been more pro-army than its rival *Avalanche*, began to fume about what it believed were insane military and political policies. When it learned that special military commissioners who investigated the deaths of eighty soldiers near Fort Phil Kearny in December 1866, had determined that the "Fetterman Massacre" was more the government's fault than the Indians, it went off on a tirade. Per the newpapers, the commissioners said, "there is no necessity for an Indian war, if the Indians are protected from the rapacity of the frontier settlers and traders." They concluded that the current conflict was really a raid upon the Treasury by frontiersmen, army, and contractors, and "Reports of atrocities by Indians are exaggerated by designing persons." The *World* was indignant, stating that it was folly to hope for any protection so long as such ridiculous reports were being made to the powers in Washington. Such reports, it claimed, were made only to "pander to the mawkish and criminal Indian philanthropy which exists in Congress," with "no regard or sympathy for the white sufferers from Indian outrages. . . ." These cowardly "Miss Nancy and philanthropic military officers" with their Indian friends condemned others from a place of safety, but so long as the Indians only "shoot, or maim, or steal from, only the privates, or settlers, frontiersmen, and overland emigrants, it is very likely that they will join in advising the Government to let the Indians have full swing and go on with the work of massacre and general outrage without interruption from the army."[10]

The *Avalanche* shared these opinions, but its latest outburst came not from the pens of the Wasson Brothers. On August 17, notice was placed in the paper announcing its sale to J. W. Hill and H. W. Millard. The new proprietors injected their own brand of toxin. For any officers or politicians who kowtowed to the Indians, they said they would "enjoy the spectacle of Bigfoot and his co-friends in the hair-dressing operation upon some of those sanctimonious, cheese-brained craniums that uphold the murderous savage." If the Eastern philanthropists only once experienced what the pioneers had to face almost daily, "they would sigh for the land of 'yellow-legged chickens' again, where a white cravat and a few religious tracts are commonly a passport to a 'square meal' among the credulous 'brethren and sistern'."[11]

The soldiers at Fort Boise, Camp Lyon, Camp Winthrop, and other posts, who were usually starved for reading material, undoubtedly read these venomous newspaper diatribes and wondered just what they were doing there. The Indians wanted to kill them and the civilians, who they were supposedly there to serve and protect, seemed to hate them with a passion. Soldiers, who received poor pay, poor food, harsh discipline, and spent much of their time in back-breaking manual labor, were also expected to hunt Indians and possibly be killed or maimed for an unappreciative populace. It was no wonder that many deserted, especially when privates only earned $16 per month and there were the enticements of many gold and silver mines in the vicinity. Of the three main regiments that fought during the last year of the Snake War, from September 1867 to September 1868, the enlistment and desertion rates are as follows: 23rd Infantry, ten enlistments and seventy-one desertions; 1st Cavalry, thirteen enlistments and 159 desertions; 8th Cavalry, fifty-nine enlistments and 481 desertions. Clearly, many of the ex-California miners who joined the 8th Cavalry, and ended up serving in the harsh lands of the Great Basin or the desert Southwest, came to prefer their previous profession.[12]

On August 16, in one of the seemingly constant restructurings to make the military bureaucracy run more smoothly, the Division of the Pacific trimmed down the District of Boise to include only Fort Boise. Camp Lyon, Camp Winthrop, and Camp C. F. Smith were placed in the new District of Owyhee. A few months later, Fort Boise was added to the Owyhee and the District of Boise was abolished. Crook's lobbying for another reorganization was successful, and the new District of the Lakes was created, to include Fort Klamath and Camps Logan, Harney, Watson, and Warner, and assigned to George Crook. Crook also had command of troops at Camp Bidwell while he conducted his campaign in that quarter.[13]

OWYHEE RIVER, AUGUST 11, 15, 1867

Captain John J. Coppinger returned to Camp Three Forks (Winthrop) after procuring a number of horses brought in from California to Camp Warner. After numerous unsuccessful foot patrols, the arrival of horses gave promise of better results. Coppinger was able to provide mounts for most of Companies A and E, 23rd Infantry. On August 11, he left Camp Three Forks with 60 enlisted men, Donald McKay and seven of his Cayuse scouts, and thirty-days' rations. They traveled 10 miles down Soldier Creek when they ran into a band of Paiutes, estimated by McKay's scouts at eight to ten. Coppinger ordered a charge, "notwithstanding the wild horses" that the hastily trained infantrymen rode. P. M. Currey reported that "he made a fine charge; rocks and sagebrush were not known. After running the Indians some five or six miles to the main rivers of Owyhee, where they took water, there was not an Indian seen to come out on the opposite side; they are supposed to have all been killed."

Coppinger scouted the area and circled over to the Three Forks where he set up camp on August 14. At three p.m. the scouts reported a Snake camp 12 miles from the Forks. Coppinger left late that afternoon, moving slowly and quietly, and took up position around the rancheria after midnight. He sounded the charge at two in the morning. Amidst the

A. R. Bowman Museum Crook County Historical Society, Prineville, Oregon

Chief Ocheho, ca 1900

shouting, shooting, and the staccato gun flashes briefly illuminating the night, the mounted infantryman devastated the camp. With no losses to the infantry, more than fifteen Indians were reported killed, and a woman and a boy taken prisoner. With first light, the soldiers discovered a fishery and destroyed it, along with many pounds of dried fish, plus the camp equipage. The prisoners told of four more nearby camps, and Coppinger marched upstream back into Idaho Territory in the Juniper Mountain country, but could not catch any other bands. After traveling more than 400 miles, he returned to Camp Three Forks on September 19. The camp functioned as a military prison until January 1869, when the captives were transferred to Fort Boise.[14]

CRANE MOUNTAIN, AUGUST 25, 1867

While the army was searching for a site to build new Camp Warner, the Indian scouts were, as usual, fanning out through the territory looking for targets. Archie McIntosh and eighteen of his scouts left Old Camp Warner on August 22, heading toward Surprise Valley, where McIntosh possibly hoped to get some revenge for his repulse the previous March at the hands of Paiutes under —the incident that prompted Crook to assume McIntosh was drunk and fantasized the encounter. McIntosh headed toward Surprise

Valley, but picked up a fresh trail north of the California line heading west into the Warner Mountains just east of the northern end of Goose Lake.

McIntosh was fairly certain he was trailing Ocheho again, as his band was the one he already fought twice in July. In one of the affairs, the scouts and the Paiutes taunted each other, the latter telling McIntosh to go home, "that they were doing well on horse meat," a reference to the dining they had done on all the horses they had stolen from commissary Crook. On this excursion, McIntosh captured two Paiute women, who told him 10 warriors were in one of Ocheho's hideouts in the mountains east of Goose Lake. McIntosh was ascending the steep, rocky, and brushy eastern side of Crane Mountain on the morning of August 25, hoping to surprise Ocheho, when Ocheho's warriors turned the table on him. The Snakes, in greater numbers, jumped McIntosh, and after a few shots, McIntosh sent scout Boise George to a Snake wickiup with a peace proposal. Instead of peace, the Snakes indignantly said they would kill anyone who came against them, and emphasized their point by shooting George in the arm.

The fight began in earnest, and the scouts took cover behind whatever rocks or trees they could find. One brave, but foolhardy scout who Archie called "Coppinger," got on top of a rock and taunted the Paiutes, saying that they didn't know how to shoot. His charade lasted only a few moments until a bullet knocked him dead off the rock. The Snakes charged once, but the scouts blasted them back, killing three and wounding several. McIntosh was contemplating what to do when the Snakes made his decision for him. He saw about twenty of them circling for his rear toward the only canyon with access for him to safely get out with all his horses. McIntosh called for a retreat, and the Snakes followed him all the way, sniping at his heels. One of his horses was shot down, but one Snake pursuer was also killed. The Snakes chased them most of the night, with intermittent war whoops piercing the air as if to let them know they were still not out of harm's way. McIntosh changed course, and made it to Darragh (Honey) Creek, near where new Camp Warner was being constructed, on the morning of August 26.

"Archy," as Joe Wasson called him, admitted he was "whipped back." McIntosh told him that the chief responsible for all this latest mischief was called "Chee-oh" (Ocheho). "Now I never heard of him before this affair," wrote Wasson, "and am loath to believe in his corporeal existence. No sooner had I got rid of We-ah-we-ah then here comes Chee-oh. Oh, damn Chee-oh!" Joe concluded, "I wish Chee-oh and We-ah-we-ah were dead and that Winnemucca would stay on the reservation—without any mental reservation—instead of coming back with powder, lead, guns, etc. I'm tired of writing about something I don't see and am eternally hearing of."[15]

Wasson appreciated all the hard work McIntosh and his scouts did. It was a shame they were not issued any better weapons. He said that if they had something other than ancient "Harper's Ferry, 1845" issues, and could

Author's photo

Silver Lake fight site.

"get revolvers swung to them also, their confidence would be enhanced and better accounts rendered in these skirmishes." On August 27, almost as if in answer to their wishes, several supply wagons arrived from Boise, bringing Spencer Carbines for Lieutenant Parnell's H Company; as a result, wrote Wasson, "Archie's men get the best of his Sharp's guns. He has done the most of the rough work so far with the poorest tools, and it is time that his outfit be improved."

On Thursday, August 29, Crook and Lieutenants Eskridge and Madigan brought in the last of the remaining usable items from Old Camp Warner to the new camp. They also brought one item of great interest to Joe Wasson: a copy of the August 17 *Avalanche*, in which Joe first learned that his brother had sold the paper—"the obituary notice" he called it, "letting me out of the institution." Joe read it with interest, and, finally able to digest the commentary from a more detached perspective, didn't particularly like what he read. He never realized "the little difference between it and a running, random conversation with some of the boys until I see the blasted stuff in print, and then am astonished to see what an amount of human cussedness and conceit a single individual under no restraint can produce. I will faithfully promise to be more concise and choice in my use of words from this out."[16]

SILVER LAKE, SEPTEMBER 6, 1867

While Crook was building a new Camp Warner and preparing for another campaign, the Paiutes in other parts of Oregon were given no respite. Troops were coming at them from all sides. Tennessean, Lieutenant John Foster Small joined the 1st Cavalry as a private in 1861, fought in numerous

The valley where the Summer Lake fight occurred, near Paisley, Oregon.

engagements in the Civil War, and worked his way up the ranks to corporal, sergeant, and second lieutenant. He was brevetted a first lieutenant for gallantry at the June 1864, Battle of Cold Harbor, and promoted to first lieutenant three months later. For a time in 1867, Small commanded at Fort Klamath.

Small left the fort on September 2, with fifty-one men of his Company A, 1st Cavalry, ten Klamath Indian scouts, civilian M. R. Pearson, and twenty days' rations. Small planned to search for hostile Paiutes on the California-John Day Road. Captain Darragh and his scouts operating northwest from Camp Warner no doubt aided his search and subsequent battle successes. As Darragh stirred things up, the Paiutes who avoided him moved right into Small coming from the other direction.

Small headed northeast from Klamath directly toward Silver Lake. On September 6, he struck a fresh foot trail that led four miles to a camp of about twenty-five Indians situated near the shore of an arm of the lake. Because the country was open and level, the Indians saw him coming and fled, wading and swimming to the opposite shore about 400 yards across. Small captured one woman and one child, who tried to hide in the grass. After destroying the camp they proceeded down the west shore, and at sundown surprised another camp; the advance guard attacked, killed one Indian and captured three.

SUMMER LAKE, SEPTEMBER 8, 1867

The next morning, Small continued to follow a trail that led around the south end of the lake and over a divide to the valley north of Summer Lake. The eastern shore looked barren and rocky, so Small chose to move down the west shore, which was bordered by Winter Ridge rising 2,000 feet above

246

the lake, and appeared more fertile and well-watered. At three p.m. they discovered an Indian camp part way up the ridge, but could not get there in time before the Indians abandoned it and fled high up the bluffs half a mile away. Small pitched camp an hour later and learned from a Paiute woman captured at Silver Lake, through a Klamath interpreter, that there was another Indian camp on a creek that flowed east into a large marsh about midway between Summer Lake and Lake Abert. Realizing that the Indians would be warned if he delayed marching until the next day, Small decided to break camp and make a night march.

The command headed southeast over another divide and down into the valley of the Chewaucan River, which at that point, near present-day Paisley, Oregon, makes a sweeping loop coming out of the mountains and flows southeast to the southern end of Lake Abert. Small halted at 3 a.m. on September 8, one mile from the creek and marsh, standing "to horse" until daybreak. At first light, they moved along the north side of the creek until they saw smoke rising three-quarters of a mile away. Although he was outnumbered, Small charged, sending one squad to circle around and prevent the Indians' escape into the marsh and another to block an escape route to the mountains. He hit the camp on three sides. Some of the soldiers dismounted and chased the Indians into the tules in waist deep water.

"The Snakes run in the 'grass,'" the *Oregon Sentinel* snidely reported, "but few, if any even, got out." Lieutenant Small wrote: "The Indians, seeing all chance of escape cut-off, received us with yells of defiance, shots from two rifles and one revolver and a shower of arrows. The fighting was at short range and was over in ten minutes."

The cavalrymen and Klamath scouts killed twenty-three Paiutes and captured fourteen; only three escaped. It was said that an influential medicine man was among the dead, along with two chiefs who had signed the October 1864 peace treaty, possibly Kiletoak and Skyteocket, names that Small rendered as "Chichocchox" and "Choetook." Private Simon Askins was wounded by arrows in the neck and leg, and Private Allen Boyd by an arrow in the thigh; the Klamath, Yekermsak, was hit by an arrow in the arm. One of their horses was killed and seven wounded. On September 9, Small marched to Lake Abert, but saw no more Indian sign, and being encumbered by wounded and captives, decided to return to Fort Klamath, reaching there September 22. For gallantry in charging a band of Indians and "killing and capturing more of the enemy than he had men," Small was brevetted captain.[17]

Despite all of the publicity that Crook had garnered, Small accounted for more Indian casualties in this one foray than Crook had in any of his fights since January.

Chapter 20 notes

1 Crook to AAG, August 2, 1867, RG 393, Dept. of Columbia, Letters Received, Box 3; *Owyhee Avalanche*, August 3, 1867, August 10, 1867; Clark, "McKay's Journal, Part 2," 275, 277-78. A recent reproduction of Wasson's reports are printed in Cozzens, *Eyewitnesses*, Vol. 2, 33-83, although there are some editing errors, such as misidentifying Lt. Moses Harris as William Harris, Capt. James Henton as Hinton, giving McKay's ancestry as Irish instead of Scotch, and misidentifying Goose Lake as Lake Abert.

2 Parnell, "Operations with Crook," 483-84; Clark, "McKay's Journal, Part 2," 278-79; *Owyhee Avalanche*, August 10, 1867, August 17, 1867, November 2, 1867. *Secretary of War 1868-69*, 771, totals the killed and captured at 46, but this number represents the total Snake casualties from the onset of the campaign on July 20, to the end of the month, and not in the July 27 battle alone.

3 Clark, "McKay's Journal, Part 2," 279, 281, 284; Crook to AAG, August 2, 1867, RG 393, Dept. of Columbia, Letters Received, Box 3; *Owyhee Avalanche*, August 17, 1867.

4 Crook to AAG, August 2, 1867, RG 393, Dept. of Columbia, Letters Received, Box 3.

5 *Owyhee Avalanche*, September 14, 1867. McKay reported that Crook returned on August 16.

6 Clark, "McKay's Journal, Part 2," 282-84; *Owyhee Avalanche*, September 21, 1867.

7 *Idaho World*, June 1, 1867, July 13, 1867; *Commissioner of Indian Affairs 1867*, 102-03, 253.

8 Angel, *History of Nevada*, 175-76. Angel says Lieutenant Lafferty followed Banks's killers and caught them on the South Fork Owyhee, but Angel apparently confused this with the fight near Camp Scott on October 26, 1867.

9 *Idaho World*, August 17, 1867, August 21, 1867; *Commissioner of Indian Affairs 1867*, 102-03.

10 Walla Walla *Statesman*, June 14, 1867, August 23, 1867; *Idaho World*, June 26, 1867.

11 *Owyhee Avalanche*, August 31, 1867. The passionate feelings expressed in nineteenth century newspaper editorials generally exceed any to be found in 21st Century. Frontier journalism was very partisan and newspapers had a great impact on attitudes. What is noticeable also is that much newspaper writing seemed to be aimed at an educated audience. It was not "dumbed-down" to the lowest common denominator. With no radio, television, or computer, almost everyone read and discussed the news. One historian (Terfertiller, *Wyatt Earp*, 81) believed "the literacy rate on the frontier was probably higher than it is more than a century later."

12 Rickey, *40 Miles a Day*, 126-27, *passim*; *Secretary of War 1868-69*, 768-69; Altshuler, *Chains of Command*, 64, 124. The 8th Cavalry was top in desertions that year, with the 7th Cavalry in second place with 457.

13 Bancroft, *History of Oregon*, Vol. 2, 537-38.

14 *Secretary of War 1868-69*, 69; Webb, *List of Engagements*, 32; *Owyhee Avalanche*, August 24, 1867; "Camp Three Forks," Idaho State Historical Society, http://www.idahohistory.net/Reference%20Series/0358.doc. The number of reported Snake casualties varies greatly, from three killed and two captured, to thirty killed.

15 *Owyhee Avalanche*, September 21, 1867; *Secretary of War 1868-69*, 69; Webb, *List of Engagements*, 33; Clark, "McKay's Journal, Part 2," 288. The battle is generally listed as Surprise Valley, but the fight was in Oregon on Crane Mountain, formerly called Lookout Mountain, east of the upper reaches of Cogswell Creek. Wasson said McIntosh returned to camp on 25 August.

16 *Owyhee Avalanche*, September 21, 1867, September 28, 1867; Knight, *Following the Indian Wars*, 47-48.

17 *Secretary of War 1868-69*, 69, 771; *Owyhee Avalanche*, November 16, 1867; *Oregon Sentinel*, September 28, 1867; Bancroft, *History of Oregon*, Vol. 2, 545; *Adjutant General's Office*, 29; Heitman, *Historical Register. Vol. 1*, 892. Small died February 22, 1869.

Chapter 21

"I Never Wanted Dynamite So Bad"

L ieutenant Colonel Crook was not an easy man to read. Somewhat taciturn, in the terminology of the day, he held his cards close to his chest. Lieutenant John G. Bourke, who later served with Crook for about one dozen years, said Crook "never asked any one for an opinion, never gave one of his own," but would go off to hold a "council of war" all alone. He left the campfire, strolled a short distance away, sat down, crossed his legs, held his hands over his shins, and sat thinking. When Crook "rubbed the tip of his nose with the back of his right hand," said Bourke, it "was the infallible sign by which the troops afterward learned to know that one of Crook's councils of war was in progress. He communed with himself. . . ."[1]

Actually, Crook did not mind having a reporter along, to write of things that Crook wouldn't verbalize, and when that reporter wrote positive stories he was more likely to be admitted to the inner circle and be privy to information. Crook had learned that it was not what you did, but what you were credited with doing that built a reputation, and a sympathetic reporter could help foster a positive image. Wasson was not one taken in by false charm, however. He studied Crook during three months' hard campaigning and came to like what he saw. Although Wasson would not characterize Crook in superlative terms as his close admirer John Bourke did, he did see potential. When Crook died, he was eulogized by General William T. Sherman, as the army's "greatest Indian-fighter." That was all in the future, and Crook was only beginning to build his reputation. Nevertheless, Wasson caught Crook's potential.

"The success of the command so far," Wasson wrote, "and upon success alone is everything judged in this practical world, implies that Colonel Crook's plan is as good as any, and I believe he has the Indian character a little nearer down to a scratch than any man in the regular service. By having sufficient men to surround and whip any band liable to be met, and good scouts with a change of horses, he can sweep a wide belt of country and keep it up continually."

The fighting of the past two months in the Lakes District convinced Crook that it was not the Oregon Paiutes alone who he was battling. "These Indians had evidently been getting ammunition somewhere," he said. The constant fighting did not outwardly appear to wear them down or demoralize them. He came to believe that the nearby reservations in California helped the recalcitrant warriors in their resistance. Indians could rest on the reservations, form a war party, ride a few hundred miles to raid, kill, and steal cattle and horses, and drive them back to the reservations where they could sell or trade the stock for weapons.

"There were always enough low and vicious white men...to purchase the property thus obtained by the Indians. . . ." wrote contemporary historian Hubert H. Bancroft. "By this means a never-failing supply of men, arms, and ammunition was pouring into Oregon, furnished by the reservation Indians of California."[2]

On August 30, from a camp about eight miles south of the new Camp Warner, Crook was ready to take his combined command out for what was hoped to be the big showdown. The campaign did not get off to a pleasant start; moving after dark, McKay reported "maney animals were lost during the night," others got bogged down in the mud, and one of Darragh's scouts, Jon, committed suicide in the morning. He had been sick for some time, and Wasson speculated that when the women prisoners were left behind, one of whom might have been his lover, it "may have caused him to shoot himself."

The command—360 soldiers, scouts, and packers from Companies F, H, and M, 1st Cavalry, Company D, 23rd Infantry, and McIntosh, Darragh, and McKay's Companies—moved slowly southwest toward the valley north of Goose Lake. McIntosh, his scouts, and McKay with twenty scouts, were detailed to reconnoiter around Lookout (Crane) Mountain, where Archie had his fight a week earlier, to see if they could pick up a trail. On the mountain, McKay found a fine defensive position, "one of the strongest Fortification that I had seen build by any Indians," he wrote, but the Indians already had been gone about a week. On the northeast side of the mountain was a heavy snowbank that furnished a perpetual stream of water for the fort's occupants. McKay went to the shore of Goose Lake and found the Indian trail went across the valley and southwest of the lake.

To the northwest, Crook sent some of Darragh's scouts, with Isaac Wilson in charge. Wilson was known to few in the command, but was apparently picked up by Captain Perry earlier in the summer, as a stager, freighter, and guide. The old man, called "Dad" by the younger soldiers, was somewhat eccentric, superstitious, and old fashioned, preferring an old flintlock to any "modern" weapons. Many of the soldiers did not appear impressed with Wilson's woodsman skills, kidding him at times with phrases like, "Now Dad, you must stick some feathers in your horse's tail or you won't have any luck!" "Dad" Wilson, realizing he was the object of their jokes, told them that if they'd furnish the feathers, he'd show where they could stick them.[3]

A camp was kept in Camas Prairie for three days, a valley about four miles northeast of present-day Lakeview, Oregon, while scouting parties fanned out to find the most promising Indian trails. Darragh saw about twenty Snakes, but they were apparently out of catching range. Wilson returned seeing nothing but tracks. On September 3, Darragh and his scouts took one week's rations and headed northwest to search the Lake Abert area. McKay and McIntosh moved west of Goose Lake and saw evidence of seventeen campfires, indicating that there were plenty of Snakes in the area. Wasson asked to accompany one of the scouting parties but was turned down because he was not an Indian, because they didn't think he could get himself within shooting distance of a Snake, and because one officer commented that he doubted if Wasson could shoot a hole in an army tent from twenty paces. The officer bet Wasson $4.50 to prove it. Joe showed his good-natured sense of humor and wrote, "Not having a cent, I have to endure this, but the worst feature of it is, no one will risk anything on it in my behalf. It looks bad. I think there is a combination to ruin my reputation, but never having had any in particular, they can't make a point of me there." He also made a half-serious call to the *Avalanche* readers to take up a collection for him, for all he was getting to eat was camas roots, and his clothes were so worn that they would "soon be reduced to a short breechclout, and were the rags at hand converted into paper, it wouldn't make a one-cent postage stamp."

On September 4, Crook moved across the valley into the mountains northwest of Goose Lake, where he camped for four more days, waiting for scouting reports. On upper Drew's Creek, McKay's scouts found and killed four Snakes, and added more scalps to their collection. On September 8, Crook moved west near Drew's Valley, where Captain William Kelly joined him from Fort Klamath. Kelly had been in the 1st Oregon Cavalry during the Civil War, spending much of his time at Fort Klamath. He mustered out on July 28, 1866, and on the same day enlisted as a captain in the 8th Cavalry. Kelly joined Crook only temporarily, and, as he was not under Crook's command, he marched back to Fort Klamath and then was sent to Camp Harney. The forces traveled together for a few days as Crook moved northwest toward Sprague River. On September 11, however, signs tended to show the Indians had moved southeast. Perhaps tiring of all the tramping to and fro, Crook turned around, went 12 miles south, and stopped. "The colonel," Wasson wrote, "had become satisfied by this time that the Indians he had 'lost' had gone south, but concluded to split the command and go in opposite directions."[4]

On Friday, September 13, Crook sent Captains Perry and Harris with their Companies F and M, plus Darragh and McKay's scouts to the north. Instructions were to investigate the country around Summer and Silver Lakes, go to the Deschutes River and downstream to Crooked River, then upstream and east to Camp Harney. Perry moved northwest about 10 miles, with the two scout companies keeping ahead and on his flanks. A sleet and snowstorm bogged them down until September 15. When the weather cleared they moved north to Silver Lake and west to Antelope Mountain. On September 20, Darragh broke off from the command and headed directly east to Camp Harney. He traveled over a high sage plain, labeled the "Great Sandy Desert" on early Oregon maps and shunned by superstitious native tribes, finding few waterholes and springs. Perry and McKay continued northwest to the Little Deschutes and downriver, augmenting their diets with the abundant river trout. They moved north to the junction with Tumalo Creek, near present-day Bend, then cut northeast to Crooked River, reaching there on September 26. Moving upstream they reached a point near their main camp on Cottonwood (McKay) Creek, where McKay and Darragh had spent much time hunting Paulina the previous winter.

They cut across the top of a large "U" bend in Crooked River, reaching the stream again below Eagle Rock, at what McKay called "the Scalp Camp," named for the place they had celebrated after taking 18 Paiute scalps back on January 20. Moving to the headwaters of Crooked River, they crossed into the Great Basin to abandoned Camp Currey on upper Silver Creek on October 3. The command reached Camp Harney on October 6. Captain William Kelly and Company C, 8th Cavalry, had already arrived. The next day Captain Perry and Lieutenant Harris went to Camp Watson.

Captain James Gilliss, 5th Artillery, assistant quartermaster for the district, learned of Crook's plans and his estimated time of arrival, and traveled to Portland to escort his wife, Julia, and Mrs. Mary Crook to Camp Harney. Crook had left his wife in Baltimore before coming West, and had not seen her in twelve months. Captain Perry's command had marched far, but fought no Indians. Such was not the case with Crook's command.[5]

When the force divided on September 13, Crook took the smaller part, consisting of Company H, 1st Cavalry, under Lieutenant William Parnell, the mounted Company D, 23rd Infantry, in command of Lieutenant John Madigan, belonging to Parnell's company, and Archie McIntosh's scouts. Per Joe Wasson, Crook remarked "that if his venture on this southern tour failed to in any way meet public expectations, the blame should fall upon him alone. He put little faith in a summer campaign but believed this one a necessity." One might speculate on Crook's concern about public expectations and the necessity of a successful campaign. He was well aware of Major Marshall's failure to defeat the Indians, and the public scorn he received for his seemingly incompetent leadership. In only a few of Crook's subsequent fights did he kill or capture significant numbers of Indians, and only one of his soldiers had been killed in direct combat. Was he concerned that an officer's reputation could only be secured with victories written in letters of blood? Did he need to show up Marshall?

252

Crook, uncommunicative as usual, led his men south. On the South Fork of the Sprague, they camped in a hail and snowstorm. During the halt, three grizzly bears walked into the rear of the column and when word reached the head, Crook, Lieutenant Eskridge, and a few others rushed to the rear. Wasson said that Eskridge ran smack into an old she-bear who was standing up to inspect the column, the lieutenant "mistaking her for his chief packmaster." Crook and the officers blasted away at the bears, breaking the order about unnecessary firing, which, said Wasson, "confused the men." The weather was bad. "We had constant rains and snow for several days after our party divided," said Lieutenant Parnell, "but we continued our work, looking for our 'lost Indians.'"[6]

On September 17, they crossed into California and the next night camped on the west side of Goose Lake, about 20 miles directly west of Camp Bidwell. They crossed the ground where "Dad" Wilson said he fought a grizzly bear the previous night; he told the soldiers they could find the animal in a certain willow patch, but when they looked, no bear was to be seen. Wasson and others were becoming skeptical of Wilson's reported frontier skills. They recruited the stock for two days before moving out again. On September 21 they moved to the south end of Goose Lake, and the next day, marched south 15 miles, where Lieutenant Parnell said, "Indian signs began to get plentiful and interesting." Joe Wasson phrased it differently: "Here the trouble commenced."

McIntosh and several Indians went out in one direction to look for signs, while "Dad" Wilson was entrusted with six Indians to head southwest for the same purpose. It was only the second time that summer, Wasson said, that Wilson was allowed on a responsible errand, the reason being that "the colonel don't want any stock in a person who is always talking of how many 'year' he has 'fit' Indians and of taking scalps as if it were as easily done as said." Crook's plan was to get scouts as near as possible to a camp while unobserved, get an estimation of the location and numbers, return and report, and the troops would make a night march and attack in the morning. Wilson blew it. About nine in the evening, on an open plain within full view of the army camp and likely hundreds of Indian eyes, he built a large fire. Within minutes the fire was answered by other signal fires, including one that appeared in the Warner Mountains about 25 miles to the east.

The fire caused uneasiness at headquarters, but Wilson wasn't finished. The next morning the command marched several miles south to the Pit River in the vicinity of present-day Alturas, California, while Wilson continued his scout about 10 more miles to the west. McIntosh's scouts captured two Indian boys and brought them to camp. About noon, Wilson "came puffing and sweating into headquarters with the story that early that morning he had 'fit' a camp" of at least fifty warriors and his scouts had run away. By then, several large signal fires were seen. Crook demanded that Wilson explain why he had fired and not simply reported as ordered. "The poor old fool," said Wasson, "stammered out something about wanting to find Archie and went off with his head down like a sheep." Parnell said, "This piece of stupidity of Wilson's gave the Indians the alarm at once, and signal-fires were visible in every direction, the whole country was ablaze, and our other scouts reported Indian runners everywhere."

After marching for two weeks over "the most infernal ground for the purpose of keeping under cover," said Wasson, their surprise had been blown just one night's march from its destination. The disappointment and anger were evident. Crook wrote in his report that the enemy was alerted "through the blunder of an old imposter of a white man who was along in the capacity of a scout." He discharged Wilson immediately. The officers were not the only ones incensed. Several cavalrymen caught Wilson and took him into the forest to string him up from a tree. Lieutenant Eskridge discovered them just in time to save Wilson's life. Parnell wrote, "it would have been meted justice to have let the rope serve its work then, for a few days afterwards many valuable lives were lost by his disobedience and insubordination."[7]

After the commotion over Wilson's gaffe, McIntosh and his scouts came in with the scalp and the gun of a warrior they had killed in the valley near one of the signal fires. With the Snakes and Pit River Indians thoroughly alerted, Crook made no attempt to conceal his moves, and on September 24, openly headed down the main road about 20 miles, as if he was making directly for Fort Crook. In the late afternoon they crossed to the south side of Pit River and made their way up a timbered canyon to camp. Crook released the two Indian boys caught a few days prior, and early the next morning the command marched along the foot of a forested mountain to the southeast, following a new trail that appeared to head for the South Fork Pit.

In a rough canyon the command surprised a wickiup; several males scattered and hid, and a few women and children were captured. Crook decided that the situation being as it was, holding a few more prisoners would accomplish no purpose. He gave them bread and let them go; one of the old women would be seen again soon. As they went along, the trail grew fresher, and after 15 miles they camped again. Even with clear horse and moccasin tracks, the men were morose, said Wasson; "the cup of indignation was full that night." With the skies dark and raining, Crook sat alone, whittling under a dripping pine. He considered the campaign "all up," said Wasson; the scouts' horses were on their last legs and much of the stock were weary and sick. No one believed they would catch any Indians.

INFERNAL CAVERNS, SEPTEMBER 26-28, 1867

On Thursday September 26, the gloomy command moved over a high tableland (today's Rocky Prairie). At a small lake, the trails seemed to scatter, and McIntosh moved off northeast, while the main command continued southeast down a canyon and out into the valley of the South Fork Pit River.

Site of Infernal Caverns fight, California.

They barely exited the canyon and turned north when McIntosh came galloping off the high bluffs and reported a large force of Indians in the rocks above and apparently wanting a fight.

As the main command advanced down the valley, Indians opened fire on them from a ravine coming down from the high bluff to the west. Crook moved the soldiers up the bluffs and had Lieutenant Parnell dismount half his force of forty-one cavalrymen and form a line on the south side; Lieutenant Madigan similarly dismounted half of his sixty-eight infantry and took a line on the north side. The east was open valley where the led horses, pack train, and guard formed up. A steep rock wall about 200 feet high boxed the west side. McIntosh collected his fifteen scouts and filtered into the high cliffs; Wasson, "satisfied that a good view of the performance could be obtained up there," went with them. Waiting for them in a natural rock fortress were about thirty Pit River Indians, a few Modocs, and seventy-five Paiutes under Sieta (Little Rattlesnake).[8]

The rock fortress was not something hastily thrown together that day to fight soldiers. The Achumawi, called Pit River Indians by the whites, had lived in the area for generations and had built many structures in and around the canyons on the west edge of the South Fork Pit. Horse-riding Modocs, Klamaths, and Paiutes had often raided them in the past, and this fortress in the lava rocks was designed to ward off Indian raiders. Crook may have been marginally correct in his assumption that Pit River Indians had been trading guns to the Paiutes; it was more likely that most of the weapons came from unscrupulous white traders or through the Modocs and Klamaths. The Achumawi rarely dealt with those three tribes. The reason they were there when Crook appeared was because it was a special occasion called a "Big Time," when other tribes not normally allowed in the Achumawi lands were invited for games, feasting, trade, and possible marriage arrangements.

255

The bands were not expecting trouble, but were down in the valley when soldiers appeared. "It was a sneak attack," said Ike Leaf, whose grandmother and great-uncles were present. They were "all bunched up there, right below Infernal Caverns. There's tules there, a lot of tules and swamp. . . . The Indians heard a shot, so some of their scouts. . .went to take a look. Well, they came back reporting that White men were coming." Most of the Indians clambered up the bluffs, but an old man and his son went into the tules. "The soldiers got around in front of them and so he hid right in the tules—" said Ike Leaf, "the old fellow hid and the son ran away alone. The soldiers chased the young fellow around—they chased him around the trail. . .and finally killed him."[9]

The land rose abruptly from an elevation of about 4,400 feet on the valley floor to about 5,100 feet on the tableland above. The 700-foot rise went from east to west in half a mile. Three-fourths of the way up, near the 4,800-foot level was a small plateau where the lava rock outcroppings made a natural fortification. The Indians had improved that area by moving hundreds of boulders to make barricades, forts, rifle pits, and firing embrasures. With the loss of one boy in the valley, the Indians made it to the fortress. The soldiers and scouts worked their way around, trying to get in position and learn exactly what they faced. McIntosh's scouts worked up a ravine on the south side and got to the brink of the western bluffs about one p.m. From about 200 feet above the forts, they were the only ones of Crook's command who could see the layout of the system below them, but they were exposed to fire. Madigan's infantry got into line shortly thereafter, and not understanding the troop dispositions, Wasson said, "his men gave us a volley of Springfield rifle balls—no one hurt. Some blasphemous remarks. . .in return fixed that matter." The scouts flattened down, but Wasson stood, "taking an opera-glass view of the menagerie beneath," until a few slugs spattered into the rocks around him and he dropped low with the others.

Wasson described his "birds' eye view of the enemy's works:" a perpendicular lava wall about 300 feet high on the west; a great ridge of lava boulders running down to the valley on the north side; a canyon running to the valley on the south side; a gradual slope coming up from the east side until nearing the forts where a low, sharp ridge of boulders formed a barrier. On the southeast were also two parallel rock ridges about 30 feet high making an impassible gorge in between. There were several forts on the little plateau: on the northeast point was a circular fort about 20 feet in diameter, breast-high with portholes; on the western point were two similar forts; from the forts to the bluffs on the west side was a field of immense lava boulders. Wasson believed the only practicable approach was up the eastern slope. Lieutenant Eskridge described the spot as "a plain lava rock about 500 by 300 yards in area, bounded on the west side by a wall of rock 150 feet high."

Lieutenant Parnell moved his men up the mountainside, between rocks and juniper trees, taking a sporadic fire as he ascended. When he reached the plateau, the fire increased and he halted. He described the objective as "a natural fortification, strengthened by artificial means, with loop-holes and embrasures. There was a main fort, of a basin-like formation, with a balcony near all round it, and above this a wall of rock about eight or nine feet in height, with a rocky gulch about forty feet deep completely surrounding the whole. . . ." Indians were posted almost invisibly in every nook, and Parnell could not tell where the shots came from. Nevertheless, Parnell advanced to the first rock barricade, whereupon about fifteen to twenty Indians let loose with a volley. Company H Private James Lyons, from Rhode Island, was killed instantly, and Sergeant Charles Barchet, a German who had fought through the Civil War with the 7th Vermont, was mortally wounded. Privates

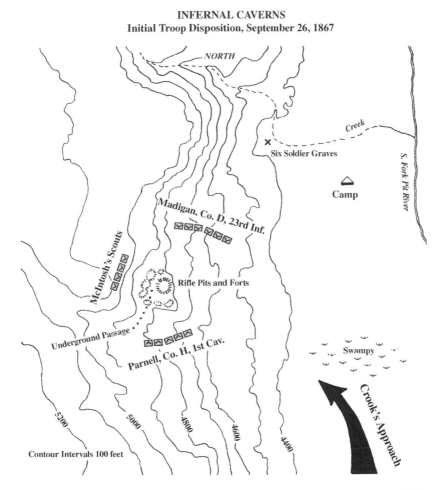

INFERNAL CAVERNS
Initial Troop Disposition, September 26, 1867

Clancy and Fisher were wounded. Parnell fell back and took cover, unable to recover Lyons's body, or rescue Barchet, who expired on the exposed slope within a few hours.[10]

McIntosh and Wasson could see the repulse from above, and Eskridge could see it from the valley. Within minutes the lieutenant began setting up a makeshift hospital. "A regular siege was inevitable," said Wasson. Everyone in the circle around the forts poured a constant stream of bullets into them, and there was a nearly continuous crack of gunshots, whining ricochets, and yelling for a few hours, but no second assault was attempted. From the bluffs to the forts was only 50 yards, at a downward angle of about 45 degrees. Hundreds of bullets smacked into the rocks, but the Indians were well protected from shots from above. On the other three sides, the soldiers could not approach without being blasted by warriors firing from caves or through loopholes.

Wasson could see about one dozen warriors in the rocky gorge, but they were in such a position where no bullets could reach them. Wasson watched who he called a "medicine man," stand in plain view and keep up a constant haranguing in a loud voice, as if he was defying the soldiers or inspiring the barricaded Indians. This kept up until about five p.m. when Crook sent a squad of Parnell's men to circle up to McIntosh's position, but not before they had shot a few times into the scouts' rear by mistake. Even with the reinforcements in that sector, one Paiute or Achumawi made his escape by snaking his way among the rocks to the northwest, near the junction of McIntosh and Madigan's commands. McIntosh thought it was one of Madigan's men trying to get in a better position, but when the warrior got near the top, "he made some saucy gestures, gave a whoop, and ran for the lava canyon north." McIntosh chased him for a while but he got away.

Crook, Parnell, and Madigan made inspections of the fortifications from as close as they could get, and Madigan was slightly wounded in the right arm for his effort. About dusk, Crook had McIntosh's scouts break off and go to the valley for supper. At dark, half the men were moved in a tighter circle around the fortifications so that the other half could get something to eat. "We had not had a mouthful since five o'clock in the morning," said Parnell. The soldiers ate in shifts, and when finished, all went back on the lines. In the gloom, Lyons and Barchet's bodies were recovered.

Parnell went up on a high point to observe, but was himself seen, "and in an instant arrows flew thick and fast around me from both flanks and front, but none hit." He went back down to check on Madigan. The soldiers on the lines had no rest, because the besieged Indians showered them with stones, "Paiute toothpicks" (arrows), and curses all night long. To make matters worse, Company D Private Carl Bross (Braus) crawled out too far ahead of the rest, and in the dark was accidentally shot and killed by his own friends. McIntosh's scouts came down off the high bluffs and moved closer to connect up more tightly with Madigan and Parnell. After dark the scouts held a war dance, "but nothing ever looked so damned ridiculous," Wasson said—the scouts apparently having a different take on the solemnity of the occasion.

From dark until midnight, rain clouds rolled in and thunder and lightning illuminated the eerie scene, "lending an infernal coloring to the black basin and wall to the west," Wasson said. The clouds above them were ominous—almost a harbinger of what was to come. During supper Joe listened as Crook opened up somewhat, telling the officers of his plans. The siege would be continued day-to-day "until the red devils were all killed or starved to death," provided they could do so with the men and material at hand. Secondly, said Crook, it had become a chronic procedure to chase Indians into the mountains only to let them escape—if this time they could hang on and defeat them, "the moral effect of such an affair would be worthy of several ordinary victories." Last, Crook believed that taking the outer fortifications by storm would shorten the siege and save more men's lives in the long run, because they would have the advantage of being behind the rock barricades with less exposure to themselves. It was a type of reasoning that made soldiers grit their teeth, tighten their belts, and perhaps curse the day they decided to join the army.

When the thunder slowly rolled away to the east, the soldiers could begin to hear the portentous sounds of boulders being rolled or piled, as the Indians strengthened their breastworks. Occasional shots were fired and yells heard, even loud talking, "sounding at times as if it proceeded from a cavern." In the darkness, a few Indians from outside the fortification attacked the pack train in the valley, and more soldiers were detailed to guard it. In the soldier camp, the casualties taken during the day got many men thinking about the possibility of their own deaths. At midnight, Eskridge went to Parnell and asked him to check again on Madigan and try to cheer him up. He found the wounded lieutenant sitting alone and looking very despondent. "I went around and gave him a drink of whiskey," said Parnell, "as his whole frame was shaking and shivering. I did all I could to cheer him up; but he evidently had a premonition of death, and nothing I could say or do had any effect whatever."[11]

At the first gray of the false dawn of September 27, Crook directed Parnell to draw in his line so they could form up for a charge. The soldiers had crawled so far forward, the brightening sky showed them to be in exposed positions and two or three were slightly wounded as they pulled back. Crook had them align below the east face, facing west; Madigan had the left with eighteen infantrymen, and Parnell the right with twenty-two dismounted cavalrymen. Joe Wasson and another civilian, Lawrence Traynor, who took the deceased Private Lyons's Spencer carbine, volunteered to go in—"it was our funeral," Wasson said. They joined in on Madigan's right, which placed them in the center of the assault. Crook moved among them and "talked to the men like a father," said Wasson. He told them that at the command they must rise up quickly, "go with a yell and keep yelling, and never think of stopping until they had crossed the ditch, scaled the wall, and broke through the breastworks—and the faster, the better."

The sun had just broken the eastern horizon. The men were told to take off their heavy overcoats, for there would be some rough climbing ahead. When the command, "Forward," was given, they rose up and rushed across the open ground toward the ravine surrounding the main fort. Madigan's command had hardly gone 20 feet when a volley knocked out more than one-third of his men. Down went Corporals Patrick McCann, Thomas Fogerty, and Edward Furman with bad bullet wounds. A bullet hit Private Frank McGuire, and arrows struck Privates William Barbes and Joseph T. Etabler (Embler). Another rifle shot wounded the packer Traynor in the thigh, and as he fell he dropped the carbine he had taken from the dead Private Lyons. The remaining dozen men could not stop, but rushed forward into the ditch in their front. Private James Kingston, also of Company D, hesitated only momentarily to drop his rifle and pick up the carbine, proving again the soldiers' preference for a lighter, faster-firing carbine over the heavier, slower rifle. Appearing on the exposed hill moments later, Lieutenant Madigan stood for a few seconds, still wearing his tightly buttoned overcoat. Whether he stopped to assess the ground or encourage his men, the delay was fatal; a bullet crashed straight through his skull and he crumpled to the ground with the same type of death wound, and on the exact spot that Private Lyons fell the day before.

In contrast to Madigan's men, Parnell's were unscathed in the first blast. "We were met by a perfect hail-storm of arrows as we rose in full view of the Indians, but not a man was touched," said Parnell. They dashed to the bottom of the ravine in an instant, where they were protected from the Indians' fire, but could not get at their foe until they crawled out. They had to climb about 40 feet of boulders too large for a man to ascend alone; two or three men had to be pushed up, and they in turn could help pull up those behind them. It took several minutes to climb the ridge until they reached the balcony level with the first line of forts. Notwithstanding the casualties they had taken, the 23rd Infantrymen reached the ravine about the same time as the 1st Cavalrymen, and the lines had become somewhat intermingled. They charged across the last open space to another wall of loose rock about eight feet high. Only a few places looked assailable, and Sergeant Bassler (Russler) of Company D, led the men on the left, while Sergeant Michael Meara and Private Willoughby Sawyer of Company H, were in the forefront on the right.

"Make a breach!" shouted Lieutenant Parnell, and "let no man stand still for a moment, but keep moving." The men tore at the rocks or shot into nooks

Author's photo

Graves of six soldiers at Infernal Caverns battle site.

and crannies, while the Indians poked their weapons through openings to fire right into the soldiers' faces. In the chaos, Wasson sidled farther to the right along the east and northeast facing of the barricade, coming up near Sergeant Meara. Meara, born in Galway, Ireland, had moved to Boston and had been in the army for 18 years. He clambered up a scalable section of the wall, peered over the top and called out, "Come on boys, we've got 'em," when a bullet bore through his head and his body crumpled on the rock parapet and fell only a foot away from Joe Wasson. The blast came from a gun fired only six inches from his head, as his face was badly powder burned.

On the left, Sergeant Bassler was the first to reach the breastworks, and he played a deadly game of hide and seek, sticking his revolver into openings, firing, ducking and dodging, and moving to other portholes. "Get out of that, you sons of bitches!" he yelled. Lieutenant Eskridge said the sergeant killed or wounded several of fifteen or more warriors who were in this section of the works.

Wasson shifted farther to his right, and near the northern edge of the wall he clambered up right behind Canadian-born Private Willoughby Sawyer. Moments later, Sawyer was "stretched out on the parapet, the brain oozing out his left temple." Regardless, Wasson got on the wall and took a firing position where he could sweep the backside of the east wall as Bassler and his crew drove the Indians out from his sector. To Wasson's disappointment, however, there were few Indians and they ran too fast; "they dropped their empty guns and slid over the west side and disappeared in the gorge in an instant like so many lizards," he said.[12]

When the soldiers were breaching the outer defenses, the Indians appeared to lose heart for a moment, perhaps not believing that the white men could survive an assault. Many dropped their weapons and headed for the next forts to the west, but only several of them who found themselves too far from a covered passageway ran exposed across the rocks. The majority of them ducked into natural tunnels and caves that led from the east fort to those to the west. A few stayed and fought.

"They went in there— [the cave] kept on going in while these others were shooting at the soldiers from outside here," Ike Leaf explained. A boy, Wa-Wa-Wok-Gee-Nay-Gee, later known as Big Pete, was with his father as the old man fired at the charging soldiers. "Finally," said Ike Leaf, "one of the older ones, old Big Pete's father—he got shot. He got shot right there. So they laid him aside, and then these others were going in. . . ." The old man had been firing with the group of warriors that had delivered the initial volley at Madigan's men. "They killed seven soldiers there," Ike said, but although the old man was hit, he said, "I want to get one more [soldier] before I go into the cave."[13]

As most of the Indians retreated to the western forts, Wasson stepped over the parapet and entered the east fort, one of the first men inside. Below him Private James Shea (Shay) of Company H, was alone farther along to the northwest. A volley of fire came from the west forts as well as from some of the natural rocks below. Bullets hit him in the wrist and in two other places. One ball shattered the stock of his rifle and knocked him down about 40 feet of rocky wall. Described by Parnell as "an old soldier and an excellent fighter," Shea climbed back up and before long "he was back with his comrades, swearing like a trooper—that he was."

Wasson quickly realized that the prospects of continuing in a "good state of health" were not very bright, and he decided to vacate the fort, and circle around back to the southeast end while Parnell fought his way inside. "In the meantime a breach was made in the wall of rocks," said the lieutenant, "and our men swarmed into the fort, using revolvers and clubbed carbines on the skedaddling Indians." When Wasson climbed back over the wall, Parnell's men were inside.

One of the last warriors to vacate the fort was Chief Sieta. As he ran across the open ground to the next fort to the west, several shots were fired at him, and two hit him square in the back as he climbed the wall. Lieutenant Colonel Crook was seen standing on the exposed spot where Madigan was killed, taking aim and firing over his own men at the running Indian. Said Wasson, "He makes few mistakes with that long Spencer of his." Parnell also gave Crook credit for the kill, stating that "General Crook, with his unerring 'Spencer,' hit him square in the spine, and Mr. Indian fell headlong down the gulch and his body buried itself between two large boulders." Eskridge described Sieta as a medicine man, "a large buck covered with hideous paint and wearing a large war bonnet, profusely decorated with feathers and silver ornaments, who had kept up a constant harangue in a loud voice throughout the previous day and night."

"After we had got possession of the fort," said Crook, "we had drawn the 'White Elephant' prize, for the Indians were deep down in the rocks, where all was darkness, and we could see nothing, whereas they, being in the dark and we in the light, they could see us." Crook had taken the east fort, but the Indians had simply shifted west, and were again behind more fortifications. There was a slight lull in the fighting, but whistling lead slugs and fluttering "toothpicks" produced a "queer music," which Wasson said a man might enjoy somewhat, if he listened from high up in a tree.

From the west forts and down in the cave labyrinths and between the rocks, the Indians still kept a tenacious hold. There were lulls, but every so often punctuated by several shots that cut clothes, ricocheted off rocks and whistled overhead. By taking the fort, said Wasson, "we had got hold of something we couldn't let go." It seemed impossible to advance, and crazy to pull back. The Indians taunted them from unseen caves and all the soldiers could do was wait and hope to see a head pop out and take a shot at it.

Private William Enser of Company H, stood up while on picket duty just to the left of where the initial charge was made; a bullet slammed deep into his right shoulder, testimony to the Indians' vigilance and sharpshooting. Lieutenant Eskridge thought he had seen action before, but confided to Wasson that the opening volleys that had decimated Madigan's charge was "the most stinging, face-slapping affair" he had ever encountered. He and Dr. Tompkins were kept busy carrying dead and wounded down to the valley hospital.

According to Wasson, if Crook was fighting mad the day before, "the morning's operations only seemed to increase it. . . ." Wasson said that everyone wished they had nitroglycerine or Greek Fire to blast the Indians. Crook was of the same mind. "I never wanted dynamite so bad as I did when we first took the fort and heard the diabolical and defiant yells from down in the rocks."[14]

Between nine and eleven in the morning, no charges were made; the soldiers were contented with tightening the circle around the remaining forts and edging into positions where they could get off a better shot. A short way to Parnell's left, Private Kingston, who had picked up the carbine that had first belonged to Lyons, and then Traynor, was carefully watching a small opening in the rocks to his front. A small twig partially obstructed his view and as he reached up to remove it, another soldier cautioned him to let it be. He replied that "it wouldn't make any difference," and he snapped it off. "An instant after," said Parnell, "a ball passed clean through his head above his ear. The shot came through that hole, for there was no other place that it could possibly have come." Incredibly enough, Kingston lived for another two weeks, dying after the command got back to Camp Warner. All three men who had held Lyons's rifle had all been killed or fatally wounded. It was not recorded if anyone ever touched that Spencer again. Down in the cave, it appeared that Big Pete's father had finally gotten his "one more" soldier before he died of his wounds.

About 11 a.m. Parnell began sending the men in shifts back to the valley to get some breakfast. After some had moved out, the Indians made an unexpected charge against the east fort and drove the soldiers out from part of it. Other men in the line rallied, however, and in turn had driven the warriors back. The upshot was that the soldiers had gotten better control of the main eastern fort, but the Indians now had command of all the approaches. The rest of the day was taken up by constant sniping and minor shifting of positions for better defense or line of fire. According to Wasson it was "a free fight—whenever you see a head, hit it." There was a stalemate. Parnell: "Their retreat was a perfect honeycomb, and they would not come out to fight." Neither would the soldiers go in after them.

The men ate supper again in shifts, but kept as tight a cordon around the Indian position as possible. A few times during the evening, showers of arrows arched into the sky and descended upon the soldiers, but no one was hit. Small parties of Indians in the valley tried to drive off the command's horses, but the packers were armed and they successfully warded off the attacks. As the night wore on, the voice of the haranguing medicine man heard the previous evening was conspicuously absent. This time, however, the plaintive "squalling of the papooses during the night" assured that the soldiers would lie awake again. It was after midnight when things quieted down. There was good reason: almost every Indian was gone. Unknown to the besieging army, there was a cave and tunnel that led underneath, up, and out.

"All the Indians were in the cave," said Ike Leaf. "Well my grandmother, and a few others, knew what the outlet was in the cave. So they went through with no lights or anything—they just knew the way. . . . They made it out—on top."[15]

The soldiers waited in anticipation for the morning, wondering if the Indians would attack, or if Crook would have them make another assault. With daylight, however, they began to breathe easier. There did not appear to be any Indians around, and no shots came from the rocks. They learned the answer when some of McIntosh's scouts discovered the Indian trail leading out of a cave about 75 yards southwest of the rear of the army line, littered with broken weapons and other items. The "trapped" Indians had simply walked out beneath them. About 8 a.m. a squad investigating the western forts captured a wounded young woman. She indicated that all the warriors were gone, and all who remained were a few wounded women and some children. She said there were about 100 warriors in the fight and she thought sixteen were killed and nine wounded.

Soon, with Crook's approval, the more daring of the soldiers began to explore the caves, even though, said Eskridge, the wounded Indians left behind "made it certain death for anyone of our party to attempt to enter." Wasson crept in only a part of them and said there must have been 10 underground acres of caverns, shelves, and fissures, crisscrossed with passages, hatchways, and tunnels in a giant maze where "ten thousand men could be stowed out of sight in fifteen minutes."

Private James (or Bryan) Carey, Company H, a long-time resident of New Orleans, boldly forged through several passageways, found dead Indians and took their scalps. He entered a large cave, head first, with revolver in hand, when a wounded warrior shot him through the heart. Carey tumbled off a ledge and down into the dark pit. No one would venture to go down and get him. Parnell went to camp, had the blacksmith fashion a long pole and make a horseshoe into a drag-hook, and fasten it to the end. Carey's comrades tied a lariat to the end of the pole and reached down into the pit as far as they could. After several tries, they hooked the horseshoe into Carey's waistbelt and hauled his body up. One man who got a glimpse into the cave said, "you could camp the command" down there.

Five dead Indians were found in one large hole, partly buried with rocks. In another cave they discovered, dead in the rocks, "An old, one-eyed, crophaired squaw, whom the command gave bread" to just three days earlier. After her release, she had beaten the troops to the Indian gathering, where she probably thought she would be safe, and where she undoubtedly warned the Indians of the soldiers' presence. While exploring the caverns about noon, one of McIntosh's scouts saw movement deep within the shadows and fired, killing another woman. She was the last casualty in the three-day affair. A total of twenty Indians were recorded as having been killed, with twelve wounded and two captured. The Indians even had horses down in the caves, and eight of them were rounded up.

After the exit cave was discovered, the soldiers and scouts rolled a large boulder into it, hoping to block it off. "After the third day," said Ike Leaf, "[the soldiers] rolled a big rock in there. That rock's still there yet. They figured that the third day [the Indians] would go thirsty and be hungry and they'd starve them out." Leaf said the soldiers left them "there for dead because they covered that hole up. But there's an outlet that they didn't know about." The few remaining Indians in the innermost recesses simply waited until the soldiers left and escaped.[16]

While rummaging around in the rocks, Joe Wasson found evidence that the Indians had been gathering up the bullets fired by the scouts from the high bluffs to the west during the first day's fight "and sent some of them back at us the next morning." Yet, the soldiers discovered plenty of bows and arrows, and powder and caps in sacks, or in a considerable number of new cans and boxes. Wasson figured that "The hammering of all the artillery extant could not have dislodged the occupants, had they decided to remain." The reason they vacated the stronghold, in Joe's estimation, was that "they had no idea of the soldiers staying with them right along . . . ."

Apparently Crook was correct in his tactics; a siege would not have worked because the Indians needed to be met hand-to-hand and rooted out. Whether Crook felt a personal need to prove that he could mix it up with the Indians and win a victory, as his predecessor, Major Marshall, had failed to do, will probably never be known. He did surpass Marshall in one respect; he lost more men. With eight killed or mortally wounded and eleven wounded, the Battle of Infernal Caverns was the costliest to the whites in the entire Snake War. Although the participants who left records seemed to agree that the battle was fought efficiently and economically, contemporary historian Hubert H. Bancroft had a different take: "That General Crook sacrificed his men in the affair of Pit River in his endeavor to achieve what the public expected of him is evident, notwithstanding the laudatory and apologetic accounts of the correspondents of the expedition."

On the other hand, Wasson was fairly convinced that Crook had done well. When the lieutenant colonel "came to Idaho last winter, he set about whipping the Indians and learning their haunts with an energy unparalleled, meeting with much success and some vexatious loss. He soon became satisfied that from the impudent nature of the depredations on the Humboldt Road and the Owyhee settlements, that the perpetrators had some far-off place of retreat and where they lived in apparent innocence." Wasson said Crook concluded that raiding Indians always attacked 200 or 300 miles from their "home" to divert attention from the peaceable portion of the tribe while the rest remained hostile. He believed the burgeoning white settlements around Carson City and Virginia City drove the Paiutes to the north, where they evicted other bands and thus, could have the Goose Lake and Pit River country all to themselves. It was nonsense, Joe said, to believe the Indians could "live round on cold rocks and horsemeat alone;" they must have a sheltered area with a good climate and adequate water, grass, food and game, just like everyone else.[17]

Later in the day on September 28, some of Crook's/Wasson's assumptions were borne out. Boise Jimmy, one of McIntosh's scouts, found the body of an Indian recognized as a leader of the band that had stolen many of Company H's horses on Donner und Blitzen River the previous winter. Boise Jimmy took the Indian's scalp, plus his fur cap, which was "tasseled off with the queues of massacred Chinamen. . . ."

The young woman captured earlier in the day "told some palpable lies at first," but when Archie's scouts took her to a tree and threatened to hang her, she spilled out much information that tallied with known events. The leader of the band at Infernal Caverns was Sieta, and he was killed in the fight. Sieta was moving north when he ran into some of McKay and Darragh's scouts operating in advance of Crook's column as it headed from Camp C. F. Smith to Warner. The confrontation convinced Sieta to turn back south to the Pit River region. Crook's fight on July 27, near Camp Warner was with Pyramid Lake Paiutes, who may have been Winnemucca's people, heading north on what was ostensibly a hunting expedition. It was Ocheho who fought with McIntosh on Crane (Lookout or North End) Mountain. The now deceased, fur-capped warrior fought with Ocheho before joining Sieta. Ocheho had moved off, saying that he would raid "up north" before the snows fell. It was Ocheho's band that had stolen Crook's horses the previous March. Ocheho took them south, along with many more he had stolen, totaling about one thousand. Ocheho used the horses for food, or traded them for weapons and supplies, mainly with the supposedly friendly Paiutes on the Pyramid Lake and Truckee Reservations. The Pit River Indians furnished the Paiutes with some weapons, but much of the trading was done between white men in Virginia City, Nevada, with the Pyramid Lake Paiutes, who exchanged ammunition for fish. The Indians were planning on holding a big meeting to discuss their best course of action when Crook struck. If so, said Wasson, the Pit River precinct would not be well represented.[18]

In the valley below Infernal Caverns, Crook packed up to return to Camp Warner. On the afternoon of September 28, less than one mile north of the campsite they buried the bodies of Barchet, Lyons, Meara, Sawyer, Carey, and Bross in separate graves side by side. They burned logs over the top and let the horses trample down the ground to obliterate any evidence of graves. Wasson commented that there was a "horror attendant in knowing that one has to be left hundreds of miles in the wilderness without so much as a little lumber to designate the line of demarcation between human and Mother Earth;" but, he realized the necessity of hiding the graves, given "the well known practices of the human hyenas" who inhabited the country. The precaution failed, however, for when a detachment of soldiers returned later to disinter the remains, no trace of them could be found, their belief being that the Indians had dug them up.

Lieutenant Parnell had his men prepare what he called "double and single travoises" for the wounded. The singles used one mule with a pole tied to either side, ends dragging the ground, secured by ropes or saplings, and overlaid with blankets. The doubles used two mules, front to back, with two long poles tied to each side, with the space of a man in between, and the poles secured with canvas and blankets, becoming, in effect, "a stretcher on mules." On a couple of mules they rigged slanted "easy chairs," padded with grass and blankets. In this manner, Parnell said, all the wounded were carried "without any unnecessary suffering." All the efforts notwithstanding, civilian Traynor died on the way back, and Kingston died after reaching Camp Warner.[19]

On September 29, the command began its march north, along the west bank of the South Fork Pit. Fifteen miles brought them to the junction of the North Fork. They crossed over, and 20 rods north and 30 rods west of the junction they stopped to bury Lieutenant Madigan. He was eulogized in a special ceremony. He was born in Ireland, and came to America where he joined the 88th New York Infantry during the Civil War, working his way from private to lieutenant. In August 1863, he joined the 2nd New Jersey Cavalry as a first lieutenant, and after the war, in February 1866, he joined the 1st Cavalry as a second lieutenant. He was posthumously breveted captain for conspicuous gallantry at the Battle of Infernal Caverns. Wasson said he was genuinely friendly, with "a droll originality and humor," and his presence around the campfire would surely be missed.

Over the next few days they moved slowly up the North Fork Pit toward Goose Lake, and on October 1, discovered a series of sites where the signal fires had been built announcing their presence on the way in, "a perfect system of telegraphy," according to Wasson. On October 3, they were in Oregon, north of Goose Lake, and continued up the valley and over the divide to Crooked Creek, which flowed north into Lake Abert. Near the southern end of the lake they cut east over the Abert Rim and, on October 4, were back at Camp Warner. Everyone was thankful to return and get a chance to rest. Newly arrived Assistant Surgeon Lieutenant Richard Powell took over from Dr. Tompkins and treated the wounded. The soldiers eagerly read the mail that had accumulated; one of the letters was to John Madigan announcing his promotion. Joe Wasson concluded his long report to the *Avalanche*, by stating: "Had a bully time and have no excuses to make."

Because Wasson praised Crook, the *Avalanche*, in receipt of his first-hand commentary, naturally took a pro-Crook stance and reported the Infernal Caverns fight as a victory. New owners Hill and Millard, although they could not have known the ultimate results one way or another, said that Crook's campaign was "the most important affair that has occurred in the way of settling the Paiutes and their allies."

It was obvious to them that in war there will be losses. "There is a queer notion that—if men get killed in an Indian fight—the victory must be on the side of the Indians, no matter what the Indians may have suffered." Other papers, like the *Idaho World*, the Jacksonville *Sentinel*, and Sacramento *Union*, more often couched their reports of Infernal Caverns in terms of "defeat" and "retreat." If the soldiers thought they were going to be able to rest on their laurels, they were mistaken.[20]

Chapter 21 notes

1 Bourke, "Crook in the Indian Country," 647.

2 *Owyhee Avalanche*, August 17, 1867; Bourke, *On the Border with Crook*, vi; Knight, *Following the Indian Wars*, 43-44; Schmitt, ed., *Crook Autobiography*, 153; Bancroft, *History of Oregon*, Vol. 2, 535-36.

3 Clark, "McKay's Journal, Part 2," 288-89; *Owyhee Avalanche*, September 28, 1867.

4 Clark, "McKay's Journal, Part 2," 289-91; Heitman, *Historical Register*, Vol. 1, 590; *Owyhee Avalanche*, September 28, 1867, November 2, 1867.

5 Clark, "McKay's Journal, Part 2," 292-97; Heitman, *Historical Register*, Vol. 1, 457; *Owyhee Avalanche*, November 9, 1867; Clark (p. 292) incorrectly identifies Lt. (brevet captain) Moses Harris as Capt. William H. Harris.

6 *Owyhee Avalanche*, November 2, 1867; Parnell, "Operations with Crook," 485.

7 *Owyhee Avalanche*, November 2, 1867; Parnell, "Operations with Crook," 485; Knight, *Following the Indian Wars*, 52.

8 *Owyhee Avalanche*, November 2, 1867; Parnell, "Operations with Crook," 486; Schmitt, ed., *Crook Autobiography*, 155n3; Eskridge, "Infernal Caverns," in Cozzens, *Eyewitnesses*, 84. Ruby and Brown, *Pacific Northwest*, 209.

9 "Crooks Canyon," http://www.farwestern.com/crookscanyon/toc.htm

10 *Owyhee Avalanche*, November 2, 1867; Eskridge, "Infernal Caverns," in Cozzens, *Eyewitnesses*, 84; Parnell, "Operations with Crook," 486.

11 *Owyhee Avalanche*, November 2, 1867; Parnell, "Operations with Crook," 486-87.

12 *Owyhee Avalanche*, November 2, 1867; Eskridge, "Infernal Caverns," in Cozzens, *Eyewitnesses*, 85; Parnell, "Operations with Crook," 487-88. Wasson said the sergeant's name was Bassler, while Eskridge called him Russler.

13 "Crooks Canyon," http://www.farwestern.com/crookscanyon/toc.htm

14 *Owyhee Avalanche*, November 2, 1867; Eskridge, "Infernal Caverns," in Cozzens, *Eyewitnesses*, 85; Parnell, "Operations with Crook," 488; Schmitt, ed., *Crook Autobiography*, 154.

15 *Owyhee Avalanche*, November 2, 1867; Parnell, "Operations with Crook," 488-89; "Crooks Canyon," http://www.farwestern.com/crookscanyon/toc.htm

16 *Owyhee Avalanche*, November 2, 1867; Parnell, "Operations with Crook," 489-90; Eskridge, "Infernal Caverns," in Cozzens, *Eyewitnesses*, 85; "Crooks Canyon," http://www.farwestern.com/crookscanyon/toc.htm

17 *Owyhee Avalanche*, November 2, 1867; Bancroft, *History of Oregon*, Vol. 2, 544.

18 *Owyhee Avalanche*, November 2, 1867.

19 *Owyhee Avalanche*, November 2, 1867; Parnell, "Operations with Crook," 490-91; Schmitt, ed., *Crook Autobiography*, 153-54.

20 *Owyhee Avalanche*, November 2, 1867, November 9, 1867; *Idaho World*, November 6, 1867.

Chapter 22
LAST OF THE WARM SPRINGS SCOUTS

While singing his praises of Crook, Joe Wasson affirmed that the lieutenant colonel's campaign had so far demonstrated to the authorities and the public, the correctness of his actions. Wasson believed that Crook's constant harassment of the Paiutes cleared the Owyhee area of large bands of Indians. He was not completely correct. Band size may have been smaller, but there were still depredations in the Owyhee and Burnt River districts. Indians, as usual, seemed to find Shea's stock easy pickings. He had just brought in 1,000 head of Texas Longhorns, and turned them loose on Catherine Creek near present-day Oreana. The Indians found Shea's new herd to be a goldmine, and ran off ninety-five head, for a loss of $6,075.

In the Mormon Basin area, about two p.m. on Sunday, September 29, a farmer, J. B. Scott, and his wife and two children, had visited a neighbor in Rye Valley and were returning home to their place on Dixie Creek. About three miles from home, Indians attacked and shot Mr. Scott in the left breast and left arm, while one gun, loaded with an iron bolt, sent its projectile through his teeth and into the back of his head. He collapsed into the back of the wagon while Mrs. Scott grabbed the reins and whipped the horses forward. Bullets hit her in the stomach and thigh, but she kept going. The pursuing Indians gave up the chase after a few hundred yards. She reached her home and neighbors came to assist her, but her wounds were mortal. She died the next day, happy, at least, that she had saved her children.

On October 2, a small band of Indians murdered an unnamed traveler near Farewell Bend on the Umatilla and Boise Road. A party of men from Mormon Basin tracked the Indians to the Snake River in the vicinity of the Weiser River before losing them.

In the Flint District on the night of October 3, Indians jumped miner Joseph F. Colwell, who was from Missouri, had lived in Jacksonville, Oregon, for a time, and moved to Owyhee in 1865. He "was shot and scalped, and his lifeless body shockingly mutilated, within a half mile of Oro and Owyhee cities." They threw his body in the fire, where part of his torso was burned to ashes. All they got from Colwell's meager possessions were a pistol and some blankets. Once again, the *Avalanche* assumed, that instead of action, "We may soon expect to hear of the Throne of Grace being besieged with orisons and supplications for 'Lo! The poor Indian,' by our Eastern countrymen. . . ."[1]

CAMP LOGAN, OCTOBER 4, 1867

On October 3, a small band of Indians plundered the cabin of a Mr. Howe, only a few miles east of Camp Logan. Lieutenant James Pike responded to the attack. Born in Ohio, Pike fought in the 4th Ohio Cavalry during the Civil War, and joined the 1st Cavalry in March 1866. In the fall of 1867, he was at Camp Logan, and at his own request was given permission to search for the Indian raiders. Pike took command of seven troopers of Company F, 8th Cavalry, and two civilian guides, and rode east toward the Blue Mountains. He may have been enthusiastic and anxious to make his mark fighting Indians, but he had little experience. The next morning, his guides found the thieves camped in a dense thicket, but Pike "imprudently gave a shout, which sent the savages flying, leaving a rifle, which in their haste was forgotten."

The Indians put up little resistance, fired only a few times and disappeared into the low underbrush. Pike's men got off a score of shots before all their targets vanished, and it was impossible to tell if they had hit any warriors. Pike made the best of it by confiscating some camp equipment and destroying the rest. When the unfortunate lieutenant found the abandoned old rifle, he foolishly grabbed it by the muzzle and struck it against a rock to break it. Instead, it exploded, sending a large caliber lead ball into his left thigh, "inflicting a dangerous wound." The troopers assisted Pike back to Camp Logan.

The next morning, Lieutenant Albert B. Kauffman led a six-man detachment of his Company F, six miles east to the Douglass Ranch, but had to wait five hours for the arrival of the two civilians who had accompanied Pike and could show him the way to the skirmish site. Kauffman then headed north into the mountains on the Mormon Basin Trail. On the way the weather turned to rain and snow, obliterating the trail, and it took another day to get to the site. He found evidence of four wickiups, but the Indian trail headed southeast and was soon lost in the new fallen snow. Incredibly, Kauffman had only taken three days' rations and had to retrace his march to Camp Logan, accomplishing nothing.

Assessing the situation through hindsight, one might conclude that the officers either did not have enough sense to take along enough supplies to accomplish their objectives, or that the commissary department ruled the roost, and, backed by a penurious government, doled out supplies enough to sustain only the briefest scouts. Numerous Indian expeditions were cut short by inadequate transportation or supplies. As for Pike's condition, his wound was patched up, but the ball had cut an artery and it proved nearly impossible to stop the persistent bleeding. Pike lingered for ten days before dying on October 14. In a standard statement, the Department of Columbia headquarters reported: "Lieutenant Pike was a valuable officer, and one who had rendered very efficient service during the past war. His loss is deeply regretted."[2]

Indians returned to Oro in the Flint District on the night of October 24. William Black, a partner in the firm, Black Brothers, was going out of his house to an underground cellar in the back, carrying a lighted candle to find his way. Indians loosed two arrows at him from behind another cabin only 40 feet away. One arrow struck Black near the heart and he died the next morning. Miners followed the moccasin tracks of five Indians before they disappeared on a rocky mountain slope.

Indian signal fires were being seen in the mountains almost every night. The Indians who shot Black, may have been in the same party that attacked a stage about five hours later near Cottonwood Station, 15 miles from Silver City. The stage, coming through at two in the morning, had only the driver and one passenger, a Mr. Brooks, aboard. The Indians shot and killed one of the horses, but the two men put out such a hot return fire, that the Indians pulled back. The two men cut the dead horse loose, the driver put out the coach lights, and galloped the three remaining horses to the station.

Captain Coppinger took fifty mounted 23rd Infantrymen and three scouts out of Camp Three Forks on October 7, to try to recover cattle that had been stolen near Silver City. He headed to Jordan Creek and upstream to Flint Creek. Going over to Boulder Creek, Coppinger picked up a trail that headed south into the Juniper Mountains. On October 10, southeast of the mountains, about eight Indians fired on Coppinger as he traversed a gorge. His men dismounted and chased the Indians on foot, up and down canyon and cliff, but the warriors always kept tantalizingly out of range, firing back whenever the soldiers seemed about to give up. Finally, the captain tired of the game and called off the pursuit. Coppinger found five slaughtered oxen, plus a cache of butchered beef hidden in the rocks, no doubt to have served as a winter food supply for the Indians. He headed west and scouted the west side of Juniper Mountain and over to the Owyhee for the next three days, and returned to Camp Three Forks on October 14, after marching 186 miles.[3]

While Crook was gone on the Infernal Caverns expedition, there were a few changes at Camp Warner. The structures planned for construction had not been started because the sawmill was not yet up and running. Twenty new recruits for Captain Perry's Company arrived, along with three new lieutenants: Thomas M. Fisher, who joined the 23rd Infantry in March 1867; John R. Eschenburg, who fought in the 2nd California Infantry in the Civil War and joined the 14th Infantry in February 1866, transferring to the 23rd Infantry in September the same year; and Duncan Sherman, who joined the 1st Cavalry in January 1867. Three privates of Captain Henton's Company B, deserted. They got near the Humboldt Road when Indians attacked them and killed Private Myers—the other two decided they would rather return to Camp Warner and take their chances with the army.

On October 7, the day Captain Gilliss had left Camp Harney to pick up his wife, Julia, and Mrs. Mary Crook, Lieutenant Colonel Crook pulled out of Camp Warner, heading for Harney. He rested only one day after returning from California. Crook, Lieutenant Eskridge, Perry's recruits, and McIntosh and his scouts headed north across the "Great Sandy Desert" wastes. They had a rough trip owing to the poor condition of the stock and lack of water; one of the new recruits died and Archie McIntosh was laid up with rheumatism. They struggled into Camp Harney on October 11. Also arriving that day was Lieutenant Frederick L. Dodge, who had fought with the Massachusetts and New Hampshire Infantry in the Civil War, and joined the 23rd Infantry in March 1867. The day before, on his way from the gold mining community of Auburn, Oregon, bringing recruits and stock, Indians attacked him on Wolf Creek near the headwaters of the Malheur River and drove off a number of his mules.

On October 12, Captain Kelly, Lieutenant William McCleave, who fought in the 1st Dragoons and 1st California Cavalry before joining the 8th Cavalry, and fifty men of Company C, 1st Cavalry, with McKay and nine scouts, left camp to look for Dodge's stolen mules. They camped at midnight on Stinking Water Creek. The next few days they explored the Malheur, Mule Creek, and Cottonwood Creek. On October 14, they remained in camp on Cottonwood while George Green, who had fought in Jennings's battle in July 1866, and five soldiers scouted for the stolen mules. The next day Kelly divided his command in half, Kelly taking one part and McCleave and McKay the other. The latter went up Horse Cock Mountain—today more genteelly called Castle Rock—and found both old and fresh signs. On October 16, they went south of the mountain to the junction of the Malheur and Little Malheur, where George Green and the five soldiers returned from their unsuccessful hunt.

On Thursday, October 17, marching in two squads on both sides of the Malheur, they saw an Indian on top of a lookout point above the river and Captain Kelly chased him four miles. The one warrior turned into several, plus some women and children. Kelly reported, "Owing to the roughness of the country could not overtake them except a squaw, child, and a mule." They were turned over to the scouts for safekeeping, but somehow, perhaps with the help of her captors, the woman took the mule and escaped the same night. Kelly, said McKay, "was much vexed" because of it.

They found evidence of a few more Indian campsites, but the occupants always fled just ahead of the soldiers, and set numerous grass fires, said Kelly, "to signalize our approach." On October 19, George Green and Sergeant Terence Sheridan left for Camp Harney to get more provisions and Kelly and McCleave moved down the North Fork to its junction with the main river, camping near the site of Lieutenant Hobart's battle in July 1865. The next day, Kelly concluded to return to Camp Harney due to several reasons, including grousing among the scouts. On October 18, Lieutenant Albert Kauffman and eleven 8th Cavalrymen made a four-day scout out of Camp Harney, but also failed to engage any Indians in battle.

Back in Camp Harney on October 12, Crook wrote to Department of Columbia headquarters that "The Indians in Capt Darragh's and McKay's Scouts are very much dissatisfied and want to go back to their families, in this dissatisfied condition they will not be of any service to me." He believed it would be a good idea to muster most of them out, keeping only enough to operate against the Snakes east of the Blue Mountains. "I much prefer these Boise Indians for Scouts," Crook wrote, expressing his partiality to McIntosh's Shoshones, "and I would like authority to enlist a company of them."

Part of the problem, in addition to wanting to see their families, was the continuing argument over the disposition of the captured horses and prisoners. The Warm Springs Indians had enlisted under the assumption that they would be able to keep the booty. Apparently the question had come up again and the scouts were having second thoughts about the deal. McKay recorded "Good news" in his journal when Kelly announced they would return to Camp Harney. On the way, they met George Green with a dispatch ordering Kelly to return immediately because of the belief that the hostile Snakes had all fled the country anyway.[4]

At Camp Harney, Crook sent Lieutenant Eskridge to Portland on October 12, with his ideas about continuing the war in the Lakes District. The contemplated move of Company F to Boise and Company H to Camp C. F. Smith, would leave Crook with few troops to finish his operation. Wasson said that Crook believed he would have more trouble with headquarters and private interests shaping his operations than from the Paiutes. Wasson complained that the hay being supplied at Harney cost $40 per ton and it was of such quality that "old doormats would be luscious nutriment in comparison," and even then, the soldiers spent all their time stacking it while being paid $16 per month, instead of chasing Indians.

On October 16, a notice was posted at Harney, stating that all civilians on the post not employed by the government, and having no visible occupation, since horse thieves and other disreputable persons were known to be in the vicinity, were to leave the reservation at once. Wasson was offended by the order. Somewhat tongue-in-cheek, he wrote that the only horse he ever contemplated stealing, "Old Buster," had died of a fever down near the Infernal Caverns. He said it was the last of the old Oregon Cavalry, had webbed feet, could live on greasewood, and carried him 1,200 miles before giving up the ghost. With "Old Buster" gone, Wasson said, "the contractors and their bummers had left nothing to steal, and I didn't come out with so much as a shoddy overcoat."

The declaration caused an exodus of non-essential personnel, including what Wasson called the "Oregon War" thieves who had robbed the government of more than it cost to fight or feed the Indians. Unfortunately, the order meant that Wasson too, would have to leave. It was Captain Perry who indicated that Wasson "came under the special ban," and Wasson hoped Perry would have to suffer by rotting at the post all winter.

Despite Wasson's dismissal, he still had good words for the efforts of the soldiers and scouts. He believed Crook's campaigning had been sound; winter fighting and the use of scouts—"make one half of the enemy oppose the other"—were the ways to win the war. He hoped another company of Shoshoni scouts would be formed and used in the Owyhee area, perhaps under Donald McKay, because they were worth more than all the "government guides, bilks, and bummers." Wasson, going out a gentleman, thanked Lieutenants Eskridge, Jack, Goodale, Rice, Stanton, and Parnell, Captain Harris, and even Captain Perry for their kindnesses over the past four months. He continued to gush over Crook. "I'd say he was one of God's own men in the right place—thoroughly in earnest; regardless of fear or favor from any source."[5]

Captain Moses Harris, with Company M, 1st Cavalry, started for Camp Lyon on October 20, and Joe Wasson joined him. The usual five-day trip took seven days because of what Wasson said were poor guides. As they crossed the Malheur they saw plenty of tracks, evidence of Kelly and McCleave scouring the area at the time. The hard march across a rough plateau between the Malheur and Owyhee, and a pull across the lava beds brought them to Camp Lyon, and all were pleased to be back. Wasson did not return to Silver City until November, but he found his brother John, still waiting for him. John went down the Columbia River and south to San Francisco, and Joe left a few days later, on November 9, taking the Humboldt Stage. He later got a job with the San Francisco *Alta California*.[6]

On October 27, Captain Gilliss pulled in to Harney with his wife and Mary Crook. Julia Gilliss was not too impressed. The post was "disagreeable," she said, "from the fact that it is situated on a flat with alkaline dust about a foot deep. I never saw such a dirty place." Crook was very glad to see his wife, Mary. "It was just one year to the day from the time that I separated from her in Baltimore until she joined me at Harney," he wrote in his autobiography.

Perhaps Crook was feeling mellower in anticipation of his wife's arrival, for the constant patrolling was curtailed somewhat, and he cut an agreement with his Warm Springs scouts. In his journal on October 23, McKay recorded that he had gotten to Harney "with all the Indian boys to settle with Genl

Crook respecting the prisoners. It was all satisfactory arranged. They got the prisoners and brot them home also the horses that was captured by them."

Apparently Crook had agreed with McKay and Darragh to let their scouts keep their captured Snake prisoners and some of the horses if the men would escort the majority of captured horses to winter quarters at Fort Walla Walla. On October 28, Lieutenant Otis W. Pollock, 23rd Infantry, the acting assistant adjutant general, issued Crook's order to allow five of McKay's men and five of Darragh's men to be excused from the Walla Walla trek, to "proceed direct to the Warm Springs res for the purpose of taking their private horses &c to that place." The order did not specify, but it is apparent that the "&c" was a reference to the human captives the Warm Springs Indians got to keep as their reward for a year's hard service. With that potentially sore point solved for the moment—after all, the army had just finished fighting a Civil War to, among other things, put an end to slavery—Crook and his officers were able to hopefully continue with their mission of fighting the Paiutes.

Crook left Camp Harney on October 30. Julia Gilliss was pleased, especially after Crook consoled her and played up the efficacies of their new destination. "We will not remain here [Harney]," Julia wrote to her parents. "Genl Crook says Camp Warner is far pleasanter. . . ." Julia would learn how pleasant Warner would be during the coming winter.

On November 1, Lieutenant James A. Rothermel, who fought in two Pennsylvania cavalry regiments in the Civil War and joined the 8th Cavalry in June 1867, took charge of moving the rest of the captured animals from Camp Harney to Walla Walla. McKay and Darragh and their remaining scouts joined in, herding 403 mules, forty-one horses, and hauling twenty sets of pack rigs. Rothermel moved from Harney to Canyon City, to the Middle Fork and North Fork John Day, to Camas Creek, Pilot Rock, to the Umatilla Reservation, and arrived at Fort Walla Walla on November 12. There were no inconvenient glitches, however, Rothermel was not happy with the service of one of his captains. McKay, in a journal he kept religiously for a full year, made no entries from November 1 through 7. Rothermel gave an indication as to why, in a report made upon reaching Fort Walla Walla. From the moment they left Camp Harney, Rothermel said, McKay "was very much intoxicated," and by the time the command reached Canyon City, McKay "became so much intoxicated that he was left behind at that place and his command marched on without him." McKay did not show up and report to Rothermel until November 14, after an absence of ten days.

The one indiscretion of a man who had been such an important part in the army operations for a full year did not prove to be a serious blemish on his record. The Walla Walla *Statesman*, like many frontier papers, generally critical of the military, did have some kudos for Darragh and McKay and their scouts for their hard work and successes, stating, "they have shown themselves admirably adapted for the peculiar service in which they were engaged. In a regular stand up fight they were greatly inferior to the white soldiers, but when it came to scouting their services were invaluable."

General Steele's, who, one year previously did not want the Indian scouts, now praised them. In a letter to General Halleck he wrote that the Indian scouts had done "most valuable service," that "they cheerfully lead the way into the middle of their enemies. In the late expeditions, they have done most of the fighting and killing." Steele believed that an additional 100 scouts "would exterminate the hostile bands by next spring, with troops enough in the settlements to prevent their [the hostiles] getting supplies from that source."

With delivery of the stock to Walla Walla done, Rothermel, McKay, Darragh, and the scouts returned to Fort Dalles on December 2, to be mustered out. In payment for their services for the past year, McKay received a check for $985.22, and Darragh received a comparable amount. The use of the two Warm Springs scouting companies was an experiment that worked, and the lessons learned by the army would be utilized in many future Indian campaigns.[7]

Chapter 22 notes

1 Cornelius Shea Depredation Claim #7644; Hanley, *Owyhee Trails*, 82; *Owyhee Avalanche*, October 5, 1867, November 2, 1867; *Idaho World*, October 9, 1867.

2 Heitman, *Historical Register*, Vol. 1, 792; *Secretary of War 1868-69*, 69, 771; Bancroft, *History of Oregon*, Vol. 2, 545-46; Kauffman to Seward, October 8, 1867, RG 393, Dept. of Columbia, Letters received, Box 3.

3 *Owyhee Avalanche*, October 19, 1867, October 26, 1867; *Idaho World*, October 30, 1867; *Secretary of War 1868-69*, 69; Coppinger to AAG, October 15, 1867, RG 393, Dept. of Columbia, Letters Received, Box 3.

4 Heitman, *Historical Register*, Vol. 1, 376, 408, 421, 881; *Owyhee Avalanche*, November 9, 1867; *Secretary of War 1868-69*, 69; Clark, "McKay's Journal, Part 2," 297-301; Kelly to Eskridge, October 24, 1867, RG 393, Dept. of Columbia, Letters Received, Box 3.

5 *Owyhee Avalanche*, November 9, 1867.

6 *Owyhee Avalanche*, November 9, 1867; Knight, *Following the Indian Wars*, 57, 325. Joe Wasson again rode with Crook as a war correspondent, joining him in the 1876 Sioux Campaign. Wasson later made several trips to Europe as a newspaperman, and reportedly had a good strike in the California gold mines. He was elected to the state legislature representing Mono County, California, and he introduced legislation creating the California Mining and Mineral Bureau. He went to San Blas, Mexico, as a U. S. consul, but his health failed and he died there in 1883.

7 Clark, "McKay's Journal, Part 2," 301-11; Gilliss, *So Far From Home*, 152-53; Heitman, *Historical Register*, Vol. 2, 848. It cost the government $17,523 to subsist the Indian scouts through their term of service. See Francis to Nickerson, January 29, 1869, RG 393, Dept. of Columbia, Letters Received, Box 1. Lieutenant Rothermel was shot by his own men in a rabbit hunting accident near the Malheur River on February 15, 1868, and was buried at Fort Boise. William McKay was appointed interpreter for the surrendered Paiutes in 1868, and served as physician at both the Klamath and Warm Springs Reservations. During the Modoc War of 1872-73, McKay turned down an offer to captain another company of scouts; instead, he accepted an offer to be the physician at the Umatilla Reservation. Living in Pendleton in 1877, he was elected vice president of the Oregon State Medical Society. He was also Umatilla County coroner from 1882 to 1886. For all he did, McKay never was financially secure. He was adopted into the Umatilla tribe, which allowed him an allotment of reservation land, which was passed down to his wife and children. He died of a heart attack on January 2, 1893, while feeding his horses. His estate amounted to $523. He was buried in Pendleton.

Chapter 23
THE DENOILLE INCIDENT

Almost every Indian depredation occurring in the Northwest during the Snake War received coverage in one or more local newspapers. Julia S. Gilliss, the army bride of Captain James Gilliss, moved from her home in Washington D. C. to the Pacific Coast, and was struck by the harshness of the land and the people. "Be thankful that you are not destined to live in this land," she wrote to her parents in 1866, "this land of cold, monstrous deeds of wicked men, whose God is Gold, and who has buried deep, deeper than its deepest caverns, all the milk of human kindness and Christian virtues. Not a paper is printed here that does not have a ghastly column of horrible murders and atrocious highway robberies."[1]

The majority of those incidents involved stock thefts and attacks on travelers or miners. Occurring infrequently were Indian attacks in which white prisoners were taken. Whereas the Great Plains tribes, particularly the Kiowas and Comanches, seemed to relish taking captives for profit, the tribes of the Pacific Northwest, although commonly keeping other Indians as slaves, were much less inclined to seize whites. There were some notable exceptions. In 1847, Cayuse massacred the Whitman Family and others at the mission at Waiilatpu, near present-day Walla Walla, Washington, killing eleven and capturing about fifty people. Some were released in the ensuing weeks, but a handful of white women and girls were kept, abused, and raped. In 1854, Shoshonis attacked the Ward Wagon Train along the Boise River. They killed Ward and seventeen others, including one would-be rescuer. The Indians burned some children over a fire, and tortured, raped, and killed some of the white female captives. In 1860, Bannocks and Shoshonis attacked the Utter/Van Ornum Wagon Train along the south side of the Snake River near the mouth of Castle Creek. About twenty-five emigrants died from bullets or starvation, while four of the Van Ornum children were carried into captivity; only one, Reuben Van Ornum, was eventually freed.[2]

It was seven years before the local presses would have another captivity to write of. Although there were nowhere near the high numbers of killings as in the Ward or Van Ornum incidents, nevertheless, the *Avalanche* announced "SHOCKING MASSACRE" in its October 26 edition.

"Again it is our painful duty to record one of the most terrible Indian massacres that has ever taken place in our midst," it reported. On Monday morning, October 21, 1867, Sergeant Nichols and Sergeant Arnold Denoille, 23rd Infantry, left Camp Lyon driving a four-horse ambulance to Fort Boise. They headed northeast out of the Cow Creek bottoms and climbed the divide to Succor Creek. Mrs. Denoille, the sergeant's wife, had been with him at Lyon, but with her pregnancy and delicate health, she was not equal to the rigors of life at a frontier outpost, and she was leaving the camp. Unfortunately for the travelers, six warriors watched their progress. Two of them, Wahi (Fox) and Oytes (Left Hand) were the husband and father of a young woman killed by McKay's scouts back in January, and both had vowed revenge.

About 10 a.m. in a canyon 9 miles up the road, midway between Camp Lyon and Reynolds Creek, they sprung their ambush. Bullets from the first volley hit driver Sergeant Denoille and he slumped in the seat. Nichols heard the shots and saw puffs of smoke from some nearby rocks, but was not aware anyone was hit until Denoille threw his hands up and cried, "My God, I am shot!"

Denoille fell from the wagon, dragging the reins with him. Nichols had a Henry Rifle and fired several shots at the Indians as the horses began running. They ran out of control for about half a mile before one of the wheel horses became entangled in the reins and dragged the others to a halt. Nichols jumped out and got Mrs. Denoille down, telling her to run to the rocks with him. She was frantic and would not go, pulled away from Nichols and ran back toward her fallen husband.

The Indians were approaching about 300 yards away. Nichols let her go and ran for cover behind some rocks. The warriors went after the woman, the horses, and wagon. Nichols saw them grab her. "The lady was near the period of giving birth to a child," the paper reported, "and if she were not immediately murdered, her fate at the hands of those devils incarnate will be infinitely worse than death." They stripped Sergeant Denoille's body and took his gold watch and almost $1,200 that Nichols believed he was carrying. Only a few Indians pursued Nichols. They fired at each other a few times as the sergeant crept through the boulders down to Succor Creek. He reached Carson's Ranch with nearly all of his clothing torn from his body by the rocks and brush. Finding no help there, Nichols continued toward the stage road leading north from Silver City.

Not far away, Indians jumped another small party that was riding through the area. Some of the men scattered among the rocks and were not seen again. One of them, a Mr. Hardy, whose horse was shot from under him, ran into the rocks, kept the Indians at bay with two six-shooters, and escaped along nearly the same path as Nichols. In the afternoon, a Mr. Strong came along the road with a wagon and two horses. The Indians shot and wounded both horses, but Strong escaped to Reynolds Creek. Later in the day the stage from Silver City to Boise City was passing along the road, about eight

Idaho State Historical Society 69-43.2

Members of the 23rd Infantry pose at Camp Three Forks, Idaho in 1868. The cannon in the photo may be the one lost in the Owyhee River during a fight and later recovered.

miles from the ambush sites, when the driver spotted a man straggling in the dust. Passenger Charles J. Bernsteil, a Silver City merchant, helped Nichols into the coach where he related his story. At the Snake River crossing, they came across Hardy and picked him up.[3]

When word of the attacks reached Silver City, W. L. Burnham, J. McCourt, and four other men went in search of the Denoilles. They found the sergeant's body, stripped but not mutilated, about $60 in greenbacks scattered about, a Bible, portions of a woman's dress, and a hat ribbon. It looked like the Indian trail went west toward the Owyhee River.

On November 6, the *Idaho World* printed a report that scouts from Camp Lyon found evidence that a white woman was burned to death about 15 miles down Succor Creek from where Sergeant Denoille was shot. They found a fire pit, long, flaxen hair, and human bones. Still, there was no solid proof of whose remains they were. The paper editorialized that they hoped "dread retribution has been dealt to Mrs. Denoille's savage murderers." A week later, a soldier who had been on an expedition to find her, claimed that no such evidence of hair or charred bones had been found; the story "is all fiction." He claimed the woman was taken to Winnemucca, "to be traded off." No one but the Indians knew what had happened to Mrs. Denoille, and they were not saying.[4]

OWYHEE RIVER, OCTOBER 26, 1867

When the army received the news of Mrs. Denoille's kidnapping, Captain John Coppinger at Camp Three Forks and Captain James Hunt at Camp Lyon were ready for action. Coppinger rode north with fifty-one mounted 23rd Infantrymen. On October 23, he joined Captain Hunt with ten men of Company M, 1st Cavalry, and three scouts, including Dave Pickett, and they picked up a trail of what appeared to be forty Indians. They rode west toward the Owyhee River in the direction of Steens Mountain. On October 25, the scouts found the embers of two campfires just east of the river. They crossed over and the next morning discovered smoke from more fires. The scouts saw an Indian on a ridge about the same time as he saw them. He turned to run. The scouts quickly notified Coppinger and Hunt, and they led the command toward the forewarned camp as fast as possible. All their haste notwithstanding, most of the Indians had scattered before the soldiers rode in. Still, they killed one warrior, and captured two women and four horses.

The captured Paiute women claimed to know about the missing white woman; she claimed she was taken to Chief Winnemucca at Steen's Mountain, but could be ransomed for blankets and supplies. Hunt freed one of the women to arrange a meeting, telling her he would pay any price to regain the white woman, except for ammunition.

Coppinger and Hunt hurried back to Camp Lyon to refit for another search attempt. Their return on October 27, luckily coincided with the arrival of Captain Harris with the majority of Company M from Camp Harney, and the appearance of a supply train from Fort Boise bringing Spencer carbines for the cavalry. Coppinger's old rifles, which were called "no better than substantial clubs," were discarded in trade for Hunt's Sharps Rifles. The *Avalanche* hoped that with better weapons, Coppinger's "*seeming* failures" would not be repeated. He returned to Camp Three Forks on November 1.[5]

On the day of Coppinger and Hunt's skirmish near the Owyhee River, Captain George K. Brady, 23rd Infantry, left Three Forks with thirty-eight men to search for Indian marauders in the Flint District. Making what appeared to be only a half-hearted scout, Brady circled around for a few days, found nothing, and returned to camp.

On November 27, Lieutenant Goodale, 23rd Infantry, left Camp Harney with 23 men of Companies F, 1st Cavalry, and C, 8th Cavalry, searching for stock stolen from civilians near the post. Goodale went east to the South Fork Malheur and on November 29 found "where an animal had been killed and very little but the blood had been left." Nearby were 17 abandoned wickiups and more mules butchered for food. Goodale recovered a few live mules left by the fleeing Indians. The trail went down the South Fork, but frozen ground and new snow obliterated the trace. Goodale returned to Camp Harney on December 1.[6]

CAMP
Three Forks of the Owyhee, Ida.
From a sketch by Lieut Geo. B McDermott 23ʳ Inf. U.S.A.
1869

Idaho State Historical Society, 69-135.0
Camp Three Forks was originally called Camp Winthrop.

CAMP WINFIELD SCOTT, OCTOBER 26, 1867

In incidents unrelated to the Denoille kidnapping, there were more flare-ups in Nevada. Captain John P. Baker had been in command of Camp McDermit for more than a year, but was succeeded by Major Albert Brackett when the district commander for Nevada shifted posts from Camp McGarry to Camp McDermit in the fall. Brackett put nearly all of the available troops out in the field looking for Indians. In late October, Captain Baker, with men of Company L, 1ˢᵗ Cavalry, scouted south of the Santa Rosas in Paradise Valley. He hooked up with Lieutenant Lafferty, with a detachment of Company A, 8ᵗʰ Cavalry, and the two of them scoured the valley and picked up an Indian trail heading east. On October 26, Baker ran into a small Paiute camp, killed three Indians and captured four. Lafferty, exhibiting the daring he had shown in the past, continued on and surprised four warriors. The fighting lieutenant was reported to have killed two of them in hand-to-hand combat.[7]

The hard campaigning, which seems to have been conducted with a bit more energy in Oregon, was bearing fruit down in Nevada, as, little by little, small numbers of Paiutes trickled in to Camp McDermit to surrender. When the Paiutes turned themselves over to the army they could expect better treatment than trying to co-exist with the white settlers.

In September and October, Paiutes had filtered back into Quinn River Valley, "making friendly demonstrations and seemingly wishing to live with the whites," reported the *Avalanche*. Although many had not surrendered, they were allowed to congregate at McCauley's Station, visit at

283

Camp McDermit, and have business with the settlers. Rather suspiciously, however, they appeared to be very interested in learning how to use the white men's new Spencer and Henry Rifles. A group of local civilians were convinced that the Indians were up to no good, and were certain they were communicating with the hostile bands regarding troop dispositions and locations of stock. In early November, a posse followed eight Paiutes thought to be spies, jumped them 5 miles below the station, and killed five. There was also an unnamed white man staying near McDermit who was thought to be selling weapons and information to the Paiutes, and, according to the locals, "needs killing worse than his pet Indians."[8]

Author's photos

The pass on Reynolds Creek Road where many stages and wagons were attacked by Indians. Above, looking north, below, looking south.

Regardless of the harsh treatment at the hands of the civilians, Paiutes continued to give themselves up. Major Brackett learned that a band of Indians wished to surrender to him, but with many of his troops in the field, he sent his acting assistant adjutant, Lieutenant Frank K. Upham, 1st Cavalry, with only a handful of troopers left at the post, to bring them in. Upham, not knowing if he was about to walk into the proverbial lion's den, traveled south near where Eightmile Creek issues from the Santa Rosas, and on November 20, thankful for his good fortune, accepted the surrender of the entire band. Said Brackett: "The savages had become disheartened by their several defeats and were only too glad to lay down their arms."

QUINN RIVER, NOVEMBER 25, 1867

While Upham was bringing in the surrendered Indians, Brackett's other patrols were still fighting. Captain James N. McElroy and Lieutenant Aaron B. Jerome, Company M, 8th Cavalry, were in the field with a detachment of the company. For much of the year, the unit had been furnishing escorts and guards or making occasional scouts. Its first fight occurred when McElroy discovered Indians in the hills south of Camp McDermit. The Indians appeared in no mood to fight, and instead of holding up in the mountains, tried to flee across the valley and get over the boggy ground at Quinn River. While they attempted to cross, McElroy's troopers caught up to them and attacked, killing two warriors. Brackett mentioned Lieutenant Jerome's bravery, writing that, "in personal conflict [he] killed an Indian who was pressing him too closely."[9]

Up north, the Denoille capture, continuing raids in the Burnt River and Owyhee Districts, and constant civilian complaints, forced the army to shift another unit into the area. Company D, 8th Cavalry, had been stationed at Fort Walla Walla for much of 1867. In early November, Captain James B. Sinclair, 23rd Infantry, commanding at Fort Boise, called for Captain Abraham Bassford to distribute men of his Company D, to the threatened areas. Bassford sent Sergeant Mark Dermont and six privates to Carson's Ranch on Reynolds Creek in the vicinity of the recent attacks. The men were to escort trains and stages between Silver City and the Snake River. Bassford was also ordered to send a sergeant and six privates to Scott's Ranch on Burnt River, where the recent murders of Mr. and Mrs. Scott had the area in an uproar. In addition, a sergeant and four privates were to go to Miller's Ranch near Mormon Basin, and were to escort stages passing from there to Olds' Ferry on the Snake. Sergeant John Adamy and 10 privates were to operate between Scott's and Miller's, escorting stages and government supply trains along that part of the road.

With all the troop, civilian, and Indian traffic crisscrossing the area, there were bound to be mix-ups. On December 3, George Hill, who had been on several military expeditions, was riding with his nephew and a Mr. Fife, hauling two hay wagons from Jordan Valley to Flint. They camped near Minear's Ranch on Big Boulder Creek. That evening they spied a fire downstream and Hill and his nephew went to investigate. Creeping close, they saw several Indians around a campfire and a few more on the hillside. George Hill opened fire with his Spencer; the Indians scattered and the two whites retreated. Mr. Fife hurried to Flint for reinforcements, while the Hills took their cattle and wagons and entrenched at Minear's. A short while later, citizens from Flint arrived, as did, most surprisingly, a detachment of soldiers from Camp Three Forks. Instead of helping to chase the Paiutes, the soldiers, Corporal Murphy and six privates from Coppinger's Company A, 23rd Infantry, demanded to know who had been firing at their Indian scouts, and suspected that there were hostile Paiutes in the area. When the Hills somewhat sheepishly explained what had happened, all parties returned to their various pursuits, thankful, at least, that no one had been killed.[10]

CRAIG GULCH, DECEMBER 12, 1867

With conflicting stories whether or not Mrs. Denoille was alive or dead, the army continued to push for an answer. On December 9, civilian packer Cal Morton, interpreter Dave Pickett, and eight Boise Indian scouts left Camp Lyon to resume the search. They rode 19 miles northwest, 14 miles northeast, and about four more miles north, when, on the morning of December 12, they found several wickiups at the head of a canyon, which is possibly today's Craig Gulch, leading west to the Owyhee River.

There appeared to be many Paiutes, including at least fifteen warriors, but the weather soon deteriorated and Morton and Pickett could not get a good estimation of numbers. They sent back two scouts for help and waited. As they sat, the weather worsened, and soon a full snowstorm pummeled them. With visibility conditions restricted, a Paiute blundered into them and rushed back to warn the camp. Pickett decided there was no time to wait and "pitched in" against the scattering Indians. Regardless of the severe weather, the unprepared Indians fled into the rugged terrain where they fought for about three hours before getting away. As the scene was described to the newspaper, "The war-whoop of the Indians on both sides was mingled with the howling of the tempest, dark forms moved hither and thither amid the elemental strife."

In the confusion, the scouts easily had the better of the fight, killing five warriors and capturing one warrior, three women, three children, three horses, and much equipage. One of the captured horses was recognized as belonging to Sergeant Denoille, but more shocking, was that one of the captured Paiute women was found to be wearing Mrs. Denoille's stockings and other articles of her clothing that the men at Camp Lyon had seen her wear on many occasions. Captain Hunt and Lieutenant Harris with forty-one men of Company M, 1st Cavalry, arrived at the scene about 9 p.m., but there was little else they could do. They destroyed the camp and returned to Lyon on the December 14.

Once in camp, interpreters questioned the captured Paiute women. "It required several applications of hanging to make the squaws tell of the place of Mrs. Denoille's captivity," reported the *Idaho World*. Whether the threats made the women tell the truth, or make up a story to save their own skin, is uncertain. In any event, this time the story was told that Mrs. Denoille was still alive, but they did not know where she was being held.[11]

In early December, raiders stole twelve oxen from A. C. Goodrich in Jordan Valley and drove them into the lava beds west of Cow Lake. Goodrich and four men trailed the thieves and recovered four oxen. The Indians had already killed the other eight, and concealed them in the rocks, undoubtedly to use as food caches for the future.

On Sunday night, December 15, Indians raided 49 Ranch and stole sixteen horses belonging to John Hailey, the proprietor of the Boise City and Umatilla Stage Line. The Indians got across the Snake River with the horses. Captain Sinclair at Fort Boise, sent Sinora Hicks with some of his Boise Indian scouts, a sergeant, and ten privates, to cross the Snake and search up the Owyhee River for sign of the horse thieves. They were unsuccessful. On Christmas night, Indians raided the Desert Stage Station on the Overland Road. They shot the station keeper and got away with two stage teams belonging to Wells Fargo.

On December 18, Captain Hunt and Lieutenant Moses Harris took forty-four men of Company M, 1st Cavalry, seven Indian scouts, and Dave Pickett, out of Camp Lyon, hoping to follow up on Pickett's success a week earlier. They crossed the Owyhee and scouted around Cedar Mountain, but found and destroyed only one recently abandoned wickiup. They returned to Lyon on December 24, having accomplished little of note.[12]

THREE FINGERS GULCH, JANUARY 4, 1868

The new year of 1868 opened with a spell of several days of below zero temperatures in the Owyhee Country and Boise Basin. The weather should have kept everyone huddling inside around warm fires, but there was a chance the Snakes would not figure that soldiers would be out looking for them.

On the last day of 1867, interpreter Dave Pickett and mixed-blood scout Sinora Hicks, took 13 Boise Indian scouts and two men of Company M, 1st Cavalry, on a hunt. On the evening of January 3, they discovered a sleeping Indian camp near the mouth of a rocky canyon on the east side of the Owyhee River 30 to 40 miles below Rinehart Springs.[13] Waiting until the next morning, the scouts crept upon the camp and delivered a volley, killing one warrior in the first blast. The Indians ran up the canyon through a narrow defile below nearly perpendicular walls. Pickett doggedly pursued until he trapped them in a nearly inaccessible dead end, where a number of them took shelter in a grotto. Overhead a rock shelf sheltered the cave, on two sides were vertical walls, and in front was a sandstone spire that shielded a direct view inside. The pass to the entrance was wide enough to admit only one man at a time. It was reported that, "it would have been madness to have attempted to charge through the defile in order to take the stronghold by storm."

It appeared as if a siege would have been the proper course of action, but Pickett and the scouts knew they could not delay, because they had only supplied themselves for a few-day's trek and were already about out of food. All they had eaten the past two days was boiled barley. Starving the Paiutes out was impossible, and it was very cold and had begun to snow. The only alternative seemed to be to try to talk the Paiutes into surrendering. An old scout volunteered to go up and talk. He needed about three hours, but finally convinced the trapped Indians to give up. They said they were tired of fighting and would surrender, provided that their lives would be spared, that they could go on the reservation near Boise City, and would not be put in the guardhouse. Jail was their biggest fear; they would rather die than be imprisoned. Pickett had his scout reply that the soldiers did not want to kill the Paiutes, but only wanted them to stop killing the whites, and gave them a pledge of safety and non-imprisonment.

With that, the first of the Indians came out of the cave. He was a crippled old man, "who looked like a veritable imp from Pandemonium." The old man's limp, his bobbing head and frightened rabbit-like glances over his shoulders, and his strange outfit, caused the scouts and soldiers to laugh. He wore his "pantaloons with the legs ripped open and sewed to the tails of the jacket behind." Their guffaws ceased, however, when they saw that he also wore a sergeant's fatigue jacket, with yellow piping. When the rest of the Indians in the cave realized the old man had not been killed, they began to file out—six men, five women, and five children. The band leader, a younger man, asked who the white chief was, and when informed, gave Dave Pickett his half-stock rifle, his bow and arrows, and a six-shooter. The pistol he had and the cap he wore were regulation army issue.

In a nearby branch of the gulch, Sinora Hicks and seven scouts captured one more warrior. Pickett and Hicks rejoined and brought in their captives to Camp Lyon on January 6. The prisoners were found to have had plenty of bullets and caps, but almost no powder. They only had one horse, which the crippled old man rode. When the Paiute women were searched they were found to have two of Mrs. Denoille's dresses, her thimble, scissors, towel, chemise, and silk stockings—it was difficult to prevent the soldiers from wanting to take revenge.

Still, the prisoners denied taking part in the Denoille murders, claiming to have gotten the articles from some Indians belonging to Old Pasego's band. They indicted that the white woman was still alive, and with Pasego's band in northern Steens Mountain. The prisoners said they were starving, that they had been eating little but roots and berries found along the Owyhee

River. They wanted to surrender and indicated that other bands across the territory were in similar dire straits. They said they would all gladly come in and make peace except they thought they would be killed. After their interrogation, Sinora Hicks and scouts escorted the twenty-two captured Indians who were being held at Camp Lyon, to Fort Boise.

If the tribes were indeed destitute, as some of the recently surrendering Indians indicated, perhaps a different tactic could be employed to bring them in. The newspapers quickly suggested that if enough friendly Indian scouts with interpreters were sent out instead of soldiers, all the Indians could be persuaded to give up. It was thought to be "the quickest, easiest and least expensive way of bringing our Indian warfare to a close."[14]

The idea made sense. It was always believed that it was cheaper to feed the Indians than to fight them. The problem was, heretofore the Indians seemed to be able to feed themselves, at least with a little nutritional help from the white men's stock. Now, at last, perhaps the nonstop warfare with soldiers constantly on their tails, with their own people tracking them down, with hiding places being discovered, and with food sources drying up, it was time to trade freedom for food and safety. It was a serious, life-altering decision to make, but the harassed Paiutes increasingly made the choice.

Still, no one knew exactly what happened to Mrs. Denoille.

Chapter 23 notes

1 Gilliss, *So Far From Home*, 40.

2 Michno, *Encyclopedia of Indian Wars*, 28-29, 80-81; Michno, *A Fate Worse Than Death*, 129.

3 *Owyhee Avalanche*, October 26, 1867; *Idaho World*, October 26, 1867; Ontko, *Thunder Over the Ochoco III*, 407.

4 *Idaho World*, October 26, 1867, October 30, 1867, November 2, 1867, November 6, 1867, November 13, 1867.

5 *Idaho World*, October 26, 1867, November 2, 1867; *Owyhee Avalanche*, November 2, 1867; *Secretary of War 1868-69*, 70.

6 *Secretary of War 1868-69*, 70; Goodale to McCleave, December 1,1867, RG 393, Dept. of Columbia, Letters Received, Box 5.

7 Angel, *History of Nevada*, 175; Brackett, "Fighting in the Sierras," in Cozzens, *Eyewitnesses*, 7; Webb, *List of Engagements*, 34; *Adjutant General's Office*, 30; Angel places Lafferty's fight in August, but the incident matches more soundly with the latter three sources indicating an October fight. Official reports state the incident occurred near Camp Winfield Scott, while Angel places it on the South Fork Owyhee.

8 *Owyhee Avalanche*, November 9, 1867; *Idaho World*, November 13, 1867.

9 Brackett, "Fighting in the Sierras," in Cozzens, *Eyewitnesses*, 7; O'Connor, "Eighth Cavalry," http://www2.army.mil/cmh-pg/books/R&H/R&H-8CV.htm

10 *Idaho World*, November 9, 1867; *Owyhee Avalanche*, December 7, 1867; Coppinger to AAG, December 11, 1867, RG 393, Dept. of Columbia, Letters Received, Box 3.

11 Hunt to AAG, December 16, 1867, RG 393, Dept. of Columbia, Letters Received, Box 5; *Owyhee Avalanche*, December 21, 1867; *Idaho World*, December 25, 1867.

12 *Owyhee Avalanche*, January 4, 1868; *Idaho World*, December 25, 1867, January 4, 1868; *Secretary of War 1868-69*, 70: Hunt to AAG, December 27, 1867, RG 393, Dept. of Columbia, Letters Received, Box 3.

13 *Owyhee Avalanche*, January 11, 1868; *Adjutant General's Office*, 31. The site of this fight is not pinpointed except as being near the Owyhee River. Rinehart Springs is not found on old maps of Oregon, but there is an old Harts Crossing shown in the vicinity of present-day Rinehart Ranch, which has two nearby springs. Downstream 30 to 40 miles from there is Three Fingers Gulch.

14 *Owyhee Avalanche*, January 11, 1868; *Idaho World*, January 12, 1868, January 25, 1868, February 12, 1868.

Chapter 24

"AS FOR GRAIN, WE HAD NONE"

Lieutenant Colonel George Crook only spent nineteen days at Camp Harney before pulling out for Camp Warner on October 30. Accompanying him and Mary Crook were Captain James Gillis and Lieutenant Otis Pollock and their families, Lieutenant Frederick Dodge, paymaster Lt. Colonel William H. Johnston, his clerk, Dr. John M. Dixon, and a few others, plus some 23rd Infantrymen as escort, and a pack train.

"We made such an imposing display in crossing the country," said Julia Gilliss, "that not a single Indian showed his face." When they arrived, the new Warner was still not finished. Remaining there to construct the post during Crook's sojourn were Company H, 1st Cavalry, and Companies B, D, and I, 23rd Infantry. The soldiers had been busily building winter quarters, but a lack of supplies and equipment slowed their progress. Many horses and mules had died due to sickness and exhaustion, and the remainder were badly worn out after four months' campaigning. New stock had to be obtained and new recruits had to be trained. The forage on hand was limited– only about three pounds of grain per day for the animals, and two or three months' worth of "moldy hay."

The men were not much better off according to Lieutenant Parnell; they only had the usual scant supply of pork, flour, coffee, sugar, and salt, with a little extra tea and sugar for the officers. There were only a few steers left to eat, Parnell describing them as so-called cattle "with their ribs and hip-bones prominently sticking out, their hides laying close down to their skeleton carcass." There was no milk for the several children in camp. The men attempted to get supplies from Camps McGarry, Bidwell, and Harney, but deep snow prevented them from getting through, and several men were badly frostbitten. Crook and his wife had the "luxury" of inhabiting one of the few partially finished structures on the post, which he described as "a log hut, with the cracks plastered with mud, no windows, and a tent fly for a covering. Our only light by day was through the roof."

Julia Gilliss soon discovered how much more "pleasanter" Warner was than Harney. In mid-November, both her husband and six-month old baby daughter had "Mountain fever." She thought the place was too windy and unhealthy. They lived in a "slab hut" with one glass window, "the only one here," she claimed. The floor was dirt, and it sloped, so that they had to put blocks under one end of the bed so they could lie level. The walls were un-hewn logs with the cracks filled with mud, and the roof made of saplings and sod. They attached a tent to the cabin so they would have two rooms. Still, it was better than the canvas tents and lean-tos that the other men shivered in. Julia was homesick and wanted very much to go east to see her parents. One thing she did like about Camp Warner over Camp Harney, however, was that it was closer to San Francisco, which would facilitate a quicker getaway, if the chance ever arrived.

Crook had selected the new campsite, supposedly because Old Camp Warner's climate was too severe in winter. The new site was no better. Parnell said the snow on the parade ground was usually three feet deep. Crook said there were drifts from ten to 15 feet high. On several occasions the thermometer registered 18 to 20 degrees below zero. Crook's larder be-came so low one day that he went out hunting and luckily shot a large white jackrabbit to supplement his rations. Years later, Parnell saw the situation through rose-colored glasses: "Yet, I heard no complaints," he wrote. "It was an illustration of heroism on the part of the women unsurpassed since the days of the Revolution. On the part of the troops it was patient endurance and discipline worthy of any age." One might have gotten a different assessment from the soldiers, and the women weren't all that happy either. Julia Gillis disliked being snowed in for more than one full month, from late December until late January, where no mail could get in or out, and "everybody is half or whole sick." Even so, she conceded, "we are not altogether miserable."[1]

On November 23, General Steele relinquished command of the Department of Columbia. His replacement was a Kentuckian, Brig. General Lovell H. Rousseau, who had fought in the Mexican and Civil War, retiring from the latter as a major general of volunteers. Rousseau made no major changes in the department; he did insist that arrangements be made to con-tinue pressing the Indians with an active winter campaign.[2]

In November and December, several scouts were made to Warner Lakes and Lake Abert, but with no sign of Indians. One reason may have been the lack of scouts. When the Warm Springs Indians were discharged it was like having lost sight in one eye. Crook thought the Boise Shoshonis were better scouts than the Warm Springs bunch, but when they were gone, he real-ized how much they were worth. On December 17, Crook sent Lieutenants Parnell and Pollock with a small escort to Boise, carrying a letter to Idaho Territorial Governor David W. Ballard for assistance in securing the services of the reservation Indians for four or five months. They reached Boise on December 30, but the Indians, said Parnell, "were very reluctant to leave their warm and comfortable dwellings for hard work and exposure in the mountains; but the prospect of a little money in the end overcame their objections. . . ." Parnell secured twenty-three scouts for "four moons" and started back for Camp Warner on January 7.

The return trip was rough. At the ferry on the Snake, the boat was frozen in solid. The ice on the edges of the 300-yard wide river was 16 inches thick, but in the middle there was open water running fast with floating cakes of ice. The ferryman could not chop the boat free. They could have crossed in a small boat, but there was no way to get the 61 horses and pack mules across. Parnell thought about returning to Boise to wait for the spring, but quickly concluded that such a course would be "cowardly," and "would frustrate all of General Crook's plans and prolong the Indian war another year." They made excursions up and downriver to see if there was a place where it was completely frozen over, but could not find any. Finally, "as a military necessity," Parnell took over the ferry. They spent a few days with a long ice saw, cutting the boat loose and sawing a channel out to the open water. Every morning they had to re-cut ice that had frozen overnight. One afternoon, with a channel open, they put aboard some animals and provisions; eight Indians took long poles to ward off the floating ice cakes and they pulled out. It went well until they got to mid-stream, when the ice floes began to batter them, coming down the river at seven miles an hour. The Indians pushed against the floes, but the boat was buffeted and pushed by the massive cakes. The ice-covered wires and ropes stretched and the boat warped downstream. "[I]t was wonderful that one or the other did not snap," said Parnell. "Had such an accident occurred the boat would have instantly capsized, and the men and horses would have perished." They finally reached thick ice on the other side and made fast to stakes driven into the ice.

The next morning they had to chop free again and repeat the trip, but could not get into their channel on the north shore without more cutting. Only small loads could be taken, because too much weight would place too great a strain on the cables when battered by the ice. It took them seven full days to cross the river, but with no loss of animals or supplies.

Next, snow five feet deep was encountered in the Blue Mountains, and the men, about thirty altogether, had to break trail so the animals could follow in their paths. The grain supply was insufficient, so the animals ate by stripping the bark off trees everywhere they camped. The men had to melt snow in camp kettles to give the animals water. One day the going was so slow they only made one-quarter mile. On the Malheur they found a wagon train that was caught in the snow. One man had a badly frozen foot that had swelled up and burst. "The flesh appeared to be dropping off in flakes as large as an egg," Parnell said. His comrades had nothing to dress it with but coal oil and rags. Parnell took the man with them to Camp Harney, where a surgeon took care of him for four months before he could walk again. To show his appreciation, one night the man stole two blankets from the hospital and rode away.

As Parnell and Pollock struggled through the mountains, Captain Bassford, trying to comply with orders to give the Indians no rest during the winter, led a detachment of Company D, 8th Cavalry, out into the wilderness. On January 16, near Kenny's Ranch on the Malheur River, they discovered a small Indian camp, but deep snow and bad weather prevented them from approaching before the Indians caught sight of them and escaped. The cold, tired command returned to Harney empty-handed.[3]

On January 24, Parnell, Pollock, the Shoshoni scouts, and animals struggled into the post. The soldiers at Harney figured they had either decided to stay at Boise or had perished in the mountains. They had come 210 miles from Boise, but still had 140 miles to go to reach Warner. They rested a few days and continued the trek, finally reaching Warner on February 1—the final 48 hours of marching without provisions or forage.

The soldiers and families rejoiced to see the long-lost detachment, supposing that they had all died. Much of the winter campaigning season was already over, but uncooperative weather was blamed—somewhat incongruously, since bad weather making the Indians easier to catch was the *raison d'etre* for a winter campaign. The papers continued to support Crook, and printed private letters from Camp Warner indicating that he was still determined to make a winter campaign. The *Avalanche* was convinced that the Indians could be taught "that the whites can follow them into their winter fastness. . .and made to feel that there is no day in the year when he is secure." All that was needed was the authorities to "properly back up" the army.

There was more to it than proper backing. It was one thing to vow to pursue the Indians to their winter quarters, but the severe weather that kept the Indians in their villages played no favorites with the hunters. In another irony, the army that once believed it had no use for Indian scouts, but proved less effective when not using them, became unwilling to move at all without Indian scouts, which made it completely ineffective.

The storms that had plagued the army in the Great Basin had been ravaging the entire Pacific Northwest. They began with heavy rains in northern California in late December. On the December 22, San Francisco papers reported "The most terrific storm which has swept the coast for twelve years past is now raging." Heavy rains and gale force winds pummeled the coast and inland to the Sierras and Cascades. Stages out of Placerville could not get out because of mud and swollen streams. At Marysville, the levee broke and the Yuba River left its banks and cut across to the Feather River, cutting a new channel eight feet deep. Much of the Sacramento Valley was submerged. Roads over the Sierra Nevada were impassable. It was said, "Such a disastrous storm was never heretofore known in the mountains." There was flooding from Portland to Puget Sound, and houses, barns, mills, dams, and fences were swept away, along with much livestock.

In January, temperatures dropped drastically and the rains turned to snow. The snow blew so hard and heavy on Owyhee's War Eagle Mountain that the employees of the Poorman Mine could not go 200 yards from the mess hall to their lodgings and had to spend the night in the boardinghouse. By January 11, several days of 12 below zero weather caused the Columbia River to freeze. At Camp Harney, on January 22, the mercury dropped to 28 below zero, and two herders froze to death. One paper called the winter of 1868 the severest ever in southeast Oregon.

Perhaps it was the weather as much as the army that caused more and more Indians to surrender. At Camp McDermit, a one-time Owyhee miner named Jennings Smith talked to Captain Baker and convinced him that if furnished with a packmule and two Indian interpreters he would go into the mountains and bring back plenty of Indians willing to surrender. Smith searched at campsites known to the interpreters, and soon had plenty of Paiutes who wanted to give up but were afraid of punishment for things they had done. Smith assured them they would not be harmed, and soon, was making trip after trip to induce small bands into turning themselves in at McDermit. Smith brought in forty-two Indians on the last day of December. More camps were located at the head of Quinn River. By early January he had talked 102 Indians into giving up and was going out for more. It was a policy the newspapers had recently proposed and it seemed to work.[4]

The bad weather continued unabated. On February 7, 1868, at Camp Watson, Captain Eugene Baker took a detachment of Company I, 1st Cavalry, out on a scout. They spent four days just trying to get through the snow near the post and gave up. On February 11, Crook, finally getting his Boise scouts, left Camp Warner with Parnell's H Company, 1st Cavalry, thirty men of Company D, 23rd Infantry, under Lieutenant Frederick Dodge, and Donald McKay and thirteen scouts, for an expedition to Steens Mountain. They moved northeast to Warner Valley about 15 miles, and crossed one of the lakes—five miles of ice—to the eastern shore where the wall of Warner Mountain and Poker Jim Ridge protected them somewhat from the winds. They took no tents, so the men bedded down for the night by laying a piece of rubber blanket or heavy canvas on the snow, wrapping in a blanket, and throwing a rubber coat or canvas on top. As the heat of their bodies warmed the snow beneath, they sank down below the snow level and got out of the direct wind.

Once out of Warner Valley, the soldiers had to break trail in the snow for the animals. On the fifth day they reached the middle Donner und Blitzen River. The Boise scouts came in to report Chief Weahwewa's camp about eight miles down the valley. The command moved slowly through snow 18 inches deep with a hard crust that broke and scraped the legs of men and animals. Crook moved through the night, hoping to be in a position to surprise the Indians at daybreak, but after midnight they ran into a small band camped in the willows along the river. The Indians ran into the thick underbrush and neither side could see the other—the only intimation of position came from gun flashes. They skirmished with each other for an hour, but Crook realized it was a useless exercise, and pulled away to edge closer to the main camp by sunup—if it was still there. At three a.m. the scouts indicated they were close and Crook called a halt, while the men and horses stood in single file, freezing, for nearly four hours. The thermometer showed ten below zero. While the men stamped their feet to keep warm, the horses, said Parnell, looked "humped up" like enraged cats, "their bodies a mass of frost, and mane and tail almost a solid mass of icicles."

At first light they pushed on, readying weapons and forming up for a charge, but the camp was empty. Crook's scouts managed to round up a few prisoners, one of them a "young buck" he called "Little 'Howlark.'" This Paiute was captured by Darragh or McKay the previous summer, and had admitted to his participation in the Chinese massacres in 1866, but had escaped in the fall. Now he was captured again and indicated that Weahwewa and the Malheur and Harney Lake bands were all camping together. Crook, despite his seemingly unconcerned demeanor, was worried about his reputation, and deep down, wanted some of the "glory" of Indian-fighting, In a letter to Joe Wasson dated February 28, he wrote that he feared Captain Perry "may find those fellows on Dunder and Blixen and make an attack on them before I can get there."

Crook marched until 11 a.m. before stopping for breakfast along the river, and for the first time in five days, the horses were able to drink water from the stream, instead of melted snow in kettles. If the scouts had really seen any camps downriver, the encounter in the dark forewarned them to vacate the premises, but no tracks out of the area were found. Since they had only a few days' rations left, Crook decided to call it off and head back to Camp Warner. Parnell blamed a shortage of packmules for cutting short the expedition, with the majority of them being down at Camp Bidwell getting grain and flour—but Crook knew that before he started.

The use of packmules allowed the army more mobility than when pulling wagons, but in the winter, the mules had to haul so much of their own forage just to survive, there was little room for other supplies, and the men had to constantly feed and care for them. It was a situation that could be likened to an Abe Lincoln aphorism, written to General Nathaniel P. Banks in November 1862: "You would be better off anywhere, and especially where you are going, for not having a thousand wagons doing nothing but hauling forage to feed the animals that draw them, and taking at least two thousand men to care for the wagons and animals, who otherwise might be two thousand good soldiers."

Poor logistics had caused Crook to retreat again.

"We reached the post on the 22nd of February," Parnell recorded, "and immediately commenced putting things in order for a longer scout early in March."[5]

Two days later, Crook reported to General Rousseau, rationalizing his most recent failure. Since he had not captured the whole bunch in his initial attack and the main camps were stirred up before he got there, he "deemed it expedient to return to camp and allow them to become quiet again." Crook figured the only way to capture or kill the Snakes was to "get upon them unawares" because complete surprise was necessary for success. He wanted the two companies at Camp Harney to join him in the next campaign, because "in the event of our not being able to surprise them, I wish to have force sufficient to completely surround them and if possible starve them out."

Crook's reasoning is suspect. Certainly surprise was a factor in most successful Indian fights, but did he really believe that he could besiege a band of Snakes and starve them into submission? He blamed his failure on the Boise Indians, "for which I have to depend upon," and whose late arrival "has interfered with my plans." Earlier, Crook dismissed the Warm Springs Indians because he thought the Boise bands were better scouts. Crook suggested a scheme to solve his difficulties obtaining reliable scouts that bordered on the bizarre. He hoped to "make captures enough of the younger portion of the hostile Indians, who with proper care and training make very good scouts, so that at the expiration of this campaign I shall not have to depend on the Boise Indians for scouts."[6]

What Rousseau might have personally thought about Crook's idea to take young boys and nurture them into scouts, a process that might have taken years, is not recorded. Perhaps Crook believed he would be fighting in Oregon for another decade.

Up north the story of bad weather and inadequate supplies was much the same. On February 17, Captain Baker left Camp Watson with twenty troopers of Company I, 1st Cavalry, on a scout. He went to the South Fork John Day, crossed the Ochoco Mountains, went to Beaver Creek, and to the headwaters of Crooked River. On February 23 and 24, Baker tried to break a trail through the snow that "was from two to five feet deep with a heavy crust on it and getting deeper as we advanced. We made only seven miles in the two days." They saw no Indian sign, and "Finding it impossible to proceed in any direction," Baker returned to Camp Watson.

On February 19, Captain David Perry left Camp Harney with forty-two men of Company F, 1st Cavalry, and 12 Indian scouts. On February 29, the scouts reported Indians on Clover Creek, east of the Blue Mountains and north of the Malheur, but the Indians saw Perry approaching and fled into the deep snow, that averaged from ten to 30 inches in depth wherever they went. In early March, he was almost out of grain for the animals, and ordered a detachment to rush to Fort Boise after grain. Even so, the animals could haul little more than forage enough to feed themselves. Nevertheless, Perry persevered, and on March 10, his scouts captured four Indian women and one child. They returned to Harney on March 19, after marching 347 miles.

Perry, trekking through higher mountains and deeper snows, had kept in the field twenty-nine days; Crook had only managed eleven.[7]

In February 1868, additional information came to light about the fate of the abducted Mrs. Denoille, who had been missing since the previous October. Sinora Hicks took the Paiute women captured in January, to Fort Boise for more questioning. This time they changed their story; instead of indicating the white woman was alive and being held at Steens Mountain, the women admitted that she was dead. They did not kill her outright, they explained, as if that would make it more acceptable; they had only beat her and treated her cruelly and she must have died from injuries and exposure to the cold temperatures.

It was no excuse to the local whites. The *Idaho World* argued that this ought to be sufficient reason to convict them of murder and execute all the warriors in the party. But no chance, the editor, James O'Meara, sarcastically countered his own argument; the sanctimonious philanthropists in the East would probably have their way. Instead of execution, he believed the culprits would probably be "fed and caressed by a vile system of error" until the spring arrives, when they can be set free, and "with a full stock of powder and lead, they can carry on their treacherous warfare. . . ." O'Meara continued to spill out his rage. The "dirty she-brutes," he said, were traipsing around Boise City with "the remnants of the clothing stripped from the slaughtered Mrs. Denoille." He argued that they should continue to barter their charms to the degraded soldiery in exchange for ammunition, by which they could supply all the Indians in the Snake River Country. Would they be executed, he railed? No! But if the culprits were Irish, German, or Scotch, there would be vigilantes aplenty to hang them all. "'Poor Lo,' you are in luck!" he cried, because otherwise intelligent people "suffer themselves to be over-ridden and down-trodden by Puritan apologists for savage tribes, and savage atrocities."[8]

As the constant army pressure and bad weather caused more Indians to surrender, the newspapers had another issue to chew on. "What shall be done with them?" one reader asked the *Avalanche* editors. Among the suggestions were that the Indians should not be put on reservations at or near their old haunts, because it was thought that as soon as the army left and the Indians were fed, they would be back on the warpath again. It was believed that frontier reservations never succeeded; the Indians were too uncivilized and the country too rough to constantly campaign in. The Paiutes did not have any central leadership; dealing with a score of minor chiefs meant that no binding treaty on all of them would ever be kept. There was evidence that frontier reservations, like the Truckee, were simply feeding grounds for the Indians in the winter, and in the summer were sources of warriors and weapons. It was suggested that the Paiutes be removed to a reservation on the coast, the reasons being they could be watched more closely and fed more economically in an area of abundant food supplies and cheaper transportation costs. Left unsaid was the "not in my backyard" attitude—the settlers east of the Cascades and Sierras were simply tired of the problem and wanted others to deal with it. What course to follow was yet to be determined.[9]

What should have been evident, even to the most ethnocentric, was that the Indians were hungry and would continue to steal to live. On the night of March 9, Paiutes rode to Jordan Valley, broke into Alexander F. Canter's cabin, destroyed or stole his provisions, clothing, cooking utensils, and other items, and stole five yoke of oxen and a yearling heifer, to the value of about $1,145. Two nights later they tried to steal stock from Baxter's Ranch, but were discovered and pursued into the mountains in the direction of Camp Three Forks. "The miserable wretches are in a starving condition," the *Avalanche* stated, "and as long as any of them run at large, they must have food, and we may therefore expect to hear of their occasional depredations."

The road along Reynolds Creek between Silver City and the Snake River Ferry had been comparatively safe since November 1867, when Captain Bassford distributed some of his men to protect travelers. Early in 1868, however, probably because it was determined that the roads would be peaceful during the winter, the soldiers were recalled.

On Wednesday, March 18, George Jarvis left his wife and three children at his home in Boise Valley, and was driving a wagon-load of eggs, cabbages, potatoes, and other vegetables to Silver City, when Indians attacked and killed him in the canyon between Carson's Ranch and Fruit's Ferry, almost one year later and in the same spot that Ullman and Younger were killed. A Mr. McDowell came along the next morning and found the trail leading a short way from the road, noticed a burned wagon, and hurried back to the road, where he flagged down the next stage and got help. McDowell and a few others returned to the scene, searched through the burned wagon and found all the eggs smashed and vegetables scattered. They found Jarvis's body, shot in the abdomen and breast, stripped, but not scalped. They put the body in the stage and took it to the ferry for burial.

The locals immediately pointed fingers at Lt. Colonel Washington L. Elliott, 1st Cavalry, in command of the District of Owyhee. He had once issued orders for soldiers to protect that very area, "but they were taken away again and the road was left without protection, and why was it?" the *Avalanche* asked. "Why is it that soldiers are kept in the barracks at Fort Boise, where they are of no earthly benefit, and our lines of travel are left unprotected?" There were now eight men killed in that area. When would the army realize that it had to maintain constant vigilance?

The violence was not always one-sided. On Friday, March 6, near Boise City, four drunken white men were involved in rape and murder. The various stories were contradictory, but in essence, the men assaulted two Indian women, and when a man called Bruneau Jim tried to intervene, the whites killed him—three of the men involved claimed the murder was committed by John Brady. The men were taken into custody, but what became of them is unknown.[10]

Down at Camp Warner, after the abortive expedition to Donner und Blitzen River in February, Lieutenant Colonel Crook was ready to take the field again. "Whenever a thaw took place, which made it possible for us to get out into the snowdrifts, slush and ice, we went," said Lieutenant Nickerson, albeit with some exaggeration.

They had gotten most of their animals back and collected enough grain and supplies to be out in the field for one month. Because the "blazing mid-day sun shone like a mirror" off the snow the last trip, several men became snow-blind. As a precaution, this time they wore goggles, broad-brimmed campaign hats, and blackened their cheeks with burnt cork to dull the "terrible glare of the sun and snow." On March 9, they started out again for Steens Mountain: Company H, 1st Cavalry (fifty-two men); Company I, 23rd Infantry, mounted (twelve men); Company D, 23rd Infantry, mounted (27 men); Donald McKay's Boise scouts (14); Lieutenant Nickerson as Crook's adjutant, and Assistant Surgeon Dickson. Parnell said the blue-goggled, black-faced men presented a comical appearance, some looking "as if they had been in the prize-ring for half a dozen rounds."

Crook's plan was to have all his forces meet at the head of Warner Lake, "and if we can get after them and get them into the rocks, to have enough to completely surround them and freeze them out. If I can be successful in doing this, it will about end the war up in this country." He again lamented his late start. "I lost the best portion of the winter in not having the scouts," he said. As they reached the rendezvous, Captain Kelly, with Company C, 8th Cavalry, from Camp Harney, joined them. As Crook explained it, "all available mounted troops were ordered to rendezvous at the north end of Warner's Lake, but, owing to non-arrival of supplies, was unable to reach there as soon as expected." For all their planning and supply gathering, they never seemed able to successfully achieve the logistics part of the equation.

With the hindsight of an armchair general, one might question Crook's tactics as well as his logistics. If he had planned to go after the Indians in the Donner und Blitzen area, he would have been much better off by wintering at Camp Harney after the Infernal Caverns campaign. There was much effort, expense, and time spent building a new Camp Warner in a location farther from the Steens Mountain/Donner und Blitzen country, in a place where the winter proved to be as bad, or worse, than it was at the old Camp Warner. Warner was about 90 miles from the Donner und Blitzen, while Harney was half that distance. Instead of moving men and supplies to Warner, and then going back, they could have all more economically just stayed at, and started from, Harney. A case in point is Crook ordering all the mounted troops to

A. R. Bowman Museum, Crook County Historical Society, Prineville, Oregon
New Camp Warner, 1870.

meet him at Warner Lake (although only Captain Kelly could comply) and then turning him about face, and marching right back to the country he had just left.

DONNER UND BLITZEN RIVER MARCH 14, 21, 1868

Nevertheless, Crook reached the bluffs above Donner und Blitzen River on March 13, where it was bitterly cold, several degrees below zero. The scouts reported fires in the valley, and about ten o'clock the next morning, the command came upon one of Winnemucca's rancherias at the edge of a rocky canyon near the river.

The differences in terrain were drastic, with half the field a flat, frozen marsh, lined with brush and willows, and the rest a hillside with large boulders and loose, sliding rock. Parnell's Company H dismounted and went up the canyon with his line extended from one bluff to the other. The Indians hid behind large boulders and it was difficult for the soldiers to get a shot at them without coming up very close. A shower of arrows hit the troopers; one passed through a man's arm, stopping with equal lengths sticking out both sides; one arrow penetrated two inches into Parnell's hip, a few other troopers took lesser wounds. Using revolvers, the troopers dodged among the rocks and drove the Indians out, but they only found one body, of "a great big savage-looking fellow" who had been riddled with bullets breaking his legs, arms, and piercing his torso. Three bullets had gone through his head, with one through his right eye. Farther, on the soldiers found more "good" Indians who had succumbed to their bullets.

In the creek bottom, the infantry had much trouble finding the Indians hiding in the willows and undergrowth. Crook and civilian guide James Luckey rode around a tangle of brush right into a wickiup; the Indian dogs barked and snarled and the occupants scampered out the back and down a bank and across an unfrozen branch of the creek. Rifles and revolvers popped in the frigid air, while occasional arrows whistled out of the brush, but few were hit on either side. An Indian boy who was with Crook was shot at, and the bullet passed diagonally across his body, between his shirt and skin, but without cutting him at all. The Indians got away on hidden pathways and across comparatively high and dry trails through the half-frozen marsh. Most of the fighting was done farther up the canyon, where scattered skirmishing continued for three hours.

Said Crook, "We could not cross this slough or creek in time to have caught any of them. We did not attempt it." They did see smoke several miles down the valley and decided to start immediately for what they assumed was another village, to catch it at dawn the next morning. The fight on March 14 cost Crook five wounded; two Indians were captured, and the best guess of Indian casualties was seven killed. Lieutenant Nickerson, who always tended to exaggerate the exploits of his hero, said that marching through the bitter weather, "was a terrible punishment to us, but the complete surprise and utter annihilation of the entire band amply repaid the toil and suffering."[11]

The "annihilated" Indians were still around. The command marched in the darkness to a point as near to the next camp as possible without giving themselves away. Again they stood there in the darkness, stamping their feet and pounding their bodies with their arms to keep warm. Freezing sleet blew in and made everyone more miserable, if that was possible.

"Our beards were one mass of ice," said Crook. At daylight, they found another partly frozen slough barring their path, and by the time they sloshed across, the Indians got away. In the afternoon, a warm Chinook blew in out of the southwest, rapidly melting the snow. They marched northeast, toward the southern end of Malheur Lake. "It was not very pleasant camping;" said Parnell, "the winter was breaking up and the snow in the valleys was melting, so that we had to pack sagebrush on the ground to lay our blankets on in order to keep out of the mud and slush."

The march toward the east end of Malheur Lake was alternately over ridges of deep snow, or in valleys through "slush up to our saddle-girths, with frequent blizzards of snow, sleet, or rain beating in our faces." The horses' legs were lacerated by breaking through crusted snow, and the men had to take much time caring for them. Realizing that the difference between a successful campaign and a disaster was a very thin line depending for the most part on the health of their mounts, many men tore off the sleeves of their own shirts to wrap around their animals' limbs, and even shared their limited supply hardtack with them. The horses, said Parnell, "would eat the hard biscuit with very much relish, but salt pork or bacon they respectfully declined."

Once again the supply situation was intolerable. "As for grain," said Parnell, "we had none after being out for a week or so. When it is remembered that the allowances of hard bread is one pound per day per man, it will be seen that the man and horse had not very much to make a square meal on."

The enlisted men and their animals led a spartan existence and endured much when they went to war; it was a shame that their officers were not more adept at getting them a modicum of essential supplies with which to wage a successful campaign. Crook had supposedly taken one month's rations, but strangely enough, only one week later the horses' grain was gone.

On March 17, they camped on a hill overlooking the valley below, which the melting snow had turned into a vast lake. A mile from camp they found some grass for the horses—their first grazing since they left Camp Warner. Late in the afternoon they spied mounted men moving down the valley about five miles away. Field glasses revealed them to be cavalry. Donald McKay rode out to learn that it was Captain Perry, who had been scouting the area with Company F since February 19. Perry had marched through snows from two feet to 30 inches deep, and on March 10, had captured four Indian women and one child. He was on the twenty-eighth day of his scout with only two day's rations left and was returning to Camp Harney, after a march of nearly 350 miles.

After learning the results of Perry's operations, Crook, for some reason, determined that it was useless to proceed further, and decided to return to Camp Warner. Since he was only two days' march from Harney he directed Captain Kelly to return there with his company, and carry the wounded with him, rather than have them endure several extra days of hard marching. If Crook had any thought of continuing his pursuit of the Indians into the Donner und Blitzen or Steens Mountain country he should have taken the entire command to Harney—unless he had already decided to wash his hands of the entire campaign.

Crook turned around and headed southwest, across the valley that had become more lake than solid ground. The worn down horses could hardly carry a man on their backs, and the soldiers led their mounts through water that was sometimes waist-deep. They found a relatively high and dry place to camp, and in the morning were surrounded by a thin sheet of ice, which again caused more cuts and discomfort to men and animals as they broke through with every step.

On the night of the March 20, they camped near the canyon where they had the fight six days earlier. That night, Corliss, the chief packer, quietly awoke Lieutenant Parnell and told him he thought Indians were creeping about. Parnell sprang from his blankets, fully dressed because of the cold, and went with Corliss to the picketed mules. Corliss's favorite saddle mule had three arrows in it. Parnell immediately called for the guards to bring in the entire herd. The animals had been roped and hobbled on a slight plateau only 200 yards from the camp, and ten men were surrounding them, yet, Indians had infiltrated, shot several animals with arrows, cut the lariats, and stolen seven horses and twenty-one mules. Among the missing horses was Crook's favorite, "Old Buckskin." "Commissary" Crook had been robbed again.[12]

In the first gray of dawn, Lieutenant Duncan Sherman went out with seventeen men to follow the trail. On the bank of the Donner und Blitzen, less than three miles from camp they found the animals—all dead. The Indians had driven them as far as they could before they got bogged down in the marsh. Some of the animals were half-butchered for the meat. The angry soldiers returned to camp with the news.

After breakfast, March 21, they discarded their spare aparejos (Mexican-style pack saddles), moved another four miles and camped again. Parnell had a plan, and Crook gave him permission to take Donald McKay, Surgeon Dickson, and six men back to where the animals had been killed. Parnell was certain the Indians were in the process of cutting up the animals to get the meat, were interrupted when the soldiers arrived, and would return to finish the job. Sure enough, as Parnell's squad approached, they saw six Indians busily cutting up the animals. They dismounted, left one man with the horses, and crept up on the unsuspecting Indians. The creek was over its banks and the land was a bog, but the soldiers, thoroughly soaked, crept through the tall ryegrass to within 300 yards of them before they would have to emerge from their cover and ascend a slight slope in the ground. They got another 80 yards before one warrior, tired of cutting, stood up to stretch and saw them coming. Parnell gave the order to fire. A few were hit, but the others ran for the river. Some swam, and some hid in the tules, but Parnell's squad shot five out of six; one warrior was shot, fell, and jumped up to run three times in succession before ceasing to rise again. Only one got away.

After the fight, Parnell thought of a way to deny the Indians their meat. "We sprinkled every carcass liberally with flour; in this condition the Indians would not dare to touch it, supposing it to be poison. We then returned to camp very well satisfied with the result of out trip."

The next morning they pulled out for good. At Warner Lake the ice was breaking up, and Parnell likened the sound to "heavy peals of thunder or distant cannonading." They marched over the ice with a foot or more of water running on top of it. Crook, who at times waxed loquacious about his hunting excursions, had little to say about the Donner und Blitzen excursion after the fight on March 14.

"The snow at once commenced melting," he wrote, "so that the next morning we had to pack up and leave the country for fear of being

Chapter 25

THE FOURTH SPRING

Spring of 1868 marked the fourth year since the start of the Snake War. For all the campaigning and fighting, there were few indications that the upcoming year would be any different than the previous four. Indians still raided near the settlements. The Paiute, Egan, kept to the upper Malheur country, striking west toward Canyon City or east to the Burnt River. In March he drove off stock in Mormon Basin and captured two wagon trains. The settlers organized a company of men, and in conjunction with troops who occasionally occupied old Camp Colfax on Willow Creek, chased unsuccessfully after Egan.

The strategy and tactics of the regular army were basically the same as the volunteer army that preceded it. Yet, there were encouraging signs for the army that some Indians were hungry, tired of fighting, and willing to call it quits. Camp McDermit had taken in a couple hundred Paiutes, yet, not all were truly ready to give up, but may have feigned surrender simply to rest and obtain food. In March, six Indians, labeled "pet prisoners," who had been accommodated at the post all winter, were allowed to freely come and go, and, according to the *Avalanche*, "in order to manifest their appreciation of the good treatment they had received," they rode off with forty head of stock. The editors sarcastically queried if the remaining Indians would all be furnished good horses and sent out to murder settlers and travelers. The *Idaho World* characterized the incident as simply another "proof of the criminal carelessness which is exercised towards the Indians all over that region by the military in command."

OWYHEE RIVER, MARCH 26, 1868

In an effort to chase down the thieves, Sergeant John New led a small detachment of Company D, 8th Cavalry, with a few Indian scouts, in a circuitous pursuit toward Steen Mountain and back to the Owyhee River. On March 26, they trailed the Indians driving some of the stolen stock into a canyon. New attacked, but the Indians were prepared and repulsed the charge. New claimed killing one warrior, but William Harris, one of his teamsters, also was killed.[1]

Reacting again to criticism, particularly as a consequence of the March 18, murder of George Jarvis along Reynolds Creek, the army shifted soldiers from Fort Boise to the Owyhee District. Captain James Sinclair, with Lieutenant Charles Bird, 23rd Infantry, personally led seventy-five men of Company H, 23rd Infantry, and twenty men of Company D, 8th Cavalry, to Silver City. They stayed in a large hall owned by Brigham & Weeks and impressed the townsfolk with some martial displays of marching and drumming. The locals commented that the soldiers appeared to have been big and strong Danes and Swedes, professional in manner, and, most notably, "not one of them was known to be intoxicated." As was the case so often, once the soldiers arrived, the Indians disappeared. Sinclair did not stay long; on April 8, after less than two weeks, he tramped back to Fort Boise. Like the Noble Duke of York, he marched them up the hill, and he marched them down again.

About the time Lt. Colonel Elliott issued orders to recall Sinclair to Boise, he received his own recall. Major Elmer Otis, 1st Cavalry, was replacing him as commander of the District of Owyhee. The locals could not see the sense in it. Just about the time one commander got used to the situation, he was pulled, and a fresh body stepped in to start the breaking-in process all over again.

MALHEUR RIVER, APRIL 5, 1868

In the Harney Valley country, Captain David Perry was busier than his superior officer, George Crook. Perry was tramping about Harney Valley, Malheur Lake, and the Donner und Blitzen country before Crook got there in March, and was back at work after Crook returned to Camp Warner to rest for a couple of months.

After meeting briefly with Crook on March 17, Perry returned to Camp Harney to refit. Several days later he was back in the saddle with three officers and ninety-eight men of Company F, 1st Cavalry, Company C, 8th Cavalry, and Company K, 23rd Infantry, plus Archie McIntosh and twelve Indian scouts. Having scoured the area to the south in March, Perry headed up the main Malheur River, where his scouts were certain they would find the Paiutes. On April 1, the scouts saw campfires 10 miles ahead, and the next day, because of high water and deep snow, Perry left the pack train under a ten-man guard and continued. On April 3, conditions worsened, and the men had to dismount to break a trail in the snow for their horses to follow. Finally the snow stopped the animals in their tracks. Perry left the horses behind with another ten men. They continued the pursuit another 10 miles, crossing streams fifteen times in the process, and with everyone exhausted, wet, and cold.

Perry crept up to the Indian camp high in the mountains near the upper Malheur, and waited in concealment, freezing in the deep snow the entire evening of April 4. At midnight, all were in place, and the nearly full moon reflecting off the snow made it light enough to coordinate an attack. When Perry gave the order to charge, the soldiers, all on foot, thundered into the rancheria like a herd of bison. The Indians, said to have been part of Weahwewa's, Oytes's, or Egan's bands, were high in a secluded camp in the snow-covered mountains, and probably never thought the soldiers could find them. They were completely surprised and devastated by the attack. Many could not even grab weapons before they were shot down, barely clothed, while emerging from their shelters.

Captain Kelly of Company C, was conspicuous in leading his men in the thick of the fight, earning a promotion to brevet major for gallantry. Lieutenant Alexander H. Stanton, Company F, was later brevetted captain for gallantry in the engagement. Without the loss of a soldier, Perry killed thirty-two Indians—twelve males and twenty women and children were gunned down in the moon shadows. One woman and one child were captured, and it appeared that only two escaped. They also captured three cattle, one horse, and gathered up 5,000 pounds of dried salmon. The camp was destroyed and the salmon thrown to the flames in a massive fish fry. Any Indians remaining near enough to see or smell the destruction of their food supply, no doubt suffered a severe blow to their morale. Perry returned to Camp Harney on April 8.[2]

INDIAN CANYON, APRIL 17, 1868

Lieutenant Colonel Elliott, while in command of the District of Owyhee, did not keep his troops as busy during the winter of 1867-68, as did Crook in the District of the Lakes. When Major Otis took over in the spring, the infantry at Camp Three Forks (Winthrop) finally began to stir. Captain George K. Brady left camp on April 14, with twenty mounted men of Company E, 23rd Infantry. He scouted the Three Forks area and moved down the Owyhee.

On April 17, Brady found a small camp of eleven Paiutes—seven men, one 14-year-old boy, one woman, and two children—in Indian Canyon about eight miles below the Forks. Brady attacked, but there was little resistance. He killed five of the men, captured the boy and two children, while only three escaped. Three good weapons were taken. Brady sent the children back to Camp Three Forks in care of a three-man detail.

The captain discovered another trail that led down Indian Canyon toward the Owyhee. He followed it until it became quite large, with all indication that a considerable rancheria was somewhere below. Brady discreetly decided it would be wise to pull back to camp and return another day with more soldiers. When the *Avalanche* received a report of the fight, it reported, "We believe that this is the first opportunity the Colonel has had for demonstrating his good will to the Lo family, and he certainly shows a disposition to treat them in a proper manner. Three cheers for Colonel Brady! This is the first installment of the Spring campaign."[3]

It was not Brady's first opportunity, and he did not return to find the Indians.

On April 23, Archie McIntosh and several of his Shoshoni scouts were patrolling out of Camp Harney, when they caught and killed a lone Paiute who got too close to the post. In Nevada and California, just when it appeared that things had quieted down, another Indian raid shocked the local settlers. The Virginia *Enterprise* and *Trespass* reported that on April 17, Indians killed five people, including the William H. Pierson family traveling to their ranch at Red Rock near the neck between Lower and Upper Long Valley near the California-Nevada line. Pierson, his wife, and daughter were in one wagon, and John Sutherland and a man named Cooper were in another. A 14-year-old boy who was herding sheep in the hills nearby saw the attack. Cooper fell from the wagon, but drew his revolver and fired several times before he was killed. The others did not make it one mile before being run down and killed. Pierson's 18-year-old daughter was shot and axed in the head. The boy said the Indians chased him nine miles before he made it to safety at another ranch.

Paiutes at the Pyramid Lake Reservation had indicated that Pit River Indians were planning on raiding the area, but the boy was said to have understood a bit of the Paiute tongue, and insisted the warriors who attacked the ranch were Paiutes. Settlers from Long Valley and Honey Lake took up the trail, but to no avail.[4]

DEEP CANYON, APRIL 29, 1868

There hadn't been any trouble in the Paradise Valley area since October 1867, and when Paiutes began surrendering at Camp McDermit, the settlers may have relaxed their vigilance. The winter of 1867-68 was severe in northern Nevada, just as it had been in most of the Pacific Northwest. By April, Paradise Valley was still covered by a few feet of snow and several families were forced to subsist on wheat and barley, ground in coffee mills.

The snow was not gone in late April, when Howluck and his band revisited the area. Mark Haviland, one of the first settlers in the area, who had fought at Willow Point in July 1865, and persevered through good times and bad, was Howluck's first victim. The raiders stole ten of Haviland's large workhorses, worth $2,000, during the pre-dawn of April 29. Settler John Rogers also had one horse missing.

When reports came in to Camp Winfield Scott, Lieutenant Joseph W. Karge, Company A, 8th Cavalry, decided action was needed. Karge, who had emigrated from Germany before the Civil War, fought in the 1st and 2nd New Jersey Cavalry, being brevetted a brigadier general in 1865. Now, reduced to a lieutenant in the regular army, he was assigned to one of the most isolated posts in the West. He had arrived at Camp Winfield Scott in November 1867, and right away there was friction between him and Lieutenant Lafferty. John Lafferty had seen action fighting Indians in the California Cavalry and in the 8th Cavalry, showing good judgment and bravery in several fights. His exploits had appeared in the newspapers and his reputation and profile were not consistent with being a subordinate lieutenant at a wilderness outpost. He did not adjust well to Karge, who had attained higher rank in the Civil War, and had one month's seniority over Lafferty, but had never fought Indians. Karge soon found that the laurels he won in the Civil War did not translate to the frontier. He may have felt he needed to make his mark in order to be promoted and gain a name for himself. Karge's first scout against the Indians back in November 1867, produced no results.

When Howluck hit Paradise Valley in April 1868, Karge discounted the raid. When he first learned of John Rogers's missing horse, he said he believed "at the time that the horse had either strayed or been taken by some white men." As if it was just another bothersome chore to keep responding to settlers who continuously cried "wolf," Karge ordered Lieutenant Pendleton Hunter to take three men and investigate. Hunter, a Michigander who had joined the 8th Cavalry as a second lieutenant in October 1867, was new to the frontier. Nevertheless, he chose only Sergeant John Kelly, and Privates James C. Reed and Thomas Ward to accompany him in pursuit of the thieves. Only Kelly had previous experience with the Indians, being wounded in the hand in the Eden Valley fight in January 1867. Civilian John Rogers joined the patrol.

When Lafferty heard of the mission, he went to Karge and complained that it was "committing murder" to send a green lieutenant out after Indians. The two had a heated argument, and finally Lafferty obtained permission to gather another squad and join Hunter. Karge, in his account of the affair, made no mention of any argument with Lafferty. He said only that, "I cautioned Lieutenant Hunter, in case he struck an Indian trail, to be careful and not allow himself to be drawn into a snare."

About 11 a.m., Karge said he finally learned of other stock being stolen in the valley. "No longer doubting Indians were the perpetrators," he said, "I immediately ordered Lieutenant Lafferty. . .to proceed with six men and one day's rations in the direction taken by Lieutenant Hunter. . .and afford him such assistance as circumstances might require."

Hunter, meanwhile, tracked Howluck to the mouth of Deep Canyon in the Santa Rosa Range, only eight miles from Camp Winfield Scott. Hunter rode six miles up the canyon, finally climbing a mountain with a gradual slope of 2,000 feet, marked with protruding horizontal cones of black rock about 500 feet from the summit. From one of these rock projections, Howluck and about seventeen warriors blasted Hunter's party from only 20 feet away. Three horses were shot through the head. Hunter, Kelly, and Ward were hit. Reed and Rogers returned fire, and all five abandoned the horses and scrambled down the mountainside. Reed and Rogers tried to drag and carry the three wounded men and fire at the warriors who pursued them, but, thankfully, they would not come right out in the open for a final charge to finish them off.

For nearly two miles the five men stumbled over rocks or slid downhill on snowfields. At last they found an oblong cave about 100 feet in circumference, surrounded by perpendicular rocks, with an opening only about six feet across. It was not fully covered on top, and there was deep snow still covering much of the ground inside. Reed took a position where he could guard the entrance for a long time, provided he had enough ammunition. Rogers, unhit, volunteered to go for help. He threw off his hat and coat and made a mad dash down the canyon.

Howluck surrounded the cave and fired at the opening for a few hours, but would not assault it. Private Reed, the only defender, fired out of the opening at any Indian who showed his head. Ward was dying with a bullet through his lungs, Kelly was wounded with a shot that broke his collarbone and first rib, and Hunter was hit by a bullet in the right hip that ranged upward and lodged near his bladder. Another bullet had gone through his clothing and exited to strike him in the right wrist.

It was six p.m. before Rogers stumbled, exhausted, into Camp Scott, stating that they had been ambushed, all the horses were dead or captured, and the four troopers were trapped in a cave. Since Lafferty was still out, Karge asked Captain Frederick Mears, 9th Infantry, the paymaster who had stopped at the post, to take charge of the camp while Karge, Rogers, an Indian guide, and 10 men rode out to rescue Hunter. A short way from camp, Karge met Lafferty, who was riding in, having been unable to pick up Hunter's trail. Karge told Lafferty to return to the post, while he continued on. Karge reached the mouth of Deep Canyon at sundown, and with Rogers showing him the way, continued on to the cave.

Howluck was already gone—bullets from Private Reed having convinced him that it would be folly to assault the cave entrance. Despite his wounds, Hunter was able to mount a horse, and Karge sent him and five men to a ranch in the valley. Karge tried to make the wounded as comfortable as possible. Before leaving the post he ordered Assistant Surgeon Hays to get his instruments and an ambulance and follow him up the canyon. Hays got lost and Karge spent the night in the cave with the wounded, covering them with the horses' saddle blankets to keep them from freezing; in his haste, Karge brought no overcoats, blankets, or canteens. Some of his men found water in a small creek about a half mile away, and carried it to the wounded men in their boots. They used their own shirts and drawers for bandages and compresses.

The next morning, while waiting for the ambulance, Karge examined the two-mile path of Hunter's retreat. He found the initial ambush site and three dead horses, but the others had been captured and taken away. When he returned, Surgeon Hays and some soldiers had arrived with stretchers and were preparing to carry the two wounded men four miles down to the ambulance.

In his report to headquarters, Department of California, Karge commended Private Reed for his "heroic behavior." Hunter survived his wounds, but mustered out of the service in January 1871, as did Karge. Private Reed won the Medal of Honor for his valiant defense. It was the only such medal awarded to any soldier during the Indian wars in Nevada. Lafferty later went with Company A, 8th Cavalry, to Arizona, where, in the Chiricahua Mountains in October 1869, he was seriously wounded when his jaw was shot away by Apaches as he tried to retrieve the bodies of fallen comrades.[5]

OTSEOS LODGE APRIL 29, 1868

On the same day as the Deep Canyon fight, Lieutenant Azor Nickerson had a run-in with Paiutes near Old Camp Warner. Crook had done little since returning from his trek to the Donner und Blitzen in March, other than to hunt and look for vegetables to prevent scurvy. They rested for one month before another scout stirred up some action. On April 27, Lieutenant John Eschenburg, Company D, 23rd Infantry, accompanied by Crook's adjutant, Lieutenant Azor Nickerson, went out with seventeen mounted men, Donald McKay, and one scout. They crossed Warner Lakes at the stone causeway, and went south, when they came across an abandoned lodge that evening, and followed what they hoped was a trail up a creek bed until midnight.

The next morning, McKay was certain the Indians went farther south, up the lake, and they continued in that direction until finding the tracks of one footman and two horses leading on almost an opposite course back to the northeast toward Old Camp Warner. They continued on into the night, when a scout named Louis discovered a campfire in a canyon at the foot of a mountain ahead of them. The rancheria, southeast of Warner (Hart) Mountain, was said to belong to Otseos (spelled "Oitz-oi-ou" by Lieutenant Parnell).

Just who was running the operation is uncertain. Lieutenant Parnell said Eschenburg was in command of the detachment and was "thoroughly conversant with Indian warfare." Lieutenant Nickerson, who was Crook's adjutant, later wrote up the report stating he was in charge.

Accompanying them was Captain Henry B. Clay, who should have been in charge, but was currently under arrest, yet for some reason was allowed to tag along. Parnell said that Eschenburg planned to approach the camp in the darkness, surround it, and attack the next morning. Nickerson, however, by virtue of his seniority of five months, pulled rank and took command. Lieutenant Parnell described the takeover thus: Nickerson, because he was "acting assistant adjutant-general of the district, arrogated to himself the honor of making the attack and the disposition of the troops for this purpose."

Nickerson later wrote, "Leaving the animals in charge of a guard, I proceeded with the remainder of the detachment consisting of Lieut.

Eschenburg and fourteen men," plus Captain Clay and a clerk named Mr. Day, to the edge of the canyon. As the moon set, they followed the shadow of the canyon side "to within about one thousand yards of them where we laid till day light." The troops got so close to the Indians in the thick sage and ryegrass that they could hear the warriors "gambling and enjoying the discomfort of the losers," according to what Parnell later learned. The fire finally died out about two in the morning.

Nickerson, in a plan he indicated was by mutual agreement, divided up into three squads: Eschenburg took the left, Nickerson took the center, and Sergeant McGuire took the right. Eschenburg's instructions were to go to the foot of the mountain, turn right, and advance slowly toward the lodges until he saw Nickerson's squad or heard firing. McGuire was to go across the creek and work his way behind the camp, and advance cautiously until he heard firing. Nickerson said, "I endeavored to impress all with the necessity for silence, but my squad and that of Sergeant McGuire made quite a splashing in fording the creek," which he believed caused the Indians "to take alarm."

When Nickerson called for the charge at daybreak, the Indians were gone. He reached the empty camp, but McGuire and Eschenburg, not having heard any firing, did not move forward. The Indians backed out of the opening, but not before brushing up with McGuire, who succeeded in capturing three horses. Nickerson had to send for Eschenburg, and when he came in, Nickerson sent his squad up into the rocks to find the missing Indians. After all the confusion, the warriors were ready for the soldiers, and blasted them with several volleys as they climbed up the slope. Five soldiers were wounded, one fatally and one severely. Nickerson could not tell where the fire from the concealed Indians came from; Eschenburg thought it was from some caves halfway up the slope and McGuire thought it was from the plateau on top.

Nickerson didn't believe he could dislodge the Indians with the number of unwounded men he had left, and Captain Clay and Mr. Day volunteered to carry a message to Lieutenant Parnell, who Nickerson figured was only about 15 miles away across the causeway. McKay rode to Camp Warner with instructions to get Dr. Dickson and bring him up—Nickerson believing one of the wounded men, with a bullet-shattered knee, would need his leg amputated. Nickerson then took the wounded out of gunfire range and directed Eschenburg to take his squad to gain the plateau in the rear. When Eschenburg got up, he "disclosed the fact that they had gained the top, scattered and gone."

Nickerson sent another messenger to intercept Parnell and tell him that he need no longer assist them. Nickerson destroyed the lodges and about 1,500 pounds of dried fish, more than 400 pounds of "dried spawn, some mule meat, roots, etc." Nickerson estimated that there were twelve to eighteen warriors in the camp, with several families, and well stocked with rifles, bullet molds, and percussion caps.

"It was evident," wrote Nickerson, "that they were what might be called rather high-toned, aristocratic scoundrels of the first water." The number of Indian losses varied with the reports, depending on which side one wanted to believe. Parnell and Crook weren't there. Parnell heard from Eschenburg that there were no Indian losses; Crook heard from Nickerson that there were considerable losses. Crook, no doubt supporting the man who idolized him, later wrote that Nickerson attacked, "inflicting severe loss; the number could not be determined." With small consolation, they destroyed the camp and returned to Camp Warner on the last day of April. Concluding his report on May 1, Nickerson wrote that he regretted to add "that Private Fonda, Company D, 23rd Infantry, died while undergoing the amputation of his leg."[6]

National Archives
Lieutenant William Parnell
in later years.

The next day, Indians raided Camp Warner, shot two mules with arrows, and ran off eight more. Lieutenant Parnell took twenty-six men of his Company H, and went in pursuit. He proceeded to the north end of Warner Lake near Ish's Ranch, found tracks, but lost them in the rocks. He then went west to Lake Abert and south, picking up tracks in Goose Lake Valley. When the trail headed toward Pit River, Parnell gave up, "as it would take several days to overtake them, and not having rations for a sufficient length of time, I returned to camp. . . ."

Why couldn't Parnell simply have taken more rations? It seemed as if every effort by the army was for naught, and that nearly every scout set itself up for failure by not carrying enough supplies. Then again, perhaps the soldiers had long since taken the civilian attitude that, "I haven't lost any Indians."[7]

Crook, in his autobiography, did not mention this less than stellar performance by his lieutenant friend, and Nickerson never mentioned it in his own manuscript. Crook's thoughts, after his own mediocre showing on Donner und Blitzen River in March, were more concerned with resting and hunting.

"In the spring," Crook wrote, "we were in the habit of going to the lake for a day or so to hunt." He and Nickerson enjoyed camping near the lakeshore, shooting wildfowl, and telling stories around the fire at night, accompanied by only a teamster and orderly. One night, as had happened so often to "Commissary" Crook, Indians stole a pony right from under his nose. His reaction was simply to be amazed at how the Indian(s) could have distinguished the pony in the dark, amid a number of mules.

On April 1, George Crook was temporarily assigned to command the Department of Columbia, to replace General Rousseau, who was called east. Before he got the word and prepared to leave Camp Warner, the month was nearly over. Crook headed southwest to Camp Bidwell, Fort Crook, and to San Francisco, and then took a steamer up to Portland, "to assume command of the department, and acquaint myself with my new duties." The papers lamented Crook's moving up to headquarters, because it would remove him from immediate field command. They called him "a thorough soldier, a splendid Indian fighter, and a gentleman in every sense of the word."[8]

HOAG'S BLUFF, MAY 7, 1868

After Nickerson's excursion, the troops at Camp Warner went into a holding pattern while Crook went to Portland. South of the line, in the Department of California, the soldiers at Camp Bidwell kept scouting. On April 28, Captain Samuel Munson, who fought in the 5th Maine Infantry early in the Civil War before joining the 9th U. S. Infantry, led a scout north toward Old Camp Warner. The command consisted of 19 men of Company G, 8th Cavalry, and 31 men of Company C, 9th Infantry, under Lieutenant Hayden De Lany, a post surgeon, and guide Daniel Hoag.

On May 1, they discovered about 40 Indians on the side of a mountain about 35 miles northeast of Camp Bidwell, at the edge of Warner Valley, southeast of today's Crump Lake. The Indians may very well have been the same band stirred up by Nickerson and Eschenburg in the same area just a few days earlier. Munson gave the order to attack, but the Indians put up a stiff resistance, and were only slowly pushed back up the long slope about three miles to the bluff top. Munson said that the Indians appeared new to the country, as they all seemed to have fresh, shod horses, many wore civilian's clothes, and many had rifles. It took four hours to push the Indians to the mountaintop. Once there, the Indians fought bravely behind well-fortified positions. De Lany, an Ohioan who fought in the 30th Ohio Infantry during the Civil War and attended two years at West Point before joining the 9th Infantry in September 1867, was shot through the arm. Private Charles Amstedt, 8th Cavalry, was wounded, and Dan Hoag was killed.

"On arriving at the summit," said Munson, "they attempted to hold it, but we pressed forward, and they scattered and fled in different directions." Munson reported killing several Indians, but the number could not be confirmed since it was nearly dark when they took the peak. De Lany was brevetted first lieutenant for gallantry. The mountain where the fight occurred took the name Hoag's Bluff, after the unfortunate guide, but the name has not survived on modern maps.[9]

While Otseos was fighting on the southern Oregon border, Egan and Oytes were still running wild from the Malheur to the Powder River. Citizens in Baker and Union Counties were up in arms. On May 3, Indians stole four horses from some miners near Auburn. They gave chase, but only found one horse, stabbed to death. The next day Indians attacked A. Bailey, while camped on Powder River not far from Baker City, and ran off twelve of his horses. That night, six horses and twelve cattle were taken from a nearby ranch. On May 6, Indians hit the long-suffering Fred Brougham for the fifth time, stealing five head of work cattle at Ten Mile Creek, just north of Camp McDermit. In early May, Indians of Howluck's band attacked packers in Ives Canyon near Butte Creek Station. One of the packers was wounded, but they reported killing one warrior and wounding several more.

While the raiding and fighting continued in the Northwest, a peace commission was in the process of treaty-making with the Plains Indians—tribes that were always in the national spotlight more than the isolated bands of the Great Basin. In 1867, Congress authorized the president to appoint a peace commission. Of the appointees—Generals William T. Sherman, William S. Harney, Alfred H. Terry, and Christopher C. Auger, Senator John B. Henderson, Commissioner Nathaniel G. Taylor, Samuel F. Tappan, and John B. Sanborn—some served with relish and some with reluctance.

One of the reluctant members, Sherman managed to miss some of the tedious proceedings, as did a few others on occasion, yet the commission did conclude a treaty with the Comanche, Kiowa, Cheyenne, and Arapaho at Medicine Lodge, Kansas, in October 1867. In March 1868, Taylor and Governor A. C. Hunt of Colorado, made an agreement with the Utes. Most of the commission was back together in the spring of 1868, and on April 29, while soldiers battled Howluck and Otseos's Paiutes in the Great Basin, they concluded a substantial treaty with several bands of Sioux and Arapaho at Fort Laramie. The Crow signed an agreement on May 7, and the Cheyenne and Northern Arapaho made their marks three days later. The peace-making and hand-shaking continued in June, when the Navajo signed a treaty, and in July, when the Eastern Shoshoni and Bannock signed an agreement at Fort Bridger.

The commissioners no doubt saw the process as successful, and a beginning of the end of the Indian wars that had plagued the West for years. In the Northwest there was mixed reaction to the brief mood of optimism.

"OUR INDIAN WAR STOPPED" read a caption in the May 19, Sacramento *Union*. The article reflected the changing editorial opinion in communities that were removed in time and space from the ongoing fighting. It censured "thieving Indian Agents, camp followers and Government leeches," for causing the trouble, abused frontiersmen, justified Indian actions, and berated whites for killing them.

General Sherman, who realized that the Indian "problem" could only be solved by harsh measures, yet knew that whites were a significant part of the problem, was lambasted or praised, depending on the politics of the complainant. The *Union* stated, "General Sherman has shown a high-souled sympathy for the Indian and a keen appreciation of his sad condition." The *Avalanche*, closer to the action, thought it would be better for any sympathizer "of Lo to take a trip in the interior and have a fellow-passenger killed, himself shot full of arrows and scalped, and the bloody work commenced while having a friendly (?) shake of the hand."[10]

The *Idaho World* blamed Congress for the continued Indian troubles, not the frontier settlers. Again, it was the Eastern representatives and senators "who have never seen anything of the Indian," and only know about him "through publications of the Coopers novels' order, or of the 'noble red son of the forest' style." In truth, the *World* said, whenever Indians kill a settler, traveler, or miner, no amount of eyewitness testimony will convince "these friends of the Indians" that they did not have reasonable and just cause for the butchery. If the army catches and chastises the perpetrators, likely as not, the commanding officer will be censured. As a case in point, the *World* cited Missouri Senator Henderson in the *Congressional Globe*, one of the commissioners "who went out to buy a peace with the savages on the Plains." Henderson said, "Somehow or other there is a war being carried on in Idaho now. Somebody has got it up; I do not know who it is, but my impression is that it is Gen. Crook. I think the Indians would be peaceable but for the conduct of General Crook."

The *World* was justifiably outraged by Henderson's uninformed accusation. Crook, for all his hard campaigning and "soldierly conduct," was censured in the U. S. Senate with the insinuation "that he is to blame for having *provoked* the Indians to hostile action!" With such ignorance in Congress, basing what they thought they knew about Indians on "Eastern trashy publications," and refusing to listen to the truth of the reports coming from the Western states and territories, the *World* concluded they had but "small hope for adequate protection" from hostile Indians.[11]

The American press created and disseminated much of what white Americans thought they knew about Indians, much as the print and film media do in the twenty-first century. The press was then a major force in defining American society and culture, and played a large part in creating our nation's myths. Indians were barbaric, heroic, romantic, noble, or ignoble, depending on the year and point of view, and were embraced or despised as the country's needs changed. The Indians received much "bad press" in the nineteenth century, but they also received "good press," and much of the division was geographical between West and East.[12]

Almost as if to prove the *Idaho World*'s contention, Indians hit the area with another spate of depredations. On May 21, Nicholas Arb, from San Francisco, was killed by Indians near Bear Creek on the Canyon City to Boise Road. On Saturday, May 23, Indians stole nine horses from a corral in Amelia City, Oregon. The next morning, five men went in pursuit. Near the head of the Malheur, the Indians set up an ambush. In the ensuing fight, Jonas Belknap, the Amelia City butcher, was killed, and his four companions retreated to a defensive position. Belknap was 22 years old and had moved to Amelia City from the Willamette Valley the previous fall. The Indians cut his body into pieces and stuck them "full of pointed rods with slices of fat bacon on the ends." Robert Young, the stable-keeper, was mortally wounded with bullets in the abdomen and thigh, but his companions carried him back to Clarksville near Burnt River. The distraught old Mr. Belknap, Jonas's father, got four men to go out and recover his son's body.

In the meantime, on May 29, ten more men went out to hunt the Indians, said to be a band of fourteen and armed with repeating rifles. The next day they camped on the Harney Road, probably on South Willow Creek about 10 miles east of where Belknap was killed. While eating supper, Indians fired into them, killing Alex Sutherland with a bullet through his head. The rest beat a hasty retreat to Creighton's Camp about six miles farther east. Eventually there were four parties of men searching for the Indians and Belknap's body. Most of them joined up and discovered Sutherland's remains, which were scalped, mutilated, and staked to the ground with a pick that was brought to dig a grave for Belknap. The Indian hunters moved to the Little Malheur and downstream, and, unknowingly, would play a part in the upcoming Battle at Castle Rock on May 31.[13]

Indians also raided the Jordan Creek settlements. About two in the afternoon on May 23, Hosea Eastman, Ben Abbott, David Smith, and David Wooden were riding in a wagon between Sheep Ranch and Inskip's Station. Eastman and Abbott were long-time Owyhee miners who were returning after a winter sojourn in California. In a small pass four and one-half miles west of Inskip's, at a place now called Holdup Rock or Dixon's Rock, one of the men commented that the place was a good spot for an ambush. At that moment, Indians, estimated at between five and eight, rose up and fired from only yards away. Smith was severely wounded by a bullet that went through his chest and out his side. Wooden was creased in the neck. Abbott, sitting at the rear of the wagon, was so startled at the initial shots that he hopped down, when a bullet tore through his coat sleeve. He went for a horse that was tied up and walking behind the wagon, but it broke loose and the Indians got it. Eastman, the driver, whipped the team into a run at the first fire, leaving Abbott behind.

When Eastman looked back he saw Abbott running for his life with two warriors chasing him. He pulled to a halt, grabbed his Spencer, and ran back to help his partner. He got off several shots at the Indians, but they ducked down behind sagebrush and he lost sight of them, however, the way one of them fell, Eastman was sure he hit him. They got back to the wagon to find one of the horses in the team also wounded. Nevertheless, Eastman got all aboard and continued to ride hard for Inskip's, hoping to warn them there before the next stage was due in.

The small garrison of soldiers immediately headed west, but they were too late. The stage, less than an hour behind, came through the same small pass and the Indians again attacked. The driver, Nathan Dixon, was killed instantly, and as he slumped over, a young man named J. W. Patton, who was sitting next to Dixon, grabbed the reins. He lashed the horses forward, but had only gone a short way before a wheel struck a rock, splitting the axle and sending Patton in a somersault to the ground.

The stage was crowded with ten passengers, who came scrambling out of the disabled vehicle. Several of them were well armed, including Samuel Black and Charles S. Peck, who began firing rapidly at the pursuing warriors. The Indians, apparently surprised by the large number of men issuing from the stage, pulled to a halt and fell back. The eleven survivors walked to a rocky eminence and made a defensive position, where Patton departed and ran for Inskip's to get the soldiers. He met them already on their way. They brought a wagon to load up the passengers and took them to the station.

The next day the soldiers went back to get Dixon's body for burial in Silver City, where he was known by many as a courteous and generous man. Dixon was a native of Indiana, about 35 years old. He had gone to California in 1853, before moving to Boise Basin in 1864. Since 1866, Dixon worked as a driver for Hill Beachey's stage line. At his funeral, people said that fate had decreed his death: first, he was not driving his regular route, having agreed to change off at the request of another driver; second, he said there was no use for the guard dog that usually ran alongside the stages between Sheep Ranch and Inskip's, because of the large number of passengers aboard; third, Dixon, told the soldiers who rode escort to the stages to stay at Sheep Ranch and rest. Dixon thought there would be no danger that fatal day. After the preacher finished the service, muttered curses and oaths of vengeance were heard. "Thus another mound," the *Avalanche* reported, "a monument commemorative of savage atrocity was added to the many scattered here and there among the mountains."[14]

Chapter 25 notes

1 Bancroft, *History of Oregon*, Vol. 2, 548-49; *Idaho World*, April 1, 1868, April 8, 1868; *Owyhee Avalanche*, March 28, 1868; Webb, *List of Engagements*, 36.

2 *Owyhee Avalanche*, April 11, 1868, April 25, 1868; *Idaho World*, April 18, 1868, May 6, 1868; *Secretary of War 1868-69*, 70-71; Heitman, *Historical Register*, Vol. 1, 590; Webb, *List of Engagements*, 36.

3 Webb, *List of Engagements*, 36; *Adjutant General's Report*, 32; *Owyhee Avalanche*, April 25, 1868. This fight is usually listed as Camp Three Forks or Owyhee River, but the actual fight appears to have taken place in Indian Canyon.

4 *Adjutant General's Report*, 32; *Idaho World*, May 2, 1868; *Owyhee Avalanche*, May 2, 1868.

5 Rathbun, *Nevada Military Names*, 128-30; Mark W. Haviland Depredation Claim # 4646; Angel, *History of Nevada*, 176; Heitman, *Historical Register*, Vol. 1, 558, 585, 611; Karge, "Indian Affairs," *Army Navy Journal*, in Cozzens, *Eyewitnesses*, 87-90; *Adjutant General's Office*, 33; *Secretary of War 1868-69*; 773. Private Reed's (sometimes spelled Reid) citation is as follows: "James C. Reed. Rank and organization: Private, Company A, 8th U.S. Cavalry. Place and date: Arizona, 29 April 1868. Entered service at:------. Birth: Ireland. Date of issue: 24 July 1869. Citation: Defended his position (with 3 others) against a party of 17 hostile Indians under heavy fire at close quarters, the entire party except himself being severely wounded." The Medal of Honor Citation is incorrect in that it lists Arizona as the site instead of Nevada.

6 Nickerson to Perry, May 1, 1868, RG 393, Dept. of Columbia, Letters Received, Box 5; *Secretary of War 1868-69*, 71; Parnell, "Operations with Crook," 633; Henton to AAG, May 2, 1868, RG 393, Dept. of Columbia, Letters Received, Box 5; Webb, *List of Engagements*, 37; *Adjutant General's Office*, 33. The latter two sources list no Indian casualties and only two soldiers wounded.

7 Parnell to Dodge, May 9, 1868, RG 393, Dept. of Columbia, Letters Received, Box 5.

8 Schmitt, ed., *Crook Autobiography*, 157-58; *Idaho World*, May 27, 1868.

9 Munson letter, in Cozzens, *Eyewitnesses*, 90-91; Brackett, "Fighting in the Sierras," in Cozzens, *Eyewitnesses*, 7-8; Heitman, *Historical Register*, Vol. 1, 365, 736; *Adjutant General's Office*, 33.

10 Frederick P. Brougham Depredation Claim #7988; *Idaho World*, May 13, 1868; *Owyhee Avalanche*, May 30, 1868; Kappler, *Treaties*, 977-1024; Athearn, *Sherman*, 172. It did take such an incident to make Sherman finally realize that the settlers were not exaggerating Indian danger, when in Texas, in May 1871, he was nearly killed by a party of Kiowas lying in ambush.

11 *Idaho World*, May 30, 1868.

12 Coward, *Newspaper Indian*, 5-10. The reading public of the nineteenth century was probably better served by being offered two points of view of "good" or "bad" Indians, than the twenty-first century public is shown through a monocular lens where all Indians get "good press."

13 *Idaho World*, June 10, 1868, June 13, 1868; *Owyhee Avalanche*, June 20, 1868; Bancroft, *History of Oregon*, Vol. 2, 549.

14 *Idaho World*, June 3, 1868; *Owyhee Avalanche*, May 30, 1868, June 6, 1868.

Chapter 26
"I DID NOT COME HERE TO SHAKE HANDS WITH HIM"

CEDAR MOUNTAIN, MAY 29, 1868

On Monday, May 25, while Nathan Dixon was being buried at Silver City, Camp Lyon was responding to the murder. Early the next morning, Sergeant Henry Miller, seven enlisted men of Company M, 1st Cavalry, scout Jim Beebe, six Boise Indians, and civilian B. G. Hooker, rode south to pick up the trail of the Indians who had killed Dixon. The tracks led northwest, across the Owyhee in the neighborhood of Rinehart's Springs and toward Cedar Mountain, about 30 miles below the Owyhee Ferry and the same distance west of Camp Lyon. In the evening of May 28, the scouts found fresh tracks. Miller halted and they went on to discover five wickiups about five miles distant. Miller let his command eat supper, and when dark, moved them cautiously to the Indian camp.

In the first gray of dawn, everyone was up and prepared, and when it became barely light enough to distinguish objects, Miller charged. As was so often the case in a dawn attack, the Indians were caught asleep, completely surprised, and fled without putting up much resistance. Only a few might have escaped. The soldiers and scouts tore through the wickiups, blasted those who emerged, and chased down anyone who tried to run. Not one of Miller and Beebe's men were injured, but the Indian camp was devastated. Thirty-four bodies were counted—seven warriors, which matched up with the estimate of Indians who attacked Eastman and Dixon six days earlier, and twenty-seven women and children.

If these were the same warriors who attacked the men near Inskip's Station, they had brought a terrible vengeance upon their families. As Beebe explained it to the newspaper, "No captives were taken, and every living thing was killed." One of the women ran a short way, turned, held out her infant, and inexplicably said, "Camp McDermit." A few soldiers presumed she must have meant she was one of the "surrendered" Indians who had been fed all winter at McDermit, but if she had hoped to save their lives, she was mistaken.

It was not said whether the Boise scouts did all the killing of the women and children, but as there was barely light enough to distinguish targets, the 1st Cavalrymen certainly had a hand in it. One thing was certain: Sergeant Miller apparently didn't see reason to halt the firing. Both sides were inured to the killing. The soldiers found only one good rifle and a five-shooter, but plenty of bows and arrows, furs, and camp equipment. The band had no horses, mules, or cattle; what they did have was a fine, long, dark brown human scalp, and immediately word passed that it was the hair of Mrs. Denoille. Miller and Beebe returned to Camp Lyon with their own scalp collection. Beebe brought in a number of them to Silver City, where the *Avalanche* reported that they "can be seen posted up in several places round town. Three cheers for Jim Beebe! He is the kind of Indian missionary adapted to this country."[1]

CASTLE ROCK, MAY 31, 1868

What would turn out to be one of the most decisive fights in the Snake War began as just another scout—one of hundreds of similar expeditions occurring over the past four years. On May 24, Lieutenant Alexander H. Stanton, Company F, 1st Cavalry, left Camp Harney with thirty-seven men of Company F, and twenty-four of Archie McIntosh's Boise Indian scouts.

Lieutenant Stanton, from Ohio, was a captain in the 16th U. S. Infantry during the Civil War, until being cashiered for some indiscretion in December 1864. He became a captain of the 8th U. S. Veteran Volunteers in July 1865, before mustering out in April 1866. The next month he joined the 1st Cavalry. He was cited for gallantry at the Malheur River fight on April 5, 1868. Little did he realize that the upcoming action would be the proverbial first domino to fall in a series of events that would end the Snake War.

Stanton's command crossed the Stinking Water Mountains to the South Fork Malheur and hunted along its tributaries. While working their way north up the North Fork Malheur, the scouts found a ten-lodge Paiute camp near Horse Cock Mountain (Castle Rock) in present-day northwest Malheur County about 18 miles north of Juntura, Oregon. The Paiutes, mainly from Egan's (Pony Blanket) band, had been the ones involved in the killing of Belknap, Young, and Sutherland just a few days earlier. They repulsed two posses of white men hunting for them, but now the whites had joined together and were approaching their hideout from the north, coming down the Little Malheur River. With Egan's attention focused on the white civilians, Stanton was closing in on him up the North Fork Malheur from the south. The two forces unknowingly approached from canyons on opposite sides toward a junction with a third canyon where the Indians waited.

Stanton attacked the ten-lodge camp, drove the surprised Paiutes off, and captured twelve horses. Six Paiute warriors returned and fought a brief skirmish, wounding one soldier. In a quick counter-attack, Stanton swept in and captured five of them. The minor action had major results. With the civilian posse on one side, and the soldiers and Boise scouts on the other, the Paiutes realized that the game was over. Many Indians began throwing up their hands in surrender. Egan signaled for a parley. After years of fighting, he and his people were exhausted, starving, and realized that they could not win.

Stanton, with some Boise scouts interpreting, was not sure what to make of the situation. Was it a ruse to buy time for the Indians to escape? Apparently there was no deception. Within a day, Egan had brought in sixty-one of his people. The next day, Lieutenant William McCleave and Lieutenant James M. Ropes of the 8th Cavalry, rode in from Camp Harney with eighteen men of Company F, 1st Cavalry, and fifty-seven men of Company C, 8th Cavalry. Egan approached McCleave, who was now in command, and asked for a council. McCleave confronted him point blank: did he want peace or war? Egan asked to have one more day, until June 3, to talk it over with his warriors. McCleave gave him the time, and Egan did return with his answer. He would advise all of his people to surrender. He said that many other Paiutes were willing to stop fighting, and said he could bring in other chiefs to talk peace.

Messengers quickly went out to find Lt. Colonel Crook, who had been to Portland and had just returned to Camp Warner via The Dalles and Camp Watson. When notified of the surrender, Crook contacted General Halleck for instructions because of a standing order that stated no officers in Halleck's division could make a treaty without consulting him first. Crook sent an inquiry to San Francisco, and headed north to Camp Harney, where the Indians were gathering.[2]

While Paiutes were congregating at Camp Harney and word of the surrender was spreading among the other bands, scout Sinora Hicks had been out with his Boise Indians in the mountains. The result of his scout was to finally solve the mystery of Mrs. Denoille's fate. Jim Beebe's discovery of the long, brown scalp had renewed interest in the story.

Hicks had taken with him one of the Paiute warriors captured earlier in the year, who claimed that the white woman was dead and he knew where the remains were. The Paiute informant may not have realized what he was getting himself into. As the party approached the site of the Denoille attack near Succor Creek, the guide indicated, rather proudly, that he was the one who had killed Mrs. Denoille. He may not have thought the action was of much consequence, and since he had surrendered and was helping the soldiers now, that all was forgiven, or, perhaps he was only making the tale up.

In any event, he played a dangerous game. The man showed Hicks where the Denoilles were attacked, where they had captured her, and where they took her. It was only half a mile from the attack site. "After stripping," the report read, "they dragged her by the neck some distance, and then laid her head upon one stone while they took another and beat it to a jelly." Wolves had scattered the remains to such an extent that Hicks was unable to gather up more than a handful. As the man told his tale, Hicks, no doubt, grew angrier by the minute, especially since the Paiute "appeared to glory in killing her."

One might speculate if the Paiute wondered what had gone wrong when Hicks and the scouts riddled his body with bullets. Hicks, who returned to Boise on June 8, reported that the guide "endeavored to escape." The Denoille incident faded from memory.[3]

Although initial surrenders had been made, there were plenty of Indians still fighting. Down in Nevada, a small band of Paiutes raided into Paradise Valley, makng an appearance there for the first time since Howluck's April raid. On June 10, Aaron Denio was "plowing with oxen for late barley." That evening he turned six oxen out for pasture, and in the morning they were gone. Denio followed the moccasin trail into the Santa Rosa Mountains. At the edge of the rocks where he lost the trail, he found two carcasses butchered for meat. He estimated his loss at $600.

SNAKE CANYON, JUNE 9, 1868

Operating out of Fort Boise, Corporal J. Moan, with a detachment of Company H, 23rd Infantry, and some Indian scouts, ran into a small band of Paiutes in the Snake River Canyon. They attacked on June 9, in exceedingly rough terrain, killed three Paiutes, and drove the rest off. While some of Captain Sinclair's men were out hunting Indians, he was having a tough enough time confining his own prisoners at Fort Boise. On June 13, thirty Paiutes escaped from custody on "a very dark and stormy" night. The next morning Sinclair took a detachment of 23rd Infantrymen and Captain Bassford took a detachment of 8th Cavalrymen, and went chasing the escapees. Eleven of them were recaptured on June 15, and seven more within the next three days. All were returned safely to the fort. "Under ground, *safe*, would be a fitter place for them," the *Idaho World* figured.[4]

BATTLE CREEK, JUNE 24, 1868

In June 1868, Captain John Coppinger took forty-five men of Company A, 23rd Infantry, and five Indian scouts, out from Camp Three Forks as escort for an exploring party seeking a shorter route from a proposed railroad depot on the Central Pacific route in Nevada to the northwest coast. The explorers had hard traveling through the rough upper Owyhee country of southwest Idaho, a trip not made any easier by Indians threatening the party. In an area said to be "east of the Red Mountain" and near Battle Creek, in remote terrain northwest of present-day Riddle, Idaho, Coppinger ran into a band of Indians. In a short fight he killed three, captured three women and a boy, while two escaped. Coppinger's Indian-hunting and escort duties kept him in the field for one full month.[5]

During June 1868, both the army and the Indians were uncertain whether to continue to fight, or pursue peace. Some bands heard word of the initial surrenders and decided to give up, while others continued to resist; it was difficult for the army to divine the Indians' intentions. Indians approached Camp Harney in handfuls and scores. Weahwewa arrived, stating that he wished to stop the fighting.

At Camp Warner, about thirty Indians came in to surrender. On June 26, Crook, Lieutenants Nickerson, Parnell, and a small escort, left Camp Warner for Camp Harney. Parnell was certain why the Indians were giving up. "The constant harassing, winter and summer, day and night, by the regular troops. . . had so demoralized the Indians, by destroying their provisions and lodges, capturing their women and children, and killing many of their chiefs and braves, that nothing was left them but to surrender and beg for clemency." They arrived at Harney on June 29, riding up the canyon near the post, passing wickiups that lined Rattlesnake Creek for more than one mile.

The next day a grand council was held, with Crook representing the U.S. and Weahwewa, Egan, Pasego, and Bighead, speaking for the Paiutes. In a move that may not have been very safe, but was likely calculated to present the Indians with a show of bravery and unconcern, Crook had his wife and Julia Gilliss stand near him at the point of contact. Julia said that the Indians "were very imposing in their panoply of war," with several of them "perfectly frightful," painted red and black and looking "as hideous as one can imagine." They came in by twos and threes until the camp was full. "The troops were all on a keen watch" Julia said, "with small arms concealed on their persons, but pretended to be carelessly strolling around unarmed." Julia and Mary Crook stood close behind the lieutenant colonel, trying to be "as unsuspicious as if we were receiving at a ball. In reality everyone was alert, and the officers behind us were keenly watchful. *Nobody* trusts a live Indian."

One might wonder about the cleverness of Crook's bluff, placing the soldiers *behind* the women. "They massed in front of us," said Julia, "on their ponies, with their guns slung across, they certainly were an ugly looking party. The General with his quiet dignity told them he would have nothing to say to them until they all dismounted, and laid down their arms."

One "turbulent spirit" broke forward, scowled, shook his head and gestured while whirling around on his pony. The situation, said Julia, "looked for a moment pretty serious." While a few rabble-rousers tried to stir up the crowd, a few others just as forcefully tried to defuse the situation. Soon, said Julia, one warrior rode among "the hundred screaming, gesticulating imps and with some strong influence brought them down to a sullen, muttering crowd."

Crook, hardly turning his head, said in a low voice to the women, "do not look frightened, be as calm and indifferent as you possibly can, and stand still right where you are." To Julia, "It *seemed* as if we stood there for hours, while those ugly braves refused to retreat unless they could retain guns and ponies." But Crook stood there "immovable as stone," and finally one after another Indian dismounted and laid his gun at Crook's feet. One furious warrior wheeled about and rode off on his pony as fast as he could, but no soldier touched his weapon. Julia did not believe that "any man living but General Crook could have brought those Indians to even the semblance of yielding. . . ." Crook was successful, but he may have owed much of his triumph to the bravery of two women standing beside him.[6]

When the Indians had calmed down and deposited their weapons, they all sat in a large semi-circle on the parade ground. Crook and his officers, fully uniformed, approached from one side, while the chiefs entered from the other. Weahwewa was in the lead. Said Nickerson: "The old rascal came up smiling, childlike and bland as the proverbial heathen Chinese, and when he and Crook met, he held out his dirty, bloodstained paw to shake hands with the General." Crook kept his hands behind him, looked him in the eye, and said to the interpreter, "Tell him that I did not come here to shake hands with him. He has been too bad an Indian, has murdered too many people. I came here to hear what he has to say for himself."

When Crook's words were translated, Weahwewa, according to Nickerson, "was very much non-plussed at first, but managed to say that he and his warriors were tired of war, and wanted to make peace."

"I am sorry to hear this," Crook replied. "I was in hopes that you would continue the war, and then, though I were to kill only one of your warriors while you killed a hundred of my men, you would have to wait for those little people (pointing to the children) to grow to fill the place of your braves, while I can get any number of soldiers the next day to fill the place of my hundred men. In this way it would not be very long before we would have you all killed off, and then the government would have no more trouble with you."

Weahwewa, perhaps realizing that it would do little good to dispute Crook's logic, insisted once more that he only wanted peace, and indicated that about half of all their people had been killed. Parnell recorded that several other chiefs made speeches "expressing sorrow at having done so much deviltry," that they looked forward to having the soldiers as their friends, and that they had "buried the rope," meaning that they would not steal any more horses.

One chief, following up on Crook's reasoning, drew on the ground with a stick as he spoke. "Your great white people are like the grass; the more you cut it down the more it grows and the more numerous its blades. We kill your white soldiers, and ten more come for every one that is killed; but when you kill one of our warriors, or one of our people, no more come to replace them." Any soldiers in hearing distance may have had concerns over the Indians' and their own commander's apparent conception of them as no more than cannon fodder, but the allusion was effective.

Crook, apparently having the Indians very concerned that he might not make peace, hammered his advantage home. He told them, according to Parnell, "that the soldiers were there to fight when it was necessary; they did not ask the Indians to make peace; the soldiers would follow them day and night, winter and summer, until the last one of them was killed, as long as they (the Indians) remained hostile and continued to kill people and to rob and steal; but if they were sincere in their pledges, and continued to be good Indians, the soldiers and the government would be their friends."

First Cavalry Lieutenant Washington I. Henderson recalled that Crook told Weahwewa that the Indians must make peace on their own free will, because he (Crook) was not ready to make peace. If they still wanted to fight, Crook said he would kill them all within two years. They could do "just as they pleased—fight till they were all dead or yield now." Weahwewa said again, that he was tired of fighting the "Bostons," that he fought them for four years already, starting with more warriors than he could count, but now he had only a few left and the white men had nearly all of his land. The chiefs appeared sincere, and Crook, said Nickerson, "consented to make peace, though apparently very reluctantly."[7]

Armed with a short dispatch from General Halleck, that read, "You are authorized to make peace with the Steen's mountain Indians; but we can give them no supplies unless they surrender as prisoners of war, to be disposed of hereafter," Crook laid out his terms. Considering that much of his stance was a bluff—he did not have 100 soldiers for every fallen Indian and did not have the means to physically corral all the Indians if they did not want to be corralled—Crook's requisites were lenient, and in hindsight, wise. He never was a believer in the reservation system as it was set up, and did not see any sense in feeding Indians while they could still hunt and gather subsistence on their own.

Crook would not confine them. He agreed that Weahwewa and the others could stay in the vicinity of Castle Rock on the upper Malheur. The soldiers would not enter the area to attack them, but they must cease their raiding, make their living by fishing and hunting, return all stolen property, and live in peace.

Crook appeared more concerned about the white citizens who congregated at Camp Harney, wishing to see harsher terms imposed on their enemies. They had no faith in Indian promises, he said. "Some had lost friends, relatives, and stock at the hands of the Indians, and were necessarily bitter, and had sworn vengeance against all Indians. But when I explained it was to all's interest to have peace so the citizens could develop the country, etc., that I had not [made] peace out of friendship for the Indians, they finally agreed not to throw any obstacles in the way by committing any unlawful acts."

Crook realized one of the best ways to secure a peace would be to make known the terms of the agreement and get as many people as possible to buy into it. On July 1, he wrote a letter to Idaho Governor Ballard, starting off, "I made a treaty yesterday with the concentrated rascality of all the Piute tribe." He told Ballard that he indicated to the Indians that he was not anxious for peace, that they had lied to him in the past and he did not fully trust them now, and that he had more soldiers coming to kill them if they did not behave. Yet, since they said they had lost half their tribes in the war, Crook figured they would make an honest try to remain at peace.

"The only thing I fear now," Crook wrote, "is that white men will commit outrages on the Indians in retaliation. If this thing can be controlled I feel satisfied that the bloody scenes of the last four years are at an end, and we will have a permanent peace with the Indians." Crook believed that Ballard could play a great part in maintaining the peace if he could publish the agreements in all the papers in the territory "and enjoin upon all good citizens the necessity of refraining from retaliation." He said if the Indians are given a chance, "I feel satisfied that our troubles with them are over."[8]

Crook remained optimistic—perhaps overly so. In his report to General Halleck, he said he had "made peace with all the hostile Indians from the Humboldt, on the south, to Fort Hall, on the north, they all acknowledging the one chief, Weahwewa, leaving no hostile Indians within the department or on its borders, except the Pitt River Indians, in California, and probably a few scattering ones between Nevada and the Three Forks of the Owyhee." This was not quite accurate. The agreement more realistically included only the Malheur River, Harney Valley, and Warner Lake bands, but it was a start.

To give the recently surrendered Indians at Camp Harney an investment with their new soldier "friends," as soon as the council was over, Crook asked Weahwewa for some help. He requested that the chief loan him ten men to serve as scouts on an expedition to the Goose Lake country to search for hostile Pit River Indians. "In an instant," said Lieutenant Parnell, "ten fine strapping young bucks stepped out as volunteers, only too anxious to get a chance at another tribe, or even some of their own, for that matter, as long as it was the excitement of war." Parnell could think of nothing more illustrative of "the character and ambition of the Indian. Just from the field of defeat and subjection by their historic foe, the white man, they were ready in a moment to join him in any enterprise of a warlike nature that would give them an opportunity to heal their wounded spirit by wreaking vengeance on a weaker foe. . . ." The ten Paiute scouts were equipped and clothed in "Uncle Sam's uniforms," and the next morning, Crook was off to California.[9]

Chapter 26 notes

1 *Secretary of War 1868-69*, 71; *Owyhee Avalanche*, June 6, 1868; *Idaho World*, June 6, 1868; Webb, *List of Engagements*, 37. Reports usually list the fight as occurring near the Owyhee River. Descriptions seem to place it in the vicinity of today's Cedar Mountain.

2 *Secretary of War 1868-69*, 71; Schmitt, ed., *Crook Autobiography*, 158; Corless, *Weiser Indians*, 48; Webb, *List of Engagements*, 37; Bancroft, *History of Oregon*, Vol. 2, 548-49; Heitman, *Historical Register*, Vol. 1, 916; *Owyhee Avalanche*, June 20, 1868; McCleave to AAG, June 24, 1868, RG 393, Dept. of Columbia, Letters Received, Box 5.

3 Bancroft, *History of Oregon*, Vol. 2, 547; Boise *Democrat*, June 9, 1868, as cited in *Owyhee Avalanche*, June 13, 1868. A twist in the postscript adds more mystery to the Denoille story. Several contemporary newspapers followed the events, all of them stating that a Sergeant Denoille was killed and a Sergeant Nichols escaped. None ever cited the sergeant's first name or unit. Inquiry at the National Archives discovered a Sgt. Arnold Denoille, 45 years old, reenlisted for the fourth time in 1869, and was assigned to the 23rd Infantry. With his uncommon surname and assuming there were no other Denoilles serving in that unit and locale at the time, it appears that Sergeant Denoille was not killed at the time of his wife's capture. Perhaps it was sergeant Nichols who had been killed and Denoille escaped, and perhaps the papers got the names switched, or purposely changed them to make more exciting copy.

4 Aaron Denio Depredation Claim # 9806; Sinclair to AAG, June 15, 1868, RG 393, Dept. of Columbia, Letters received, Box 4; *Idaho World*, June 17, 1868, July 4, 1868; Webb, *List of Engagements*, 37.

5 *Secretary of War 1868-69*, 71; Webb, *List of Engagements*, 38. *Adjutant General's Office*, 33, indicates eight Indians killed.

6 Parnell, "Operations with Crook," 634; Gilliss, *So Far From Home*, 176-77.

7 Schmitt, ed., *Crook Autobiography*, 307-08; Nickerson, "George Crook and the Indians," 11-12; Parnell, "Operations with Crook," 634; *Owyhee Avalanche*, July 11, 1868.

8 *Secretary of War 1868-69*, 71; Schmitt, ed., *Crook Autobiography*, 159; Bancroft, *History of Oregon*, Vol. 2, 530; *Owyhee Avalanche*, July 11, 1868; *Idaho World*, July 25, 1868.

9 *Secretary of War 1868-69*, 72; Bancroft, *History of Oregon*, Vol. 2, 531; Parnell, "Operations with Crook," 634-35.

Chapter 27
THE WAR WINDS DOWN

Although about 300 Indians gave up at Camp Harney and another thirty came in to Camp Warner, it took time to get the word to the scattered bands, and even so, they were not governed by the actions of other chiefs. In mid-July, south of Silver City on Boulder Creek, H. S. Murdoff and a few others were leisurely doing some prospecting and fishing. Murdoff became separated from the rest when three Indians sprang out of the brush. They fired guns at him, but luckily, all snapped and misfired. Murdoff turned, ran, and got back to the others in his party, but not before a warrior struck him "with one arrow in the part of his body nearest the saddle." The wound was painful but not dangerous.

About the same time, Captain John Walker and Lieutenant John W. Lewis, with a detachment of Company C, 23rd Infantry, and Indian scouts, left Camp C. F. Smith and marched over Steens Mountain. Walker had been back East for the past several months, and had recently returned to find the situation changed from when he had left. Even though peace was the word of the day, Walker was looking for Indians—whether to battle or to accept their surrender would be up to them.

On July 17, Walker's scouts met up with some Paiutes, who claimed to be of Winnemucca's Band. They wanted to give up. Although the greater part of Winnemucca's people were still holed up and uncertain of what to do, about seventy Indians turned themselves in to Walker and returned with him to Camp C. F. Smith.

An expedition with a similar purpose left Fort Boise on July 16, heading for the Weiser River in Idaho to find a "band of thieving Snakes." Captain James Sinclair, Company H, 23rd Infantry, nine enlisted men, and Sinora Hicks and seven Boise Shoshonis, headed for the upper Weiser, where settlers reported the Indians to be camped. Moving fast, and with only eight days' rations, Sinclair reached the site, but found the camp vacated. He tracked the Indians into the mountains, and on July 23, overtook them at the junction of the Little Salmon and Salmon River. Sinclair wrote that he "surrounded a band of hostile Snake Indians, capturing Eagle Eye and his band forty-one in all including thirteen bucks, not one escaping." Eagle Eye's people, however, were Weiser Shoshonis who had not participated in any of the depredations and willingly surrendered. They peacefully accompanied Sinclair back to Fort Boise. It was well that they did, because in what was an all too familiar litany, Sinclair reported "that having taken only 8 days' rations along," his detachment had to live on fish and roots for some time.

There was no evidence of plunder among the Weiser Indians, but one thing they found looked suspicious. There was a pair of moccasins about sixteen inches long, stuffed with fur, that "could be used to make a fearful looking track," enough to convince the uninitiated that it was made by an Indian seventeen feet high." Here, perhaps, was another part of what grew into the legend of Bigfoot.

Sinclair looked around for more Indians, and, running out of food, was forced to take some of the Indians' supply before getting everyone back to Boise. There, it was again determined that these Indians were not hostile Snakes. Eagle Eye met with Governor Ballard and army commanders. They talked over whether to send the band to Camp Harney with Weahwewa's people, send them to the agent in charge of the Bruneau Indians, or let them go. Ballard decided to let them return in peace to their old hunting grounds on the Weiser. The rest of the Indian prisoners being held at Fort Boise were sent to Camp Harney.[1]

Lieutenant Moses Harris left Camp Lyon about July 10, with twenty-eight men of his Company M, 1st Cavalry, and Jim Beebe as interpreter. They scouted down the Owyhee to its mouth, then up the Malheur. On July 15, near the forks of the Malheur, they picked up a trail and followed through the mountains for a day before Harris's scouts contacted three Paiutes. As they talked, the rest of the soldiers rode up and frightened the Paiutes away. Harris continued to pursue them, but for some strange reason they now appeared to be heading in a beeline for Rattlesnake Creek in Harney Valley.

"I had now become convinced that the Indians I was in pursuit of, were peacefully disposed and would give themselves up at Camp Harney," Harris said. Because he had "but three days' rations on hand," he concluded to go to Harney to get supplies and see if his hunch was right. He arrived on July 18, and discovered that the Paiutes he had been chasing had arrived at the camp the day before. Re-supplied, Harris rode back to Camp Lyon, arriving there on July 27. It appeared as if all the Indians in the area were coming in to surrender.[2]

JUNIPER CANYON, JULY 26, 1868

Perhaps the last fight of consequence in the Snake War occurred near Camp Three Forks. Captain Coppinger had just returned from a month-long scout and road exploration. He ordered Lieutenant George McMannis Taylor, an Ohioan who fought in the 73rd Ohio Infantry in the Civil War, to lead the next expedition, the purpose of which was to apprehend the Indians who had attacked and wounded Mr. Murdoff on Boulder Creek. On July 24,

Taylor took eighteen men of Company E, 23rd Infantry, on a scout into the Juniper Mountains only about 20 miles south of the post.

The first day out they marched 14 miles and camped on the North Fork Owyhee, and the following day they went to Willow Creek. On July 26, the scouts found a band of about twenty Indians in Juniper Canyon, about 12 miles from Taylor's camp. When they returned with the news, Taylor immediately headed out and attacked before the day was over. The command killed five warriors, captured four, and wounded a number of others. They found "three Kentucky rifles" in the camp, along with a large number of bows, "several quivers filled with poisoned arrows, a large quantity of bullets and powder," furs and other camp items. They also discovered a nearly new U. S. Infantry dress coat. Taylor believed these last "good Indians" were the ones who had committed the depredations in the Flint District of late. On the way back to camp, it was reported that, "two prisoners attempted escape and were killed." It was Taylor's last action in the Owyhee country. After returning to Three Forks, he was sent to Fort Vancouver to take command of Company F, 23rd Infantry.[3]

Although the major fighting appeared to be over, there were still isolated raids. Another in a long line of stock thefts from Con Shea took place on August 1, 1868. This time the rancher lost thirty head of pack and saddle animals that he valued at $2,250. By the time the Snake War drew to a close, Con Shea and his partners, John Catlow and John McMahon, lost an estimated 630 animals worth more than $55,000.

Raiding parties, however, slowly dwindled. Throughout the month of August and into early September, more Indians were captured or gave up in southwest Idaho Territory. Sergeant T. Slater, with interpreter S. E. McCanless out of Camp Three Forks with a detachment of Company A, 23rd Infantry, and several Indian scouts, made the largest capture, rounding up five men, five women, and six children in the Juniper Mountains. At the post, three of the captives were freed with the promise to bring in fourteen more Indians, and Captain Coppinger commended Slater's "intelligence and tact" in convincing them to give up. All of them professed to want to give up and have peace, "at least," said the cynical *Avalanche*, "till they recruit and obtain a fresh supply of arms and ammunition."[4]

On September 6, six more Indians came in to Camp Three Forks, all Bruneau Shoshonis under Soya-Poga. They said that back in the summer of 1866, Winnemucca was in the area with 200 warriors, and he forced them to go along with them to fight the whites. Others were forced to join Winnemucca also, until they escaped and moved south to the Humboldt River area where they had been hiding for two years. Coppinger believed the story, adding, "it is well understood that the Pah-utes at that time threatened to kill the Bruneaus, unless they joined them. . . ." Soya-Poga wished to be able to take his people to the Boise area to live in peace.[5]

One of the largest surrenders was brought about with the help of Sarah Winnemucca and her brother, Natchez. Sarah, who had been to school in California and learned English, was sticking to her conviction that all talk of raids and killings by Indians was one vast white conspiracy concocted by them to make money. Although she intensely disliked "white people," somehow she thought better of the soldiers, even though she blamed Captain Wells and his soldiers for killing her people at Mud Lake in March 1865, and driving her father into the hostile camp. Said Sarah, somewhat inconsistently, "Because white people are bad that is no reason why the soldiers should be bad, too."

In the summer of 1868, Sarah, who had been staying in the Virginia City, Nevada, area, was summoned to Fort Churchill. Since some Indians were surrendering, the army hoped that Sarah could talk to her father, Winnemucca, and convince him to give up. Sarah and her brother, Natchez, who sometimes raided with the Paiutes in the north, talked it over with their people on the Pyramid Lake Reservation. Some thought they should try to get the old man in, while others thought it was a ruse. They said to Natchez, "You and your sister know what liars the white people are, and if you go and get him and he is killed by the soldiers, his blood will be on you."

Despite their misgivings, Sarah and Natchez started for Camp McDermit on July 1, with a detachment of Company M, 1st Cavalry. The leisurely journey took about three weeks. At McDermit, they met Captain Dudley Seward, who had fought as a major in the 2nd Ohio Cavalry for most of the Civil War, and in July 1866, enlisted in the 8th Cavalry. Seward had them come to his office and extended to them all possible courtesies.

"He was a very nice man," Sarah said. He asked Natchez if he thought he could bring his father in. "I would like to have him come in, so he can be taken care of," said Seward. "He is too old to be out in this bad country. If Gen. Crook should find him and his people, he might make him some trouble." Sarah said she didn't know why the whites constantly persecuted her father; "My good papa has never done anything unkind to the white people," she claimed. The soldiers killed many of his people at Mud Lake, she said. "This is what drove my poor papa away; we have not seen him for two years."

Sarah's assessment of her "poor papa" was not shared by some Shoshonis. Captain Coppinger, on a long scout out of Camp Three Forks in July, went almost to the Humboldt River and met "Captain John's" and "Captain Jim's" bands of Shoshonis—people whose good character was vouched for by interpreter McCanless. "Captain Jim" said that his people had "good heart" for the white men, and wanted to help them, because "hostile Pah-utes sometimes raided on them; always plundering and sometimes murdering them—that they desired to see Winnemucca's people made prisoners, or forced to make peace; that they would willingly assist to that end. . . ."

A "head man" that Coppinger called Sam, asked to come along and help with negotiations. Coppinger moved his command toward Camp McDermit about the time that Sarah and Natchez arrived there.

At McDermit, Captain Seward asked Sarah to stay and be the post interpreter for $65 per month, and told Natchez he would pay him five dollars a day while he looked for Winnemucca. He asked how many soldiers he needed to escort him. Natchez did not want any, for fear the Indians would think they were coming to fight.

"I will find my father sooner by going alone," he said. After speaking with other Paiutes camped along Quinn River, Sarah and Natchez learned that, under the soldiers' protection they got food and clothing and the work they had to do was "only child's play," and they were "as happy as we can be." With such good reports, Natchez got five other Paiutes to accompany him to help convince the others that they had nothing to fear. When Coppinger

From Owyhee Trails, *Caxton Press*
Sarah Winnemucca

arrived, he said he sent Sam, "at his own request, to go with Natchez, the Truckee chief, to try to find Winnemucca."

Before Natchez rode out on July 20, W. J. Hill, proprietor of the *Avalanche*, who was at McDermit on business, spoke to Sarah Winnemucca. He called her "a well educated girl and is daughter of the famous old chief of that name." She told him Natchez and a few other Paiutes were going to ride for Steens Mountain, about a two-day journey, to her father's hiding place "to try to persuade old Winnemucca to come in."[6]

While Natchez combed Steens Mountain, setting signal fires to alert the Paiutes of his presence, Major Elmer Otis, District of Owyhee commander, was on a tour of inspection and stopped for several days at Camp C. F. Smith. There were about 200 surrendered Indians up at old Camp Alvord, two-thirds of them coming from the Surprise Valley and Humboldt areas.

At C. F. Smith, Otis met with about twenty-five warriors from the band that had surrendered to Captain Walker two weeks earlier. Through the interpreter, Otis talked to their spokesman, "Pahoui," in much the same manner as Crook had done with Weahwewa. They told Otis that they had been fighting for four years, were tired of it, and wanted to make peace. He asked them if there were any less white men around since the war began; they said there were more. He asked them if there were more Indians; they said there were less. Otis replied that this would always be the situation as long as the war continued—more white men and less Indians. He said that if they would stop fighting, stealing, molesting travelers, and stay in their own country, they would be left alone. "Pahoui" agreed, saying that they would live by those rules, but the soldiers must realize that they were not part of Weahwewa's people, although they joined with them on occasion, and they wished to have their own land south of Steens Mountain "where white men did not live." Otis agreed, but said final word still rested with Crook.[7]

Crook agreed in theory, but not in practice. As the surrendered Indians began filtering down to Camp C. F. Smith, they were fed out of the government stores. Crook complained to Halleck: "Some of these Indians, after promising to come into Camp Harney, were met by the troops from Camp C. F. Smith, and induced to go in the vicinity of that post, where there seems to be a disposition to feed them, contrary to repeated instructions from these headquarters."

Crook believed the Indians needed to be concentrated at a few posts, but made to hunt and forage for their own food, unless in a starving condition. He recommended the abandonment of Camps Logan, Lyon, and C. F. Smith, and Brig. General Edward O. C. Ord, commander of the Department of California, ordered the abandonment of Camp McGarry.[8]

When Crook left Camp Harney on July 1, he headed back to Camp Warner, where he figured to make one more expedition into northeastern California to deal with the Indians who had taken part in the April murders of the Pierson Family. In mid-July, several units were sent to rendezvous in Goose Lake Valley. Captain Baker brought Company I, 1st Cavalry, from Camp Watson; Company A came from Fort Klamath; Company H moved out of Camp Warner; and Company C, 9th Infantry, traveled west from Camp Bidwell.

Crook left Camp Warner on July 24, and assumed command. He moved south to the South Fork Pit, near the scene of his fateful fight at Infernal Caverns nearly one year before. The scouts found several trails from what Crook called "marauding expeditions" crossing the area, appearing to come up from the south and head toward the Pit River. Crook went down Pit River to Big Valley, 40 miles northeast of Fort Crook. On August 6, his scouts exchanged shots with warriors from several camps in the vicinity. The Indians fled downriver, but Crook had his scouts press on to make contact and assure them that he only wanted to parley.

A number of the braver Paiutes and Pit River Indians returned—Crook called them a "few of the more friendly ones." They arrived carrying provisions of "young ducks in various stages of putrefaction," said Crook, "and smelt so that I would not allow them to camp on our side of the river." Whether the Indians were friendly or brave, they were certainly impertinent. In trying the same sort of tactics that worked on Weahwewa and other chiefs at Camp Harney, Crook asked if they remembered how he fought them a decade earlier. Yes, the warriors replied, "they remembered how they had pounded" Crook and chased him away. Crook, getting angry, said that if they did not stop lying, "I would give them another opportunity of pounding me right then and there, whereupon they changed their tactics."

Crook then bluffed them, saying that he knew all about them murdering the Pierson Family in Honey Lake Valley in the spring. "Not knowing how much I did know," said Crook, "they confessed the whole thing." The Indians said that nine of their tribe had indeed killed the Piersons and others, but they had run away and could not be brought in at that time.

Crook told Captain Munson, who commanded at Camp Bidwell, to visit the area again in two months and round up the murderers. Crook catechized the Indians, telling them that for too long they had been getting away with depredations that had been blamed on the Paiutes; that they were now exposed; that they must deliver up the murderers to authorities; and that their bad behavior would no longer be tolerated. If there were any more depredations the entire band would be punished, and if any of them came into the upper country at all, they would be killed. With his rules laid out, Crook headed back for Camp Warner on August 10.[9]

Crook turned over the troops to Captain Eugene Baker to continue the sweep in search of hostiles. Baker went south toward Susanville, searched around Eagle Lake and east across the Madeline Plains. There, he detached Captain Munson with his 9th Infantrymen to continue the search as he marched north to Camp Bidwell. Baker determined that there were "no signs of the Indians having been there since early last spring," so he called off the hunt and headed to Camp Warner, reaching it on August 19.

Parnell, who led Company H on the expedition, said, "the roving bands had followed the example of those at Harney and had sought shelter and protection on some of the reservations either at Harney, Klamath, or the Pyramid Lake, Nevada." Parnell painted a sanguine picture of the recent events. "Thus was concluded one of the most determined and successful campaigns ever organized against the bands of hostile Indians that kept Northern California, Oregon, Washington Territory, Idaho, and Nevada in perpetual commotion, retarding the prosperity of the country and a constant menace to life and property."[10]

The "Snakes," of course, would have a different opinion about whose lives, property, and prosperity were menaced.

It was not quite over yet. There were still bands in the mountains and deserts that would make their own tough choices whether to submit or struggle to maintain a free life. One large group that chose to surrender was Winnemucca's. Natchez had found his father and convinced him to come in. In August, 490 more Paiutes arrived at Camp McDermit, where, Sarah Winnemucca said, "they were kindly received" and were given clothing, "good bread, coffee, sugar, salt, pepper, pork, beef, and beans."

The influx of Indians strained the camp's resources, but they made the best of it. More bands came in, with about 400 more Indians congregating at Camp C. F. Smith, where the land was harsher, there was less game, and supplies were strained to the breaking point. At McDermit, Captain James N. McElroy, 8th Cavalry, asked Sarah Winnemucca, employed as post interpreter, if she thought the Indians would come to McDermit. She thought they would. When McElroy asked how many soldiers it would take to bring them in, she said "none;" she and her brother could do it.

Supplied with fifteen wagons, drivers, and extra food and supplies, Sarah and her brother escorted the Paiutes in. Now there were more than 900 Indians at Camp McDermit. Sarah, caught between two physical worlds and a dichotomous frame of mind, still disliked "whites," but liked soldiers (enough to marry two of them). She said her people weren't fond of being cared for by the army, "but they know more about the Indians than any citizens do, and are always friendly." Their time at Camp McDermit was a welcome respite from the previous four years of war. "So we lived quietly for two years," Sarah said.[11]

George Crook left Camp Warner for Portland on August 26. In his report to General Halleck, he wrote: "I am now of the opinion that the Indian war in this country has closed, and that there are no hostile Indians in the country extending from the Truckee, in the south, to the northern boundaries of Idaho and Oregon."

Crook's and Baker's last foray into California seemed to have subdued that region also. Captain Thomas McGregor, 1st Cavalry, who accompanied the expedition, returned to Fort Klamath, and on September 1, wrote, "The Indians are played out; it was impossible to get the least show of a fight out of them. . . . All the Snakes and Pitt Rivers have come in, and I do not believe there is a hostile Indian from the Sacramento to the Columbia."

In mid-September, a band of Paiutes who had been in the Summer Lake-Silver Lake region, moved to Sprague River and made contact with the Klamaths to ask about surrendering. The Klamaths contacted Agent Applegate, and he got William McKay, who went out and convinced the Paiutes to come in to the agency. In command at Fort Klamath, Captain McGregor accepted them in his charge.[12]

Crook could be well satisfied with the results of his campaigning, but his peace plan was not being implemented as he envisioned. He wanted the surrendered Indians to stay in restricted areas where they would be unmolested and self-sustaining. "I do not approve of subsisting them at government expense," he wrote, "or getting them into a way of thinking that they must be subsisted," yet, he believed that many of them had not the time to lay in winter supplies, so a government supply of fresh beef should be used to help them through the first winter. After that, Crook believed the Indians should be on their own to care for themselves. It was a wise vision that, sadly, did not develop.

In early September, there were about 125 Paiutes staying at the foot of Steens Mountain, near Camp C. F. Smith. When Captain John H. Walker visited their camp, he determined that they were hungry, and considered it "an absolute necessity that they should have the flour and meat ration. . . ." Crook had only authorized beef distribution in the direst circumstance in the winter, and said nothing about flour, so Walker wrote for permission to Lt. Colonel Marcus Simpson, the assistant commissary general. He said he had plenty of beef, but little flour. Simpson told Walker that beef issues would be acceptable, but no additional flour would be supplied, however, he indicated that since Camp McGarry was being abandoned, there would be 40,000 pounds of flour at that post, a quantity he claimed would be enough to feed the Indians all winter. In a postscript, Simpson added that Walker should note that 40,000 pounds of flour "is a four months' supply of breadstuff rations for 300 persons."

Secretary of War John M. Schofield got drawn into the affair, and authorized the issue of meat to the Indian prisoners, but neglected to address the flour issue. General Halleck got involved, stating, "General Crook's application was limited to *Meat* rations, and nothing is said about *flour.* . . ." If Walker wanted to issue flour, he needed to check with Crook. Perhaps disgusted with the red tape, Walker fed the Indians. It was still late summer, and Crook's plan to have the Indians subsist themselves, except for a possible emergency beef issuance during the coming winter, had already fallen by the wayside.[13]

Crook issued orders to discharge most of the citizen employees in the district. His tone in his report to General Halleck was somewhat apologetic, saying that the expenses he incurred to run the various campaigns "may have seemed large, yet the results will show that it has been true economy." As usual, the government remained concerned about money, with a niggardly Congress generally hampering wartime efficiency and peacetime treaty making. Posts were abandoned and companies were shuffled about, with the 23rd Infantry headquarters vacating Camp Warner and moving to Fort Vancouver. More companies of the 8th Cavalry were sent to Arizona.

Citizens from the Owyhee region compiled and sent at least four petitions to Lt. Colonel Crook, requesting that Camp Lyon be kept open, "until after the approaching winter at least," because history showed "it is the most dangerous section of our frontier." They wanted the soldiers to remain to give the Indians "a reasonable trial before trusting to their promises." Camp Lyon was kept open until March 1869. Camp Three Forks remained in business until October 1871. Fort Harney was closed in June 1880.

In October 1868, a familiar face was back near some of his old haunts. James A. Waymire was tired of the volunteers and the petty bickering among its officers, and resigned from the 1st Oregon Cavalry in November 1864, but apparently he still had a love of the service. He joined the 1st Cavalry in 1867, and in October of 1868, was in command of Camp Lyon. Waymire led a scout out to Sheep Ranch on Jordan Creek to search for Indians who reportedly stole several horses on October 9. A few days later, Waymire was back at Camp Lyon. The entire affair, he wrote, "was a mistake—the horses having been found and no Indians having been in that vicinity recently."

Waymire, who had started the army's participation in the Snake War with his over-enthusiastic expedition beyond Steens Mountain in April 1864, conducted what was probably the last scout of the conflict four and a half years later.

Lieutenant Colonel Crook would make his home base in Portland, where he remained until relieved by General Edward R. S. Canby in 1870. "Nothing of note occurred during these two years," the terse Crook wrote.[14]

The Snake War that began, not with a bang, but with a whimper, ended in the same fashion. It proved, however, to be the deadliest war, in terms of human lives lost, of any of the Indian wars in the West.

It only took until September 1868, for one concern about the recently concluded war to be expressed in General Orders No. 32. It seems that none of the post cemeteries had been enclosed or judiciously cared for. While fighting a war, subsisting from day to day, and being more concerned with a myriad of seemingly more pressing issues, the graves of American soldiers and civilians were not deemed a great priority. Cattle had been grazing in the cemeteries and wild animals were running about, knocking over the primitive wooden headboards. The grass and weeds did their perpetual work, and the wind and sun performed their aging processes.

The native peoples had their own remembrances, while the military had to suggest some mild coercion to enjoin its officers to take measures to have the graveyards enclosed, cared for, and have proper headstones erected. The war was hardly over, and it was already difficult, the Order stated, "to recognize them as resting places for the Nation's dead."[15]

Chapter 27 notes

[1] *Idaho World*, June 10, 1868, July 29, 1868, August 8, 1868; *Owyhee Avalanche*, July 18, 1868, July 25, 1868; *Secretary of War 1868-69*, 71; Webb, *List of Engagements*, 38; Corless, *Weiser Indians*, 50-51; Sinclair to AAG, no date, RG 393, Dept. of Columbia, Letters Received, Box 5.

[2] Harris to AAG, July 28, 1868, RG 393, Dept. of Columbia, Letters Received, Box 5.

[3] *Secretary of War 1868-69*, 71; *Owyhee Avalanche*, August 15, 1868; Heitman, *Historical Register, Vol. 1*, 946; *Adjutant General's Office*, 34.

[4] Cornelius Shea Depredation Claim #7644; Coppinger to Hammond, September 5, 1868, RG 393, Dept. of Columbia, Letters Received, Box 5; Webb, *List of Engagements*, 38; *Owyhee Avalanche*, September 12, 1868.

[5] Coppinger to Hammond, September 7, 1868, RG 393, Dept. of Columbia, Letters received, Box 5.

[6] Winnemucca Hopkins, *Life Among the Paiutes*, 85, 99-102; Coppinger to Hammond, August 10, 1868, RG 393, Dept. of Columbia, Letters Received, Box 5; *Owyhee Avalanche*, August 1, 1868.

[7] *Owyhee Avalanche*, August 15, 1868. "Pahoui" could have been Pohave (Race Horse) or Pasego (Sweet Root), or possibly a reference to the Pohoi Band (Wild Sage People).

[8] *Secretary of War 1868-69*, 72; Frazer, *Forts*, 94; *Owyhee Avalanche*, August 15, 1868.

[9] Schmitt, ed., *Crook Autobiography*, 158-59; *Secretary of War 1868-69*, 72-73; Parnell, "Operations with Crook," 635.

[10] Baker to Nickerson, August 19, 1868, RG 393, Dept. of Columbia, Letters Received, Box 4; Parnell, "Operations with Crook," 635.

[11] Winnemucca Hopkins, *Life Among the Paiutes*, 90-93, 103; Angel, *History of Nevada*, 184.

[12] Crook to AAG, August 22, 1868, RG 393, Dept. of Columbia, Letters Received, Box 5; *Oregon Sentinel*, September 5, 1868; McGregor to AAG, September 14, 1868, RG 393, Dept. of Columbia, Letters received, Box 5.

[13] Crook to AAG, August 22, 1868, RG 393, Dept. of Columbia, Letters Received, Box 5; Walker to Simpson, September 10, 1868, Simpson to Walker, September 19, 1868, Halleck to Simpson, September 28, 1868, RG 393, Dept. of Columbia, Letters received, Box 5. Walker, perhaps frustrated by all the ruckus he had started, only fed the Indians in September, and then sent them all to Camp Harney, where they continued to receive rations.

[14] Crook to AAG, August 22, 1868, RG 393, Dept. of Columbia, Letters Received, Box 5; Waymire to AAG, October 15, 1868, RG 393, Dept. of Columbia, Letters Received, Box 1; Schmitt, ed., *Crook Autobiography*, 159.

[15] *Owyhee Avalanche*, September 26, 1868.

Chapter 28
CONCLUSIONS

The Snake War is little known to most people, other than some folks living in the Pacific Northwest, the occasional Indian Wars student, or Western History buff. Surprisingly, the fighting caused more casualties than any of the other Indian Wars in the trans-Mississippi West.[1] The breakdown is as follows:

	Soldiers		Civilians		Scouts		Indians				
	Killed	Wounded	Killed	Wounded	Killed	Wounded	Killed	Wounded	Captured		
1864	6	8	4	8	4	1	69	12	5	=	117
1865	6	17	14	2	0	0	288	30	79	=	436
1866	9	22	101	3	0	3	307	139	53	=	637
1867	11	18	1	2	2	4	228	22	126	=	414
1868	8	8	2	0	0	0	98	5	37	=	158
Total	40	72	122	15	3	6	985	209	303	=	1,762

The above figures only represent the casualties in what were formally recognized as "battles." Added to these are the numbers of the civilian and Indian casualties that occurred in scores, probably hundreds, of incidents across the frontier that were little noted outside the local area, and then mostly forgotten. When adding in the casualties from the Indian raids mentioned in this study, which is not a full accounting, we find approximately an additional ninety civilians killed, thirty wounded, and sixty Indians killed or wounded. The depredations on the civilian front during the Snake War echoed the worst of the raiding in the most dangerous areas of the frontier West.

When one compares the above losses to some of the bloody Civil War battles where there were often thousands of casualties in a single battle, the numbers may appear insignificant, but it is like comparing apples with oranges. The Indian Wars were in a completely different category, more of a guerrilla war with much smaller numbers engaged and where one side rarely sought to meet the other in a pitched battle. Comparing the Snake War with other Western Indian wars, however, we find that the casualty count stands far above the rest.

Perhaps the most famous of wars has been called the "Great Sioux War" of 1876-77, in which the Battle of the Little Bighorn was the main

345

showpiece. That conflict produced about 847 casualties on both sides, only about half the numbers of the Snake War. In third place is the Red River War of 1874-75, with about 684 casualties. The Apache War of 1871-73, in which Lt. Colonel George Crook was in charge much of the time, produced about 652 casualties. The Nez Perce War of 1877 had about 418 killed and wounded, while the Modoc War in 1872-73, produced about 208 casualties. Wars that lasted longer than the Snake War, such as the Apache fighting from 1885 to 1891, produced only 136 killed and wounded.

With the Snake War being so costly in terms of lives lost, one might wonder why it has never achieved a place in the American consciousness, as did the fighting with the Lakota, Cheyenne, Comanche, and Apache. There are a number of possible reasons, many of them speculative. First, some of the Paiute people were not taken seriously as warriors. Many of the tribes of the Great Basin were among the last to get guns, and those in the southern basin never used horses as a societal and cultural mainstay, because of the lack of grass and water for horses, and the lack of large game animals like the bison, to justify a mobile, horse-based lifestyle. Early white explorers gave the local Indians the pejorative title, "Diggers," because their scarce food supply meant that much of their sustenance had to be taken from the earth. If there was racism inherent in the appellation, it did not come solely from the whites. The Paiutes to the north, or Shoshonis to the north and east, also looked down on these people as *Shoshokos* ("walking people") because they couldn't chase big game and were seen as "earth eaters."[2]

Writing in the 1880s, historian Hubert H. Bancroft, like many of his contemporaries, was surprised when he learned that the Paiutes and Shoshonis could fight. First they were "treated with contempt, as incapable of hostilities, other than petty thefts and occasional murders for gain." When they first began to attack the Warms Springs Agency, state representative Robert Newell, for one, "laughed at the terror they inspired, and declared that three or four men ought to defend the agency against a hundred of them." But, said Bancroft, a change had come over them. With firearms they had changed from "cowardly, skulking creatures, whose eyes were ever fastened on the ground in search of some small living thing to eat," into people to be feared.[3]

Perhaps it was not the "Diggers" who had changed at all, but only the white perceptions of them. If so, the subsequent impressions reverted back to the original uncomplimentary view. A century later, Peter Farb, in his 1968 book, *Man's Rise to Civilization*, traced economic and technological factors in the development of cultures, using various Indian tribes in North America as his examples. Little had apparently changed in a century, for in Farb's opinion also, the "Diggers" were about the lowest tribe on the technological totem pole. If an educated anthropologist could make this assessment, the reading public could probably be expected to share the opinion of Robert Newell.

The Paiutes rarely inspired fear, except in their enemies. They never seemed to catch the imagination of the American public. One of the reasons may be because the Snake War came in the middle of the last forty-year flare-up of the Indian Wars from 1850 to 1890. It was followed by more spectacular battles, with more famous army and Indian personalities who made the headlines. There was no Custer, Sheridan, Miles, or Mackenzie in the Snake War. Crook had not yet made a name for himself. There was no Red Cloud, Sitting Bull, Crazy Horse, Satanta, Cochise, or Geronimo. There was no 7th Cavalry.

One reason that few people knew of the battles or warriors of the Snake War was because there were few reporters who covered it. Joe Wasson was one of the first "war correspondents" to go in the field with the army. He covered part of Crook's campaign for the *Owyhee Avalanche*. When Crook fought the Lakotas in 1876, five reporters rode with him, representing a dozen national newspapers from coast to coast.

The Paiutes never attracted the artists and photographers like the Great Plains tribes did. They had no Remington, Russell, Schreyvogel, Barry, or Soule. There was no great battle like the Little Bighorn, depicted in books, paintings, and movies thousands of times, with wild, colorful prints of the fight displayed in countless beergardens across the land.

There were, however, battles similar to other celebrated fights on the Great Plains. For instance, Isaac Jennings's fight in July 1866, while surrounded by Indians and awaiting rescue or death is not unlike the famous civilian fight at Beecher's Island in 1868. There were incidents in the Snake War, similar to the more infamous "massacres" at Sand Creek in 1864, or Wounded Knee in 1890, that never received such notoriety. For instance, Mud Lake in 1865, inflamed the Paiutes much as Sand Creek did the Cheyennes. There were fights at Leonard Creek in 1865, Guano Valley in 1866, Steens Mountain in 1867, or the Owyhee River in 1866, where many Indians were killed, and some in circumstances where the word "massacre" might be fairly applied—but who has heard of them?

The battles and personalities were obscured by the concurrent fighting elsewhere, and were painted over by later, more colorful, and more publicized events. It is almost as if the Paiute warrior was like the proverbial tree in the forest—was there any sound made when he was shot dead and no one was there to hear it?

The Paiutes, never being taken seriously as warriors, didn't elicit a serious military effort, at least early in the war. When Crook and his adjutant, Lieutenant Azor Nickerson, first arrived in the Owyhee area, Nickerson was not convinced the situation was all that serious, saying that "A semi-Indian war had been in progress. . .of greater or less importance" since the whites first came into the region.[4]

Each new arrival had to learn first-hand that he was indeed, in the midst of an Indian war. The army, with its many reorganizations and personnel changes, never seemed to hit upon an effective combination of commanders, tactics, and troops, at least, arguably, until Crook took over. Even then, Crook was less the initiator, and more the beneficiary of the accumulated results of a war of attrition that had been ongoing for years before he arrived.

The military never did teach standard Indian war tactics; it was much more comfortable re-fighting the Napoleonic Wars, the Civil War, or the latest battles in Europe. Officers sent out to fight Indians had to learn their trade as they went, hopefully advancing in experience from apprentice, to journeyman and master levels. Most of them had their own opinions as to which strategy would work best; some were innovative; some adhered to methods that rarely worked. The army operated the best it could with insufficient soldiers and resources, and the lack of an overall, unifying strategy.

What Crook learned, and what almost every other successful Indian war commander would have to learn, was that there would be few, if any, set-piece, large-scale battles, where the army's superior firepower could decimate an enemy. They fought a guerrilla war. As fighters, the Indians may at times be dismissed for avoiding large battles, sneaking up on their adversaries, and attacking only when they had the advantages of numbers and surprise, but that was the only way the Indians could win. Given the fact that the Indians almost always avoided a pitched battle, it was also the only way the army could win. The Indians had to be followed, found, and surprised in order to bring them to battle. Almost every successful fight for both sides was the result of a surprise attack. And in surprise attacks, there is a great chance that non-combatants will also suffer.

Although Crook carried the fighting to a successful conclusion, at least in army and white civilian terms, he did it with no new, innovative tactics. In a war that lasted about four and a half years, Crook came in for the last one and a half years; about two-thirds of the fighting and casualties had already been sustained. Crook made no radical impact, but more or less continued the fighting by attrition, which had been in going on for three years. Crook did nothing new using Indian scouts. It was done before, for 250 years, and Currey and Drake had utilized Indians to scout and fight in 1864.

Winter war was nothing new. It too, had been a tactic constantly used in the Indian Wars, initiated by the earliest colonists in the seventeenth century. Winter war, total war, civilian war, whatever title one chooses, was not something Union generals first learned in the Civil War. What Crook did was simply to continue to press a war of attrition on his foes, grinding them down day by day, until death, starvation, and exhaustion forced them to surrender or die. It was not glorious, if any warfare is, but it was effective.

CONCLUSIONS

What the military learned from the Indian Wars, if it did learn anything, was that a guerrilla war is won by attrition, and the carrot approach will not work unless a big stick is first applied. Be that as it may, the Snake War remains one of the least known of all the Western Indian Wars, although, in terms of human casualties, it was the deadliest of them all.

Chapter 28 notes

1 This includes all the 13 major campaigns for which the U. S. Government awarded Indian War Campaign medals for service from 1865 to 1891: Southern Oregon, Idaho, Northern California, Nevada, from 1865 to 1875; Comanches and Confederated Tribes in Kansas, Colorado, Texas, New Mexico, and Indian Territory from 1867 to 1875; Modoc War, 1872-1873; Apaches in Arizona, 1873; Northern Cheyennes and Sioux, 1876-1877; Nez Perce War, 1877; Bannock War, 1878; Northern Cheyennes, 1878-1879; Sheep-Eater, Paiute, Bannock, 1879; Ute War, 1879-1880; Apaches in Arizona and New Mexico, 1885-1886; Sioux in South Dakota, 1890-1891; Hostile Indians, any action in which U.S. Troops were killed or wounded between 1865-1891.
2 Ontko, *Thunder Over the Ochoco*, III, 6.
3 Bancroft, *History of Oregon*, Vol. 2, 534.
4 Nickerson, "George Crook and the Indians," 9.

APPENDIX A.
Snake War Battles and Casualties

S = soldier
C = civilian
Sc = scouts
I = Indians
k = killed
w = wounded
c = captured

1864

April 7, 1864. WILDHORSE CREEK (Andrews, Oregon) S-3k. C-1k, 1w. I-5kw.

May 18, 1864. CROOKED RIVER (Paulina, Oregon) S-3k, 5w. C-1w. Sc-3k, 1w. I-3k.

June 2, 1864. ANTELOPE CREEK (Jordan Valley, Oregon) I-6k.

June 24, 1864. JOHN DAY ROAD (Silver Lake, Oregon) C-2w.

July 11, 1864. GRINDSTONE CREEK (Paulina, Oregon) Sc-1k.

July 12, 1864. JORDAN'S FIGHT (Jordan Valley, Oregon) C-1k, 2w.

July 15, 1864. BLACK CANYON (Dayville, Oregon) S-1w.

July 20, 1864. JUNIPER MOUNTAIN (Southwest Idaho) C-2k, 2w. I-35k.

September 13, 16, 1864. THREE ISLAND CROSSING (Glenns Ferry, Idaho) I-19k, 5w.

ca. October 18, 1864. PAULINA CREEK (LaPine, Oregon) I-4k, 1w, 5c.

1864 totals: S-6k, 8w. C-4k, 8w. I-69k, 12w, 5c. Sc-4k, 1w. = 117

1865

February 11, 1865. O'REGAN'S FIGHT (Snake River) I-5k, 4c.

February 15, 1865. RUBY CITY RANGERS (Owyhee Mountains, Idaho) I-20k.

February 15, 1865. BRUNEAU VALLEY (Bruneau, Idaho) I-30k.

ca. March 10, 1865. WALKER LAKE (Hawthorne, Nevada) C-2k.

March 13, 1865. GRANITE CREEK STATION (Gerlach, Nevada) C-5k.

March 14, 1865. MUD LAKE (Nixon, Nevada) S-1w. I-29k.

March 14, 1865. JOHN DAY RIVER (Kimberly, Oregon) I-12k, 10-w.

April 5, 1865. PARADISE VALLEY (Paradise Valley, Nevada) C-2k.

April 6, 1865. COTTONWOOD CREEK (Paradise Valley, Nevada) I-7k.

April 15, 1865. CANE SPRINGS (Orovada, Nevada) I-18k.

April 17, 1865. GARBER'S FIGHT (Izee, Oregon) S-1k, 2w. I-4k, 8w.

May 7, 1865. LITTLEFIELD'S ENCOUNTER (Northcentral Nevada) I-?

May 20, 1865. GODFREY'S MOUNTAIN (Northcentral Nevada) S-2k, 4w.

July 3, 1865. JACKSON CREEK (McDermitt, Oregon) C-4k.

July 9, 1865. MALHEUR RIVER (Juntura, Oregon) S-2w. I-5k, 5w.

July 17, 1865. OWYHEE RIVER (Southeast Oregon) I-4k, 4w.

ca July 20, 1865 HOT SPRINGS (Northeast Nevada) I-70c.

July 26, 1865. WILLOW POINT (Willow Point, Nevada) S-1k, 2w. C-1k, 2w. I-21k.

July 31, 1865. COTTONWOOD CANYON (Carlin, Nevada) S-1w. I-11k.

ca August 4, 6, 1865. GRAVELLY FORD I-3k, 3w, 4c.

September 3, 1865. TABLE MOUNTAIN (Unionville, Nevada) I-10k.

September 12, 1865. WILLOW CREEK (Orovada, Nevada) S-1w. I-31k.

September 15, 1865 SILVER CREEK (Riley, Oregon) S-1k. I-3k.

September 23, 1865. SILVIES RIVER (Burns, Oregon) S-2w. I-15k.

November 17, 1865. LEONARD CREEK (Northwest Nevada) S-1k, 2w. I-55k, 1c.

ca November 19, 1865. BARRY'S FIGHT (South Fork John Day, Oregon) I-5k.

1865 totals: S-6k, 17w. C-14k, 2w. I-288k, 30w, 79c = 436

1866

January 12, 1866. BATTLE CREEK (Northwest Nevada) S-5w. I-38k, 1w. Sc-1w.

February 15, 1866. GUANO VALLEY (Northwest Nevada) S-1k, 6w. I-96k, 15w, 19c.

February 16, 1866. OWYHEE RIVER (Three Forks, Oregon) S-1w. I-1w

February 23, 1866. DRY CREEK S-1k, 1w. I-18k, 2w.

March 7, 1866. PARADISE VALLEY (Paradise Valley, Nevada) I-6k.

May 19-21, 1866. CHINESE MASSACRES (Southeast Oregon, Southwest Idaho) C-99k.

May 27-28, 1866. THREE FORKS S-5k. I-7k, 12w.

July 2-7, 1866. JENNINGS'S FIGHT C-1k, 3w. I-30kw.

July 17, 1866. STEENS MOUNTAIN (Southeast Oregon) S-1w. I-3k, 5w.

July 18, 1866. RATTLESNAKE CREEK (Harney, Oregon) S-1k. I-11k, 10w, 4c.

August 21, 26, 1866. HUNT'S FIGHTS (Owyhee Country) I-12k.

September 14, 1866. CAMP WATSON (Central Oregon) I-1k, 1c.

September 15, 1866. CLARK'S FIGHT (Prineville, Oregon) Sc-2w. I-4k.

September 28, 1866. DONNER UND BLITZEN RIVER (Frenchglen, Oregon) S-1w. I-6k.

October 3, 1866. LONG VALLEY (Northwest Nevada) I-8k.

October 5, 1866. SPRAGUE RIVER (Bly, Oregon) I-4k.

October 14, 1866. HARNEY LAKE VALLEY (Harney, Oregon) S-1w. I-3k, 8w.

October 26, 1866. LAKE ABERT (Valley Falls, Oregon) S-2w. I-14k, 28w, 7c.

October 30, 1866. O'BEIRNE'S FIGHT (Malheur County, Oregon) S-2w. C-1k. I-2k, 8w, 8c.

November 1, 1866. TROUT CREEK CANYON (Southeast Oregon) I-4k, 3w.

ca November 17, 1866. FORT KLAMATH S-2w. I-13k, 20w.

November 18, 1866. JOHN DAY RIVER (Central Oregon) I-3k, 1w.

December 3, 1866. CAMP WATSON (Central Oregon) I-14k, 5c.

December 26, 1866. OWYHEE RIVER (Southeast Oregon) S-1k. I-25k, 9c.

1866 totals: S-9k, 22w. C-101k, 3w. I-307k, 139w, 53c. Sc-3w = 637

1867

January 7, 20, 1867. CROOKED RIVER (Prineville, Oregon) I-28k, 8c. Sc-2w.

January 8, 1867. OWYHEE RIVER (Southeast Oregon) I-5kw.

January 9, 1867. MALHEUR RIVER (Harper, Oregon) S-1w.

January 18, 1867. EDEN VALLEY (Paradise Valley, Nevada) S-1w. I-2k.

January 29, 1867. STEENS MOUNTAIN (Southeast Oregon) S-3w. C-1k, 1w. I-65k, 30c.

February 7, 1867. VICKSBURG MINES (Northwest Nevada) S-2w.

February 15, 1867. BLACK SLATE MOUNTAIN (Golconda, Nevada) I-5k.

February 16, 1867. SURPRISE VALLEY (Fort Bidwell, California) I-5k, 2c.

ca February 25-26, 1867. PUEBLO MOUNTAIN (Fields, Oregon) I-2k, 5c.

March 23, 1867. SOUTH FORK OWYHEE (Tuscarora, Nevada) I-6k.

April 25, 1867. LITTLE TROUT CREEK (Ashwood, Oregon) I-4k.

April 27, 1867. SILVIES RIVER (Burns, Oregon) I-6k, 6w.

May 5, 1867. CAMP WATSON (Dayville, Oregon) I-1k.

May 18, 1867. SUMMIT SPRINGS STATION (Southeast Oregon) I-2w.

June 19, 1867. STEENS MOUNTAIN (Southeast Oregon) I-12k, 1w, 2c.

June 22, 1867. DONNER UND BLITZEN RIVER (Frenchglen, Oregon) I-5k, 2c.

July 8, 19, 1867. MALHEUR RIVER (Southeast Oregon) I-4k, 22c.

July 15, 1867. SOUTH FORK MALHEUR (Venator, Oregon) I-6k, 1w, 2c. Sc-1k.

July 27, 1867. CAMP WARNER (Southcentral Oregon) I-11k, 11c.

August 11, 15, 1867. OWYHEE RIVER (Southeast Oregon) I-3k, 2c.

August 25, 1867. CRANE MOUNTAIN (Lakeview, Oregon) I-4k, 3w. Sc-1k, 1w.

September 6, 1867. SILVER LAKE (Silver Lake, Oregon) I-1k, 5c.

September 8, 1867. SUMMER LAKE (Paisley, Oregon) S-1k, 1w. I-23k, 14c. Sc-1w.

September 26-28, 1867. INFERNAL CAVERNS (Likely, California) S-8k, 11w. I-20k, 12w, 2c.

October 4, 1867. CAMP LOGAN (John Day, Oregon) S-1k.

October 21, 1867. THE DENOILLE INCIDENT (Reynolds, Idaho) S-1k. C-1k.

October 26, 1867. OWYHEE RIVER (Southeast Oregon) I-k, 2c.

October 26, 1867. CAMP WINFIELD SCOTT (Paradise Valley, Nevada) I-5k, 4c.

November 25, 1867. QUINN RIVER (McDermitt, Nevada) I-2k.

December 12, 1867. CRAIG GULCH (Southeast Oregon) I-5k, 7c.

1867 totals: S-11k, 18w. C-1k, 2w. I-228k, 22w, 126c. Sc-2k, 4w. = 414

1868

January 4, 1868. THREE FINGERS GULCH (Southeast Oregon) I-1k, 17c.

March 14, 21, 1868. DONNER UND BLITZEN CREEK (Frenchglen, Oregon) S-5w. I-12k, 2c.

March 26, 1868. OWYHEE RIVER (Southeast Oregon) C-1k. I-1k.

April 5, 1868. MALHEUR RIVER (Drewsey, Oregon) I-32k, 2c.

April 17, 1868. INDIAN CANYON (Southeast Oregon) I-5k, 3c.

April 29, 1868. DEEP CANYON (Paradise Valley, Nevada) S-2k, 1w.

April 29, 1868. OTSEOS LODGE (Southcentral Oregon) S-1k, 4w.

May 1, 1868. HOAG'S BLUFF (Adel, Oregon) S-2w. C-1k. I-4kw.

May 29, 1868. CEDAR MOUNTAIN (Southeast Oregon) I-34k.

May 31, 1868. CASTLE ROCK (Juntura, Oregon) S-1w. I-5c.

June 9, 1868. SNAKE CANYON (Weiser, Idaho) I-3k.

June 24, 1868. BATTLE CREEK (Riddle, Idaho) I-3k, 4c.

July 26, 1868. JUNIPER CANYON (Silver City, Idaho) I-5k, 3w, 4c.

1868 totals: S-8k, 8w. C-2k. I-98k, 5w, 37c. = 158

Total   S-40k, 73w. C-122k, 15w. I-990k, 208w, 300c. Sc-6k, 2w. = 1,762

APPENDIX B.
Partial List of Indian Depredations in the Snake War, referenced in this study

2-64 H. Jones, stock stolen, Cottonwood Creek, Oregon
3-64 40 horses and mules, Davis Ranch, Canyon City, Oregon
  "   H. Smeathman killed, Disaster Peak, Nevada
4-64 Overton and Wilson killed, 23 stock stolen, Canyon City, Oregon
  "   Stock stolen, Officer's Ranch, Canyon City, Oregon
5-64 G. Dodge, H. Burton, two others killed, Noble wounded, eight stock stolen, Disaster Peak, Nevada
  "   Humboldt Rangers, one man killed, three Indians killed, Nevada
  "   P. Langdon, T. Renney killed, Drew's Road, Oregon
6-64 B. Harding killed, Rogers wounded, Mountain House, Oregon
  "   Richardson Train, two men wounded, seven cattle stolen, John Day Road, Oregon
7-64 One man killed, 40 stock stolen from wagon train, Canyon City, Oregon
  "   Two Men killed, 300 cattle stolen, Goose Lake, Oregon
  "   Burton killed, Drew's Road, California
  "   One man killed, stock stolen, Jordan Valley, Oregon
  "   M. Jordan killed, two men wounded, Owyhee River, Oregon
65-65 Wells Fargo robbed, Umatilla Road, Oregon
  "   Stock stolen, Reynolds Creek, Idaho
  "   13 horses stolen, Cottonwood House, Oregon
2-65 J. McComins, Gregory killed, 500 stock stolen, Jordan Creek, Oregon
  "   Ruby City Rangers kill 20 Indians, Idaho-Oregon
3-65 I. Stewart, R. Rabe killed, Walker Lake, Nevada
4-65 H. Floder killed, southern Oregon
  "   J. Potter, two others killed, Cottonwood House, Oregon
  "   35 mules stolen, Douthitt & Brothers, Olds Ferry, Oregon
5-65 12 horses stolen, Italian Canyon, Nevada
  "   Two miners killed, northern Nevada
6-65 Two miners killed, Pueblo Mines, Oregon
7-65 Four horses stolen, Overland Stage, Rock Creek Station, Oregon
8-65 Three Indians killed, Goose Creek Mountains, Idaho
  "   Three miners killed, Hot Springs, Nevada
  "   28 cattle stolen, Con Shea, Sinker Creek, Idaho
9-65 O. Graffan killed, Malheur River, Oregon
  "   One man wounded, Inskip's Station, Oregon
  "   20 cattle stolen, Con Shea, Sinker Creek, Idaho
  "   Property destroyed, McWilliams Ranch, Jordan Creek, Oregon
10-65 Ten horses and one ox stolen, Inskip's Station, Oregon

" 16 horses stolen, Con Shea, Sinker Creek, Nevada
11-65 Horses stolen near Warm springs, Oregon
" Stock stolen, Robinson's Ranch, five Indians killed, John Day River, Oregon
" Bellew killed, Cedar Springs, Nevada
" Clark wounded, Jordan Valley, Oregon
" Five mules stolen, McWilliams Ranch, Jordan Creek, Oregon
" Ten stock stolen, Baxter's Ranch, Jordan Valley, Oregon
" 50 cattle stolen, Con Shea, Sinker Creek, Idaho
12-65 One Indian wounded, Camp Alvord, Oregon
1-66 Four cattle stolen, John Day River, Oregon
2-66 Ten horses stolen, Babington's Ranch, Idaho
" Two horses stolen, Parson's Ranch, Idaho
" Three horses stolen, Cold Springs Station, Idaho
" A. Hall wounded, one Indian killed, 37 cattle, nine horses stolen, Jordan Valley, Oregon
" Four horses stolen, Inskip's Station, Oregon
3-66 Four horses stolen, Brownlee's Ferry, Idaho
" Cattle stolen, Miller's Ranch, Oregon
" D. Brown, M. Mott killed, Jordan Valley, Oregon
4-66 Four horses stolen, Burnt River, Oregon
5-66 J. Witner killed, John Day River, Oregon
" Stock stolen, property destroyed, Cane Springs Station, Nevada
" Stock stolen, property destroyed, Buffalo Springs Station, Nevada
" C. Bacheler wounded, three horses stolen, property destroyed, Owyhee Ferry, Oregon
" 421 cattle of Beard and Miller stolen, California Road
" 65 stock stolen, Booneville, Idaho
6-66 C. Gassett killed, Flint District, Idaho
" J. Perry killed, Sinker Creek, Idaho
" 57 cattle stolen, Con Shea, Sinker Creek, Idaho
" Stock stolen, property destroyed, Willow Creek Station, Oregon
" Stock stolen, property destroyed, Summit Springs Station, Oregon
" Stock stolen, property destroyed, Rattlesnake Station, Oregon
7-66 G. Hill kills two Indians, Jordan Valley, Oregon
" Fisher and Drake wounded, Camp McGarry, Nevada
8-66 S. Leonard killed, Canyon Creek,
" James Grett killed, Jordan Valley, Oregon
" M. Wilson killed, D. Graham wounded, Canyon City, Oregon
" 54 mules, 18 cattlen stolen, Camp Watson, Oregon
" Stock stolen, Rock Creek, Oregon
" One man killed, Dixie Creek, Oregon
" Station keeper killed, stock stolen, Summit Springs, Oregon
9-66 Stock stolen, J. Clark, Oregon
" Stock stolen, F. Thompson, Oregon
" W. Hill wounded, stock stolen, Owyhee Ferry, Oregon
" H. Paige killed, Wheeler wounded, one Indian killed, stage attack
" Six horses stolen, Clarksville, Oregon
10-66 11 horses stolen, Rock Creek, Idaho

" J. Dixon killed, two Indians killed, Inskip's Station, Oregon
" 16 horses and mules stolen, Con Shea, Sinker Creek, Idaho
" Teamster killed, one Indian killed, northern Nevada
11-66 W. Wilcox killed, D. Harrington, W. Waltermire wounded, stage attack, Owyhee Ferry, Oregon
" 12 horses stolen, C. Bacheler, Walters Ferry, Idaho
" Cattle stolen, Dean & Bayley's Ranch, Dixie Creek, Oregon
" J. Kester killed, Canyon City, Oregon
" Walsh killed, Fruit's Ferry, Idaho
" F. McCoy killed, J. Adams wounded, horses stolen, stage attack, Reynolds Creek, Idaho
" 14 cattle stolen, Sinker Creek, Idaho
" Chinese miner killed, Owyhee District, Idaho
12-66 Stock stolen, one Indian killed, Inskip's Station, Oregon
1-67 Westover killed, Camp McGarry, Nevada
" Glass killed, Boise Valley, Idaho
2-67 Mules stolen, C. Breymer, Dalles Road, Oregon
" Horses stolen, F. Thompson, Oregon
" Cattle stolen, Riley's Ranch, Canyon City, Oregon
3-67 Stock stolen, C. Gregg, Paradise Valley, Nevada
" 13 horses stolen, Miller's Ranch, Oregon
" Stock stolen, Officer's Ranch, Canyon City, Oregon
" Stock stolen, Brackett's Ranch, Cottonwood, Oregon
" Mules stolen, C. Lockwood, Canyon City Road, Oregon
" Six Indians killed, Baker City, Oregon
" 25 mules stolen, pack train, Weiser Ferry, Idaho
" 22 cattle stolen, Ray's Ranch, Reynolds Creek, Idaho
" W. Younger, J. Ullman, and Bouchet killed, stage attack, Reynolds Creek, Idaho
4-67 J. Fraser and W. Slack killed, Wagontown, Idaho
" McKnight killed, Reynolds Creek, Idaho
5-67 Cattle stolen from Shea, McMahon, Eastman, Sinker Creek, Idaho
" 17 horses and mules stolen, F. Brougham, Flat Creek, Nevada
" 21 horses stolen, Summit Springs Station, Oregon
" Two Indians killed, Miller's Ranch, Oregon
6-67 Cattle stolen, Hamlin's Ranch, Mountain House, Oregon
7-67 40 cattle stolen, Sinker Creek, Idaho
" Irishman killed, Idaho
8-67 J. Banks killed, Camp Winfield Scott, Nevada
" J. Mangin wounded, one Indian killed, Jordan Valley, Oregon
" 12 horses stolen, Briggs & Boyles Ranch, Grande Ronde, Oregon
" Three miners killed, Mormon Basin, Oregon
" A. King and Haggert killed, Rye Valley, Oregon
9-67 J. Scott and wife killed, Rye Valley, Oregon
" 95 cattle stolen, Con Shea, Sinker Creek, Idaho
10-67 J. Colwell killed, Flint District, Idaho
" W. Slack killed, Oro City, Idaho
" A. Denoille and wife killed, Sergeant Nichols wounded, Camp Lyon, Idaho

356

12-67 12 oxen stolen, A. Goodrich, Jordan Creek, Oregon
" 16 horses stolen, J. Hailey, Idaho
" Two stage teams stolen from Wells Fargo, Desert Station, Idaho
3-68 Four oxen stolen, A. Canter, Jordan Creek, Oregon
" G. Jarvis killed, Reynolds Creek, Idaho
" Bruneau Jim killed, Boise Valley, Idaho
4-68 One Indian killed, Camp Harney, Oregon
" W. Pierson, wife, daughter, Sutherland, Cooper killed, Long Valley, California
" Horses stolen, Paradise Valley, Nevada
" Two cattle stolen, F. Brougham, Flat Creek, Nevada
5-68 12 horses stolen, A. Bailey, Powder River, Oregon
" Four horses stolen from miners, Powder River, Oregon
" 18 horses stolen, ranch near Powder River, Oregon
" One packer wounded, one Indian killed, two wounded, Ives Canyon, Oregon
" Nine horses stolen, Amelia City, Oregon
" 15 mules and horses stolen, F. Brougham, Flat Creek, Nevada
" J. Belknap, R. Young, and A. Sutherland killed, Willow Creek, Oregon
" D. Smith, D. Wooden, N. Dixon killed, stage attacks, Jordan Valley, Oregon
6-68 Six oxen stolen, A. Denio, Paradise Valley, Nevada
7-68 H. Murdoff wounded, Flint District, Idaho
8-68 30 horses and mules stolen, Con Shea, Sinker Creek, Idaho

APPENDIX C.
Cost of Subsisting Troops at Oregon and Idaho Posts, 1866-1868[1]

Posts	1866	1867	1868
Camp C. F. Smith	$7,400	$13,556	$5,704
Camp Lyon	$8,636	$4,710	$6,781
Camp Logan	$1,515	$4,397	$5,213
Camp Watson	$9,795	$14,275	$8,322
Camp Harney	--	$8,686	$20,997
Camp Warner	$3,783	$16,888	$24,407
Camp Three Forks	$7,304	$11,183	$13,703
Fort Boise	$20,397	$12,032	$10,010
	$58,830	$85,727	$95,137

APPENDIX D.
Indian Casualties Caused by California Regiments

The Californians who enlisted during the Civil War caused more destruction among the native population in the West than did enlistees of any other state or territory. In five years they killed more Indians than any of the ten U.S. Cavalry regiments did in the forty years between 1850 and 1890.

When the Civil War ended, many Californians apparently had not had enough fighting. Some of them, along with many new recruits from the Sierra Nevada mines and the San Francisco area, signed up again in the fall of 1866 in a new regiment. The 8th U. S. Cavalry was made up entirely of Californians. Including the 8th Cavalry's fights, we find that Californians accounted for nearly one-fifth of all Indian casualties in the West.[2]

Regiment	Fights	Casualties Caused	Casualties Per Fight
1st Calif. Cav.	24	216	9.0
2nd Calif Cav.	28	786	28.1
1st Calif. Inf.	6	83	13.8
2nd Calif. Inf.	23	221	9.6
3rd Calif. Inf.	5	137	27.4
5th CA Inf.	14	263	18.7
6th Calif. Inf.	2	6	3.0
7th Calif. Inf.	4	15	3.8
1st Calif. Mountaineers	14	41	10.1
	120	1,868	15.5
8th U.S. Cavalry	+167	+ 688	4.1
Total	287	2,556	8.3

Appendix C notes

1 Foster to Nickerson, February 13, 1869, RG 393, Dept. of Columbia, Letters Received, Box
2 Michno, *Encyclopedia of Indian Wars*, 365.

BIBLIOGRAPHY

Adjutant General's Office. *Chronological List of Actions &c., with the Indians from January 15, 1837 to January, 1891*. Washington: GPO, 1891.

Altshuler, Constance Wynn. *Chains of Command: Arizona and the Army, 1856-1875.* Tucson, Arizona: The Arizona Historical Society, 1981.

Angel, Myron. *History of Nevada*. Oakland, California: Thompson & West, 1881.

Antone Ranch and Camp Watson Historical Tour. Prineville, Oregon: Crook County Historical Society, 1995.

Athearn, Robert G. *William Tecumseh Sherman and the Settlement of the West*. Foreword by William M. Ferraro and Thomas J. Murphy. Norman, Oklahoma: University of Oklahoma Press, 1995.

Bancroft, Hubert Howe. *The Works of Hubert Howe Bancroft Volume XXX History of Oregon Vol. II 1848-1883*. San Francisco, California: The History Company, 1883.

__ *The Works of Hubert Howe Bancroft. Volume XXXI History of Washington, Idaho, and Montana 1845-1889*. San Francisco, California: The History Company, 1890.

Bartlett, Richard A. *Great Surveys of the American West*. Norman, Oklahoma: University of Oklahoma Press, 1962.

Becher, Ronald. *Massacre Along the Medicine Road: A Social History of the Indian War of 1864 in Nebraska Territory*. Caldwell, Idaho: Caxton Press, 1999.

Beckham, Stephen Dow. *Requiem for a People: The Rogue River Indians and the Frontiersmen*. Corvallis, Oregon: Oregon State University, 1996.

Bensell, Royal A. Gunter Barth, ed. *All Quiet on the Yamhill The Civil War in Oregon*. Eugene, Oregon: University of Oregon, 1959.

Bourke, John G. "General Crook in the Indian Country." *The Century Magazine* XLI, no. 5 (March 1891): 643-660.

__ *On the Border With Crook*. Lincoln, Nebraska: University of Nebraska Press, 1971.

Brackett, Albert G. "Fighting in the Sierras." In *Eyewitnesses to the Indian Wars, 1865-1890 The Wars for the Pacific Northwest*, ed. Peter Cozzens. Mechanicsburg, Pennsylvania: Stackpole Books, 2002.

Brooks, James F. *Captives & Cousins: Slavery, Kinship, and Community in the Southwest Borderlands*. Chapel Hill, North Carolina: University of North Carolina Press, 2002.

Camp Watson Papers—Military Road Pamphlet 9. Prineville, Oregon: Crook County Historical Society, nd.

Carey, Charles H. *General History of Oregon Through Early Statehood*. Portland, Oregon: Binfords & Mort, 1971.

Clark, Keith, and Donna Clark. "William McKay's Journal, 1866-67: Indian Scouts, Part I." *Oregon Historical Quarterly* LXXIX, no. 2 (Summer 1978): 121-171.

___ "William McKay's Journal, 1866-67: Indian Scouts, Part II." *Oregon Historical Quarterly* LXXIX, no. 3 (Fall 1978): 269-333.

Cline, Gloria Griffen. *Exploring the Great Basin.* Reno, Nevada: University of Nevada Press, 1988.

Clodfelter, Michael. *The Dakota War: The United States Army Versus the Sioux, 1862-1865.* Jefferson, NC: McFarland & Company, Inc., 1998.

Coffman, Edward M. *The Old Army: A Portrait of the American Army in Peacetime, 1784-1898.* New York: Oxford University Press, 1986.

Converse, George L. *A Military History of the Columbia Valley 1848-1865.* Walla Walla, Washington: Pioneer Press Books, 1988.

Corless, Hank. *The Weiser Indians Shoshoni Peacemakers.* Foreword by Merle W. Wells. Caldwell, Idaho: Caxton Printers, Ltd., 1996.

Coward, John M. *The Newspaper Indian: Native American Identity in the Press, 1820-90.* Urbana, Illinois: University of Illinois Press, 1999.

Crum, Stephen J. *The Road on Which We Came: A History of the Western Shoshone.* Salt Lake City, Utah: University of Utah Press, 1994.

Curran, Harrold. *Fearful Crossing: The Central Overland Trail Through Nevada.* Las Vegas: Nevada Publications, 1987.

Danziger, Edmund Jefferson, Jr. *Indians and Bureaucrats: Administering Reservation Policy During the Civil War.* Urbana, Illinois: University of Illinois Press, 1974.

Dippie, Brian. *The Vanishing American: White Attitudes & U.S. Indian Policy.* Lawrence Kansas: University Press of Kansas, 1982.

Drake, John M. "Cavalry in the Indian Country, 1864." Edited by Priscilla Knuth. *Oregon Historical Quarterly* LXV, no. 1 (March 1964): 5-118.

Drake, John Miller. "The Oregon Cavalry." 1906. John Miller Drake Papers. Oregon Historical Society, MSS 80.

Dunlay, Thomas W. *Wolves for the Blue Soldiers: Indian Scouts and Auxiliaries with the United States Army, 1860-90.* Lincoln: University of Nebraska Press, 1982.

Durham, Michael S. *Desert Between the Mountains: Mormons, Miners, Padres, Mountain Men, and the Opening of the Great Basin, 1771-1869.* Norman, Oklahoma: University of Oklahoma Press, 1999.

Dyer, Frederick H. *A Compendium of the War of the Rebellion.* Three Volumes. Des Moines, Iowa: The Dyer Publishing Company, 1908.

Edwards, Glenn Thomas, Jr. "The Department of the Pacific in the Civil War Years." PhD. diss., University of Oregon, 1963.

Egan, Ferol. *Sand in a Whirlwind The Paiute Indian War of 1860.* Reno, Nevada: University of Nevada Press, 2003.

Ellis, Richard N. *General Pope and U.S. Indian Policy.* Albuquerque, New Mexico: University of New Mexico Press, 1970.

Eskridge, Richard I. "The Battle of the Infernal Caverns." In *Eyewitnesses to the Indian Wars, 1865-1890 The Wars for the Pacific Northwest,* ed. Peter Cozzens. Mechanicsburg, Pennsylvania: Stackpole Books, 2002.

Evans, John W. *Powerful Rockey: The Blue Mountains and the Oregon Trail, 1811-1883.* La Grande, Oregon: Eastern Oregon State College, 1991.

Foote, Shelby. *The Civil War A Narrative Fort Sumter to Perryville.* New York: Random House, 1958.

Franzwa, Gregory M. *Maps of the Oregon Trail*. St. Louis, Missouri: The Patrice Press, 1990.

Frazer, Robert W. *Forts of the West: Military Forts and Presidios and Posts Commonly Called Forts West of the Mississippi River to 1898*. Norman: University of Oklahoma Press, 1965.

Frederick, J.V. *Ben Holladay the Stagecoach King: A Chapter in the Development of Transcontinental Transportation*. Glendale, California: Arthur H. Clark Co., 1940. Reprint, Lincoln: University of Nebraska Press, 1989.

Freeman, Douglas Southall. *Lee's Lieutenants A Study in Command Cedar Mountain to Chancellorsville*. New York: Charles Scribner's Sons, 1943.

Fuller, Emeline L. *Left by the Indians and Massacre on the Oregon Trail in the Year 1860*. Fairfield, Washington: Ye Galleon Press, 1992.

Gilliss, Julia. *So Far From Home An Army Bride on the Western Frontier, 1865-1869*. Edited by Priscilla Knuth. Portland, Oregon: Oregon Historical Society Press, 1993.

Glassley, Ray Hoard. *Indian Wars of the Pacific Northwest*. Portland, Oregon: Binfords & Mort, 1972.

Goetzmann, William H. *Exploration & Empire: The Explorer and the Scientist in the Winning of the American West*. New York: W.W. Norton & Company, 1966.

Greever, William S. *The Bonanza West: The Story of the Western Mining Rushes 1848-1900*. Norman, Oklahoma: University of Oklahoma Press, 1963.

Hanley, Mike and Ellis Lucia. *Owyhee Trails: The West's Forgotten Corner*. Caldwell, Idaho: Caxton Printers, Ltd., 1999.

Heitman, Francis B. *Historical Register and Dictionary of the United States Army*. 2 Volumes. Washington: GPO, 1903.

Hennessy, John J. *Return to Bull Run The Campaign and Battle of Second Manassas*. New York: Simon & Schuster, 1993.

Hopkins, Sarah Winnemucca. *Life Among the Paiutes: Their Wrongs and Claims*. New York: G. P. Putnams's Sons, 1883.

Hunt, Aurora. *The Army of the Pacific, 1860-1866*. Glendale, California: Arthur H. Clark Co., 1951. Reprint. Introduction by Robert A. Clark. Mechanicsburg, Pennsylvania: Stackpole Books, 2004.

Jackson, W. Turrentine. *Wagon Roads West: A Study of Federal Road Surveys and Construction in the Trans-Mississippi West, 1846-1869*. New Haven, Connecticut: Yale University Press, 1965.

Kappler, Charles J., ed. *Indian Treaties 1778-1883*. Mattituck, New York: Amereon House, 1972.

Karge, Joseph W. and Samuel Munson. "Indian Affairs on the Pacific Coast." In *Eyewitnesses to the Indian Wars, 1865-1890 The Wars for the Pacific Northwest*, ed. Peter Cozzens. Mechanicsburg, Pennsylvania: Stackpole Books, 2002.

Kee, Wayne. *Ocheho and Ochoco An Evolutionary History*. Prineville, Oregon: Paunina Press, 2005.

Knight, Oliver. *Following the Indian Wars: The Story of the Newspaper Correspondents Among the Indian Campaigners*. Norman, Oklahoma: University of Oklahoma Press, 1960.

Lieutenant Watson Meets Paulina. Prineville, Oregon: Crook County Historical Society, 1992.

Lockley, Fred. *Conversations With Pioneer Men: The Lockley Files*. One Horse Press, 1996.

McArthur, Lews A. and Lewis L. McArthur. *Oregon Geographic Names*. Portland, OR: Oregon Historical Society Press, 2003.

Madsen, Brigham D. *The Bannock of Idaho*. Moscow, Idaho: University of Idaho Press, 1996.

___*The Northern Shoshoni*. Caldwell, Idaho: Caxton Printers, Ltd, 1980.

___*The Shoshoni Frontier and the Bear River Massacre*. With a foreword by Charles S. Peterson. Salt Lake City: University of Utah Press, 1985.

Mares, Michael A. *Encyclopedia of Deserts*. Norman, Oklahoma: University of Oklahoma Press, 1999.

Marszalek, John F. *Commander of all Lincoln's Armies*. Cambridge, Massachusettes; Harvard University Press, 2004.

Mattes, Merrill J. *The Great Platte River Road*. Lincoln: Nebraska State Historical Society, 1969.

Michno, Gregory F. *Battle at Sand Creek: The Military Perspective*. El Segundo, California: Upton & Sons, 2004.

___*Encyclopedia of Indian Wars Western Battles and Skirmishes, 1850-1890*. Missoula, Montana: Mountain Press, 2003.

Michno, Gregory and Susan. *A Fate Worse than Death: Indian Captivities in the West, 1830-1885*. Caldwell, Idaho: Caxton Press, 2007.

Moody, Ralph. *Stagecoach West*. Lincoln, Nebraska: University of Nebraska Press, 1998.

Murray, Keith A. *The Modocs and Their War*. Norman, Oklahoma: University of Oklahoma Press, 1959.

Newsom, David. *David Newsom: The Western Observer 1805-1882*. Introduction by E. Earl Newsom. Portland, Oregon: Oregon Historical Society, 1972.

Nichols, David A. *Lincoln and the Indians: Civil War Policy & Politics*. Urbana, Illinois: University of Illinois Press, 2000.

Nickerson, Azor H. "Major General George Crook and the Indians." Typescript. Walter Scribner Schuyler Papers. WS 58. Henry E. Huntington Library, San Marino, California.

Ontko, Gale. *Thunder Over the Ochoco Lightning Strikes Vol III*. Bend, Oregon: Maverick Publications, Inc., 1997.

Orton, Richard H., Brig. Gen. *Records of California Men in the War of the Rebellion, 1861 to 1867*. Sacramento, California: State Printing Office, 1890.

Paher, Stanley W., ed. *Fort Churchill: Nevada Military Outpost of the 1860s*. Las Vegas: Nevada Publications, 1981.

Parnell, William R. "Operations Against Hostile Indians With General George Crook, 1867-'68." The United Service, n.s., 5, 6 (May, June 1889): 482-98, 628-35.

Prucha, Francis Paul, ed. *Documents of United States Indian Policy*. Lincoln, Nebraska: University of Nebraska Press, 1990.

Rathbun, Daniel C. B. *Nevada Military Place Names of the Indian Wars and Civil War*. Las Cruces, New Mexico: Yucca Tree Press, 2002.

Report of the Commissioner of Indian Affairs 1864-1869. Washington: GPO, 1863-1870.

Rickey, Don, Jr. *Forty Miles a Day on Beans and Hay*. Norman: University of Oklahoma Press, 1963.

Robinson, Charles M. III. *General Crook and the Western Frontier*. Norman, Oklahoma: University of Oklahoma Press, 2001.

Rogers, Fred B. *Soldiers of the Overland: Being some account of the services of General Patrick Edward Connor & his Volunteers in the Old West*. San Francisco: The Grabhorn Press, 1938.

Ruby, Robert H. and John A. Brown. *Indians of the Pacific Northwest*. Foreword by Alvin M. Josephy, Jr. Norman, Oklahoma: University of Oklahoma Press, 1988.

Rusco, Elmer. "The Chinese Massacres of 1866." *Nevada Historical Society Quarterly*. 45, no. 1 (Spring 2002): 1-30.

Russell, Don. *One Hundred and Three Fights and Scrimmages The Story of General Reuben F. Bernard*. Mechanicsburg, Pennsylvania: Stackpole Books, 2003.

Sager, Catherine. *The Whitman Massacre of 1847*. Fairfield, Washington: Ye Galleon Press, 2004.

Schlicke, Carl. *Left by the Indians and Massacre on the Oregon Trail in the Year 1860*. Fairfield, Washington: Ye Galleon Press, 1992.

Schmidt, Martin F., ed. *General George Crook: His Autobiography*. Norman, Oklahoma: University of Oklahoma Press, 1986.

Secoy, Frank Raymond. *Changing Military Patterns of the Great Plains Indians*. Lincoln: University of Nebraska Press, 1992.

Settle, Raymond W., and Mary Lund Settle. *Saddles and Spurs: The Pony Express Saga*. Lincoln: University of Nebraska Press, 1972.

Shannon, Donald H. *The Utter Disaster on the Oregon Trail: The Utter and Van Ornum Massacres of 1860*. Caldwell, Idaho: Snake Country Publishing, 1993.

Sheridan, P. H. *The Personal Memoirs of P. H. Sheridan*. New York: C. L. Webster, 1888. Reprint. Introduction by Jeffery D. Wert. New York: Da Capo Press, 1992.

Smith, Philip Dodd, Jr. "The Sagebrush Soldiers Nevada's Volunteers in the Civil War." *Nevada Historical Society Quarterly*, 5, nos. 3-4 (Fall and Winter 1962): 1-87.

Smith, Sherry L. *The View from Officer's Row: Army Perceptions of Western Indians*. Tucson, Arizona: University of Arizona Press, 1990.

Strobridge, William F. *Regulars in the Redwoods: The U.S. Army in Northern California 1852-1861*. Spokane, Washington: The Arthur H. Clarke Company, 1994.

Tate, Michael. *The Frontier Army in the Settlement of the West*. Norman, Oklahoma: University of Oklahoma Press, 1999.

Terfertiller, Casey. *Wyatt Earp The Life Behind the Legend*. New York: John Wiley & Sons, Inc, 1997.

Thompson, Colonel William. *Reminiscences of a Pioneer*. San Francisco, California: 1912.

Thrapp, Dan. *Encyclopedia of Frontier Biography in Three Volumes*. Lincoln: University of Nebraska Press, 1991.

Trenholm, Virginia Cole, and Maurine Carley. *The Shoshonis Sentinals of the Rockies*. Norman, Oklahoma: University of Oklahoma Press, 1964.

Unruh, John D., Jr. *The Plains Across: The Overland Emigrants and the Trans-Mississippi West, 1840-60*. Urbana, Illinois: University of Illinois Press, 1993.

Utley, Robert M. *Frontiersmen in Blue: The United States Army and the Indian 1848-1865*. New York: Macmillan Publishing Co. Inc., 1967.

___*Frontier Regulars: The U.S. Army and the Indian 1866-1891*. New York: Macmillan Publishing Co. Inc., 1973.

Varley, James F. *Brigham and the Brigadier: General Patrick Connor and His California Volunteers in Utah and Along the Overland Trail*. Tucson, Arizona: Westernlore Press, 1989.

Waldman, Carl. *Atlas of the North American Indian*. New York: Checkmark Books, 2000.

Walker, Cyrus H. Cyrus Hamlin Walker Papers. *Oregon Historical Society*, MSS 264.

Webb, George W. *Chronological List of Engagements Between the Regular Army of the United States and Various Tribes of Hostile Indians*. St. Joseph, Missouri: Wing Print. and Pub. Co., 1939.

Webber, Bert. *Oregon Trail Emigrant Massacre of 1862 and Port-Neuf Muzzle-Loaders Rendezvous Massacre Rocks, Idaho*. Medford, Oregon: Webb Research Group, 1987.

Welch, Julia Conway. *Gold Town to Ghost Town: The Story of Silver City, Idaho*. Moscow, Idaho: University of Idaho Press, 1982.

Wilson, Thomas C. Advertising Agency. *Pioneer Nevada*. Two Volumes. Reno, NV: Harold's Club, 1951.

Wooster, Robert. *The Military & United States Indian Policy 1865-1903*. Lincoln, University of Nebraska Press, 1995.

GOVERNMENT PUBLICATIONS

Condition of the Indian Tribes. Report of the Joint Special Committee, Appointed Under Joint Resolution of March 3, 1865. With an Appendix. Washington, GPO, 1867.

Letter from the Secretary of War. In response to Senate resolution of June 11, 1888, report relative to the raising volunteer troops to guard overland and other mails from 1861 to 1866. Senate Exec. Doc. 70. 50th Congress.

U.S. Congress, House of Representatives. "Difficulties With Indian Tribes." 41st Congress, 2nd Session. Executive Document 240.

U.S. Congress, House of Representatives. *Report of the Secretary of War 1868-69*. 40th Congress, 3rd Session. Executive Document No. 1. Washington, GPO, 1868.

U.S. Congress, House of Representatives. *Report of the Secretary of War*. 41st Congress, 2nd Session. Executive Document No. 1, part 2. Washington, GPO, 1869.

U.S. Department of the Interior. Bureau of Indian Affairs. *Reports of the Commissioner of Indian Affairs. 1863-1869*. Washington: GPO, 1863-1870.

U.S. War Department. *The War of the Rebellion: A Compilation of the Official Records of the Union and Confederate Armies*. Washington: GPO, 1880-1901.

INTERNET SOURCES

Anderson, "Fourteenth Infantry," http://www.army.mil/cmh-pg/books/R&H/R&H-14IN.htm

"Battle of Three Forks," Idaho State Historical Society, http://www.idahohistory.net/Reference%20Series/0239.doc

"Bigfoot," Idaho State Historical Society, http://www.idahohistory.net/reference%20series/0040.doc

Bork, "History of the Pacific Northwest," http://www.usgennet.org/usa/or/county/union1/1889volumeII

"Camp Lyon," Idaho State Historical Society, http://www.idahohistory.net/Reference%20Series/0357.doc

"Camp Three Forks," Idaho State Historical Society, http://www.idahohistory.net/Reference%20Series/0358.doc

"Crooks Canyon," http://www.farwestern.com/crookscanyon/toc.htm

"Discovery of Gold in Oregon," http://www.legendsofamerica.com/OR-BlueBucket.html

"Idaho Military Posts," http://www.idahohistory.net/Reference

"The Lost Blue Bucket Mine," http://www.legendsofamerica.com/OR-BlueBucket.html

O'Connor, Lt. Charles M. "Eighth Cavalry," http://www2.army.mil/cmh-pg/books/R&H/R&H-8CV.htm

"The Snake War, 1864-1868," Idaho State Historical Society, http://www.idahohistory.net/Reference%20Series/0236.doc

Wainwright, Capt. R. P. Page. "First Regiment of Cavalry," http://www2.army.mil/cmh-pg/books/R&H/R&H-1CV.htm

NEWSPAPERS

Idaho World. Idaho City, Idaho

Oregon Sentinel. Jacksonville, Oregon

Owyhee Avalanche. Ruby City and Silver City, Idaho

Reese River Reveille, Austin, Nevada

Walla Walla Statesman, Walla Walla, Washington

National Archives

National Archives and Records Administration, Washington, D.C. Record Group 123, U.S. Court of Claims, Indian Depredation Files.

Bacheler, Chauncey D. Claim # 7239

Beachy, Hill, and Johnson, Owen. Claim # 10289

Brougham, Frederick. Claim # 7988

Canter, Alexander. Claim # 7193

Clark, James N. Claim # 1721

Clarno, Andrew. Claim # 1738

Denio, Aaron. Claim # 9806

Hall, Amanda. Claim # 6762

Haviland, Mark. Claim # 4646

Shea, Cornelius, John McMahon and John Catlow. Claim # 7644

Weir, James. Claim # 6866

RG 393 Department of Columbia, Letters Received, Boxes 1-5.

THE AUTHOR

Gregory Michno is a Michigan native. Greg attended Michigan State University and did post-graduate work at the University of Northern Colorado. An award-winning author, he has written two dozen articles and several books, dealing with World War II and the American West. His books are *The Mystery of E Troop*, *Lakota Noon*, *USS Pampanito: Killer-Angel*, *Death on the Hellships*, *The Encyclopedia of Indian Wars*,  *Battle at Sand Creek* and *A Fate Worse than Death: Indian Captivities in the West, 1830 - 1885.* He also participated in editing and appearing in the dvd history, *The Great Indian Wars 1540-1890.*

Greg lives in Longmont, Colorado.

INDEX

OTHER TITLES ABOUT
THE WEST
FROM
CAXTON PRESS

Massacre Along the Medicine Road
The Indian War of 1864 in Nebraska
by Ronald Becher
ISBN 0-87004-289-7, 500 pages, cloth, $32.95
ISBN 0-87004-387-0, 500 pages, paper, $22.95

A Dirty, Wicked Town
Tales of 19th Century Omaha
by David Bristow
ISBN 0-87004-398-6, 320 pages, paper, $16.95

Our Ladies of the Tenderloin
Colorado's Legend in Lace
by Linda Wommack
ISBN 0-87004-444-3, 250 pages, paper, $16.95

Necktie Parties
Legal Executions in Oregon, 1851 - 1905
by Diane Goeres-Gardner
ISBN 0-87004-446-x, 375 pages, paper, $16.95

A Fate Worse Than Death
Indian Captivities in the West, 1830-1885
by W. Gregory and Susan Michno
ISBN 0-87004-451-9, 512 pages, hardcover, $24.95

For a free catalog of Caxton titles write to:

CAXTON PRESS
312 Main Street
Caldwell, Idaho 83605-3299

or

Visit our Internet web site:

www.caxtonpress.com

Caxton Press is a division of THE CAXTON PRINTERS, Ltd.